American Indian Rock Art

Volume 48

With Contributions By

Peter Anick

Livio Dobrez

Patricia Dobrez

Eric C. Fuller

Michael J. Fuller

Neathery B. Fuller

Estrela C. García García

Spence Gustav

Janine Hernbrode

David A. Kaiser

James D. Keyser

Chester R. Liwosz

Stephen J. Lycett

Beatriz Menéndez Iglesias

Tomás Pérez-Reyes

César Armando Quijada López

Richard A. Rogers

Alejandro Terrazas Mata

Walter van Roggen

American Indian Rock Art
Volume 48

Edited by Amy Gilreath, Ken Hedges, and Anne McConnell

American Rock Art Research Association

Orem, Utah
2022

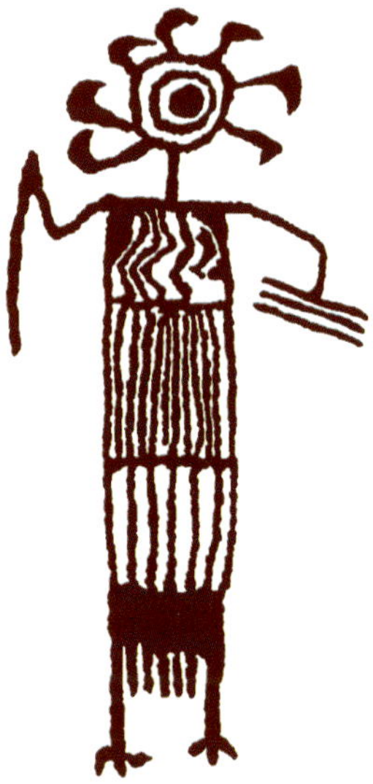

c/o Troy Scotter
569 East 320 North
Orem, Utah 84097-4817

ISBN 978-0-9888730-9-4

The American Rock Art Research Association is a 501(c)(3) non-profit organization.

Printed and bound in the United States of America.

Editors: *Amy Gilreath, Ken Hedges, and Anne McConnell*
Copy Editing, Layout, and Design: *Ken Hedges and Anne McConnell*
Cover Photographs: *Tenabo, New Mexico, by Livio Dobrez (see page 161)*
Title Page Photograph: *Cueva Blanca de La Pulsera, Sonora, by Beatriz Menéndez Iglesias (see page 55)*
Flyleaf Photograph: *Overview of Sutherland Wash, Arizona, by Janine Hernbrode (see page 80)*

About the cover:

Rock art is frequently positioned in inspiring fashion. Here, twin feathered serpents on a high ridge overshadow the observer at Tenabo, New Mexico. Photographs by Livio Dobrez.

Printed by Jostens Commercial Printing,
Clarksville, Tennessee

Table of Contents

Preface

All on planet Earth have been affected by Covid-19 as it burgeoned in 2020, then persisted throughout 2021 and well into 2022. Likewise, the regular rhythm and pace of ARARA has been affected. The 2020 Conference planned for June in Great Falls, Montana, was rescheduled for June 2021. Those originally scheduled to present their research at the 2020 conference opted to present their work in Volume 47 of *American Indian Rock Art*, edited by David Kaiser, Mavis Greer, and James Keyser. Conference planners did a reboot, with Great Falls retained as the venue for our 2021 conference. Mavis Greer and James Keyser continued to wear their mantles as Local Chairs and Field Trip Organizers, and finalized a fresh program and schedule for our June 2021 conference. But as the virus continued to morph, conference plans necessarily did too. By January 2021 it was evident that an in-person conference was untenable. Our first-ever virtual conference was held June 12–13, 2021, with members throughout the U.S. and a few stalwart international members logging in between 9 a.m. and 5 p.m. Pacific time, dependent on individuals' schedules and internet connectivity.

This volume, 48, brings forward nearly a dozen presentations from the first virtual conference. Four are single-site studies, and they include Picture Cave in Missouri (Michael Fuller et al.); the Weppler site in Montana (James Keyser et al.) with Plains Biographic rock art; another Plains Biographic rock art site but this one in west-central Colorado (David Kaiser and James Keyser); and Cueva Higuerillas with its wealth of hand images in red pigment, located within Cucurpe in northern Sonora. This last paper, by Beatriz Menéndez et al., reflects INAH's long-standing concern with rock art sites in Mexico, and is one of two papers contributed in both English and Spanish.

The American Southwest is the setting for three papers that each consider spatially proximal as well as stylistically and chronologically comparable groupings of sites. Janine Hernbrode addresses the discovery and documentation of bell rocks—in situ and portable ones—associated with both large and small Ancestral O'odham rock art concentrations in southern Arizona. Her paper describes a leave-no-trace approach for testing large rocks and boulders for resonance and provides us with examples of both seemingly amorphous and highly concentrated peck marks that denote rocks that were "rung" in the prehistoric past. Peter Anick et al. study fine-incised designs prevalent on the walls of the Red Cliffs within the Palatki Heritage Site in Verde Valley, Arizona. It, too, will especially appeal to those interested in innovative recording methods. The last Southwestern paper, by Chester Liwosz, gives attention to avian iconography at several rock art sites on Mesa Prieta in New Mexico, particularly macaw and raptor representations, and what their placement on the landscape might reveal about their cultural significance.

The second contribution in both English and Spanish is by Estrela García, who is concerned with delimiting the geographical and temporal setting for a collective of Atlantic Axis sites, found primarily in oceanside settings in western Europe and dating to pre-Roman times in the Metal Ages.

The final three papers give broader consideration to: public interpretation of rock art (Richard Rogers), the Kantian concept of aesthetics and ways that we experience rock art (Livio Dobrez), and an appreciation of both plan and profile views in prehistoric Australian rock art with continued use by contemporary Traditional artists (Patricia Dobrez).

We editors are very appreciative of the authors' efforts in contributing their work. We are grateful, too, for the assistance provided by peer-reviewers and our fellow ARARA volunteers who helped bring this publication to fruition. We particularly thank Ryan Byerly, Steven Freers, Mavis Greer, and Johna Hutira for their good works, not to mention the anonymous reviewers. Finally, rather than perceive Gilreath as the traditional lead Editor for Volume 48, we point out that our names are in alphabetical order; no one should infer that the order ranks our individual impact.

—Amy Gilreath, Ken Hedges, Anne McConnell

Picture Cave in Missouri: New Research

Michael J. Fuller, Neathery B. Fuller, and Eric C. Fuller

New insights into the chemistry of pigments and pictograph motifs were obtained in 2020 by a team using portable XRF and DStretch digital photography in Picture Cave. Our work builds on the previous research into the rich Mississippian iconography of the site (radiocarbon dated to the eleventh century A.D. by Carol Diaz-Granados). The pictographs, situated in the dark zone of the cave, are the largest concentration of rock art images in the State of Missouri. The cave and its rock art have been characterized as the "womb of the universe" based upon Osage ethnographic input. We understand this explanation and offer a second interpretation that is also nuanced by Osage ethnographic input. The physical nature of the cave and rock art imagery may have originally been biographical for specific elite warriors in Mississippian society.

Picture Cave (23WN79) is situated in the lower reaches of the Missouri River drainage. The site is situated 13.12 mi (21.2 km) west of Femme Osage (French, "Osage Woman") Creek—a well-known place-name that Bryan (1909:294–295) linked to the tradition of an Osage woman who drowned in the stream. Local folklore prefers to ascribe her death to romance/murder, but it is more likely that she met her death in a spring-time flash flood that swept down the narrow creek; she may have been gathering edible spring plants as well as seining for fish. Lewis and Clark recorded the Femme Osage place-name on 23 May 1804 (Thwaites 1904:27) during their journey up the Missouri River. Daniel Boone built a cabin along Femme Osage Creek about 1800 (Bryan 1909:297). Several scholars have drawn parallels between the traditions of the Osage Nation and the art painted on the walls of Picture Cave. In fact, the place-name could derive from an Osage woman who had accompanied a party of Osage hunters/warriors on a visit to Picture Cave. Historical documents do not record an Osage encampment in the Femme Osage drainage.

Picture Cave is located 29.5 mi (47.5 km) from the Mississippian residential and ceremonial center at Blake Mound (23SL51) and Centaur Mound (23SL33). The hundreds of pictographs in Picture Cave have been attributed to Mississippian priests and warriors based upon stylistic analysis and radiocarbon dating (Diaz-Granados et al. 2001). The site is within the zone of direct influence by the ancient city of Cahokia (Pauketat 2004:Figure 1.1); it is situated 61.0 mi (98.2 km) from the center of the Great Plaza at Cahokia.

Our research at Picture Cave is part of a larger study of the pigments utilized at pictograph sites in Missouri. Five sites were studied with pXRF and DStretch photography in 2020–2021: Picture Cave, White Rock Bluff (23TE01), Rattlesnake Bluff (23FR95), Willenberg Shelter (23FR96), and Bourbeuse Eagle (23FR152). The pigment analysis was accomplished using a handheld Niton pXRF instrument leased from EcoRental in St. Louis, Missouri. All of these sites, except for White Rock, are rich with iconography from the Mississippian period (ca. A.D. 900–1450). The research team in the field at Picture Cave included Dr. Michael Fuller, Neathery Fuller, Eric Fuller,

Michael J. Fuller
St. Louis Community College

Neathery B. Fuller
St. Louis Community College

Eric C. Fuller
Smallin Civil War Cave, Ozark, Missouri

American Indian Rock Art, Volume 48. Amy Gilreath, Ken Hedges, and Anne McConnell, Editors. American Rock Art Research Association, 2022, pp. 1–19.

Thomas Mercer, Mark Leach, Alan Westfall, and Doug Porter. The photographs in this report are the work of Fuller, Leach, Westfall, and Porter. It must be noted that the Niton pXRF instrument was checked in the laboratory before going into the field for accuracy against reference samples, checked at the entrance of Picture Cave against aluminum alloy sample AA6061 prepared by Rocky Mountain Reference Materials, and checked a final time for accuracy when the data was downloaded. This paper presents a summary of our findings in Picture Cave. Detailed listings of the individual measurements and their locations in the caves are presented on the senior author's website (Fuller 2021).

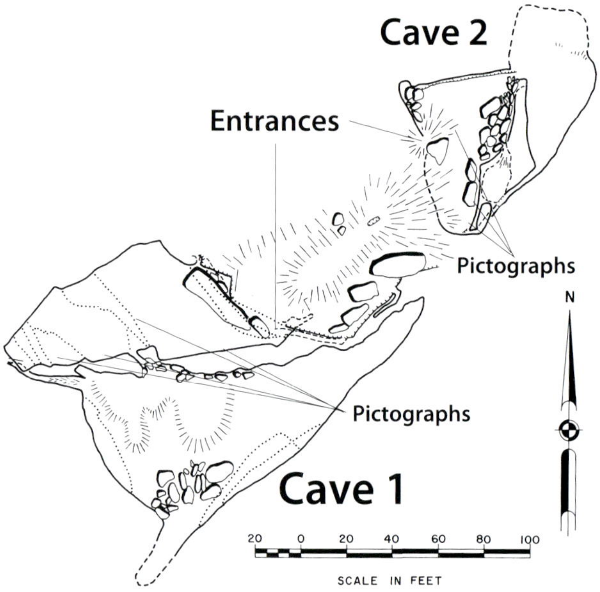

Figure 1. Map of Picture Cave adapted from base map provided by the Missouri Speleological Survey.

Fresh digital photography was carried out at Picture Cave and the other four sites; three DStretch-enabled digital cameras were in use during the fieldwork. The location of each site was double checked with GPS, and site updates were shared with the Missouri State Historic Preservation Office and the Archaeological Survey of Missouri. Five more sites were visited in 2021 to evaluate the possibility of doing further pigment analysis and to correct inaccuracies in the site locations.

Picture Cave Context

Picture Cave has two entrances which lead to independent galleries (Figure 1). Members of the Missouri Speleological Survey speculate that these galleries may once have connected but have become choked with fill and breakdown over many centuries. The main chamber of Picture Cave 1 is approximately three times larger than the chamber of Picture Cave 2. A large colony of bats generally roosts in a room below the area of the rock art in Picture Cave 1. The squeaking noises of the colony and presence of fluttering bats give Cave 1 an eerie sense of being a place inhabited by Spirit Beings.

The motifs in Cave 1 are very different from those in Cave 2. Victorious warriors, defeated enemies, warrior shields, and threatening Underworld Spirit Beings decorate the walls of Cave 1. Two male turkeys fight for dominance of a rafter of female turkeys. One portion of the sandstone ceiling above Panel 1 in Picture Cave 1 consists of fossilized ripples that leave the impression that you are underwater, in the realm of water creatures. The antlered serpent (Figure 2) in black pigment swims like a water snake and confronts/greets everyone who enters the main chamber of Cave 1.

Picture Cave 2 contains pictographs of animals, hunters, meat drying racks, sandhill cranes, and the abstract design called *kapemni* (Figure 3). Goodman (1992:16) and Lee et al. (2014:2) identified the *kapemni*

Figure 2. DStretch YBK *image of the Antlered Serpent with a vicious snarl, painted in black pigment in Cave 1, Panel 3, Glyph 43. Photograph by Mark Leach.*

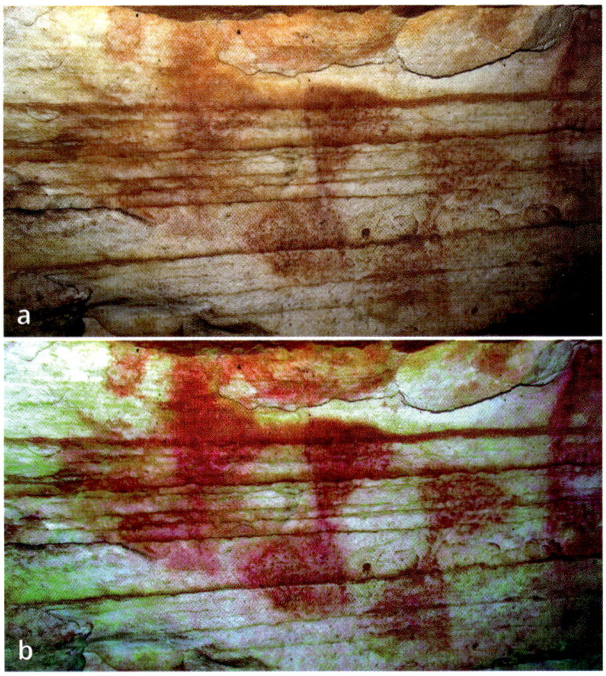

Figure 3. (a) The kapemni *pictographs in Cave 2. (b) DStretch* LRE *enhancement. Simek and Cressler (2015:300) describe this as two hourglass forms, but the DStretch image clearly shows three.*

design as a traditional Sioux motif that links the heavens and the earth. We believe that this contrast in pictograph motifs signals that the ritual use of Cave 2 was by Mississippian sky clans, while the images in Cave 1 were created for ritual use by earth/water clans.

Another way to perceive the two chambers is that Cave 2 relates to hunters of animals while Cave 1 relates to hunters of men. The physical orientation of the two caves parallels the Osage concept of sacred directionality. Among the Osage, east (the direction of Cave 2) relates to morning and life, while west (the direction of Cave 1) relates to evening, night, and death (Bailey 2004:29). Joe Hall (personal communication August 12, 2021), an elder in the Osage Nation, associates red with the east (rising sun, life, and peace) and black with the west (setting sun, death, warfare, and revenge).

Radiocarbon dates from three pictographs in Picture Cave are solid evidence that Mississippian artists were decorating the walls of the cave as early as A.D. 940 ± 80 to 1090 ± 90 (Diaz-Granados 1993; Diaz-Granados and Duncan 2000:Table 6.1; Diaz-Granados et al. 2001; Rowe 2009:1732). The cave entrance is situated in a highly isolated upland slope location at a distance of 3.5 mi (5.6 km) from the Missouri River Valley. Houck (1908:226) shows a Native American trail along the north bank of the Missouri River running from St. Charles to the "Villages of the Missouris" in Chariton County, Missouri. Picture Cave is too far from the trail along the north bank of the Missouri River to be of any use for hunters or warriors.

We suspect that Picture Cave was discovered by a group of Native American hunters tracking game such as deer, elk, turkey, bear, or bison; Bryan (1909:294) reports these were abundant in the Femme Osage Valley during the early nineteenth century. A tall grass prairie began approximately 9 mi (14.5 km) north of Picture Cave in the early 1800s (Mike Leahy, personal communication August 12, 2021). It is possible that gatherers spreading out from a base camp, such as the Cactus Cove Pictograph Site (23WN1156) (Fuller 2014:12–17), found the entrances to Picture Cave. The edible resources available in the rugged dissected landscape included wild honey, hickory nuts, acorns (white oak and chinkapin oak), blackberries, raspberries, and blueberries; all of these were used by the Osage (E. Fuller 2018) though the low density of these edible foods would have made this area "slim pickings" for gatherers (Mike Leahy, personal communication August 12, 2021).

At least 294 pictographs (Simek and Cressler 2015:273) decorate the walls of Picture Cave; there are numerous examples of overlapping pictographs indicating repeated visits by more than a single artist. We believe the actual number of pictographs to be easily over 300. We interpret the pictographs as fulfilling two functions. First, Picture Cave was a place where individuals would encounter and "refresh" their relationship with the Spirit Beings. Second, it functioned to commemorate powerful men and women who had played important roles at either Cahokia or at the closer Blake-Centaur Mississippian settlement. Keyser (1979:43), describing the Writing-on-Stone site along a tributary of the Missouri River in Southern Alberta, noted that both ceremonial art and biographic art appear at that site. "Biographic pictographs" is a concept that Keyser has put forward for several rock art sites on the Great Plains (Keyser and Klassen 2001:2443–253; 2003); his encouragement to this line of inquiry (personal communication June 13, 2021) is greatly appreciated. The concept of biographic pictographs at Picture Cave was put in print by Townsend (2015:152) in his contribution to the Picture Cave volume.

Picture Cave would be lost for centuries until rediscovered by Euro-American settlers. Harrison (1943:193) recorded that the cave was discovered by John Wyatt in the early nineteenth century when he tracked a bear to the entrance of the cave. Bears and panthers had used the cave as a den during the 1800s.

Bryan and Rose (1876:290) record that Captain John Wyatt (b. 1788–d. 1865) married Attossa Pinchney Sharp in 1817; she lived with her parents on a farm located only a few miles from Picture Cave. Wyatt was probably hunting on his father-in-law's pioneer farm when he discovered the cave.

Picture Cave became a curiosity for locals in Warren County in the nineteenth century according to Harrison (1943:193), who collected some of her information from two informants: Dr. A. W. Ebeling and Benj. Frick. There are many historic names and dates left near the pictographs; early dates written on the walls include 1878, 1886, 1888, and 1897. The surname Ebeling is written in cursive script over Glyph 1 in Cave 1, Panel 2. The 1878 date comes with a jauntily drawn woman's leg (in charcoal).

The cave came to the attention of citizen scientists in 1964 when it was recorded and mapped (Figure 1) by four members of the Missouri Speleological Survey: C. Curran, A. Schallert, R. Clark, and D. Biunno. The site was reported to the Missouri Archaeological Survey around 1986 by James F. Keeke, a member of the Missouri Conservation Commission; by that time, looters had already started digging in the floor of the cave. Looting was being carried out by both local individuals, and individuals from St. Louis. Law enforcement officers would bring Michael Weichman (State Archaeologist) and Dr. Gary Rex Walters (Contract Archaeologist with Triad Consultants) to the cave during 1988 to determine the proper handling of human remains disinterred by a local looter.

The property owners, horrified by the looting and concerned that looters would attempt to remove pieces of the rock art, were pleased that action was taken to gate the entrances to Cave 1 and Cave 2. This also marked the opportunity for careful study of the rock art by Carol Diaz-Granados, then a graduate student at Washington University in St. Louis. Her fieldwork began in 1991 and was continued in 2005; the history and results of that project are outlined in *Picture Cave* (Diaz-Granados et al. 2015). No member of the teams organized by Dr. Carol Diaz-Granados participated in our study. We have tried our best to use their reference system of panels and glyphs.

White Pigment

Our pXRF pigment analysis had a series of research questions to answer. Our number one objective as defined in the project Research Design was to obtain chemical data on the pictographs that used white pigment. Our assumption is that white pigment is rare in Picture Cave and rare at other pictographs sites in the Midwest because of the scarcity of the mineral used for the pigment. Emily Beahm (personal communication July 14, 2021) notes that the records of the rock art database developed by the Arkansas Archeological Survey have only two white pictographs; they are both situated in Rock House Cave (3CN20). Mark Wagner (personal communication August 7, 2021) knows of only one white pictograph example in Illinois, and he suspects that it may be historic.

Red Horn

White pigment in Cave 1 is present on the most famous painting in the cave, variously described as He-Who-Wears-Human-Heads-as-Earrings, Morning Star, and/or Red Horn (Figure 4), with the head drawn in black pigment and the body painted solid white. The pictograph was catalogued as Glyph 104 in Cave 1, Panel 1, by Simek and Cressler (2015:278). It should

Figure 4. White and black pigment pictograph in Cave 1, Panel 1, Glyph 104, that is often called Red Horn.

be noted that Dieterle (2010; personal communication July 11, 2021) has questioned the identification of Glyph 104 with Morning Star. We will refer to Glyph 104 as Red Horn in this article, because that is the designation used by many authors. In fact, we see the pictograph as a historic figure dressed in the regalia of the Spirit Being named Red Horn. Cuffs of the regalia are clearly seen on his left arm that carries the bow. The "head" of Red Horn is disproportionately large to the body because it is a mask—much like a Pueblo Katsina mask. He wears a large "long-nosed god maskette" as an ear ornament (Diaz-Granados et al. 2015:149–150), also painted in white. Red Horn carries in his right hand what has often been interpreted as the severed head of his father with an attached white plume. Careful inspection shows that it is more than just a severed head—the shoulders and part of the upper torso are clearly represented; it is a third of the body. Maybe it is another mask and regalia that would have been worn by another historic individual.

A cluster of faint biographic pictograms (Figure 5) is located under the left arm of Red Horn: Man + Elk slain by 2 arrows to its heart + Bow and Arrow + Broken Arrow. The slain elk pictogram was recognized by Diaz-Granados and Duncan (2000:232, Figure 6.6). Simek and Cressler (2015:278) catalogued the slain elk as Glyph 103, and the three glyphs (bow, arrow, and broken arrow) to the right of the elk as an abstract pattern that they could not recognize. They did not recognize the man's head in profile. We recognized the faint pictograms after processing our digital images with the DStretch program. A tentative reading of the biographic name glyphs suggests "Great Man, Slayer of the Great Stag, Skilled Warrior and Breaker of the Enemy."

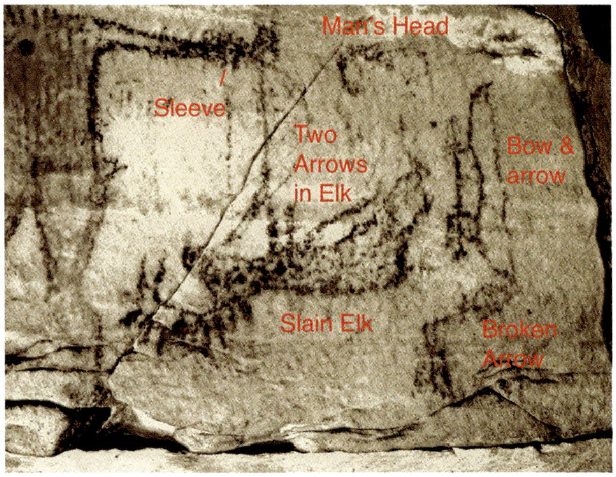

Figure 5. DStretch YBK *image of the Red Horn biographic pictograms. Photograph by Doug Porter.*

The use of pictograms in Picture Cave is evidence, admittedly limited, of a shared communication strategy within the Mississippian communities in the Lower Missouri River Valley. We have identified biographic pictograms at the Willenberg and Rattlesnake Bluff rock art sites.

Among the *Ṭsi´-zhu* (Osage, Sky clans), white is seen as representing the clear, bright, and shining stars (2009:202); La Flesche (1932:355) reports that the Osage term for white is *çka* and Quintero (2009:202) reports that the term for white is *ska'ha*. Members of the Sky moiety could see use of this color in a dark cave as inappropriate. La Flesche (1932:63, 102, 242) recorded the term *ho*^{n}*´-ba çka* as white day, meaning "daylight," and the term *mo*^{n}*-thi*^{n}*´-ḳa-çka* for white clay (possibly the pigment source). Color symbolism could easily vary between various Native American nations and possibly between the moieties of a specific nation. Joe Hall, an elder in the Osage Nation, associates white with the "Path of Life" (personal communication August 12, 2021).

There are two published proposals for the chemical composition of the white pigment used in Picture Cave. The first proposal for the white pigment of the Red Horn pictograph was offered by Diaz-Granados and Duncan (2000:105); they wrote that the white pigment used for the Red Horn pictograph was "possibly burnt bone, kaolinite, or crushed shell," but that an exact determination could not be reached without a chemical analysis. This is a reasonable explanation. Hough (1907:408) equated white pigment with either kaolin clay, limestone, or gypsum.

The second proposal for the composition of the white pigment of the Red Horn pictograph was published by Blankenship (2015:38) in her chapter on the chemical analysis of the pigments used in Picture Cave. She concluded that it was "created by abrading patinated sandstone to create white graphic in conjunction with a line drawing in black." Blankenship's explanation is straightforward, but why wasn't that technique used more widely in Picture Cave or at other sites situated in the Midwest?

A series of six sequential pXRF measurements were taken with the Niton instrument on the white pigment of the Red Horn pictograph; three were taken as percentage elemental analysis and three were taken as ppm analysis. Two readings were taken in the center of the body of the pictograph, two on the "long-nosed god maskette," and two on the white feather plume that lays across the outstretched arm of Red Horn.

Three elements are dominant in the Red Horn pictograph:

- silicon (93.143% to 96.310%)
- aluminum (3.067% to 5.46%)
- iron (0.516% to 1.246%).

We were very disappointed that lead (Pb) was not present in either the percent or ppm analysis because we felt that it was a good candidate. Likewise, the possibility that barite, proposed by a geologist at the Missouri Geological Survey, could also be immediately dismissed. The ppm readings for the three locations on the Red Horn pictograph are:

- antimony = 47.07 to 92.59 ppm
- tin = 30.61 to 77.19 ppm
- cadmium = 16.56 to 35.2 ppm
- palladium = 6.27 to 7.47 ppm
- silver = 57.55 to 125.64 ppm
- zirconium = 38.09 to 69.27 ppm
- zinc = 9.5 ppm
- tungsten = 31.52 ppm
- iron = 355.48 to 989.23 ppm
- barium = 422.09 to 548.59 ppm
- strontium = 11.54 to 17.59 ppm
- rubidium = 2.93 ppm

Numerous "clean wall" pXRF readings were taken in the cave, including one immediately to the left of the Red Horn pictograph. Nine readings were taken at several places on the unpainted cave wall; they provided ranges of silicon, aluminum, and iron that equaled and, in some cases, exceeded the values of the Red Horn pictograph.

The ppm data for the Red Horn pictograph shows no unexpected readings except for the presence of palladium that appears as 7.47 ppm ± 3.05 and 6.27 ppm ± 3.7; these appear in the center of the body of Red Horn and in the long-nosed maskette. Palladium did not appear in the white feather plume between the body and decapitated head. A trace (9.75 ppm ± 3.51) of palladium appears in one of the white eyes painted in Panel 2, Glyph 3. It also appears (4.43 ppm ± 2.74 and 5.34 ± 2.86) in the red pigment used in the red dot and red circle of Panel 2, Glyph 7 at Picture Cave. Finally, it occurs in the black pigment figure holding a bow (4.92 ppm ± 2.73) in Panel 1, Glyph 69 at Picture Cave.

Palladium appears in the background readings (7.67 ppm ± 4.58) at the Willenberg Site, and the Bourbeuse Eagle site has a natural level of 9.18 ppm ± 3.05. The presence of palladium in the unpainted bedrock at two rock art sites complicates any endeavor to explain it as a unique fingerprint for a specific mineral pigment.

Predator/Foe Eyes

Ironically, the pXRF readings on the two pairs of white predator/foe eyes (Figure 6) in Panel 2, Glyph 3 provided results very different from those of Red Horn. The right eye of the right pair of eyes measured:

- silicon = 70.08% ± 2.678
- aluminum = 26.5832% ± 0.715,
- iron = 3.278% ± 0.44.

The right eye of the left pair measured:

- silicon = 63.836% ± 2.004
- aluminum = 30.151% ± 0.534
- iron = 5.756% ± 0.515
- niobium = 0.21% ± 0.09

Figure 6. White eyes of two foes/predators that are associated with a horizontal crevice in the wall of Cave 1, Panel 2, Glyph 3. Note the dots of white paint spatter approximately a half meter to the right of the two pairs of eyes. The eyes are elliptical, as if the foe/predator is squinting to enhance its vision. Scale is 1 meter. Photograph by Eric Fuller.

These readings are so different that it is safe to say that the white paint for Red Horn and the white paint for the two pairs of predator/foe eyes are not the same. Most of the trace element values for the white eyes, in ppm, fall significantly above the parameters of the Red Horn pictograph except for:

- palladium = 9.75 ppm
- silver = 165.88 ppm
- gold = 12.94 ppm
- iron = 3726.27 and 3900.1 ppm
- barium = 691.17 ppm
- rubidium = 4.28 and 5.23 ppm

These readings are very similar to the two muscovite mica reference samples measured with the very same Niton pXRF. The traces of silver and gold could point to alum precipitated as a result of hydrothermal activity; this is an area of future research.

The two pairs of predator/foe eyes definitely remind us of a panther teaching her cub to hunt. A mature panther and cub, painted in red pigment, stalk a deer in the main panel of Turtle Shelter (23CY554) (Fuller 2011:8–11).

Red Pigment

The results of the chemical analysis of the red pigments at Picture Cave are straightforward compared to the white pigment results. Diaz-Granados and Duncan (2000:104) wrote that the common source of Missouri red pictograph pigment include hematite, iron oxides, red ochres, and possibly limonite. Blankenship (2015:Figure 4.7, Table 4.1) conducted SEM-EDS analysis of several red pigment pictographs in Picture Cave. She analyzed the red strip extending from the open mouth of a threatening carnivore (wolf?) as composed of oxygen, silicon, and iron with a minor component of aluminum. An important question that we hoped to answer about the red pigment was whether traces of sulfur could be detected, because that would indicate the possibility that the mineral gypsum had been added to the iron pigment. We were also interested in whether any traces of mercury would appear in the red pigments. Littmann (1975:Table 1) proposed that both hematite (Fe_2O_3) and cinnabar (HgS) were used to create red pigment in Mesoamerica.

The color red in the worldview of the Osage Nation has different symbolic meanings within the two moieties. The *Ho*^{n}*´-ga* (Earth Lodge) people interpret the red color as related to the destructive nature of fire. The underside of the bear claws on a bear claw necklace were painted red to represent the flames of a merciless fire. The *Ṭsi´-zhu* (Sky Lodge) people associate red with the peaceful morning sky (La Flesche 1921:81). The Osage word for red is *zhu´-dse* and dark red/crimson is *zhu´-dse-sha-be* (La Flesche 1932:228).

Cave 1, Panel 1, Glyph 122

The pXRF analysis of Cave 1, Panel 1, Glyph 122 (Figure 7) yielded results similar to those reported by Blankenship with the exception that we were able to provide greater detail. Our elemental reading indicates that the pigment is composed of:

- silicon = 85.572 %± 7.015
- iron = 7.361% ± 1.586
- aluminum = 6.913% ± 1.867

The Niton pXRF instrument does not quantify oxygen, but it can be assumed to be a major component since sulfur (the most likely bonding agent) is not represented. Two nearby readings on unpainted portions of the wall show remarkably higher amounts of silica (95.286% ±2.649), roughly equal amounts of aluminum (4.169% ± 0.883), and significantly lower amounts of iron (0.492% ± 0.108). Iron as a ppm is, as expected, greater in the red pictograph (3651 ppm ± 91.59) in comparison to the nearby unpainted rock (610.14 ppm ± 29.85).

Figure 7. Vertical band of red pigment associated with the open mouth of a wolf, lower right. Red pigment strips are also in front and above the nose of the wolf; red pigment was used to enhance the eyes of a barn owl, upper left. Cave 1, Panel 1, Glyph 122. Our identification of the heart-shaped face of a barn owl is based upon an ARARA Zoom lecture by David (2021); Simek and Cressler (2015:281) identify the heart-shaped face creature as a herpetomorph (shape resembling a reptile or amphibian).

Circle and Dot

Two very prominent red circle and dot pictographs decorate the walls of Cave 1 and we conducted pXRF analysis on the red circle and dot pictograph in Cave 1, Panel 2, Glyph 7 (Figure 8). This pictograph was first published by Diaz-Granados in her dissertation (1993:Illustration 27.2d). The chemistry of this pic-

Figure 8. (a) Circle and dot of red pigment, Cave 1, Panel 2, Glyph 7. Scale is 1 meter. Photograph by Eric Fuller. (b) DStretch enhancement of the circle-and-dot pictograph. A very faint pattern of black spokes visibly radiates from the dot to the edge of the circle. Photograph by Doug Porter.

tograph was analyzed and published by Blankenship (2015:Figure 4.9, Table 4.1); she identified the major elements as oxygen, silicon, and iron with minor elements of aluminum, phosphorus, potassium, and calcium. Our team conducted two pXRF analyses on the center of the red dot and two pXRF analyses on the widest part of the circle. Our data basically agrees with Blankenship's analysis with a few slight departures. The red pigment in the center "dot" is primarily composed of:

- silicon = 75.232% ± 1.175
- iron = 14.773% ± 0.601
- aluminum = 8.569% ± 0.37

The values for the thickest part of the red circle are:

- silicon = 65.777% ± 1.611
- iron = 16.86% ± 0.495
- aluminum = 17.329% ± 17.329

The pXRF analysis of an unpainted portion of the wall immediately to the left of the circle shows the bedrock to be primarily:

- silicon = 93.949% ± 1.852
- aluminum = 4.177% ± 0.271
- iron = 1.808% ± 0.202

For the dot and circle, the ppm data are:

- iron = 27719.21 ppm ± 171.31 (dot)
- iron = 21766.29 ppm ± 157.77 (circle)
- chromium = 121.51 ppm ± 55.45
- chromium = 89.88 ppm ± 55.72
- palladium = 4.43 ppm ± 2.74
- palladium = 5.34 ppm ± 2.86
- gold = 12.27 ppm ± 4.62
- copper = 15.59 ppm ± 7.92
- manganese = 44.43 ppm ± 25.63
- rubidium = 3.74 ppm ± 1.13

The ppm data show a predictable pattern of high elevated iron versus 1844.27 ppm ± 53.96 for a nearby spot on the unpainted wall. The remaining elements were detected in the red pigment, but not in the nearby unpainted bedrock. Some of these elements may have been contributed by the addition of small amounts of limonite (yellow ochre) and/or calcite to the pulverized red ochre (iron oxide) based upon pXRF analysis of specimens in the Missouri mineral collection of St. Louis Community College.

The DStretch photographic analysis of the two circle and dot motifs shows faint internal decorations executed in black paint. Our DStretch analysis (Figure 8b) on the circle and dot design (Cave 1, Panel 2, Glyph 7) shows a series of radial black lines extending from the edge of the dot to the outer edge of the red circle. The other dot and circle (that we photographed and will pXRF on a future expedition) has a black circle surrounding the dot, a black circle midway to the inner edge of the red circle, and two black circles enclosing the red circle. Brown and Muller (2015:Figure 8.4) describe Glyph 7 as a "dot-in-circle" motif and offer no explanation. Dot-in-circle pictographs are associated with the sun among the Klamath in the Great Basin (David 2016:44, Figure 29) and at Feather Cave in New Mexico (Ellis and Hammack 1968:26, 27, 35, 39, Figure 4). In the case of Picture Cave, we prefer to interpret the glyphs as specific shields associated with great warriors. Shield pictographs have been identified at many sites in the Plains, Southwest, and Great Basin. A large dot-in-circle red pigment pictograph has been documented on the ceiling of the Bay Creek site (11Pp52) in southern Illinois and dates to the Mississippian period (Mark Wagner, personal communication August 7, 2021). An Osage war shield with concentric circles and lines extending from the dot to the outer edges was exhibited in the Art of the Osage; the lines extending from the center were interpreted as war paths (Bailey and Swan 2004:89, Cat. 44).

The red color shield in Cave 1, Panel 2 is directly associated (on the right and left) with pictographs that portray warriors and warfare. To the left is a faint red pictograph (Cave 1, Panel 2, Glyph 4) of a warrior dancing with a severed head in his right hand and a weapon (mace?) in his left hand (Figure 9). Cressler and Simek (2015:186) describe this pictograph as a figure holding an oval-shaped human head; they do not mention that he wears a shirt with five scalps hanging

Figure 9. DStretch YRD image of the dancer with severed head and upraised mace, clearly showing the scalp fringes of his shirt. Photograph by Mark Leach.

from his right arm and five scalps hanging from his left arm; La Flesche gives *wa-do´-k.a* as the Osage term for "scalps of men" (1932:187) and *wa-ha'* as "scalp of a slain warrior of the enemy" (1932:191). Our identification of the lines under the arms is based upon parallels to George Catlin's drawing of Clermont, son of Chief Clermont of the Osage (Catlin 1841b:41, Figure 150). Scalp-fringed shirts were recorded by Catlin as symbols of great honor among warriors of the Blackfeet (1841a:29, Figure 11), Oteo (1841b:27, Figure 143), and Assiniboine (1841b:195–196, Figure 150).

Crimson Red Zigzags

A crimson red pictograph of considerable interest was analyzed with pXRF in Cave 2, Panel 4, Glyph 529. It is a pattern of twin zigzag lines that are painted horizontally (Figure 10). DStretch analysis of this pictograph did not find any evidence for additional details as in the case of the many pictographs at Picture Cave. This pictograph was observed by Diaz-Granados (1993:Figure 27.4c) and published in Diaz-Granados and Duncan (2000:Figure 5.52a). Zigzag lines are proposed as one of seven most frequently recurring entoptic forms in rock art worldwide, including the United States (Lewis-Williams and Dowson 1988). We prefer a more nuanced explanation that David (2016:53; 2021) presented based upon his study of the zigzag patterns in Klamath rock art; he suggests that the horizontal zigzag lines are "Spirit lightning giving the shaman momentary ability to see the unseen." Lightning, an electrical phenomenon in the sky, makes perfect sense in Cave 2 with its Sky clan associations. Keyser (2000:39, Figure 21) recognized that zigzag lines radiating from a medicine bundle on the Five Crows Ledger drawing number 3 literally represent power rays. Keyser (2004:12, Figure 7) identified the zigzag pattern decorating a tipi petroglyph at the Names Hill site in Wyoming as evidence of the owner's medicine power. The relationship of the zigzag with lightning is very clear at the Jeffers Site in Minnesota where horizontal lightning streaks from both shoulders of a thunderbird (Keyser 2004:63, Figure 57).

Figure 10. Twin zigzag horizontal lines on the wall of Cave 2, Panel 4, Glyph 529. Scale is 10 cm. Photograph by Eric Fuller.

The crimson zigzag was analyzed by Blankenship (2015:Figure 4.3, Table 4.1); she reported that the major elemental components are carbon, oxygen, and silicon with minor elements being aluminum and iron. Our pXRF analysis indicates that the pigment's composition includes:

- silicon = 91.494% ± 1.229
- iron = 4.467% ± 0.3
- aluminum = 2.859% ± 0.267

with elevated traces of:

- antimony = 118.36 ppm ± 12.16
- tin = 88.76 ppm ± 11.15
- cadmium = 17.21 ppm ± 7.61
- silver = 179.53 ppm ± 13.15
- barium = 704.79 ppm ± 44.48

versus background readings of:

- antimony = 43.02 ppm ± 8.28
- tin = 36.76 ppm ± 7.61
- cadmium = 17.21 ppm ± 5.71
- silver = 88.8 ppm ± 31.71

It is interesting that the crimson pigment contained traces of rubidium (3.7 ppm ± 1.7) and mercury (10.31 ppm ± 4.61), while these elements were not present in the nearby clean wall above the crimson zigzag. Mercury and rubidium do show up in the ppm readings from two unpainted walls in Cave 1 (readings 58 and 61), so they may simply be flukes though that assumption deserves more careful study.

The level of iron in the crimson zigzag is remarkably higher (3233.9 ppm ± 90.49) than the nearby unpainted wall (919.75 ppm ± 37.73), but far less than many of the red pictographs in Cave 1 such as the red circle (217766.29 ppm ± 157.77) or red dot (27719.21 ppm ± 171.31).

At least one mineral was combined with the iron pigment to produce the crimson color at both Picture Cave 2 and Willenberg. The elevated levels of antimony, tin, cadmium, silver, barium, and mercury could reflect the addition of a kaolinite clay to the powdered iron ore. We found those elements present in trace ppm when analyzing a piece of kaolinite clay in the St. Louis Community College Geology collection. The addition of wood charcoal would also help darken a red pigment into a shade of crimson, but it is unlikely that charcoal was the only additive.

Meat Drying Racks

One of the most impressive red pictographs in Cave 2 is an elaborate image of meat drying racks (Figure 11). The percent elemental analysis of the red pigment

Figure 11. Red pictograph of meat-drying racks in Picture Cave 2, Panel 6, Glyph 562. They are overlain with black pigment pictographs of cranes (see Figure 15). Image by Mark Leach.

indicates that it includes:

- silicon = 93.638% ± 1.363
- aluminum = 3.659% ± 0.314
- iron = 2.68% ± 0.265

The ppm measurements showed the expected higher amount of iron (3247.47 ppm ± 61.47 versus 760.34 ppm ± 43.78) when compared with a nearby piece of unpainted wall. The red pigment contains mercury (4.83 ppm ± 2.5) and nickel (22.17 ppm ± 14.59) which are absent in the nearby unpainted wall, but within the range of several unpainted tests made in Picture Cave 1.

The drying racks are an interesting motif in Picture Cave 2. Diaz-Granados and Duncan (2000:126) interpret racks heavy with drying meat as linked to the Oglala Sioux concept of heaven. *Htaa puze* (literally, dried deer) is the Osage phrase recorded by Quintero (2009:278) with a similar term, *ṭa'-pshe* (pemmican), recorded by La Flesche (1932:138). Pictographs of racks with drying animal hides appear at the Cactus Cove Pictograph Site (23WN1156) which is only a few kilometers distant from Picture Cave (Fuller 2014).

Rattlesnake

Among the red pigment pictographs of Cave 2 is the remarkable image in Panel 1, Glyph 505, that measures approximately 2 meters in length and was created by hundreds of short dots and dashes of pigment (Figure 12). Simek and Cressler (2015:295) identify this pictograph as a herpetomorph—specifically a rattlesnake. The pXRF analysis of the pigment for this pictograph shows a composition of:

- silicon = 93.498% ± 1.825
- aluminum = 4.731% ± 0.586
- iron = 1.613% ± 0.203

The analysis of a nearby portion of unpainted bedrock demonstrated a much lower percentage of iron (0.668% ± 0.122) and aluminum (3.949% ± 0.358). The ppm analysis found a significant increase in iron between the red pigment and unpainted bedrock (1625.55 ppm ± 45.04 versus 621.56 ppm ± 28.55). The pigment is certainly iron based with a slight chance of an intentional or unintentional addition of a mineral such as mica that could contribute the slight increase in aluminum.

We puzzled over this pictograph while inside Cave 2, and during the DStretch analysis of the images. The

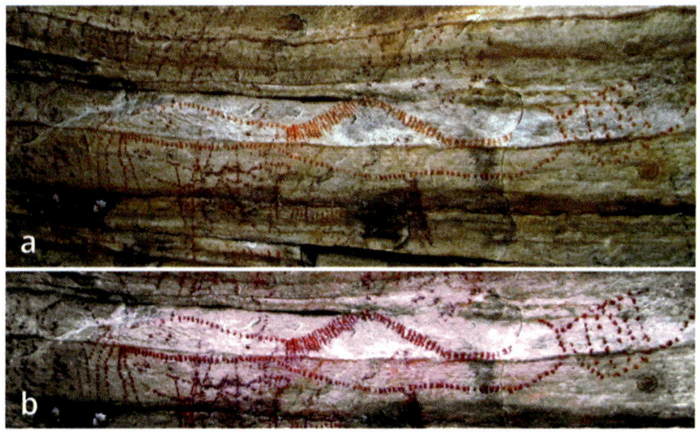

Figure 12. (a) Snakelike red pigment pictograph created with hundreds of dots and dashes in Picture Cave 2, Panel 4, Glyph 532. (b) DStretch RGB0 enhancement to clarify the design.

right hand "end" of the pictograph resembles a segmented rattlesnake tail like the one at Groeper Shelter (23WN1177). Snakes are very common in the Mississippian rock art in Missouri and two snakes are shown in black pigment in Cave 1 (Figures 13 and 14). Red pigment was used to create the winged serpent pictograph at the Bourbeuse Site, the horned serpents at the Groeper Shelter, and a serpent at Painted Rock (23OS5). Black pigment serpents are found at Rattlesnake Bluff, Willenberg, and Picture Cave 1. There is not a specific color preference for serpents in terms of shelter or caves

Figure 13. Serpent with threatening mouth in black pigment in Picture Cave 1, Panel 2, Glyph 15. Photograph by Mark Leach.

Figure 14. Serpent and a large frog (bullfrog? cane toad?) stalk a flock of turkeys with either the help or hindrance of a thunderbird. Picture Cave 1, Panel 1. Photograph by Mark Leach

in Missouri. It is significant that no other snake pictograph in Missouri was created using this technique of small dots and dashes. A second explanation, problematic, is that this pictograph represents the Milky Way. That is plausible in Cave 2 because it is decorated with other examples of Sky clan imagery.

Black Pigment

A common concept in North American archaeology is that black pigments were created either from charcoal or manganese ore (DeBoer 2005:84). Littmann (1975:Table 1) lists the source of black pigment in Mesoamerican art as including carbon, pyrolusite (MnO_2), and manganite (MnO). Koenig et al. (2014:176–177) report that manganese black pigment as "light" as 426 ppm has been documented in the Lower Pecos Canyonlands of Texas.

Ça´-be (La Flesche 1930:28), the color Black within Osage tradition, has a rich, symbolic association. Quintero (2009:267) renders the word as *sápe*. The *Ho^{n}´-ga*, Earth clans among the Osage, associate the color black with the west—the direction of the setting sun (Bailey 2004:29), construed as the place of death when the tribe was at war (La Flesche 1930:550). Carbonized redbud or yellow willow wood were used to create pigment that was applied to the face of warriors and their horses (Dorsey 1884:118, 124; La Flesche 1932:226). The verb *i´-ḳi-no^{n}* was recorded by La Flesche (1932:73) for the ritual act of a warrior painting himself ceremonially. The charcoal used for pigment by the Earth clan warriors was prepared ritually by an elder of the Sky clans, specifically the *Wa-ça´-be Zhu-dse*—Red Black Bear clan (La Fleche 1939:18). The term Red Black Bear clan was recorded by Mathews (1961:37–38) as the seventh *Ṭsi´-zhu* (Sky) clan; each clan had its main name with auxiliary titles related to their multiple life symbols and clan functions. The charcoal used for pigment by Sky clan warriors was ritually prepared by an elder of the Earth clans, specifically the *Wa-ça-be* (Black Bear) clan; each elder was given an article of value as payment for his work in preparing the charcoal pigment(La Flesche 1939:18). Redbud and willow trees are sacred and symbolize long life (La Flesche 1928:55, 1932:174); they are the only species identified as being suitable for ritual charcoal (La Flesche 1939:18). The fire to create the charcoal was made outside the war tent, the "houses of the warriors" (Dorsey 1884:118–120; La Flesche 1932:226), and the act of crushing the charcoal and applying it to the face and body was a symbolic act expressing determination to show no mercy in battle, and to symbolize, at one level, the enemy that will be broken, burnt, and displayed as a trophy of victory (Dorsey 1884:124; La Flesche 1928:226).

Sandhill Crane

Several black pigment pictographs were analyzed in Picture Cave 1 and 2. Of particular importance is a faint black pigment image of a bird with long legs and neck (Figure 15) that was painted on top of the red meat drying racks. The bird's head is partially obscured by another black pictograph painted on top of it (or emerging from its head), but its long beak can be clearly recognized. This is a representation of a sandhill crane that was the totem of the Great Crane clan within the *Ṭsi´-zhu* Sky People of the Osage. La Flesche

Figure 15. (a) Black pigment cranes painted on top of the meat-drying racks in Picture Cave 2, Panel 6; (b) DStretch YBK *enhancement.*

recorded the term *pe´-ṭo^{n}-hiu-stse-dse* for the sandhill crane and *Pe´-ṭo^{n} ṭo^{n}-ga Zho-i-ga-the* for the clan of the Great Crane People; he noted that elders of this clan played an important role in peacemaking (La Flesche 1928:123; 1932:127).

Black Warrior

One of the most impressive black pigment paintings at Picture Cave is of a warrior in Cave 1, Panel 1, Glyph 12 (Figure 16a). His face is decorated with the forked-eye pattern, and he holds a trilobed mace at head height as either as a display or a threat to strike. His nocked arrow touches (penetrates?) the swirling lower torso of a barn owl with red eyes (Figure 16b). Duncan and Diaz-Granados (2018:Figure 2.11) identify this pictograph as the "Man of Mystery, Gray or Dark Wolf." Dye (2017:72) speculates that this pictograph could be identified as "Wild Twin or Spring Boy aka Lightning Boy, Long Teeth and Thrown-Away." The identifications proposed by Dye, Duncan, and Diaz-Granados are of powerful Spirit Beings; our perspective is that it is a historic person who was portrayed in his warrior regalia in a manner similar to the powerful Spirit Beings. We will refer to him as Black Warrior.

A small, faint bust, without the eye paint or regalia headdress, is painted directly in front of Black Warrior, and we believe this marks the painting as a biographical representation of a historic warrior. The mouth is open in the act of speaking or singing for both the warrior and biographic representations. We believe that he is one of at least three biographic pictographs in Picture Cave 1. La Flesche (1928:31, 41) recorded that the second son *(Ksho^{n}´-ga)* born to a family in the Puma/Panther clan of the Osage, a powerful clan among the *Ho^{n}´-ga* (Earth clans), would be named *I´-e-çka-wa-the* meaning Giver-of-Speech. The same name is also recorded for males in the Black Bear and Elk clans (La Flesche 1928:135, 141).

The pXRF analysis was conducted on the darkest patch of pigment in the center of the painting of Black Warrior. The pigment consists of:

- silicon = 96.189% ± 3.144
- aluminum = 1.973% ± 0.892
- iron = 1.651% ± 0.256
- niobium = 0.115% ± 0.041

The reading on a portion of unpainted wall directly beneath the bow of Black Warrior discovered a much lower natural iron content (0.492% ± 0,108). Niobium was not identified as either a percent or a ppm presence in the unpainted wall sample, but it does appear in three other unpainted readings at Picture Cave—that suggests it is just an uncommon part of the bedrock. Likewise, the Black Warrior pigment sample had a very small ppm presence of:

- selenium = 3.6 ppm ± 2.02
- chromium = 180 ppm ± 68.22
- arsenic = 4.92 ppm ± 2.96

These were absent in the nearby unpainted wall, but that is of no consequence. Selenium and chromium show up in several unpainted wall samples at Picture Cave. The iron ppm is significantly greater in the Black Warrior pigment (2512.53 ppm ± 67.89 versus 610.14 ppm ± 29.85); that can best be explained as the intentional (or unintentional) mixing of a small amount of iron pigment with the charcoal. The DStretch image of the Black Warrior does not show a hidden red pigment pictograph beneath the Black Warrior.

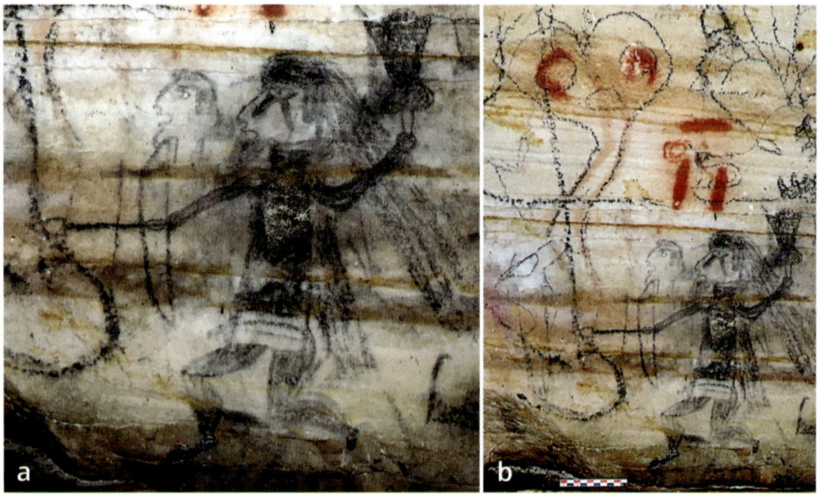

Figure 16. (a) Black Warrior with biographic glyph on the wall of Cave 1, Panel 1, Glyph 12. (b) Black Warrior in panel context. Scale is 10 cm. Photographs by Eric Fuller.

Antlered Serpent

Definitely one of the most interesting black pigment pictographs in Picture Cave is the antlered serpent with teeth shown in a threatening snarl (Figure 2). Diaz-Granados and Duncan (2000:Plate 15, Figure 5.18) identify this image as the Underwater Spirit; Townsend (2015:149) labels it the "Guardian Antlered Piasa." We agree that the image is powerful and definitely meant to deter anyone who does not know how to tame or master this powerful Spirit Being. We interpret the image, influenced by our research at Washington State Park (Fuller et al. 2019), as a malicious and powerful Spirit Being that we identify as the *Ṭs'a´-ṭo*$^{n´}$*-ga*, literally big snake, equated by La Flesche (1932:157, 215) to the Christian concept of Satan. For simplicity, we will refer to it as the Antlered Serpent. This glyph has an uncorrected ^{14}C date of A.D. 1000 ± 100 (Diaz-Granados et al. 2001).

The pXRF analysis of the "nose" of the Antlered Serpent shows that the elemental composition is:

- silicon = 94.905% ± 1.44
- aluminum = 3.712% ± 0.267
- iron = 1.186% ± 0.182
- niobium = 0.13% ± 0.045

The pXRF analysis of the "left eye" of the Antlered Serpent shows that the elemental composition is:

- silicon = 87.767% ± 4.883
- aluminum = 4.221% ± 1.404
- iron = 1.076% ± 0224

Iron percentage was elevated in the nose and eye in contrast to the unpainted wall immediately to the right of the face where the iron was 0.695%. We believe that the small increase in iron in the Antlered Serpent represents the charcoal pigment being mixed with a trace of red pigment or applied with the same brush as the red pigment without careful cleaning.

Black Arm

Another important black pigment painting is the "Black Arm" (Figure 17) that is found in Cave 1, Panel 5, Glyph 212. This glyph has an uncorrected ^{14}C date of A.D. 950 ± 70 (Diaz-Granados and Duncan 2000:Table 6.1). This pictograph has been identified by Duncan and Diaz-Granados (2018:Figure 2.12) as belonging to the Spirit Being named "Sky Chief" who has a rich tradition among Sioux. The pictograph shows an arm that holds an animal puppet (of a bison? a rabbit?) and an animal pelt (an otter?) draped over the arm. These attributes are problematic because they do not immediately correlate with the stories of Sky Chief. For simplicity, we will refer to this pictograph as Black Arm. Keyser (2018:119) noted that "Long Arm," who interferes with humans, can be found at several northern Plains rock art sites; Matthews (1877:69–70) is the earliest source on this powerful Spirit Being as recounted to him by the Hidatsa.

The pXRF analysis of the Black Arm pictograph demonstrated elemental components of:

- silicon = 92.034% ± 4.22
- aluminum = 5.188% ± 0.57
- iron = 2.719% ± 0.549

Figure 17. Black arm with animal pelt extends from a crevice in the wall; Cave 1, Panel 3, Glyph 43. Scale is 10 cm. Photograph by Eric Fuller.

An unpainted portion of bedrock beneath the arm has less iron (1.37% ± 0.197). The DStretch analysis of the Black Arm pictograph does not show an underlying red pictograph, so we assume the trace of iron must be either intentional or an accidental admixture of a small amount of red pigment with the black pigment.

Mantled Warrior

The scale of the Black Arm pictograph is very large compared to the majority of the pictographs in Picture Cave. Two other "large" scale pictographs are the "kneeling warrior with forked eye" (Cave 1, Panel 4, Glyph 192), and "Mantled Warrior" (Cave 1, Panel 1, Glyph 130). A sample of the black pigment of the "Mantled Warrior" (Figure 18) was used for radiocarbon dating; the uncalibrated ^{14}C date is A.D. 1010 ± 80 (Diaz-Granados et al. 2015:Figure 5.2, Table 5.1).

Diaz-Granados and Duncan (2000:Plate 14, Figure 5.48) described this pictograph as a "Kilted Figure"; the term "kilt" is odd because the garment appears to expose one shoulder and is wrapped around the upper and lower torso—a kilt covers only the waist. Specialists studying the preserved Mississippian textiles from Spiro Mound generally classify the garments as mantles versus skirts (Sievert 2011:60). We have chosen the term "Mantled Warrior" instead of "Kilted" or "Skirted" warrior. An Osage warrior wears a blanket or robe with

Figure 18. Wrapped warrior with forked eye and brandishing a mace; Cave 1, Panel 1, Glyph 130.

his weapon arm free to reflect the fact that he is capable of defending against attack; the specific term in Osage for such a cape/mantle is *a´-ga-ha-mi* (La Fleche 1932:8, 239; Joe Hall, personal communication August 12, 2021). Catlin (1841b:Plates 152, 153) illustrated Osage warriors Tal-lee and Tchong-tas-sab-bee each wearing a trade blanket off one shoulder and holding a lance or tomahawk in his free hand. A "King" of the Timucua Nation (modern Florida and southeast Georgia) is shown wearing a one-shoulder mantle in a painting by Jacques Le Moyne de Morgues in 1564 (Dye 2020:154).

Diaz-Granados (2004:146, Figure 17), in a later article, identified the Mantled Warrior pictograph as the "Giant" in the story of the Hero Twins; this identification was based on the two elite warriors, much smaller in scale, in front of the Mantled Warrior. We believe that the identification of the Hero Twins is plausible, but it is unlikely that the painter who created them was the same artist who created the larger figure; style and execution are very different. Likewise, the two arrows in the chest of the Mantled Warrior were most likely painted by the artist who painted the two warriors in smaller scale.

Roediger (1991:115) notes that men wearing an over-the-shoulder mantle signified a special person of eminence among the Pueblo populations of the Southwest United States. Among the Aztecs, a mantle/cape was called a *tilmátli* (Aguilar-Moreno 2006:365; Berdan and Anawalt 1992:Folio 65r) and a decorated mantle was one of the gifts sent by Moctezuma to Cortes when the Spaniards ships were anchored in Veracruz (Markman and Markman 1989:97).

The pXRF analysis of the pigment smear beneath the chin of the warrior showed no significant difference with the nearby clean wall; suggesting the black pigment is charcoal without a trace/residue of red pigment. There was actually a lower amount of iron in the black pigment (872.81 ppm ± 40.44 ppm) than the unpainted bedrock directly above the head of the figure (1335.6 ppm ± 63.31).

Black Anthropomorph

Another important black pigment pictograph (Figure 19, right) in Picture Cave 1 is found in Panel 1, Glyph 69. Blankenship (2015:Figure 4.8, Table 4.1) describes this as an anthropomorphic image and characterized its major chemical elements as carbon, oxygen, and silicon with minor components of aluminum, potassium, phosphorus, and iron. Our pXRF analysis indicates that the black pigment is composed of:

- silicon = 94.846% ± 1.459
- aluminum = 4.018% ± 0.304
- iron = 1.013% ± 0.176

The nearby unpainted wall has almost identical percentages of silicon and aluminum, but half the amount of iron (0.518% ± 0.116). Cressler and Simek (2015:275) note that the figure holds a bow with an unnocked arrow in its right hand; they characterize the

Figure 19. Anthropomorphic figure with head regalia and a bow/arrow to the right of the thunderbird, Picture Cave 1, Panel 1, Glyph 69. Photo by Mark Leach.

head as distinctly drawn in a V shape, though we see the head as wearing trailing regalia. The black figure is immediately to the right of an equal size bird with outstretched wings and a flared tail (Figure 19, left); it resembles a thunderbird as represented at several rock art sites in Missouri and the Plains.

Black Deer

A black pigment pictograph of a deer (Figure 20, right) rendered as if it had been penciled versus painted in black pigment is situated in Picture Cave 1, Panel 4. Glyph 203. Blankenship (2015:41, Figure 4.6, Table 4.1) analyzed this pictograph and reported that it was primarily carbon (58.37%) with "minor impurities from the underlying sandstone." Our pXRF identified the major elements as:

- silicon = 92.033% ± 1.996
- aluminum = 5.699% ± 0.382
- iron = 2.152% ± 0.274

These are within the range of the nearby unpainted wall; in fact, the iron content of the bedrock was greater (2.89% ± 0.306) compared to the pictograph. The ppm readings did not identify any trace elements in the pigment that were not represented in roughly equivalent values in the unpainted bedrock. The unbranched

Figure 20. Two deer with upturned tails painted in black pigment. The animal on the right has tall unbranched horns or antlers; Picture Cave 1, Panel 4, Glyphs 202 and 203. Photograph by Michael Fuller.

versus branched antlers may be less significant than "big" antlers versus "small" antlers. One way to read this image is that a young buck is shadowing a mature buck as often happens in Missouri during the winter.

Anthropomorph with Shield

A black pigment pictograph (Figure 21) in Cave 2, Panel 4, Glyph 532, has been interpreted as an anthropomorphic image with a rectangular shield (Blankenship 2015;39, Figure 4.2, Table 4.1). This does not contradict our interpretation of Cave 2 as primarily dealing with Sky clans and peace; Osage men of the

Figure 21. Black pigment figure interpreted as holding a rectangular shield from Cave 2, Panel 4, Glyph 532.

Sky clans fight alongside the Earth/Water clans during times of war (La Flesche 1939:13, 16). It is also possible that the figure does not hold a shield, but a hide or textile. Blankenship characterized the pigment of this figure as either carbon black or iron-rich clay (ochre). Our pXRF analysis identified:

- silicon = 96.141% ± 1.233
- aluminum = 2.357% ± 0.225
- iron = 1.437% ± 0.189

The percentage of iron in the nearby unpainted bedrock was lower (0.918% ± 0.174) than in the pigment, but not exceptionally different. Likewise, the ppm of iron was higher in the pigment (1950.0 ppm ± 0.174) than in the unpainted bedrock (862.9 ppm ± 39.07).

A Possible Biographic Composition

A fascinating cluster of pictographs (Figure 22) in Picture Cave 1 has not been extensively discussed—it is a combination of red and black pictographs immediately to the right of the red dot and circle that we interpret as a war shield. This is the third biographic pictograph we have identified in Picture Cave.

At first glance, we saw the cluster of red and black pictographs as an allegory related to hunting taboos—the small black figure on the left side of the composition as a hunter trapped in his own pound/corral by an avenging Spirit Being. Professor Alice Kehoe (personal

Figure 22. DStretch LDS image of the scene rendered with both red and black pigments in the same composition, Cave 1, Panel 2, Glyphs 10, 11, 12, and 13.

Figure 23. DStretch of paddlers painted in Cave 1 above Panel 4. Photograph by Mark Leach.

communication June 6, 2021) kindly pointed out that the design around the single black figure makes better sense as war regalia, and Jim Keyser (personal communication June 13, 2021) suggested that the two small figures under the large red archer could well be name glyphs. Their observations are very convincing. The two pictograms under the large red archer include a slain deer and a seated figure (another deer?) near the head of the slain deer. Using Osage naming traditions reported by La Flesche (1928:48), it is possible that the seated figure is making an offering of a bowl of water or a bowl of shelled corn. Was the name something like "Mourner" or "Avenger" of the slain deer? This series of red and black pictographs was not pXRF analyzed, but that is planned for a future expedition.

Canoe with Four Paddlers

We were surprised while doing DStretch analysis in Picture Cave 1 to recognize the representation of a large canoe with four paddlers (Figure 23) painted in black pigment above Panel 4. This pictograph is not discussed in *Picture Cave* (Diaz Granados et al. 2015). Only half of the canoe is shown, as if saying that it is emerging from the stone, like men paddling out of a fog bank. The first and second paddlers clearly have a single feather in their hair; the fourth paddler is either standing or is at least a head taller than the other three. The Piney Creek site (11R26) in southern Illinois has a red pigment canoe pictograph that shows a full canoe with six short figures and one tall figure (Wagner et al. 2018:Figure 5.57); most of the Piney Creek pictographs can be dated to the Mississippian period based upon motif and degree of preservation.

Paddlers in a dugout canoe appear on fragments of engraved shell cups found at Spiro Mound (Page 1981:8–9; Wood 2018:Figure 3). Paddler gods in Maya cosmology are involved with recreating earth after a cataclysmic destruction (Aveni 2019:18). There are several examples of carved bones and a painted Maya pottery vessel showing canoes and paddlers (Freidel et al. 1993:89–93). The long bones decorated with scenes of paddlers were uncovered by the University of Pennsylvania excavation inside Temple I, the tomb of Jasaw Chan K'awiil, one of the most powerful kings who ruled Tikal from A.D. 682 to 734.

It may well be that the paddlers painted on the wall of Picture Cave 1 are Spirit Beings as in the case of Maya art, but there is also the possibility that this pictograph is biographic and celebrates the moment that a great ruler (the larger figure) arrived on a journey of conquest or diplomacy. A canoe with seven warriors is represented as decoration on one side of an eighteenth-century Osage war club carved out of Osage orange (Bailey and Swan 2004:98, Cat. 55); the reverse of the war club shows three headless corpses and "the arrow of death."

Summary

Over 300 pictographs decorate the walls of Picture Cave 1 and 2. The pXRF data for the pigments show that red was created from iron minerals and black from charcoal; this was expected and indicated by the initial XRD analysis by Blankenship (2015). A few black pigment pictographs also contained traces of iron. The white pigments are still problematic. The two sets of fierce eyes in Cave 1 can best be explained as a pigment probably containing either mica and/or kaolinite. The white pigment of Red Horn is most definitely not lead; additional study is certainly needed.

We interpret the motif differences between Cave 1 and 2 as reflecting the symbolic associations between Earth/Water clans versus Sky clans. The use of biographic pictographs in Cave 1 is particularly significant as these may be significant historical figures either from Cahokia or one of its sister communities such as the St. Louis Mound Group or the Blake Mound/Centaur Mound Group.

References Cited

Aguilar-Moreno, Manuel
2006 *Handbook to Life in the Aztec World.* Facts on File, New York.

Aveni, Anthony F.
2019 *Star Stories: Constellations and People.* Yale University Press, New Haven.

Bailey, Garrick
2004 Osage Cosmology. In *Art of the Osage* by Garrick Bailey and Daniel C. Swan, pp. 27–38. University of Washington Press, Seattle.

Bailey, Garrick, and Daniel C. Swan
2004 *Art of the Osage.* With contributions by John W. Nunley and E. Sean Standing Bear. University of Washington Press, Seattle.

Berdan, Frances F., and Patricia R. Anawalt
1992 *The Codex Mendoza.* University of California Press, Berkeley.

Blankenship, Sarah A.
2015 Geochemical Analyses of Prehistoric Pigment Materials from Picture Cave. In *Picture Cave: Unraveling the Mysteries of the Mississippian Cosmos,* edited by Carol Diaz-Granados, James R. Duncan, and F. Kent Reilly II, pp. 37–45. University of Texas Press, Austin.

Brown, James A., and Jon Muller
2015 Tradition and Horizons in Southeastern Representation. In *Picture Cave: Unraveling the Mysteries of the Mississippian Cosmos,* edited by Carol Diaz-Granados, James R. Duncan, and F. Kent Reilly II, pp. 113–124. University of Texas Press, Austin.

Bryan, William S.
1909 Daniel Boone in Missouri. *Missouri Historical Review* 3(4):293–299.

Bryan, William S., and Robert Rose
1876 *A History of the Pioneer Families of Missouri.* Bryan, Brand & Co., St. Louis.

Catlin, George
1841a *Letters and Notes on the Manners, Customs, and Conditions of the North American Indians, Volume* 1. Published by the author, London. Facsimile reprint 1965, Ross and Haines, Minneapolis, Minnesota. Electronic document, http://archive.org/details/39002055099585.med.yale.edu, accessed January 12, 2022.

1841b *Letters and Notes on the Manners, Customs, and Conditions of the North American Indians, Volume* 2. Published by the author, London. Facsimile reprint 1965, Ross and Haines, Minneapolis, Minnesota. Electronic document, http://archive.org/details/39002055099593.med.yale.edu, accessed January 12, 2022.

Cressler, Alan, and Jan F. Simek
2015 Illustrated Catalog of Picture Cave Art. Appendix in *Picture Cave: Unraveling the Mysteries of the Mississippian Cosmos,* edited by Carol Diaz-Granados, James R. Duncan, and F. Kent Reilly II, pp. 273–301.

David, Robert J.
2016 *Spirit Fire and Lightning Songs: Looking at Myth and Shamanism on a Klamath Basin Petroglyph Site.* University of California Press, Berkeley.

2021 Spirit Songs and Sacred Fire: Considering Native Perspectives through an Understanding of Klamath Basin Myth. Zoom presentation, American Rock Art Research Association lecture series, May 8, 2021. Electronic document, https://www.youtube.com/watch?v=10JdDIJN1iw, accessed May 4, 2022.

DeBoer, Warren R.
2005 Colors of a North American Past. *World Archaeology* 37(1):66–91.

Diaz-Granados, Carol
1993 *The Petroglyphs and Pictographs of Missouri—A Distributional, Stylistic, Contextual, Temporal and Functional Analysis of the State's Rock Art.* Ph.D. dissertation, Department of Anthropology, Washington University, St. Louis, Missouri.

2004 Marking Stone, Land, Body, and Spirit: Rock Art and Mississippian Iconography. In *Hero, Hawk and Open Hand: American Indian Art of the Ancient Midwest and South,* edited by R. Townsend and R. V. Sharp, pp. 139–150. Yale University Press, New Haven.

Diaz-Granados, Carol, and James R. Duncan
2000 *The Petroglyphs and Pictographs of Missouri.* University of Alabama Press, Tuscaloosa.

Diaz-Granados, Carol, James R. Duncan, and F. Kent Reilly III, eds.
2015 *Picture Cave: Unraveling the Mysteries of the Mississippian Cosmos.* University of Texas Press, Austin.

Diaz-Granados, Carol, Marvin W. Rowe, Marian Hyman, James R. Duncan, and John R. Southon
2001 AMS Radiocarbon Dates for Charcoal from Three Missouri Pictographs and their Associated Iconography. *American Antiquity* 66:481–492.

Dieterle, Richard L.
2010 The Redhorn Panel of Picture Cave: An American Star Map. The Encyclopedia of Hočąk (Winnebago) Mythology (online). Electronic document, https://hotcakencyclopedia.com/ho.RedhornPanelStarMap.html, accessed July 9, 2021.

Dorsey, James Owen
1884 An Account of the War Customs of the Osages. *American Naturalist* 18:113–133.

Duncan, James R., and Carol Diaz-Granados
2018 The Big Five Petroglyph Sites: The Place on the Landscape and Relation to the Creators. In *Transforming the Landscape: Rock Art and the Mississippian Cosmos,* Carol Diaz-Granados, Jan Simek, George Sabo, and Mark Wagner (editors). Oxbow Books, Havertown, Pennsylvania.

Dye, David H.
2017 Animal Pelt Caps and Mississippian Ritual Sodalities. *North American Archaeologist* 38(1):63–97.

2020 Mississippian Symbolic Weaponry at Spiro. In *Recovering Ancient Spiro: Native American Art, Ritual, and Cosmic Renewal,* edited by Eric D. Singleton and F. Kent Reilly III, pp. 152–173. National Cowboy & Western Heritage Museum, Oklahoma City.

Ellis, Florence Hawley, and Laurens Hammack
1968 The Inner Sanctum of Feather Cave, a Mogollon Sun and Earth Shrine Linking Mexico and the Southwest. *American Antiquity* 33(1):25–44.

Freidel, David, Linda Schele, and Joy Parker
1993 *Maya Cosmos: Three Thousand Years on the Shaman's Path.* Quill William Morrow, New York.

Fuller, Eric C.
2018 *Osage Wild Plants in Missouri, Arkansas, Kansas and Oklahoma.* Manuscript version January 14, 2018. Copies on file with Cameron Pratt at the Daposka Ahnkodapi School, and with Vann Bighorse at the Osage Nation Language Department in Pawhuska, Oklahoma.

Fuller, Michael J.
2011 Turtle Shelter Rock Art Site. *Missouri Archaeological Society Quarterly* 28(2):8–11.

2014 Cactus Cove Pictograph Site (23WN1156). *Missouri Archaeological Society Quarterly* 31(3):12–17.

2021 Picture Cave. Michael Fuller (website). Electronic document, http://www.profmichaelfuller.com/picture-cave.html, accessed May 11, 2022.

Fuller, Michael J., Neathery B. Fuller, and Eric C. Fuller
2019 Total Solar Eclipses and Rock Art in Missouri. *Missouri Archaeological Society Quarterly* 36(1):12–19.

Goodman, Ronald
1992 *Lakota Star Knowledge: Studies in Lakota Stellar Theology.* Sinjfe Gleska University Press, Rosebud Sioux Reservation, Mission, South Dakota.

Harrison, Eugenia Lillian
1943 *The Place Names of Four River Counties in Eastern Missouri.* Master's Thesis, University of Missouri, Columbia.

Houck, Louis
1908 *A History of Missouri: From the Earliest Explorations and Settlements until the Admission of the State into the Union.* Volume 1. R. R. Donnelley & Sons, Chicago. Electronic document, https://archive.org/details/historyofmissour01houc/page/n9/mode/2up, accessed May 18, 2022.

Hough, Walter
1907 Dyes and Pigments. In *Handbook of American Indians North of Mexico,* Volume 1, edited by Frederick Webb Hodge, pp. 407–408. Bureau of American Ethnography Bulletin 30. Electronic document, http://www.archive.org/details/bulletin-3011907smit, accessed January 13, 2022.

Keyser, James D.
1979 The Plains Indian War Complex and the Rock Art of Writing-On-Stone, Alberta, Canada. *Journal of Field Archaeology* 6(1):41–48.

2000 *The Five Crows Ledger: Biographic Warrior Art of the Flathead Indians.* University of Utah Press, Salt Lake City.

2004 *Art of the Warriors: Rock Art of the American Plains.* University of Utah Press, Salt Lake City.

2018 Warriors and Weapons: Late Prehistoric/Protohistoric-Period Warfare in Bear Gulch Rock Art. In *Archaeological Perspectives on Warfare on the Great Plains,* edited by Andrew Clark and Douglas Bamforth, pp. 66–119. University of Colorado Press, Boulder.

Keyser, James D., and Michael A. Klassen
2001 *Plains Indian Rock Art.* University of Washington Press, Seattle.

2003 Every Detail Counts: More Additions to the Plains Biographic Rock Art Lexicon. *Plains Anthropologist* 48(184):7–20.

Koenig, Charles W., Amanda M. Castañeda, and Carolyn E. Boyd
2014 Portable X-Ray Fluorescence Spectroscopy of Pictographs: A Case Study from the Lower Pecos Canyonlands, Texas. *Archaeometry* 56(51) Supplement 1:168–186.

La Flesche, Francis
1921 *The Osage Tribe: Rite of the Chiefs; Sayings of the Ancient Men.* Thirty-sixth Annual Report of the Bureau of American Ethnology 1914-1915, pp. 35–604.

1928 *Osage Tribe, Two Versions of the Child-naming Rite.* Forty-third Annual Report of the Bureau of American Ethnology 1925-1926, pp. 23–164.

1930 *The Osage Tribe, Rite of Wa-xo-be.* Forty-fifth Annual Report of the Bureau of American Ethnology 1927-1928, pp. 523–833. Electronic document, https://www.biodiversitylibrary.org/item/10771#page/565/mode/1up, accessed June 24, 2022.

1932 *A Dictionary of the Osage Language.* Bureau of American Ethnology Bulletin 109, pp. 1–406.

1939 *War and Peace Ceremony of the Osage Indians.* Bureau of American Ethnology Bulletin 101, pp. 1–280. Electronic document, https://repository.si.edu/handle/10088/15407, accessed June 24, 2022.

Lee, Annette S., Jim Rock, and Charlene O'Rourke
2014. *D(L)akota Star Map Constellation Guide: An Introduction to D(L)akota Star Knowledge.* (Native Skywatchers, St. Cloud, Minnesota.

Lewis-Williams, J. David, and Thomas A. Dowson
1988 The Signs of All Times: Entoptic Phenomena in Upper Palaeolithic Art. *Current Anthropology* 29(2):201–245.

Littmann, Edwin R.
1975 Methods for the Identification of Pigments. *American Antiquity* 40(3):349–353.

Markman, Roberta H., and Peter T. Markman
1989 *Masks of the Spirit: Image and Metaphor in Mesoamerica.* University of California Press, Berkeley.

Mathews, John Joseph
1961 *The Osage: Children of the Middle Waters.* University of Oklahoma Press, Norman.

Matthews, Washington
1877 *Ethnography and Philology of the Hidatsa Indians.* United States Geological and Geographical Survey Miscellaneous Publication 7, Washington, D.C.

Page, Barbara
1981 Spiro Mound Artifacts Reveal 12th Century Culture. *Gilcrease Magazine* 3(3):2–11.

Pauketat, Timothy R.
2004 *Ancient Cahokia and the Mississippians.* Cambridge University Press, Cambridge.

Quintero, Carolyn
2009 *Osage Dictionary.* University of Oklahoma Press, Norman.

Roediger, Virginia More
1991 *Ceremonial Costumes of the Pueblo Indians.* University of California Press, Berkeley.

Rowe, Marvin W.
2009 Radiocarbon Dating of Ancient Rock Art Paintings. *Analytical Chemistry* 81:1728–1735.

Sievert, April K.
2011 Fiber Artifacts. In *Artifacts from the Craig Mound at Spiro, Oklahoma,* edited by April K. Sievert with J. Daniel Rogers, pp. 55–72. Smithsonian Institute Scholarly Press, Washington, D.C.

Simek, Jan F., and Alan Cressler
2015 "Tracings in the Idleness of Art": Picture Cave in the Context of Southeast Prehistoric Cave Art. In *Picture Cave: Unraveling*

the Mysteries of the Mississippian Cosmos, edited by Carol Diaz-Granados, James R. Duncan, and F. Kent Reilly III, pp. 9–27. University of Texas Press, Austin.

Thwaites, Reuben Gold
1904 *Original Journals of the Lewis and Clark Expedition 1804–1806,* Volume 1. Dodd, Mead & Co., New York.

Townsend, Richard F.
2015 The Cave, Cahokia, and the Omaha Tribe. In *Picture Cave: Unraveling the Mysteries of the Mississippian Cosmos,* edited by Carol Diaz-Granados, James R. Duncan, and F. Kent Reilly III, pp. 145–165. University of Texas Press, Austin.

Wagner, Mark J., Kayeleigh Sharp, and Jonathan Remo
2018 Transformed Spaces: A Landscape Approach to the Rock Art of Illinois. In *Transforming the Landscape: Rock Art and the Mississippian Cosmos,* edited by Carol Diaz-Granados, Jan Simek, George Sabo, and Mark Wagner, pp. 100–154. Oxbow Books, Oxford.

Wood, Peter H.
2018 Missing the Boat: Ancient Dugout Canoes in the Mississippi-Missouri Watershed. *Early American Studies* 16(2):197–254.

Keeping Score—A Crow (*Apsáalooke*) War Tally

James D. Keyser, David A. Kaiser, and Stephen J. Lycett

First reported in 1960 and mentioned again in an article about 25 years later, the Weppler site (24ST560) has always been an enigma, not obviously related to any other rock art in the Yellowstone and Musselshell River drainages of central Montana. However, recent research into the ways Plains warriors tallied their various war honors coupled with the first photographs of the site have finally enabled us to understand the Weppler images as a bar tally documenting the honors of Crow warriors.

Plains Indian warriors "kept score" by tallying their war honors in many ways. Enemies overcome, slaves captured, weapons or scalps taken, the times a man or his horse was wounded, service as a war-party scout, and horses stolen or gifted are but a few of the deeds these men enumerated on various "scoresheets" (Table 1). Tallies were painted on bison robes, a man's body, various clothing items, and even some utilitarian tools (Figures 1–3). Tallies were also drawn as ledger drawings and painted and carved at rock art sites (Figure 3a, d).

Figure 1. Tracing of a Crow robe dating prior to 1837 that illustrates both an enemy tally (top half) and a bar tally (bottom half). Adapted from Brownstone (2001:70) with additions from photographs in Keyser's possession.

James D. Keyser
Oregon Archaeological Society, Portland, Oregon

David A. Kaiser
Oregon Archaeological Society, Portland, Oregon

Stephen J. Lycett
Department of Anthropology, University at Buffalo, The State University of New York (SUNY) Amherst, New York

American Indian Rock Art, Volume 48. Amy Gilreath, Ken Hedges, and Anne McConnell, Editors. American Rock Art Research Association, 2022, pp. 21–37.

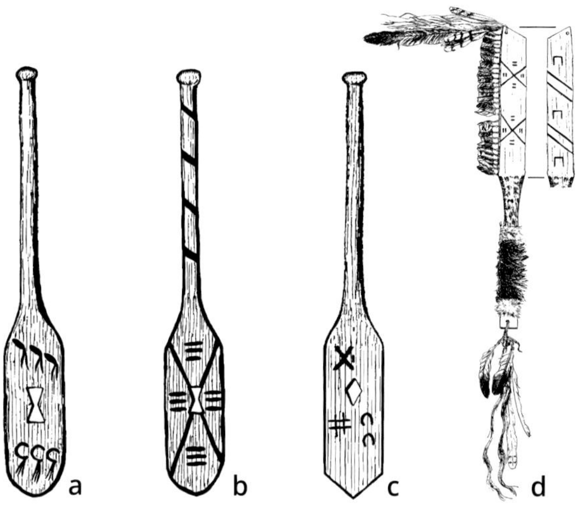

Figure 2. Tallies were recorded on a variety of personal possessions: (a-c) Bullboat paddles; (d) Lumpwood Society officer's emblem; a-c adapted from Wilson (1924:257) and Mallery (1893:442), d adapted from Lowie (1913:261).

Brownstone (2001:78–80) has named two types of tallies: Bar tallies, which count the number of an artist's war parties (and often the deeds accomplished on each); and object tallies, which usually count captured war trophies but sometimes list objects gifted to others to increase a man's prestige. To these two basic types of tallies, we add "enemy tallies" showing vanquished or abducted enemies (and often the weapon used to strike or kill them), and "action tallies" showing the number of times a warrior or his horse has been involved in some honorific activity. Among the many such actions commemorated by these tallies are the number of wounds the warrior or his horse received in combat, the number of times he led a war party or served as a war-party scout, the number of times he has fought from behind breastworks; and the number of times he took a picketed horse (Table 1).

Table 1. War Honors Found in Tallies.

War Honors Found in Tallies	Crow	Blackfoot	Sarsi	Hidatsa	Mandan	Arikara	Lakota	Other
Count First Coup in a Fight [1]	X							
Take Weapon in Combat [1, 2]	X	X			X			X
Take Picketed Horse [1]	X	X					X	
Lead War Party [1]	X	X					X	
Take a Horse	X	X	X	X	X	X	X	X
First to Strike an Enemy	X	X	X	X	X	X	X	X
Second to Strike an Enemy	X	X	X	X	X	X	X	X
Third to Strike an Enemy	X	X	X	X	X	X	X	X
Fourth to Strike an Enemy	X	X	X	X	X	X	X	X
Kill an Enemy [3]							X	
Hand to Hand Combat with Enemy							X	
Capture an Enemy		X					X	
Serve as War Party Scout	X	X	X				X	X
Suffer a Wound	X			X	X	X	X	
Horse Suffers a Wound				X	X	X		
Take an Enemy Scalp	X	X	X					
Participate in a War Party	X	X		X	?	?		
Fight Behind Breastworks [4]	X			X	X	X		
Face a Fusillade of Fire		X						
Trample an Enemy								X
Rescue a Comrade							X	
Give Away a Horse	X			X	X			
Give Away Other Captured Property				X	X	X		X

[1] These are the four primary coups for Crow chieftainship.
[2] Some tribes rated taking a gun highest, but all war trophies were tallied.
[3] In some tallies this may be different than striking an enemy.
[4] Only some tribes recognized this as an honor.

All four types of tallies summarize a man's brave deeds (or, in the case of an object given away, his generosity), and were advertised to bolster his status as an accomplished warrior and tribal leader. All four types of tallies occur in all major Biographic art media—robe art, ledger drawings, and rock art—throughout the Plains. Most common in rock art are object tallies and enemy tallies, both of which have a common objective—to show close-quarter battle actions resulting from directly engaging and overpowering an enemy. Their similar function means they were often combined in rock art tallies and both types have each been recognized at

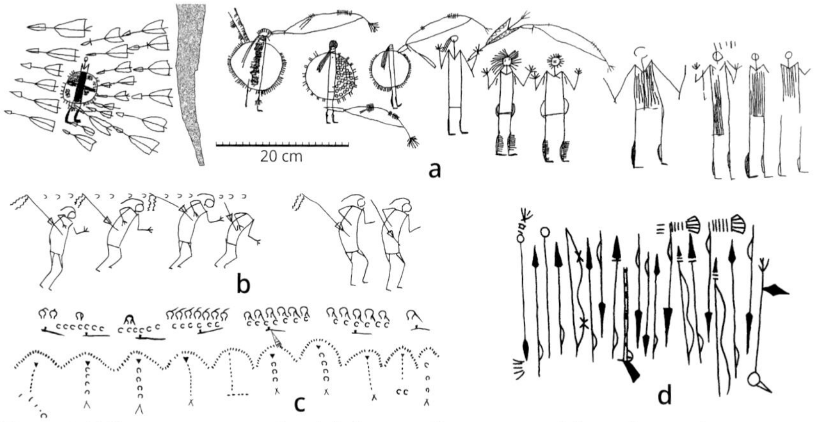

Figure 3. Tallies in various media: (a) Enemy tally at Bear Gulch site (24FR2), Montana; (b) enemy tally by Red Feather (Adolphe) in the Five Crows ledger; (c) action tally on the robe of Crow warrior Charges Strong; (d) object tally at Mujares Creek, Texas.

more than a half-dozen rock art sites (Table 2). Tallied objects in rock art include gun, lance, coup stick, sword, tomahawk, quirt, scalp pole, arrows, bow, bow-spear, shield, and partisan's pipe. Although this is a slightly less diverse assemblage of items than that painted in robe art (lacking scalps, bags, medicine bundles, knives, powder horns, and shot pouches), it is still an impressive array of objects.

Action tallies are less common in rock art, and correspondingly show fewer "actions." Such tallies are largely dependent on a vocabulary of exploit (or honor) marks developed and repeatedly used by the artists of a tribe or an affiliated group of tribes. On the northern Plains there were two primary vocabularies (Figure 4), one used by the Blackfoot confederacy (Blackfoot, Blood, Piegan, and Sarsi) and another used by the Crow and the three affiliated Upper Missouri River tribes (Hidatsa, Mandan, and Arikara). The Lakota also used the vocabulary of the Upper Missouri tribes but in a far less formalized manner.

Table 2. Rock Art Sites with War-Honor Tallies.

Rock Art Site	Bar Tally	Object Tally	Enemy Tally	Action Tally	Combination
EiPl-19		X	X		
DgOv-83			X		
DgOw-9					X
DgOw-27 (at Writing-on-Stone)				XX	
DgOw-30			X		
24FR2 (Bear Gulch)			XX		
24ML508			X		
24ML560			X		
24RB1019			X		
24ST560 (Weppler)	X				
24YL82			X		
24YL417			X		
24YL419 (Nordstrom-Bowen)	XX	X			
24YL1190		X			
39FA79			X		
39HN210		X			
Tensleep Canyon, Wyoming*					X
48CO287 (Little Boxelder Cave)			X		
48SW82			X		
5BL4885			X		
14RU304		X			
Conant Springs, New Mexico			X		
Mujares Creek, Texas		X			
41VV327			X		

X is one occurrence XX is two occurrences.
* Site described and illustrated in Keyser and Poetschat 2014:281.

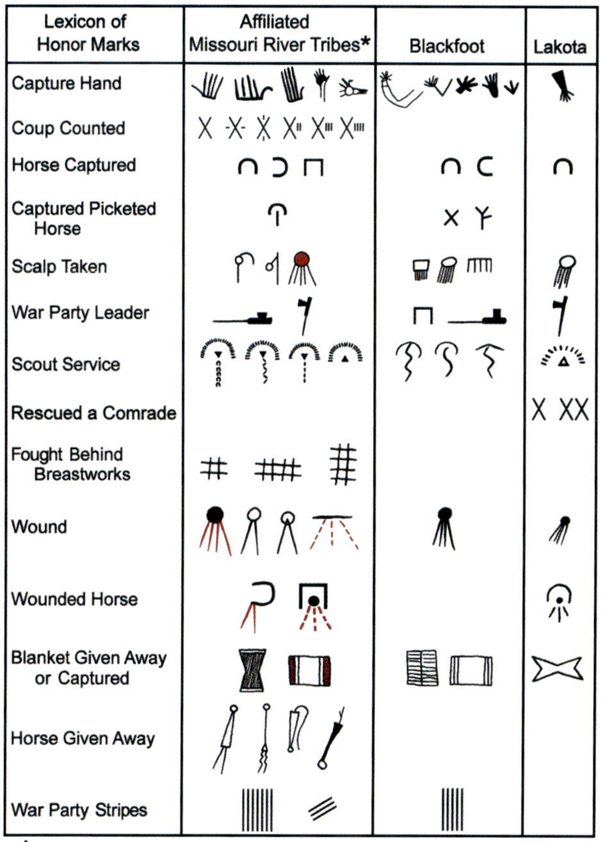

*Crow, Hidatsa, Mandan, Arikara

Figure 4. Vocabularies of honor marks used on the northern Plains.

Site DgOw-27 at Writing-on-Stone, Alberta, shows two warriors' tallies of war parties led and picketed horses taken (Figure 5). These tallies have been fully described (Keyser and Klassen 2003:10–12) and recently dated to the turn of the twentieth century by comparing them and their unique "vocabulary" with that used in Blackfoot robe art at that time (Lycett and Keyser 2021). So far, other action tallies of scout-service symbols, wounds, and less common honors (Table 1) have not yet been recognized in rock art, even though wounds and scout-service tallies are relatively common in the robe and ledger art of Blackfoot, Crow, Hidatsa, Gros Ventres, and Lakota warriors, all of whom are known to have carved and painted rock

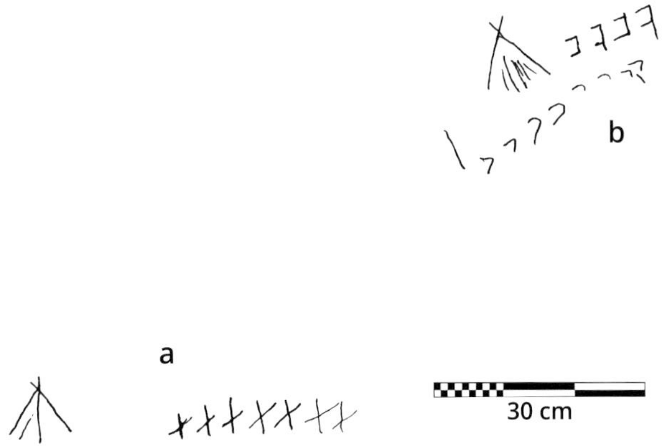

Figure 5. This action tally at DgOw-27 at Writing-on-Stone, Alberta, records two warriors' success as horse raiders.

art (Barbeau 1960:Figures 101, 111, 134; Cowdrey 2010:Figures 4, 11; Dempsey 2007; Feder 1980:59; Greene 2006:Figures 3, 14; Lessard 1991:73; Schoolcraft 1854:251, Plate 31; Taylor 1998:28).

Bar tallies have been recognized at two rock art sites. At Nordstrom-Bowen (24YL419), there are what appear to be two such tallies (Figure 6). One is part of a much more-extensive tally inscribed as the top row of images on one panel at the site. A sequence of 13 tall vertical lines forms the right half of this row. Most of these lines have shorter oblique lines extending to the left from near their tops. Although these were originally identified as 13 scalp poles (Keyser and Cowdrey 2008), only six of them have small "tailed" circles among the oblique "danglers." Based on other Biographic drawings (Keyser 2000:58–60; Keyser and Poetschat 2009:18, 27), these small, tailed circles represent scalps. But three of the poles with scalps also have simple oblique lines, five other verticals have only two to seven short oblique lines with no obvious scalps, and two have no lines at all.

Figure 6. These tallies at the Nordstrom-Bowen site in Montana combine bar tallies, an object tally, and a vignette combat scene.

Comparing this structure to other bar tallies (cf. Brownstone 2008), we now believe that these vertical lines represent "war-party stripes," some of which are made into "compound strokes" by the attachment of oblique lines representing various war deeds that serve as what we term "modifier" marks (Figure 7).[1] Each vertical stripe represents a single war party; but, in order to keep track of various honorific deeds, warrior-artists made these stripes "compound" by attaching one or more small pictograms or ideograms representing the deed(s). Thus, a horse-hoofprint pictogram stood for a stolen horse while an **X** ideogram stood for a coup counted. Among the deeds depicted at Nordstrom-Bowen are scalps taken, represented by the small, tailed circles. Both Lowie (1912:231–236; 1913:163; 1922:253–255) and Bauerle (2003:99–104) document that scalps were frequently taken on the warpath and displayed in a variety of ways to indicate success upon the war party's return. The short, oblique lines without scalps could represent almost any warfare action from taking a picketed horse, to striking or killing an enemy, to capturing a weapon. Quite similar marks are shown as modifiers on several bar tallies (Figures 1, 8) and on one are actually identified as representing people killed (Mallery 1893:274). Because this bar tally is carefully aligned with the group of captured weapons forming the left part of the longer sequence—a com-

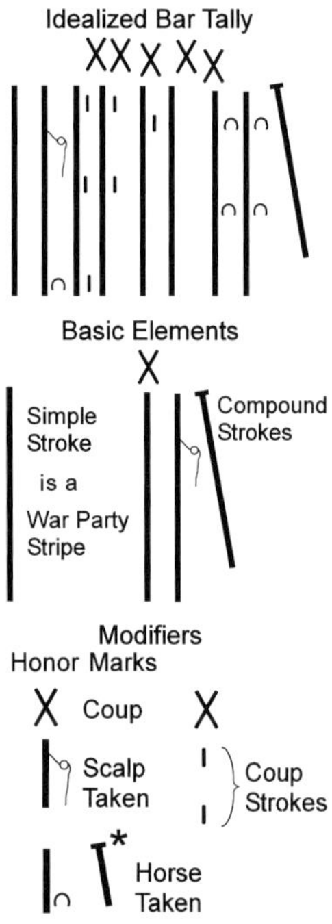

Figure 7. Terminology used in describing bar tallies. The asterisk at bottom indicates a possible interpretation.

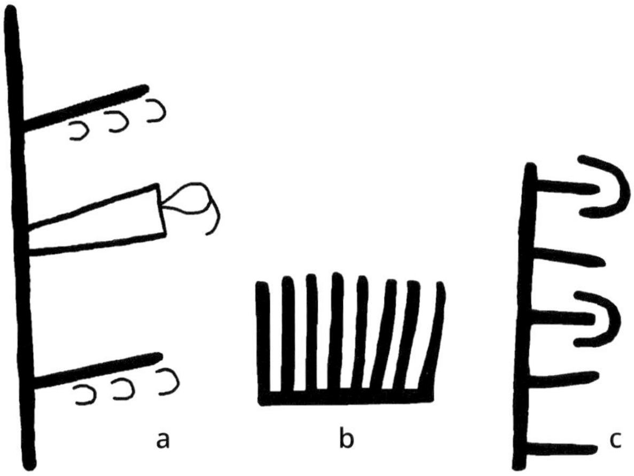

Figure 8. Simple modifiers used with bar tallies: (a) Painted Crow bison robe; (b) Lakota winter count; (c) Mandan woman's dress (painted with husband's honor marks).

position that illustrates one of the most detailed and expansive lists of tallied objects in Plains rock art—we propose that all the images forming this upper row are the work of a single artist.

What is likely a second bar tally on this same panel is a row of 15 vertical lines incised just below the left end of the upper combination object-and-bar tally (Figure 6). What these vertical bars actually count is open to interpretation, but we propose they are either war-party stripes carved on the panel by the first artist to augment the upper tally by adding his additional war expeditions, or (seemingly more likely) war-party stripes added by a different warrior-artist to represent his own war record. A single incised combat scene aligned just to the right of this lower bar tally is a relatively simple drawing, suggesting it belongs with the simpler bar tally.

The Nordstrom-Bowen object tally is a horizontal row of nine weapons plus two quirts. The weapons are (from left to right in Figure 6) a gun, two spears, two tomahawks, a crook-neck coup stick, a feathered lance with no point, a broadsword, and a recurved bow. Several of the weapons are elaborately decorated with tabs, fur-wrapped handles, and a fringe of feathers.

Inscribed next to the upper end of several objects in this tally are relatively large circles. In our own drawings, made from color slides taken in 1996, there are five of these placed between various weapons, but in a second drawing published by Arni Brownstone (2001) there are two additional circles, one located between the two tomahawks and one to the left of the gun on the far-left end of the tally. Both of the circles in Brownstone's drawing are slightly smaller and incomplete. We do not know what these circles represent, and Brownstone (2001:81) suggests they are "incidental to rather than a part of the adjacent objects." He further notes that similar small circles are illustrated in much the same position in a tally of war trophies painted on a Crow war shirt (Brownstone 2001:81). When asked specifically about these circles, Tim McCleary (2020) offered the following:

> ...the circles must mean something, but what exactly I was never able to [discover]. ... a few images...confirm they are 'something.'...[some] tally counts have modifiers between the objects (or lines)...My own speculation is the circle must mean something like, 'I was the first' or 'This was my first' or something of that nature. Obviously, [the circle indicates] that [the object] is somehow different than the others.

We agree with Brownstone that these circles are not a physical part of each object, but McCleary's observation makes sense to us. We know that tallies drawn by artists from the Crow and the three affiliated Missouri River tribes (Hidatsa, Mandan, and Arikara[2]) included various sorts of modifiers, some of which now seem essentially idiosyncratic. This is due to the difficulty of formulating "rules" for or "patterns" among the few such extant tallies preserved in the Historic record when there is little relevant ethnographic information. Thus, as of now, these circles remain an enigma, although we believe they did modify the adjacent weapons in some manner.

Based on other object tallies, however, these weapons certainly represent war trophies captured by the artist who drew them. The quirts could be captured war trophies, but they might just as easily represent horses gifted to others to increase the artist's prestige. Drawing quirts as honor marks in this way was documented by Prince Maximilian (1906:264) when he visited the upper Missouri villages in 1832-1834. While there, he wrote: "Another mode of painting their robes is, to represent the number of valuable presents they have made. By these presents, which are often of great value, they acquire respect and reputation..." These designs included "...whips, indicating the number of horses given, because the whip belonging to the horse is always bestowed with the animal."

Whether all the honors tallied on the accompanying 13 war-party stripes represent the deeds of one man is not known. For several groups, when using such war-party stripes to represent war-party leadership, an artist was permitted by tribal convention to illustrate all the deeds performed by members of his war party and, by extension, all the objects they had taken (Bowers 1965:258, 279–280; Brownstone 2001:78–79; 2008:18).

The Weppler Site Rediscovered

A newly reassessed pictograph site northwest of Billings, Montana, is an even better example of a Plains rock art bar tally. Drawn with charcoal on the back wall of a shallow rockshelter in a minor tributary to a larger drainage, the Weppler site (24ST560) was first reported in the professional literature by George Arthur (1960), who provided a sketch that misleadingly separates the large linear tally into two sections (cf. Figures 9, 10a). About two decades later Tom Lewis, a local avocational archaeologist, visited the site and published his sketch (Figure 10b)[3] of part of the imag-

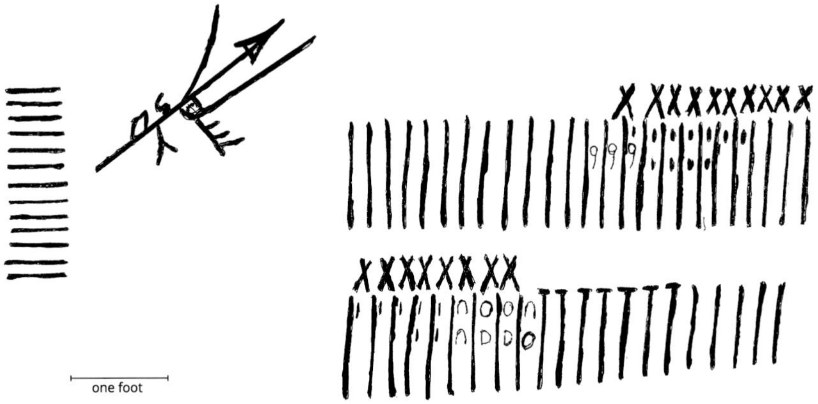

Figure 9. George Arthur's original sketch of the Weppler site imagery. Adapted from Arthur 1960.

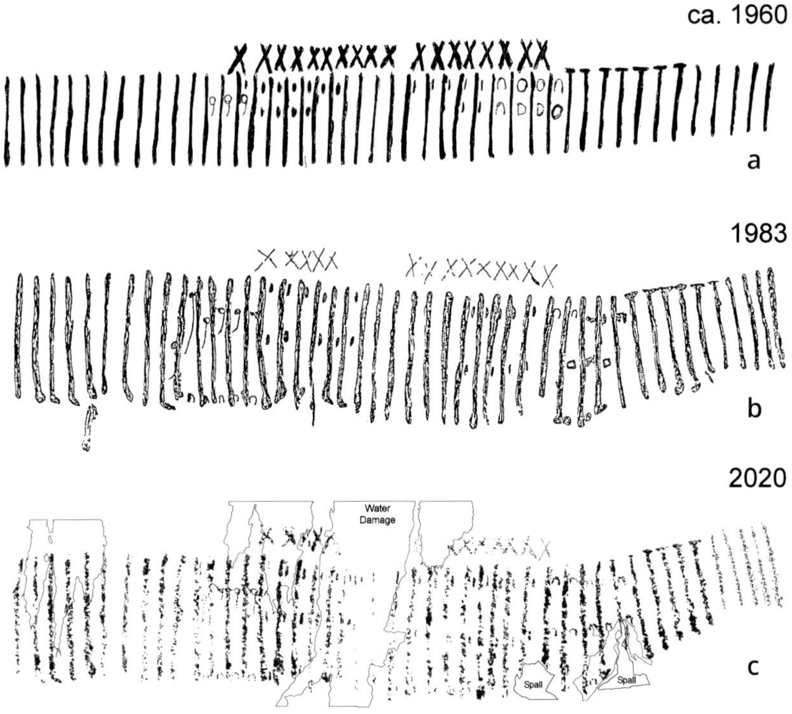

Figure 10. Comparison of previous sketches of Weppler site bar tally with authors' photo-tracing. (a) Arthur; (b) Lewis; (c) current photo-tracing.

ery (Lewis 1986:245, 248). Neither Arthur nor Lewis recognized the site for what it actually was, despite recognizing the horse hoofprints. Lewis proposed that the charcoal-drawn pictographs were some sort of solar notations with enigmatic "coefficient glyphs" and "subsidiary notations" and that in order to understand the imagery one might use "permutations of 46 and 14 or 46 and 18" (Lewis 1986:245). Our interest in the site was kindled as we were doing background research for a larger volume on Biographic rock art, and we recognized Arthur's drawing as showing a classic Plains bar tally with associated honor marks.

Due to the site's relevance to our larger work, in the spring of 2020, Keyser contacted an avocationalist colleague, Loren Haar, who lives in the general site area. By the late summer of 2020, Loren was able to visit and photograph the site with current and former landowners. Loren's photographs are the only ones presently available of the site, but they show the imagery to be in approximately the same condition as sketched by Tom Lewis, with only minor loss of smaller components (Figure 11). Unfortunately, both the Lewis sketches and the Haar photographs show that considerable erosion occurred in the 20-plus years between when Arthur saw the site and Lewis then visited it. Nonetheless, a wealth of information is preserved in the remaining Weppler site pictographs.

Loren Haar took nearly 100 photographs of the site with a smartphone, most of which were focused on the imagery, but a few showed an overall view of the rockshelter. We asked Mark Willis to take these photographs and provide a panorama view. He stitched together a panorama of the rockshelter's back wall using a commercial Structure from Motion (SfM) photogrammetry package called Metashape (Version 1.5.3). This software takes a set of overlapping photographs; analyzes the location of visually similar objects in them; and from these, constructs a single graphic of the entire panel by stitching together the best portions of each of the many photographs taken. In addition to the panorama, Mark also constructed a 360-degree rotatable model. This model helped us see that the slight change in orientation of the images is real, rather than a function of a change in the orientation of the cliff face. From these photographs, we were able to do a photo-tracing of the images (Figure 10c) while eliminating problems of parallax by laying it over the panorama using the Corel Paintshop Pro graphics program.

Even a cursory examination of the three recordings of the Weppler bar tally shows there to be several

Figure 11. Current photographs (some enhanced with DStretch) show essentially the same condition for the Weppler site bar tally as described and sketched by Lewis. Photograph on right is DStretch enhancement YBK.

places where the different recordings are not precisely in alignment. For instance, Lewis indicates five scalps starting with bar 9 (counting from left to right) and five horseshoes starting with bar 10, the final horseshoe only being associated with a single, poorly defined line modifier. Conversely, Arthur shows only three scalps starting with line 13 and the last one being next to line 15, which has an X and one short modifier stroke just above it. Our photo-tracing shows the scalps associated with lines 11–14 and line 15 having an X above it and two short modifier strokes.

Obviously not all of these can be accurate, so we carefully compared our version to both others and overlaid Lewis's image onto the panorama we developed. It appears to us that the illustrations by both Arthur and Lewis demonstrate the difficulty of keeping track of which of the many bars have modifiers when one must record a long series of nearly identical marks without benefit of a photograph to use as a template. We have ourselves suffered disorientation when comparing these to the panorama template, and we suspect there simply is some degree of "drift" or "duplication" in the notations illustrated by Arthur and Lewis. The differences between the earlier sketches and our photo-tracing have been carefully compared to available photographs and there is no indication of any of the "extraneous" Arthur or Lewis marks now visible. In sum, all of the nine extraneous marks (two scalps, three hoofprints, one coup-stroke, two T-tops, and one X) recorded by Arthur and Lewis no longer exist at the site. While it is possible that some of these have been lost to erosion, we could find no evidence indicating this was the case, suggesting their presence was the result of initial recording errors.

The Weppler Site Imagery

The images at Weppler are charcoal pictographs. The primary composition is an extensive bar tally formed of 46 vertical war-party stripes aligned in a long horizontal row (Figures 10c, 12). Counting from left to right, the last ten stripes are slightly shorter than the others, and this group is oriented at a slightly more upward oblique angle than the main sequence. The morphology of these last ten stripes and the absence of modifying marks on the last five of them make them appear to have been made as two groups of five. The first 36 bars are all uniformly about 30-cm tall with the first 10 having no modifier marks. The first 41 bars and most of the modifying marks are painted with a thick liquid or pasty black paint, as indicated by the even application of pigment that fills slight indentations in the cliff surface in combination with the absence of drips or spatters. Only three of the Xs (those above bars 24, 32, and possibly 31) appear likely to have been dry-applied with raw charcoal based on their sketchy, thin-

Figure 12. A schematic reconstruction of the Weppler site bar tally using information from all three recordings (see Figure 10). Black marks are currently visible at the site; red marks have been removed by water erosion and are reconstructed from earlier recordations.

line form, but many of the 18 Xs have been more affected by erosion than most of the vertical bars.

More than half of the war-party stripes (26 of 46), located in the exact middle of the composition, have coup-mark modifiers located above and/or to the right of each stripe. We know this rightward orientation because three of the four scalps are attached to the stripe on their immediate left. The coup-mark modifiers include Xs above 18 stripes (which serve to make them compound strokes in Brownstone's terminology); and scalps, horse hoofprints, and short vertical coup-strokes drawn in various combinations next to 25 stripes.

This composition is a classic Plains bar tally (cf. Figures 1, 8, 13) characteristic of the art of the Crow and the three affiliated Upper Missouri River tribes, which included the Hidatsa (close linguistic cousins of the Crow)[4], the Mandan, and the Arikara. These four tribes had the most highly developed and complex "vocabulary" of war-honor -exploit marks on the Plains[5] (Mallery 1893:438–440). The Hidatsa claimed to have originated this lexicon of honor marks and it was most formalized among their affiliated tribes, while the Crow used the same marks in a slightly less-structured fashion.

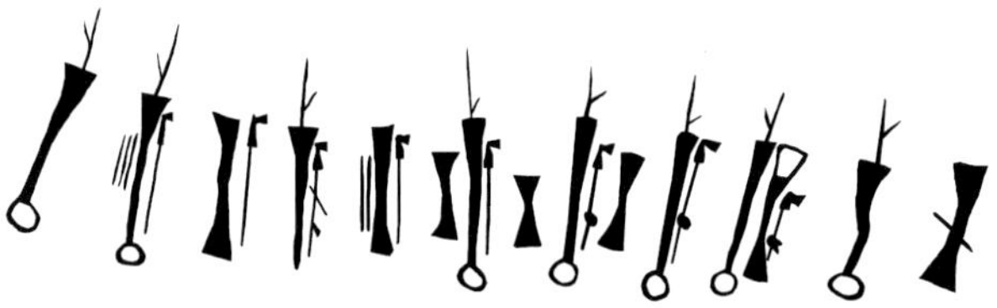

Figure 13. This tally of objects given away to increase a man's prestige is painted on an Hidatsa bison robe. Elongate hourglass shapes are blankets, long trapezoids (most with a circle at the bottom) are quirts, thin elongate objects are pipes, lines to the left of quirts indicate multiples of those items. Adapted from Brownstone (2001:79).

Bar tallies were used among these four tribes in a variety of ways. Primarily they decorated painted robes, war shirts, and leggings (Brownstone 2001, 2008), but they are also known to have been painted on horses (Berlo 2000:88; Bethke 2016:220–221; Cowdrey 2010:2–3) and even a woman's dress (Brownstone 2008:16–17).[6] The actual war-party stripes in these bar tallies are sometimes compound strokes, but both compound and simple strokes routinely include numerous modifier marks including horses captured, enemies killed, and scalps taken. Using various examples of Crow, Mandan, and Hidatsa bar tallies in combination with their exploit-mark vocabulary, we can understand quite a bit about the war record commemorated at Weppler.

Referencing the schematic drawing in Figure 12, we see there are the first ten stripes which lack any ancillary coup marks. Apparently, these represent either war parties in which the artist participated but did not perform any specific deeds worthy of recognition or a simple tally of war parties not intended to document specific deeds. Given that the medium—charcoal applied across a rough-hewn sandstone surface—is not conducive to the carefully controlled, even-edged lines like the finger-painted bar tallies on robes and clothing, we believe the slight "foot" at the bottom of stripes 2 and 3 does not denote anything meaningful. We found no evidence of the feet noted by Lewis on a few other stripes (e.g., 9, 19, 20), but we did find the "widening" he recorded at the bottom of stripe 16. That (and other slightly wider bottoms Lewis recorded on several other stripes) also appears to us to be a function of the medium rather than a meaningful part of the composition.

Beginning with stripe 11, the artist illustrated four war-party stripes, each with a scalp and a hoofprint just to the right. These marks indicate the taking of scalps and capture of horses. The scalps are placed just above the midpoint of the war-party stripe, and three of them are connected to the stripe by a short line. The single horse hoofprints are placed at the bottom of each war-party stripe.

Then beginning with stripe 15, each of the next 18 war-party stripes is overtopped by an X indicating the counting of a coup. The photographs taken in 2020 show that five of these superimposed X-marks (those surmounting stripes 20–23 and 25) are no longer visible and four others (those surmounting stripes 17, 19, 24, and 26) are badly eroded by water that has flowed down over the drawing. Fortunately, the Lewis drawing shows X-marks above stripes 24 and 25 as visible in 1983, and the Arthur sketch shows all 18 of these marks in place. Thus, we know that these 18 war-party stripes were all originally topped by an X.

Of the first 16 stripes with an X above, 15 have from 1 to 3 small vertical dashes—which we term "coup-strokes"—visible as coup-mark modifiers. In every instance, these short coup-strokes are drawn singly and aligned just to the right of each stripe. They are variously placed near the top, in the approximate middle, or at the bottom of the stripe. None of these stripes has any other ancillary marks. The combinations with one or two coup-strokes include top only (two), bottom only (one), top-middle (seven), and top-bottom (one). Four stripes have all three coup-strokes.

Stripe 22 has an X above, but no modifying coup-stroke. The last war-party stripe surmounted by an X (number 32) has no coup-stroke but, instead, has a single horse hoofprint painted in both the upper and middle positions.

Following the war-party stripes surmounted by X-marks, there are four more simple stripes with from one to three individual hoofprints as honor marks. These include two stripes with hoofprints at the upper and middle positions, one with a single hoofprint at all three positions, and one stripe with a hoofprint only at the middle position.

The first 36 war-party stripes are all approximately the same length. Thirty of these are still sufficiently well-enough preserved to measure them on our phototracing using an arbitrary scale so they could be relatively compared one to another to ascertain if the size groupings apparent on visual inspection could be supported statistically.

Following the 26 modified war-party stripes are the two groups, each comprising five shorter stripes, aligned at a slightly more upward angle than the first 36. The first set of five stripes (37–41) are compound strokes, each with a narrow T-top.[7] Pigment density of these stripes is the same as the first 36. These are all drawn so their tops are aligned with one another, but they vary in length more than any other group of stripes, and they are only 70 to 86 percent as long as the mean length of the first 36 stripes.

The last five stripes (42–46) are simple strokes different from any other stripes in this composition. All five are drawn with a markedly lighter and spottier application of charcoal pigment than any of the first 41 stripes. Although these five are aligned with stripes 37–41, none has the T-top. They do not exhibit as much variation as stripes 37–41, but four of them are markedly shorter than any in the preceding five stripes (and thus far shorter than any of the first 36).

There are three other much smaller images drawn with a raw lump of charcoal at Weppler (Figure 14). All of these can be easily recognized as charcoal "drawings" rather than "paintings" by the spotty application of black pigment along their form. About 50 cm to the left of the bar tally is a curvilinear scrawl (Figure 14c) that seems to show two humans engaged in sexual intercourse. The scrawl was identified as a sex scene by Tom Lewis in his site notes, but in its current state (at least from photographs) it bears only a sketchy resemblance to such a scene. In fact, we could see it as such only after reading Lewis's field notes.

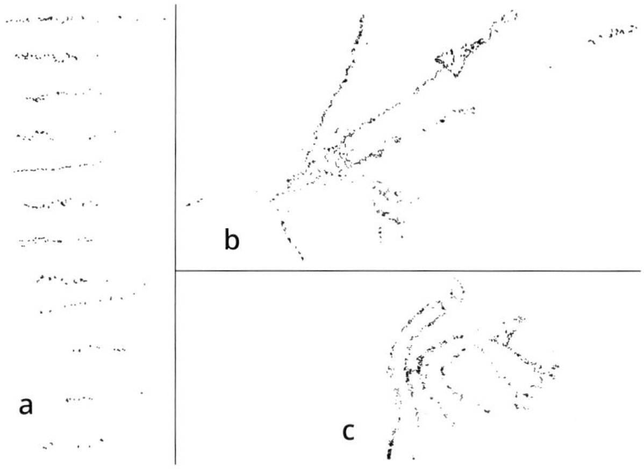

Figure 14. These Weppler-site images were drawn with a raw lump of charcoal.

Further to the left, about 60 cm distant, is another much larger scrawl (Figure 14b). We call this the "spear scrawl" because it consists of straight lines with one obviously representational component. This is a lance with an exaggeratedly long triangular point, which is drawn through the central meeting point of several long lines and tilted up at about a 40-degree angle from horizontal. At least four other straight lines converge near the midpoint of the spear shaft. Arthur (1960) provided a sketch of this (Figure 9) that quite closely resembles what we can record from current photographs. Lewis (1983), on the other hand, did a fanciful sketch that made the scrawl into a mounted warrior with shield and spear (Figure 15). We give the Lewis sketch little credence since what is currently visible is much closer to what Arthur originally recorded.

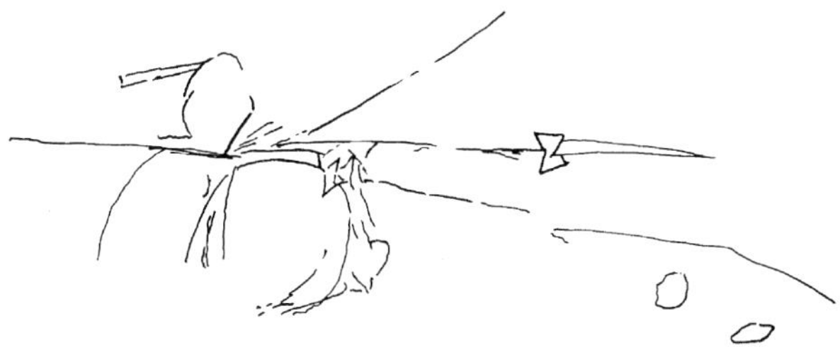

Figure 15. Lewis's sketch of the "spear scrawl" bears little resemblance to what is actually drawn on the rock surface. Compare to Figure 9 and Figure 14b.

Finally, slightly further to the left of the "spear scrawl" is a vertical column of 13 short horizontal strokes stacked one above the other. In current photographs we could find only 12 such strokes (Figure 14a), but Arthur sketched and Lewis noted one more. The faintness of these lines in our photographs and the spottiness of the charcoal pigment make it highly likely that we simply cannot recognize the other line. These strokes are all about the same length and spaced approximately equidistant from one another in the column.

Interpreting the Weppler Imagery

Despite the obvious function of the main Weppler composition as a bar tally, the site imagery presents serious challenges to interpretation. Initially, we note that Arthur did not record the curvilinear "sex act" scrawl. Lewis seems confident in his identification of this as sexual intercourse between two humans, and we can see how he interprets it as such. Possibly it was clearer in 1983, but Lewis apparently made no drawing of it. A sex scene of this sort would not be out of place in a Crow rock art site devoted to a warrior's "accomplishments." Similarly graphic scenes (Figure 16) are found at No Water and Joliet (e.g., Keyser and Cowdrey 2008; Keyser and Poetschat 2009:13, 47–48). We only wish that the image at the Weppler site were clearer in order to confidently identify it as a sex act.

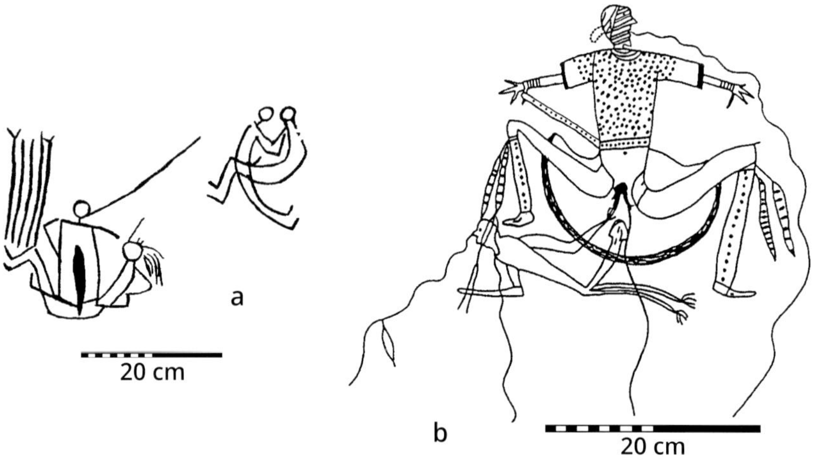

Figure 16. Sex scenes drawn at other Crow rock art sites. (a) No Water (48WA2066), Wyoming; (b) Joliet (24CB402), Montana.

The spear scrawl presents its own set of issues. Certainly the Lewis rendition is nothing more than wishful thinking, but, at the same time, when we first noticed Arthur's rendition, we suspected this showed a warrior armed with a spear (and possibly mounted). This is one of the most common types of scenes in Crow Biographic art and such mounted men are frequently paired with a stacked array of simple weapons to denote either a supporting or opposing force of warriors (Figure 17a, c), Conversely, since we have no way of determining if the spear scrawl actually represents a warrior, it is possible that these stacked strokes are another bar tally drawn in slightly different form. Unless much older photographs of this site are discovered, these interpretations are simply not verifiable.

In any case, these two scrawls and the stacked array of lines appear to represent an artist other than the one who drew most of the bar tally. Only the last five vertical strokes of the bar tally composition and a few small coup marks (the four scalps and a couple of the Xs) are drawn with similarly sketchy lines. Even those last five war-party stripes, however, are more firmly drawn and more heavily applied to the cliff surface, and it would have been nearly impossible to draw the much smaller scalps and Xs without using a raw chunk of charcoal.

The main Weppler composition is indisputably a bar tally, recording warriors' performance of brave deeds while members of war parties. Those vertical war-party stripes with a scalp and a hoofprint record the art-

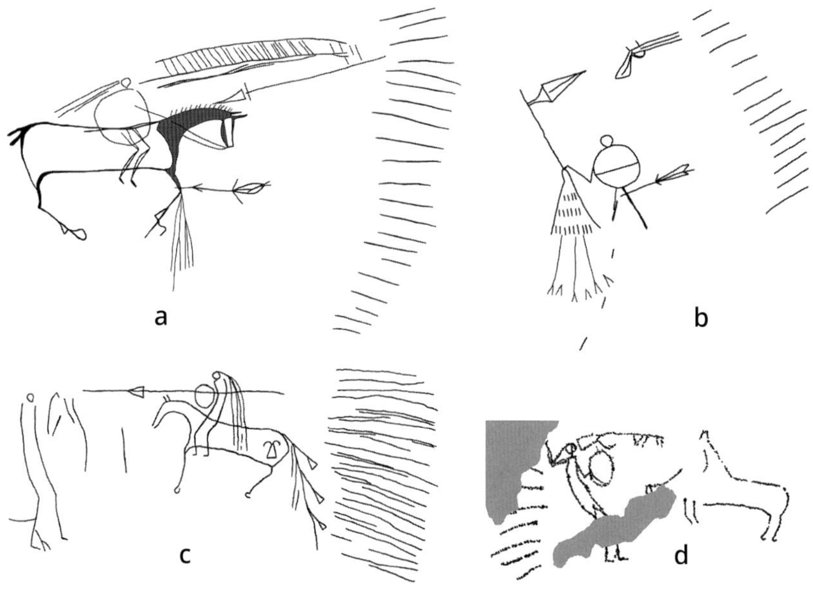

Figure 17. Stacked arrays of lines representing generic weapons are shorthand for groups of warriors opposing or supporting the main actor. (a, b) 24GV191, Montana; (c) 48HO9, Wyoming; (d) 48SW9532, Wyoming.

ist's horse-raiding expeditions where he (or the men he commanded) took enemy horses and killed and scalped enemy warriors. The individual modifier marks almost certainly represent multiple enemies killed/scalped and horses stolen, since it stretches credibility to believe that only one of each was accomplished on four separate trips. Such synecdoche is characteristic of many bar tallies and Plains Biographic art in general.

The next 18 war-party stripes document expeditions on which the warrior/artist had counted coup—and in one case stolen horses during the same action. As noted above, the Crow, Hidatsa, Mandan, and Arikara shared the most detailed and complex lexicon of honor marks used to express a warrior's brave deeds. The most complex of these honor marks is the X. Plains Indians typically counted four coups on an enemy by hitting or touching the person (either alive or dead) with anything from the bare hand, through all sorts of weapons, to a quirt. The person counting the initial coup claimed a slightly greater honor than those who followed, but all four were able to record their coup with an honor mark. In the Upper Missouri system, the coup-strike exploit mark was based on an X (Figure 4). Among the Mandan, Hidatsa, and Crow the X stood for first coup counted in a fight and dashes were added in the spaces between the arms of the X (e.g., X- or -X-, =X=, etc.) to denote three subsequent coup-strikes on any opponent. The Arikara used the X to denote killing an enemy and an X with one through four dashes as the four coups (Mallery 1893:438–439). None of the half dozen other tribes living in this part of the northern Plains used the X in this way. Although the Lakota used an X to indicate a killed enemy, they did not use the dashes to indicate different sequential coups.

Among the Crow, striking first coup was a very important accomplishment. It was one of the four war honors (along with taking an enemy's weapon in hand-to-hand combat, stealing a horse picketed within an enemy village, and leading a war party) that were required for a man to assume the status of chief.

These 18 compound war-party stripes, consisting of a stripe surmounted by an X, document various coups counted. The X above the war-party stripe documents the act of counting coup, while the coup-strokes positioned below the X and alongside the stripe modify the X to reflect its sequential value. Those without a coup-stroke represent the striking of first coup. One such unmodified coup mark is above stripe 22. While it is possible that any modifying coup-stroke below has been eroded away, DStretch analysis shows other coup-strokes visible in this water-damaged area, so we suspect this is an unmodified X—as it is shown also on both the Arthur and Lewis sketches. The second example is atop stripe 32, and there are two horse hoofprints but no coup-strokes in the "modifying" positions. Both instances, then, seem to document a war party where the artist struck first coup in a fight. The small dashes modifying the other Xs include four examples with one coup-stroke, eight with two, and four with three, denoting times the artist struck second, third, and fourth coup, respectively. Crow rock art at the Bear Gulch site (Figure 18) contains one other example where an X with three adjacent strokes apparently represents the striking of fourth coup (Keyser et al. 2012:169–170; McCleary 2016:65).

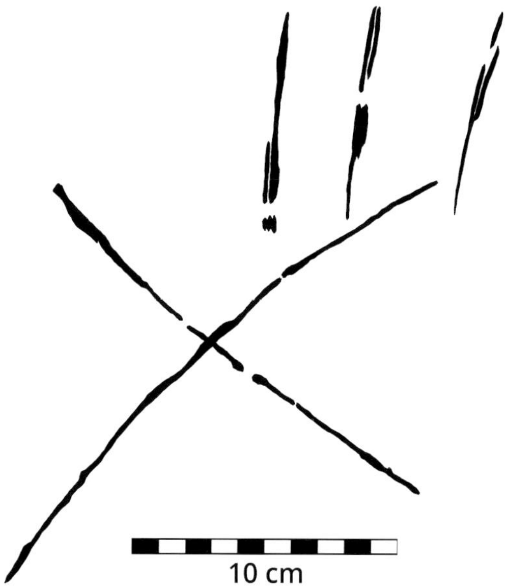

Figure 18. Coup mark at Bear Gulch, Montana, denoting the striking of fourth coup.

Just to the right of stripe 32 are four stripes with one to three horse hoofprint modifiers. These represent four war parties where the artist recorded the taking of horses only, with the multiple hoofprints apparently indicating the capture of greater numbers of animals.

Immediately to the right of these 26 war-party stripes with modifier marks are two groups of five stripes each, seemingly drawn by two different "hands" than the first 36 stripes. In the first group of five stripes, all have a distinct T-top creating a compound stroke. Given the uniformity of these strokes and the absence of tops on any others, we suspect they represent something specific, but we can only guess what these represent. One possibility is they represent picket pins indicating picketed horses taken, but we know of only a single possible analogue—a **T**-topped picket pin with a short cut rope drawn in a horse-stealing scene at the Joliet site (Figure 19)—to support this suggestion. Finally, in the last group, all five stripes are plain, and apparently simply indicate war-party participation.

*Figure 19. Crow-style horse carved at Joliet, Montana, shows a **T**-top picket pin with cut picket rope to indicate that the horse was stolen. The horse wears a forehead ornament and a cloth necktie while a large metal knife is painted as an honor mark on its left flank.*

How Many Artists are Represented?

The question of how many artists drew the various parts of the Weppler site bar tally is a complicated one. At first glance it seems obvious that the last ten stripes are drawn by different hands than drew the first 36 and—as we noted earlier—the position, composition, and arrangement of these final sets of stripes indicates a total of three separate groups. Contrasts between the three groups of stripes are clearly evident if their relative length values are plotted as box-and-jitter graphs (Figure 20). The relatively low variation in the lengths of stripes in the first group—despite their far greater number than in the other groups—is evident in the small (interquartile range) box compared with the other two groups. Moreover, using a non-parametric Mann-Whitney *U*-test, the relative median lengths of the stripes in Group 1 are shown to be statistically greater than those of Group 2 (z=3.567, p <0.001). Likewise, the stripes in Group 3 are significantly different from those in Group 2 in terms of relative median lengths (z=2.312, p=0.02). In sum, such contrasts support the idea that these three groups represent the work of three different artists.

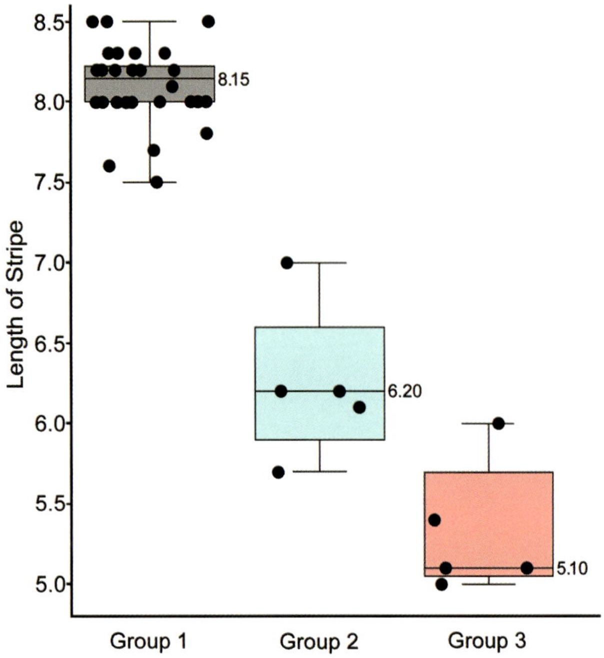

Figure 20. Box-and-jitter plots comparing relative lengths of stripes in each of the three identified groupings. For each group, the boxes display the 25–75 percent interquartile ranges and median length is indicated by horizontal line within each box. Minimal and maximal values are indicated by horizontal lines at the termination of the whiskers extending from each box. Individual dots represent the relative length values for the stripes within each group. Stripe lengths are in centimeters measured from a photograph, and so display relative rather than absolute length of stripes on the rock surface.

Who Were the Weppler Artists?

We can be reasonably confident that the artists who recorded their war deeds at Weppler were Crow warriors. The site is directly in the heart of Crow country during the 1800s (Figure 21) and there are many other indisputably Crow rock art sites all around this one. However, based on its location, the site might also have been painted by a marauding war party from either the Mandan or Hidatsa tribes—and we must not forget that Hidatsa raiders from the Knife River area in North Dakota had captured Sacajawea more than 100 miles (160 km) west of the Weppler site near Three Forks, Montana, in 1800. But neither the Mandan nor Hidatsa fought with the Crow, and it seems unlikely that a war party from either group would have left this sort of calling card in Crow territory—especially if they typically practiced the same sort of "painting-up" rites as the Crow did to announce a war party's successful return.

Other groups who regularly raided into this area (Flathead, Shoshone, Lakota, Cheyenne, and Blackfoot) did not use the vocabulary of war deeds that are

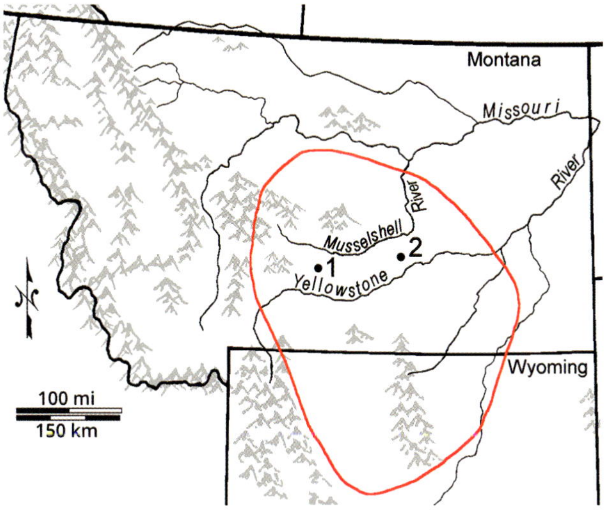

Figure 21. Both the Weppler (number 1) and Nordstrom-Bowen (number 2) sites are in the heart of Crow territory (red outline), between the Musselshell and Yellowstone rivers. The Mandan and Hidatsa homeland is just off the right side of the map.

drawn at Weppler. In contrast, the Crow did use exactly this vocabulary and were active raiders throughout the 1800s.

But why would Crow warriors stop at Weppler? The site is a secluded location in a minor draw with a water source directly in front of the small rock shelter. The location would provide shelter from the weather and from the prying eyes of other war parties. Crow men reported that war parties returning from successful expeditions routinely stopped short of home to rest and stay the night (sometimes after escaping pursuit by those they had raided). At such a stop, the group "painted-up." In this practice, successful men who had counted specific coups painted their faces and/or clothing with black paint (charcoal mixed with buffalo blood) so they could triumphantly ride into camp the next day with much celebration (Lowie 1912:234–235, 1922:255). Lowie (1912:235) describes this painting-up action in detail:

> Members of a victorious war party killed a buffalo on their return and put the blood into a paunch. Then all took their robes and whitened them with wetted clay. Dry pine wood and. . . grass were burned separately to make. . . ashes. The two kinds of charcoal and the blood were mixed in warm water, which was stirred. Four or five eminent men recited their deeds and began to paint each warrior's robe with the symbol of the first coup struck. . . .Then each of the eminent men instructs the privates [less accomplished warriors] how to paint so many horse tracks or so many slain enemies, corresponding to their former exploits.

Lowie (1912:235–237) further documents additional details of such war parties "painting-up." These include how various coup-strikers' shirts, robes, and faces were painted in preparation for announcing their successful return. Interestingly, he notes that the number of human figures painted on these "announcement" robes represented the number of enemies on whom coup was counted, but one informant reported that these did not necessarily represent the actual number of enemies struck.

Since this site is deep within Crow territory, it would have served very well as a returning war-party's bivouac, and village sites in both the Musselshell and Yellowstone River drainages are within a relatively easy horse ride. One can readily imagine a successful war party overnighting here to paint-up, and an accomplished warrior or the war-party leader using some of the black paint to document his war record in the small rockshelter. Later warriors could easily have added the last ten war-party stripes at different times.

Deciphering This War Record

Given the observable and statistically supportable separation of the bar tally into three distinct groups of stripes, the obvious conclusion is that at least three artists drew the large bar-tally composition. The first artist recorded 36 war-party stripes, 26 of which are modified in different ways by the addition of exploit marks denoting the accomplishment of recognized coups. Brownstone (2008:18) has noted that bar tallies "ideally display accomplishments in both primary classes of warfare: horse raids and scalp raids," and that would certainly seem to be the case here. Thus, a total of 36 war parties, resulting in multiple stolen horses, scalps taken, and coups counted would seem to be a war record of a very accomplished warrior, especially considering that neither the taking of a weapon nor the leadership of a war party is expressly documented at this site. In trying to determine why an artist would draw ten war-party stripes with no associated coups, and yet illustrate 26 with various combinations of coup-count modifiers, we have examined two different scenarios discussed below:

Scenario 1. Do the ten plain war-party stripes indicate a different sort of participation than the modified ones? Most frequently, ethnographically collected bar tallies from the Crow, Hidatsa, and Mandan contain some sort of modifier marks for each war-party stripe, but a few Blackfoot examples show only the stripes (Brownstone 2008:11). However, the Crow warrior, White Arm, drew his horse in a ledger drawing with just ten horizontal stripes painted on its hip. Cowdrey (2010:2–3) identifies these as war-party stripes, each one indicating White Arm's participation in a war party. He further suggests there would have been a matching ten more on the opposite hip. Thus, it seems possible that plain stripes simply denoted participation. It seems odd, however, that at the start of a tally there would be ten war expeditions that resulted in no war honors of note for the artist. While it could happen, this seems like quite a "dry spell" for an otherwise notably successful warrior, especially one who counted some sort of coup on each of the following 26 war-party stripes.

Scenario 2. If we reject simple participation, then it might be reasonable to suggest that these ten stripes recorded the war parties the artist had led. Among some groups a successful war captain was entitled to claim credit for all the deeds accomplished under his leadership (Bowers 1950:72, 1965:258, 279–280; Smith 1943:115), but there is no direct report of the Crow doing this. Therefore, it seems plausible to us that these first ten, unmodified stripes represent the war expeditions led by the artist and the following 26 represent war expeditions on which he performed various brave deeds. If such were the case, it is possible that the same war expedition may have been represented by two stripes—one in the "leadership" group (stripes 1–10) and one in the "deeds accomplished" group (stripes 11–36).

In either case, this warrior had an enviable war record. Based on the number of times he illustrated each of the honor-mark symbols, we can see that he killed (and scalped) at least four enemies, stole horses on nine expeditions (with four of these apparently recording greater numbers of animals), and he counted coup 18 times—twice as first coup. We examined the Historic record for the number of coups recorded by accomplished Crow warriors in the last decades of the 1800s and found that a war record like this would be notable but not without parallel. For instance, Lowie (1912:231–232) reports that *Itchupdéete* (No Shinbone), a famous war leader and pipe owner, recounted a list of his deeds in which he indicated he "went to war about fifty times." In a later work discussing war honors, Lowie (1922:253) summarized the war records of three highly regarded chiefs of the late 1800s. These included Bell-rock, Plenty-coups, and Gray-bull, each of whom had between 12 and 25 primary coups to his credit (Table 3). Finally, Tim McCleary (2021) indicated that Plenty-coups' war record at Chief Plenty Coups State Park in Montana commemorates more than 100 war parties in which he participated. McCleary further noted that, in his opinion, many warriors went to war between 20 and 50 times. In sum, a warrior who was able to record 36 war-party stripes would not have been out of the ordinary.

Table 3. Primary Coups of Three Crow Warriors.

Warrior	Gun Captured	Picketed Horse Taken	First Coup	War Parties Led	TOTAL
Bell-rock	5	3	6	11	25
Plenty-coups	4	4	7	9	24
Gray-bull	3	3	3	3	12

The two groups of five bars at the right end of the larger composition are more difficult to interpret. Morphologically these appear to have been done by a different artist than the one who drew the first 36 war-party stripes, and this conclusion is supported by statistical analysis. The first five-bars groups, stripes 37–41, all have the same form, appearing to have been painted with a liquid pigment but drawn with a pronounced T-top. These may simply be stripes added to the larger tally by a later artist to document his war expeditions. However, if these are actually a compound stroke done to intentionally represent a specific war honor, they may represent picket pins, indicating the capture of a picketed horse. A similar T-top picket pin is carved as part of a horse-stealing scene at the Joliet site (Figure 19), but it is the only example we know of. If these strokes represent the taking of picketed horses, we do not know why they are not also modified in other ways.

The last five war-party stripes (42–46) were drawn using a different technique than the other painted stripes. We can only surmise that these were added by a third artist to represent his own war honors in a generic form. Whether these are related to the other dry-charcoal drawings showing a possible pair of copulating humans, the spear scrawl, and the vertical column of horizontal lines is unknown, but drawing them as five war-party stripes to accompany the others at the site is the most parsimonious explanation.

Finally, it has been suggested that the war-party stripes in groups 2 and 3 were added by the original artist on subsequent visits. We think this is unlikely, given the significantly different morphology of the three groups and the absence of coup-mark modifiers in either of the last two groups.

Later artists adding to an initial war record is an activity supported by evidence from other sites. It is not uncommon in Biographic rock art to have an artist repurpose an earlier drawing to tell his own war story. Reworked scenes have been described from DgOw-32 at Verdigris Coulee and at 24GV191 and Joliet here in Crow country (Greer et al. 2019:60–61; Keyser and Kaiser 2022; Keyser et al. 2022). At Joliet, the image is a woman in a dance scene. Crow consultants say the woman is included to show her metaphorically giving birth to the Hot Dance (McCleary 2016:43–44). However, the scene was repurposed by a later warrior-artist who added himself into it and modified the woman to document his sexual capture of a rival military society member's wife.

Tallies are also augmented by later artists. For example, a tally found at Bear Gulch (Keyser 2011:51–53) is a Blackfoot enemy tally with four additional enemies added by a second artist, recognizable by his different artistic style (Figure 3a). Similar modification is probably shown at Nordstrom-Bowen as well (see above). Such reuse of imagery may have been intended to link the second artist with the reflected glory or power of the original artist.

Summary

The Weppler site pictographs are dominated by an extensive bar tally almost certainly painted and drawn by members of returning Crow war parties. Crow ethnography describes in detail the painting-up rituals of a returning war party that involved drawing bar tallies on warriors' robes and painting their other clothing in various ways. These rituals happened at a secluded bivouac close to the warriors' main camp, which provided a staging area for the triumphant return of successful raiders. The Weppler bar tally appears to be painted with pigment like that described in the ethnographic record, and the site location would have served as an ideal war-party bivouac.

The primary bar tally painted at Weppler documents one man's impressive war record and shows two much smaller groups of war-party stripes apparently added by two other artists. One of these later artists likely also drew additional narrative scenes that have not been preserved as well as the bar tally, either because the tally is mostly painted rather than drawn or because it is painted in a slightly more sheltered location. The artist who drew the primary tally was an accomplished raider proficient in taking horses and scalps and who counted numerous coups—including two first coups. This man's illustrated war record would put him in the company of the best Crow warriors of the last half of the 1800s.

We do not know when the Weppler pictographs were painted and drawn. Obviously, they postdate the introduction of horses into this area, but that provides only a *terminus post quem* of about A.D. 1700–1730 (Ewers 1955:15–18; Haines 1938:430; Medicine Crow 2000:23; Secoy 1992:105). But we know that bar tallies of this sort were in use by the Crow, Mandan, and Hidatsa from at least the first decades of the 1800s into the Reservation period (Brownstone 2001, 2008; Cowdrey 2010; Ronan and McLeod 2019). Given this known timespan, our best estimate is that the site was painted sometime in the early to mid-1800s.

Though abstract on first viewing, comparison with similar bar tallies in other media and a knowledge of the complex iconographic symbolism of honor marks among the Crow, as well as the Hidatsa, Mandan, and Arikara allow us to largely decipher the messages in this pictographic tally. An accomplished Crow warrior left a record of his war honors on the rock wall of a small shelter for all to see. He participated in 36 war parties, ten of which he led. He captured horses on nine expeditions, took scalps on four, and counted 18 coups. This impressive war record apparently attracted other warriors to add their deeds nearby. Almost two centuries later, his pictograph still extols his warrior status.

Acknowledgments. We thank Arlene Weppler and Kim Herzog for permission to visit and photograph the Weppler site, and Loren Haar for taking photographs for us. Mark Willis created a panorama and a 360-degree rotating model of the site that proved invaluable. Mavis Greer and David Wade were instrumental in obtaining the Tom Lewis field notes. Arni Brownstone's work with bar tallies was an indispensable foundation for our work. And finally, Tim McCleary willingly shared his extensive knowledge of Crow ethnography, rock art, and culture to help make our task of interpreting the site imagery so much easier and more complete.

Notes

1. Brownstone (2008) first coined the term "compound strokes" to differentiate "simple" strokes from those variously modified by the addition of symbols at their top. We have further distinguished "modifiers" as both those marks which can be used to make a simple stroke "compound" and also those that can be added next to a war-party stripe or a captured weapon to provide further information.

2. Although we know of no identified example of a robe art bar tally drawn by an Arikara artist, ledger drawings from the tribe show warriors wearing such robes and painting tallies of war honors on their legs (Greene 2006). They also painted these exploit marks on personal equipment (Mallery 1893:441).

3. Although Lewis (1983:1) indicates that he made "tracings" of the imagery at Weppler, our close comparison of his recording against the Haar photographs and the Willis panorama indicates that some of what he recorded does not exist. For instance, one hoofprint is simply not there in the Haar photographs, and DStretch of that same image shows no remnant of it. Nevertheless, the vertical stripes on each side of this "missing" image are easily seen both in ambient light and in DStretch transformed photographs. We suspect that Lewis did do some sort of tracing (his version fits reasonably accurately on our panorama), but that he either added some things later based on photographs or was particularly generous with his interpretation of marks. For these reasons we refer to his work as a sketch—albeit a much more accurate one than that of Arthur.

4. The Crow and Hidatsa were closely related enough that their languages were mutually intelligible.

5. As shown in Figure 4, tribes of the Blackfoot confederacy and the Lakota had their own vocabularies of exploit marks, but these were less extensive and less formalized than that of the Mandan-Hidatsa/Crow, and both of these groups rarely used bar tallies (Brownstone 2008).

6. The honor marks painted on this dress were those of the dressmaker's husband, painted on the garment by him (Brownstone 2008:17).

7. Arthur and Lewis illustrate seven and six **T**-topped bars, respectively; but like their other "extra" coup marks, these seem to be mistakes in their sketches. We checked each of these stripes for possible tops but found no evidence of such, despite this area having suffered little or no erosion.

References Cited

Arthur, George
1960 Pictographs in Central Montana: Part III, Comments. *Montana State University Anthropology and Sociology Papers* 21:41–44.

Barbeau, Marius
1960 Indian Days on the Western Prairies. *National Museum of Canada Bulletin* 163.

Bauerle, Phenocia
2003 *The Way of the Warrior: Stories of the Crow People.* University of Nebraska Press, Lincoln.

Berlo, Janet Catherine
2000 *Spirit Beings and Sun Dancers: Black Hawk's Vision of the Lakota World.* George Braziller, New York.

Bethke, Brandi Ellen
2016 *Dog Days to Horse Days: Evaluating the Rise of Nomadic Pastoralism Among the Blackfoot.* Ph.D. Dissertation, School of Anthropology, University of Arizona. Electronic document, https://repository.arizona.edu/handle/10150/621102, accessed January 24, 2022,

Bowers, Alfred W.
1950 *Mandan Social and Ceremonial Organization.* University of Chicago Press, Chicago.

1965 *Hidatsa Social and Ceremonial Organization.* Bureau of American Ethnology Bulletin 194.

Brownstone, Arni
2001 Seven War-Exploit Paintings: A Search for Their Origins. In *Studies in American Indian Art: A Memorial Tribute to Norman Feder,* edited by Christian F. Feest, pp. 69–85. European Review of Native American Studies, University of Washington Press, Seattle.

2008 Composition and Iconography in Painted Plains Indian Shirts. in *Generous Man Ahxsi-tapina: Essays in Memory of Colin Taylor, Plains Indian Ethnologist,* edited by Arni Brownstone and Hugh Dempsey, pp. 8–34. Tatanka Press, Wyk auf Foehr, Germany.

Cowdrey, Mike
2010 Drawings by White Arm, Crow, c. 1889. *Splendid Heritage: Treasures of Native American Art.* Electronic document, http://www.splendidheritage.com/Notes/WC8708086.pdf, accessed January 24, 2022.

Dempsey, L. James
2007 *Blackfoot War Art: Pictographs of the Reservation Period, 1880–2000.* University of Oklahoma Press, Norman.

Ewers, John C.
1955 *The Horse In Blackfoot Indian Culture.* Bureau of American Ethnology Bulletin 159.

Feder, Norman
1980 Plains Pictographic Painting and Quilled Rosettes: A Clue to Tribal Identification. *American Indian Art Magazine* 5(2):54–62.

Greene, Candace S.
2006 Arikara Drawings: New Sources of Visual History. *American Indian Art Magazine* 31(2):74–85, 99.

Greer, Mavis, John Greer, and James D. Keyser
2019 Armored Horses in Northwestern Plains Rock Art. *Archaeology In Montana* 60(2):53–99.

Haines, Francis
1938 The Northward Spread of Horses Among the Plains Indians. *American Anthropologist* 40:429–437.

Keyser, James D.
2000 *The Five Crows Ledger: Warrior Art of the Flathead Indians.* University of Utah Press, Salt Lake City.

2011 These Brave Deeds I Have Done: The Earliest Blackfeet War Record. *American Indian Art Magazine* 36(2):48–55.

Keyser, James D., and Mike Cowdrey
2008 Northern Plains Biographic Rock Art: Ethnography Written on Stone. *Archaeology in Montana* 49(1):19–34.

Keyser, James D., and David A. Kaiser
2022 War Stories: Reading Plains Indian Biographic Rock Art. Berghahn Books, New York. (In press.)

Keyser, James D., David A. Kaiser, George Poetschat, and Michael W. Taylor
2012 *Fraternity of War: Plains Indian Rock Art at Bear Gulch and Atherton Canyon, Montana.* Oregon Archaeological Society Press, Publication 21.

Keyser, James D., David A. Kaiser, and Mark D. Willis
2022 Using Remote Control to Reconstruct the Remote Past: UAV Photography along the Milk River. In *New Approaches to Rock Art in Canada: Indigenous Knowledges, Sacred Landscapes and Cultural Heritage,* edited by Dagmara Zawadzka, Oscar Moro Abadia, and Bryn Tapper. (In press.)

Keyser, James D., and Michael A. Klassen
2003 Every Detail Counts: More Additions to the Plains Biographic Rock Art Lexicon. *Plains Anthropologist* 48:7–20.

Keyser, James D., and George Poetschat
2009 *Crow Rock Art in the Bighorn Basin: Petroglyphs at No Water Wyoming.* Oregon Archaeological Society Press, Publication 20.

2014 *Northern Plains Shield Bearing Warriors: A Five Century Rock Art Record of Indian Warfare.* Oregon Archaeological Society Press, Publication No. 22.

Lessard, F. Dennis
1991 Pictographic Sioux Beadwork: A Re-examination. *American Indian Art Magazine* 16(4):70–74.

Lewis, Thomas H.
1983 *Rock Art Site Survey Form and Accompanying Notes for Weppler #2, 24ST560.* On file at Bureau of Land Management, Billings Curation Center, Billings, Montana.

1986 Counts, Coups, and Tally Marks: Evidence of Notational Systems in the Pictographic/Petroglyphic Record. *Northwest Science* 60(4):243–248.

Lowie, Robert H.
1912 Social Life of the Crow Indians. *Anthropological Papers of the American Museum of Natural History,* Vol. 9, Part 2, 179–248.

1913 Societies of the Crow, Hidatsa, and Mandan Indians. *Anthropological Papers of the American Museum of Natural History,* Vol. 11, Part 3, pp. 143–358.

1922 The Material Culture of the Crow Indians. *Anthropological Papers of the American Museum of Natural History,* Vol. 21, Part 3, pp. 201–270.

Lycett, Stephen J., and James D. Keyser
2021 Changing Patterns of Stylistic Diversity in Blackfoot Biographic Art across the Nineteenth Century. *Plains Anthropologist* 66:242–266.

Mallery, Garrick
1893 *Picture-Writing of the American Indians.* Tenth Annual Report of the Bureau of Ethnology 1888-'89, pp. 1–822.

Maximilian, Alexander Philipp (Prince of Wied)
1906 *Travels in the Interior of North America,1832–1834,* Part 2. Volume 23 of *Early Western Travels 1748–1846,* edited by Reuben Gold Thwaites. Arthur H. Clark Company, Cleveland, Ohio.

McCleary, Timothy P.
2016 *Crow Indian Rock Art: Indigenous Perspectives and Interpretations.* Left Coast Press, Walnut Creek, California.

2020 E-mail message to Keyser dated December 24, 2020.

2021 E-mail message to Keyser dated January 10, 2021.

Medicine Crow, Joseph
2000 *From the Heart of Crow Country: The Crow Indians' Own Stories.* University of Nebraska Press, Lincoln.

Ronan, Kristine K., and Allan McLeod
2019 Counting Coup Marks Owned and Drawn by Red White Buffalo (Numak'aki) in 1884, Explained by Beaver (Numak'aki) and Butterfly (Minitari) and Copied by Gilbert L. Wilson in 1909. In Káma-Kapúska! Making Marks in Indian Country, 1833–34. Nineteenth-Century Art Worldwide: A Journal of Nineteenth-Century Visual Culture 18(2). Electronic document, https://scalar.usc.edu/works/kama-kapuska-making-marks-in-indian-country-1833-34/counting-coup-marks-owned-and-drawn-by-red-white-buffalo-numakaki-in-1884, accessed January 24, 2022.

Schoolcraft, Henry R.
1854 *Information Respecting the History, Condition and Prospects of the Indian Tribes of the United State: Collected and Prepared Under the Direction of the Bureau of Indian Affairs, per Act of Congress of March 3rd, 1847.* Part IV. Lippincott, Grambo & Co., Philadelphia, Pennsylvania.

Secoy, Frank Raymond
1992 *Changing Military Patterns of the Great Plains.* University of Nebraska Press, Lincoln. (Reprint of 1953 original).

Smith, DeCost
1943 *Red Indian Experiences.* George Allen and Unwin, London.

Taylor, Colin
1998 *Buckskin and Buffalo: The Artistry of the Plains Indians.* Rizzoli International Publications, New York.

Wilson, Gilbert L.
1924 The Horse and The Dog in Hidatsa Culture. *Anthropological Papers of the American Museum of Natural History,* Vol. 15, Part 2, pp. 127–311.

The Art of Attack—A Plains Biographic Pictograph in Western Colorado

David A. Kaiser and James D. Keyser

A Historic-period attack on a group of entrenched defenders was illustrated at 5GF1339 in far west-central Colorado. This panel unfortunately collapsed before it could be fully studied. However, a handful of historical photographs of the panel showing the battle still exists. A recording based on these photos reveals a detailed narrative using Plains Biographic style conventions, unusual in the area. Employing the Biographic art lexicon to interpret the image, we can decipher the elements used to tell the story of fortified defenders overwhelmed by a group of determined attackers who came from the east to raid the local Ute inhabitants.

During a 1985 Colorado Department of Highways archaeological survey conducted along State Highway 139 between Loma and Douglas Pass, Colorado (Figure 1), an agency field crew found and recorded an extensive rock art site, 5GF1339 (Mahaney 1986; Rhodes 1986). Unfortunately, the site was only recorded with color-annotated sketches since an "in-depth study of the site was...not within the scope of this project" (Mahaney 1986). The authors noted, however, that they did consult with Sally Cole about the site. Based on Cole's statement that the imagery was uncommon (if not unique) for the area, they recommended that a full-scale comparative study of 5GF1339 be eventually done (Mahaney 1986:85). Sadly, that work was apparently never undertaken, although Cole (1990:219–222) did do some preliminary interpretation of Mahaney's sketches using concepts of the Biographic art lexicon proposed by Keyser (1987).

Sometime later, between 1985 and 2009, the site was visited and partially documented further with three black-and-white photographs. We know these photographs postdate 1985 because a part of Panel 4 (present in the site sketch) is missing from all three photographs, apparently because it had broken away given the visible natural fracture. These three photographs were scanned in 2009 by personnel at the Grand River Institute (GRI) and shown to Keyser in June of that year while he was consulting for GRI on a Class I Cultural Resource Overview for the Grand Junction Field Office of the Bureau of Land Management (Berry 2011).

During that consulting project, GRI personnel took Keyser to visit site 5GF1339 and showed him that nearly all of Panel 4 (as well as parts of other panels) had collapsed. Evidence of this was large pieces of the fallen cliff jumbled together and lying face down in the small alcove. In 2020, while working on a book about the Biographic rock art lexicon (see Kaiser and Keyser 2020; Keyser 1987, 1996; Keyser and Klassen 2003; Keyser and Kaiser 2022; Parsons 1987; Petersen 1971:269–308, 1988:xvii;), we obtained the photographs Keyser had seen in 2009 from Rich Ott at the GRI. We made phototracings of the images drawn across most of Panel 4. Despite the difficulties

David A. Kaiser
Oregon Archaeological Society

James D. Keyser
Oregon Archaeological Society

of working only with a partial photographic record and field sketches by archaeologists lacking expertise in rock art recording, we attempt here to build on Cole's (1990:219–222) initial efforts to do some of the comparative work called for by Mahaney (1986:85), emphasizing two battle scenes depicted in Panel 4.

The Rock Art at 5GF1339

As originally recorded, 5GF1339 consists of six separate panels delineated by the site recorders in a large alcove formed in a massive Mesa Verde formation sandstone outcrop just north of State Highway 139 right-of-way, which follows the upper reaches of the East Salt Creek drainage, a tributary of the Colorado River. Although the six concentrations of rock art are more properly thought of as three loci, we retain the original panel designations in order to facilitate comparison with the previously published site information. The smallest and least complex panel occurs on a point of rock at the southwest edge of the alcove, while the other five are closely clustered at the top of what was a nearly four-meter-high rockfall at the alcove's deepest extent (Figure 1). The imagery faces east and south in the alcove and was originally somewhat sheltered by overhangs above. Panels 1 and 2 consist of a few small geometric scrawls drawn with red ochre crayons and charcoal. All color designations used here are taken from Mahaney's (1986) written descriptions and the labels on the sketches. A single incised geometric petroglyph was recorded. None of these images appears to be related to the Biographic tradition art on the other panels, and they are not reproduced here.

Panel 3 contains a large, curved, abstract petroglyph as well as other geometric pigment-drawn shapes, but it also includes a line-drawn horse above a pictograph of eight spears converging on two zoomorphs that appear to be horses, although it is difficult to verify this given the sketchiness of the panel drawing (Figure 2). All of these are loosely scribed line-drawn figures in a dark red ochre.

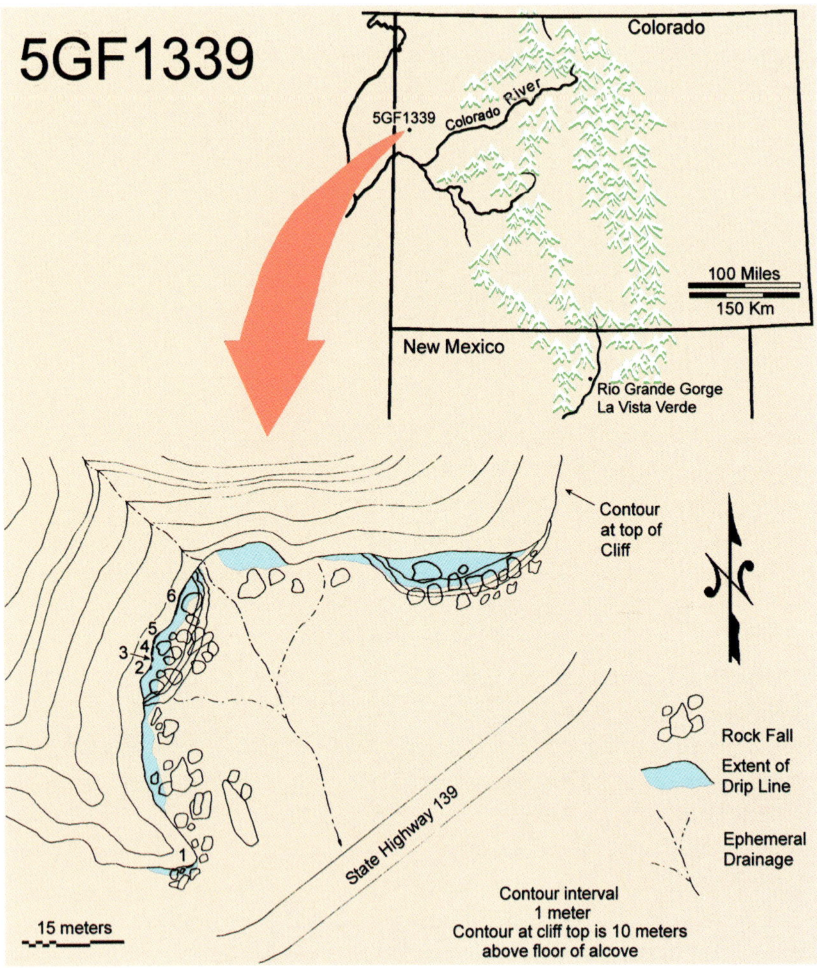

Figure 1. Location of 5GF1339, and panel locations at the site.

Figure 2. Biographic elements at Panel 3, adapted from Mahaney 1986:87.

Panel 4 shows two complex groups of horses, tipis, humans, and weapons arranged into two narrative battle scenes that use many elements of the Biographic art lexicon to tell war stories in considerable detail (Figure 3). In addition, in the lower left corner of the panel is a stacked array of three long guns, probably flintlocks, but the subject they are pointing toward is indecipherable. These guns are not visible in the photographs we have. The imagery on Panel 4, drawn with ochre "chalk" in various shades of red, is mostly done as relatively carefully scribed lines with a much less-dense smudging used to fill in the bodies of some horses, humans, and rifle buttstocks (Figure 4). Examination of the photographs strongly suggests that the pigment was dry applied in the relatively precise lines and then some of the open areas (bodies, buttstocks) were filled in by blending the pigment in a process artists term stumping. That is, the thicker chalked pigment is smeared or smudged with the fingers or with much lighter pressure from the chalk piece itself.

Figure 3. Original sketch of Panel 4 by Mahaney (1986:89). Color references removed, and cracks labeled by authors.

In the photographs we have, the darker red color of what we label Scene A contrasts markedly to a lighter, more washed-out color typifying the Scene B images. These color differences were also noted on the original sketch of the panel (Mahaney 1986:89). This suggests that the two scenes represent different episodes, done with chalks of slightly different composition and color. Smudging to infill the bodies also appears to be done with a lighter "touch" in Scene B than in Scene A.

An earlier pictograph episode underlies Scene A. Two connected ovals of differing size may represent

Figure 4. Photograph of Panel 4 taken some time between 1985 and 2009. Courtesy of the Grand River Institute, Grand Junction, Colorado.

an unidentifiable zoomorph. This image is much more faded than the biographic scene and may have been applied with a liquid pigment as indicated by its much wider and smoother lines. Photographs also show an episode of seemingly random abrasion across the upper part of Panel 4. These abrasions superimpose this earlier image but lie beneath the chalked ochre battle scene.

Panel 5 consisted of two parts spanning a large face measuring more than 3.5 by 2.5 meters in dimension (Figure 5). Images scattered across this face include at least four horses with riders, a few other anthropomorphs, two groups of tipis, some guns, and other miscellaneous designs. Both red and white pigments were used to draw these figures. Several of the images are grouped in various combat scenes. In the upper left corner, a gun points toward a group of six tipis (Figure 5a), while in another part of the panel a horseman points a gun at what appears to be a falling human (Figure 5b). Two other horses appear to be engaged in a chase, one following the other in the center of the panel. Between the animals is a large, ghost-like, trapezoidal-body anthropomorph more than 40 cm tall. Mahaney (1986:88) reports that this figure is superimposed over part of one horse. This anthropomorph is not typical of Historic-period Biographic art in this region; and, in fact, shows formal similarities to earlier Barrier Canyon, Basketmaker, and Fremont rock art—all of which commonly occur in this general area of western Colorado/eastern Utah. Given the difficulty in many cases of determining superimpositions without close analysis of small details, we suggest that further study of this image (if it can be exposed) would be needed to verify its chronological placement. Overall, however, Panel 5 appears to be primarily biographic drawings of the same genre as those on Panel 4.

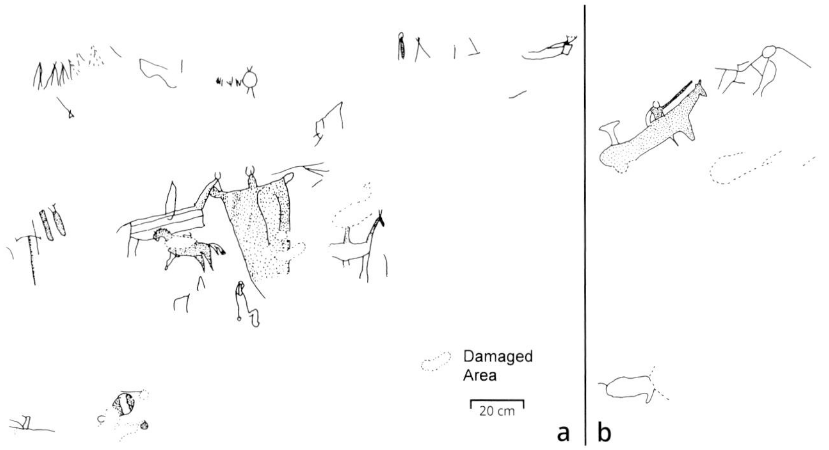

Figure 5a and b. Both parts of Panel 5 featuring Biographic art as sketched by Mahaney (1986:90-91). Relabeled by authors.

Panel 6 comprises four areas with paintings, again composed with red and white pigment. Similar to Panels 4 and 5, the art on this panel also consists largely of biographic drawings, interspersed with geometric shapes (Figure 6). Some of these geometric designs are circular and may represent shields. Recognizable images include five mounted warriors, one at the top of the panel appearing to hold a gun and a small, equestrian-period shield, as well as a shield-bearing warrior with a scalloped design around the shield's perimeter. The horse ridden by the man carrying a shield and gun wears some sort of decorated bit represented by an arc of six straight lines extending from its nose.

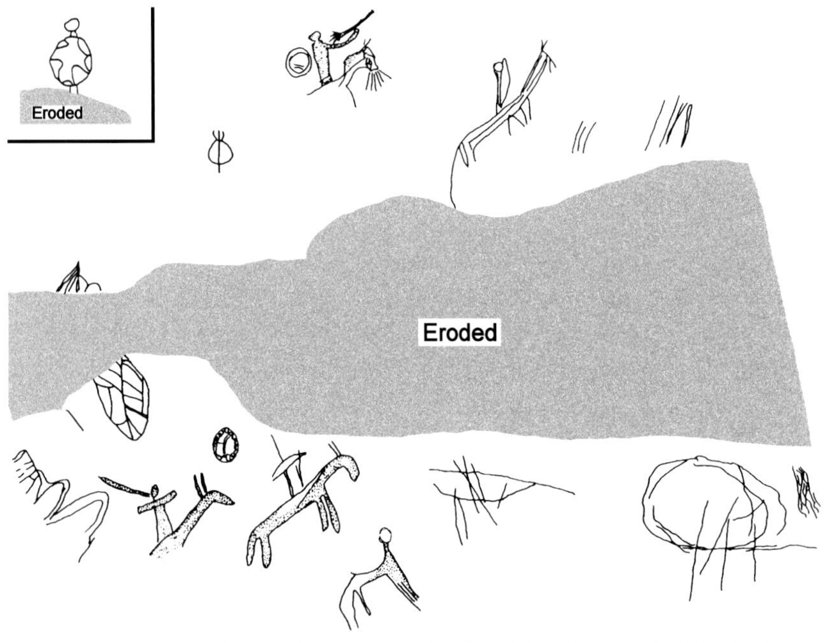

Figure 6. More Biographic art shown on Panel 6. Sketch by Mahaney (1986:93). Erosion in center relabeled by authors. Shield-bearing warrior inset in upper left from separate part of panel.

Analysis of the Scenes on Panel 4

The two scenes on Panel 4 are the subject of this paper. Fortunately, the photographs in our possession enable us to do photo-tracings of the entire Scene A and about half of Scene B. For purposes of analysis, we have incorporated Mahaney's sketch of the "missing" half of Scene B into our interpretation.

One element on Panel 4 that resists identification is a roughly circular shape filled with diagonal and crisscrossed lines. This image is more faded than Scene A that appears to overlap a portion of it. It is unclear if this element was originally part of Scene B, or another, unrelated episode.

Scene A

This battle scene (Figures 7and 8), which shows a fortified defending force being overwhelmed by attackers, uses many Plains Biographic conventions to tell its narrative. The prominent circle on the left side of the scene represents a fortification, possibly some kind of constructed bulwark against attack, but it could also be a natural hollow or other defendable location. The fortification is large enough to contain several people and horses. Similar circular fortifications are found across the northern Plains (Figures 9, 10). Drawn as if seen from above, people inside are generally shown from a side view. While humans might be lying down in some cases, horses are always shown standing in side view as well, indicating a multi-plane perspective (Kaiser and Keyser 2020:31-32).

To the right of the circle, a group of fighters defending this fortification are represented only by a stacked array of weapons—in this case nine long guns, indicated by the long barrel and triangular buttstock, and four spears, shown as simple horizontal lines. This is another typical Plains convention, which

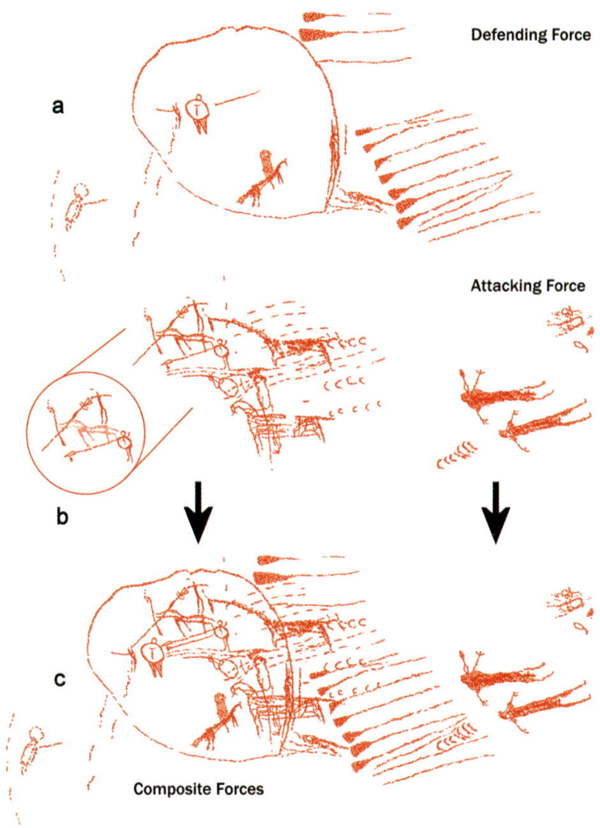

Figure 7. Photo-tracing of Scene A. (a) Defending force, including circular fortification. (b) Attacking warriors with track sequences. (c) Complete scene.

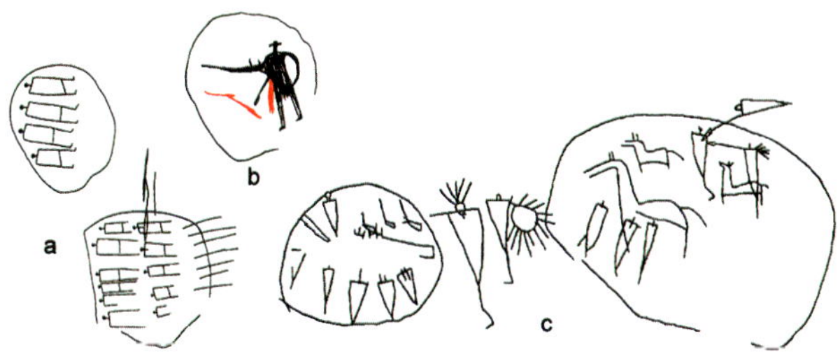

Figure 9. War parties shown within circular fortifications at other Plains Biographic rock art sites. (a) Entrenched combatants with stacked weapon array at DgOw-32, Alberta; (b) A wounded gunman inside a fortification at DgOw-20, Alberta; (c) Warriors and horses inside fortifications at Turner Rockshelter, Montana. Note the breaching of the entrenchment by the enemy.

Attackers are coming from the right-hand (north) side of the panel. Two of these attackers are killed, and lie prostrate with their arms outstretched, one with an arrow in his head or neck (Figure 8C/7). This indicates that while not shown in the stacked array of weapons, defenders also used bows and arrows to try to repel the attackers. In the original sketch a third defeated assailant is shown just above the first two (Mahaney 1986:89), and while this is logically consistent, there is insufficient detail in the photographs we have to confirm this identification. Cole (1987:232) indicates that these three horizontal figures "are drawn on a portion of rock which has fallen from its original position and would have originally presented the figures as upright." This is incorrect. One of the photographs clearly shows that, while divided by cracks in the rock face (indicated by a vertical line on the original sketch), these images are in their original position (Figure 12) and intentionally drawn horizontally to indicate the death of these attackers.[1]

Undeterred, the remaining invaders overwhelm the defenses and break through their line. Multiple rows of dashed footprints and lunate hoofprints show attackers on horseback as well as on foot. Two hoofprint sequences lead directly to mounted warriors breaching the fortification. Beneath the lower horse breaching the defenses and directly behind the stacked guns is a series of horizontal lines (Figure 8B/5). While indistinct, this may have been intended to represent another defeated enemy, either killed by the rider or trampled by his horse. This rider confronts a defender

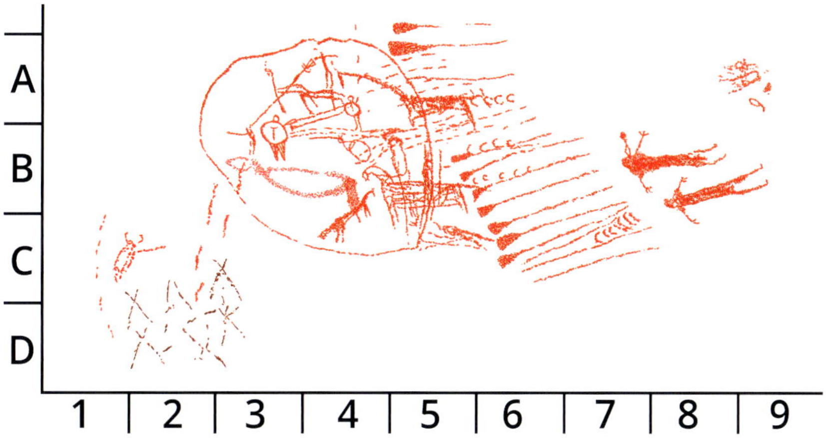

Figure 8. Scene A at 5GF1339. Note earlier joined ovals inside circular fortification and reuse of the village-scape from the earlier Scene B in the lower left.

is shown in exactly the same spatial relationship at DgOv-81 at Writing-on-Stone (Figure 10). Compared with other guns shown in the scene at 5GF1339, the elongated barrels of these weapons likely indicate they are firing, since a bullet's path in this artistic tradition is sometimes shown by a line extending from the barrel towards the intended target (Figure 11).

Figure 10. Large battle scene at DgOv-81, Alberta. Note circular fortifications and stacked weapon arrays similar to those drawn at 5GF1339.

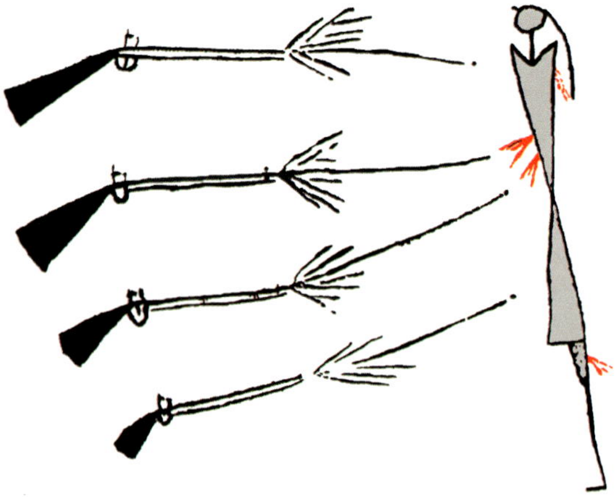

Figure 11. Firing guns as shown on the Maximilian Robe. Redrawn from Robe IV B 199, Ethnological Museum, Berlin.

Figure 12. Close up photograph of the prone figures on Panel 4. Courtesy of the Grand River Institute, Grand Junction, Colorado.

also on horseback, though no weapons are shown. The attacker's horse is shown with a rein and a possible bit decoration, indicated by two pendant lines.

Two other track sequences represent unseen horses that may not have penetrated the stronghold as they do not lead into the fortification. A dashed track sequence starts at one of the lines of hoofprints, indicating the rider dismounted and continued forward on foot Figure 8C/5). A third, roughly depicted, riderless horse is shown within the fortification (Figure 8D/4). Because it faces left, we suspect this was the mount of one of the invaders, likely the warrior shown just above, shooting a gun.

Multiple rows of footprints are shown breaching the defenses, leading to a group of warriors fighting inside the fortification. More track sequences are shown than the number of attackers depicted within, indicating a larger attacking force. One series of tracks leads to an attacker shown only by his shield and gun (Figure 8C/4). Additional tracks show the path of an attacking shield-bearing warrior with a spear who enters from the top of the panel (Figure 8D/4). From the bottom of the scene, track sequences lead to two pedestrian defenders within the circle.

Another series of tracks appears to be associated with a warrior to the left of the fortification, who carries a lance and wears a bison-horn headdress (Figure 8 B/1), although he does not appear to engage in the battle. These tracks running from below the fortification are drawn in a darker pigment than that of the lower scene but appear to have served to incorporate the tipi village from the previous episode, possibly to show that the defenders in Scene A moved from their village to a more defendable position. These tracks may also suggest some defenders may have fled from their ransacked and ravaged village, possibly to seek refuge in whatever geographic feature might be represented by the cross-hatched oval—possibly the rugged Book Cliffs region nearby.

Within the fortification, the uppermost attacking warrior, drawn as a stick figure, has likely dismounted from the sketchy horse below it (Figure 8D/4). His gun is shown with a trigger guard as well as exaggerated hammer and frizzen, indicating a flintlock long gun. The warrior shoots the gun at a lower stick figure, who leans backwards in defeat (Figure 8C/3). The path of the bullet is depicted as a long line connecting the gun to its victim.

These weapons may first have been introduced in the area by the Spanish Dominguez-Escalante expedition in 1776. The ethnohistoric record indicates that southern Plains tribes began acquiring flintlock firearms in very small numbers by the first decades of the 1700s (Secoy 1992:79-83) and continued to obtain these weapons in increasing quantities into the 1800s.

However, flintlock and caplock weapons continued to be used well into the mid-1800s as evidenced by both ledger and robe drawings.

To the left of this attacker is a floating gun, possibly a pistol, using synecdoche to represent a second, otherwise unseen, attacker (Figure 8D/3). This gun fires at a defending shield-bearing warrior with T-shaped shield heraldry (Figure 8C/3). Again, a long line extends from the muzzle of the pistol. However, this attacker misses his target, as a dash in front of the shield warrior shows the bullet wide of its mark.

The attacker shown only by his round shield and flintlock rifle, also aims at this same defending shield-bearing warrior, but this man does not appear to fire his gun. Above this figure, another attacker holds a shield and a long spear tipped with a large triangular point that touches the defending shield figure (Figure 8C/4). A parallel line below the attacker's spear likely indicates the defender's lance, however it is not connected to him and is shown floating towards the attacker, a common Biographic convention for a captured weapon.

This defending shield-bearing warrior suffered a concerted attack by numerous enemies. He was likely a principal defender, or a warrior of some importance to have so many attackers focused on his defeat. Numerous other dashes lead to this same figure. While unclear, these dashes may indicate additional flying bullets aimed at the defenders, or they could be the paths of the attackers as they advanced further into the defender's stronghold.

While the lower two warriors on horseback are not shown with any weapons or specifically engaged in combat (Figure 8B/4-5), the depiction of the smaller horse and rider in a subordinate position likely represents the defender's defeat, a fate shared by the other fighters, unable to stop the overwhelming attack by their enemies.

Although entrenching in their fortification and being well armed, the defenders were overcome by the attacking force. Using warriors on horseback and on foot, the attackers broke through the defensive line and breached the fortification. After a heated battle, the attackers defeated the warriors within.

Scene B

Scene B (Figure 13) is reconstructed here from a photo-tracing of the upper leftmost part of the panel that can be seen in the site photographs, to this we have appended a portion of the Mahaney (1986) sketch to fill in the now-missing portion. In carefully comparing this photo-tracing to Mahaney's sketch (both during the reconstruction and afterward), we note that the sketch is only a moderately accurate representation of what we know to have existed at the site. That is, the animals, tipis, weapons, and humans are generally accurately placed in the scene, but their specific forms are not particularly faithful to what was actually drawn on the cliff. Thus, horses appear bulkier, humans are more amorphous, and weapons often lack detail. Additionally, there is no careful delineation of what lines on the sketch are cracks in the rock, and what possible differences in shades of pigment might say about some seemingly random shapes that may not be related to the scene itself. This is, of course, the primary disadvantage of working with a non-specialist's tracing; but, in terms of overall interpretation of the scene, we are encouraged by the general correspondence between the sketch and the photographs.

Figure 13. Scene B at 5GF1339. Red images from photo-tracing. Black images from original sketch by Mahaney (1986:89). Gray area spalled off in photographs taken between 1985 and 2009.

Scene B shows an attack on a village, indicated by three stacked rows of simply drawn X-shaped tipis illustrated in a typical Biographic compositional style in which higher images represent objects further away without diminishing in size. The attackers are shown in a similar fashion, preventing the closer images from blocking the further ones. The bottom row of tipis could be right-side up, but they may also be upside-down. Either configuration is known from various depictions of Plains tipi villages.

The large group of attackers is represented by about a dozen (or possibly more)[2] warriors on horseback. Most warriors hold circular shields, some possibly showing geometric heraldry. The heads of some warriors peek above these shields, while other attackers are shown only by their shield and weapon. Some of these weapons are indistinct, but several appear to be spears, one with a distinctive crosspiece near the tip indicating a metal weapon (Keyser and Kaiser 2010). Other warriors carry long guns.

Behind the horses are a series of dashes representing tracks. While these might be intended to show the route of the mounted warriors, the tracks are not obviously hoofprints. More likely, the tracks show a group of foot soldiers following behind, using synecdoche to represent the pedestrian warriors only by their tracks.

At the head of the mounted attackers, a warrior wears a dramatic bison-horn headdress, carries a gun, and rides what appears to be horse covered in leather armor. The body of this animal is significantly wider than others shown on the panel and is depicted in a solidly painted bulky rectangular shape, likely indicating an armored horse. Horses illustrated clad in leather armor—some quite similarly drawn—are found across the Plains (Fowles and Montgomery 2019:114; Greer et al. 2019). Horse armor, used by the Shoshone, was described by Meriwether Lewis as late as 1805 (Moulton 1988:150), and consisted of overlapping hides reinforced with glue and sand. Such horse armor is depicted in the Segesser I hide painting (Hotz 1991). Like the horse leading the charge in Scene B, the armored horses on the Segesser I hide were used to break through the enemy lines, while other comrades—both mounted and afoot—followed up to engage the disrupted enemy. Armored horses were used primarily in pre-gun warfare since their leather protection could deflect a spearpoint but was less effective against bullets. However, the use of armored horses did overlap with early gun warfare, and these weapons also occur together at the West Ryegate site in Montana (Greer et al. 2019:60).

In the far left of the scene, a rectangular-body human holds one arm bent upwards and the curve of his legs gives the appearance of falling backwards, in a typical Biographic posture of defeat. The figure might be holding a weapon facing the attackers, but the details are unclear. Two floating coup strike weapons point at this figure, representing the actions of otherwise unseen attackers. A lance with a clear triangular spear tip points towards his head, while a gun fires at his torso. Clearly this warrior was the victim of a focused attack because he was likely a person of some importance.

Some elements of Scene B are not clear. A cluster of several lines to the right of the lower tipis cannot be identified. It is possible that details were missed on the sketch, or natural cracks became confused with the art, as evidenced by the long vertical line through the middle of the scene that conforms to the area that spalled off the cliff prior to when the photographs were taken that we have. It is possible that some of these other lines represent some sort of constructed defensive rampart, but this is only speculative due to the unclear nature of the sketch. Below these lines is what appears to be another horse. If correctly identified, it has a starburst of short lines at its nose. This could represent a bit decorated with feathers or other streamers. Similarly shaped bridle decorations are found on armored horses at Arminto, Wyoming (Greer et al. 2019:77), while a decorated bit of another style is also shown in Scene A.

A circular shape behind the group of horses may represent an entrenchment used by the village defenders but overwhelmed by the larger attacking group. However, there are no clear depictions of people, animals, or weapons inside the circle, so this must remain a tentative identification.

At the top of the spalled area in the photographs is an animal, likely a horse. However, it is facing the opposite direction to all the others. Assuming this is not a mistake in the sketch, and without a rider shown, it might represent a stolen horse taken after the battle. No other conventions are used to indicate a stolen animal (McCallister et al. 2021), but some individual or isolated animals are thought to represent war trophies.

Finally, two groups of dashes, representing tracks, lead away from the extreme left of the village. One group extends straight to the left. These tracks could indicate attack from both sides via a pincer movement, but as no other attackers are shown the tracks more likely indicate part of the village fleeing in that direction. Another group of tracks goes behind the pedestrian warrior wearing a bison-horn headdress and terminates at the cross-hatched oval area above. This warrior and the tracks are composed with a darker pigment than the rest of Scene B and were likely added later as part of Scene A (Figure 8A-B1).

Some Observations on Panel 4 Art

Both scenes on Panel 4 would almost certainly have been drawn by the victorious attackers. While suffering some losses, in both cases the raiders overcame the defenders and commemorated their victories at this site. Both battle scenes seem likely to have been composed by artists of the same group at different times, who returned to this locality to record their victories.

While any identification of the groups' identities based on stylistic criteria must be considered speculative (especially since we are not able to examine the imagery first-hand), the shape of the horses and the overall simplicity of the human figures provides some clues. The use of several widespread Plains Biographic artistic conventions indicates the artists were raiders from further east or southeast on the Plains. Historic Plains style art is found elsewhere in western Colorado at Craig Sandrocks (Keyser 2008), about 133 km (70 miles) to the north of the site.

Cole (1987:222) ascribes the art at 5GF1339 to possible Comanche or Shoshone artists. From her discussion of the site, we suspect that her attribution is based on stylistic criteria combined with the "remarkabl[e] similar[ities] to early, pre-A.D. 1830-1850, Biographic Style art from the northwestern Plains" expressed by the compositions at 5GF1339 (Cole 1990:220). But we cannot rule out Cole knowing of the ample evidence that the Shoshone/Comanche occupied the East Salt Creek drainage during the Late Prehistoric and Historic periods. Surface collections and limited test excavations during highway salvage operations at two groups of sites in a 10 km (six mile) stretch of the East Salt Creek valley extending just north and south of 5GF1339 recovered artifacts that include Intermountain Ware pottery from three sites, tri-notched arrowpoints at seven sites, Native-made metal arrowpoints at two sites, and a "Shoshone" knife at one site (Rhodes 1986:61-83). In all, seven sites in the upper reach of this stream valley contained artifacts strongly suggestive of a Shoshone/Comanche presence spanning the Late Prehistoric to Historic-period transition.

We agree with Cole's assessment that this rock art appears far more "Plains-like" than the typical Ute rock art—even that focused on horses and riders. Having extensive experience recording and evaluating both Shoshone and Ute "horse and rider" rock art (Conner and Keyser 2019; Keyser 2011; Keyser and Poetschat 2005, 2008), we both were immediately struck by the strong Plains "feel" of many of the compositions at 5GF1339. While some of the simpler horses and riders are reminiscent of those at Ute sites, the multiple stacked arrays of weapons, flying bullets, track sequences (both horse and human), and fortified positions all have multiple counterparts in Plains rock art but not in Ute rock art of the Colorado Plateau.

However, when we began seeking comparative compositions elsewhere on the Plains, the closest similarities seem to be with the Comanche rock art found at the La Vista Verde site complex in northern New Mexico's Rio Grande Gorge (Fowles and Arterberry 2013). The 5GF1339 scenes and several compositions at La Vista Verde (Figure 14) share the same characteristically "loose" compositional style, coupled with the somewhat sketchy, elongated form for horses and the even sketchier human figures.

Fowles (Fowles and Arterberry 2013:72-77) has argued that the fluidity and stylization of the Rio Grande Gorge style art is based on its "mimetic gestural" aspects, by which the artist is actually physically re-enacting the event as he creates the battle imagery. Certainly there are aspects of 5GF1339 that fit very well with this hypothesis. Most of the Colorado horses have the same extremely fluid style, though their riders and the riders' weapons show much less detail at the scale of these large battle scenes. Humans are shown both as simple stick figures as well as rectangular or oval-bodied warriors. Some guns are shown as a simple line with a triangular buttstock, but others are depicted with a detailed flintlock firing assembly, and shots are expressed by long streaks exiting the gun barrel and extending to the target. While such variations in forms of basic components (horses, humans, weapons) might be attributable to individual artistic skill and style, we suspect that these scenes are each the product of an individual artist, so that should not be a major causative agent. Rather, it seems to us to indicate a broad view of accepted variation in the depiction of these objects, with an emphasis on the act of drawing being more important than a tight boundedness of style. While this makes direct comparison with stylistically similar examples difficult, if one accepts the premise that the drawing of the image was actually part performance, it equates this art to that of the Rio Grande Gorge (Fowles and Arterberry 2013, Fowles and Montgomery 2019). Thus, we believe the art at 5GF1339 is most similar to Fowles's Rio Grande Gorge style imagery.

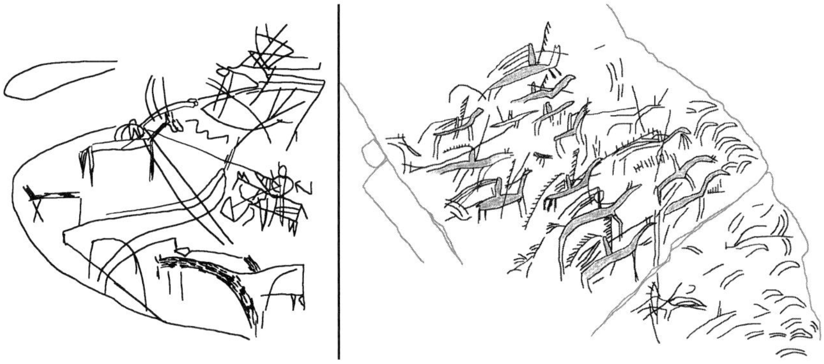

Figure 14. Panels at La Vista Verde in New Mexico with horses, riders, a gun, spears, and geometric images, composed in a similar loose style to that at 5GF1339. Images courtesy Severin Fowles.

Additionally, if we are correct in the identification of an armored horse in Scene B, this would also concur with the Comanche's early acquisition of the horse and the use of armored mounts in warfare. Other rock art examples of armored horses attributed to the Comanche are found in southeast Colorado (Mitchell 2004), and La Vista Verde in New Mexico (Fowles et al. 2017:171-173). Likewise, Comanche use of the stacked array convention representing armed warriors is also shown at La Vista Verde (Fowles et al. 2017:175)[3] and at site 5LA5569 in the Pinon Canyon Maneuver Site in southeastern Colorado (Loendorf and Kuehn 1991:191, 206-207).

If our tentative identification is correct, the use of multiple Plains Biographic style conventions in composing the narratives at 5GF1339 suggests the scenes show successful raids by a Comanche group on local Ute people. This fits quite well with Comanche history (Newton 2011).

Separating from the Shoshone on the northern Plains, the group that became the Comanche migrated south where they encountered the Plains Apache, a more established and powerful group. Withdrawing to the mountains and foothills to the west the Comanche allied with the local Ute people, both wishing to acquire horses and European trade goods. However, once the Comanche amassed horses and weapons through trade and raids, their alliance with the Ute dissolved, and they quickly expanded their territory. Unlike the part-time agriculturalists in the region, the Comanche, as mobile bison hunters, were able to parlay their acquisition of the horse and their widespread use of them in raiding neighboring territories to establish what Hämäläinen (2008) has termed the "Comanche Empire" and called Comanchería (Figure 15).

While expanding their powerbase in the southern Plains, the Comanche retained ties with the Shoshone in the north, trading horses and captives (Newton 2011:11). These trade routes took the Comanche through Ute territory in what is now central and northwestern Colorado. About midway through their approximately two-century domination of the southern Plains (ca. 1770-1820), the Comanche experimented with a transhumant settlement pattern "that moved [part of their population]...from Comanchería to...Ute territory in the Colorado Plateau" (Hämäläinen 2010:196). This occupation of the Colorado Plateau appears to have involved seasonal migrations from the Plains to the highlands and back and coincided with violent raids on the local Ute tribes, whose former alliance with the Comanches had disintegrated (Hämäläinen 2010:197).

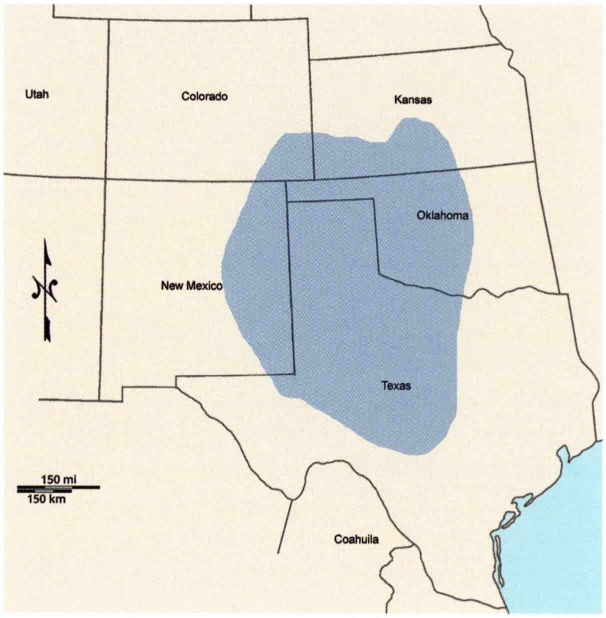

Figure 15. Area of the Comanchería, though raids took place well outside their main territory.

The art at 5GF1339 seems likely to have been created during a raiding expedition on a trip north to trade with the Shoshone, or at the time of Comanche expansion back into the Colorado Plateau (or both). The horses and guns suggest a full-fledged Plains warfare pattern, but the fewer guns and the armored horse in Scene B suggest a date sometime in the last half of the eighteenth century. Moving into this area of the Colorado River valley, the Comanche would have met local Ute villages and conflict would certainly have arisen. It appears that the battle scenes at 5GF1339 record two sequent Comanche attacks on the same local population separated by a few years during the time when Comanchería extended into west-central Colorado.

Summary

The details in Scene B are less clear than those in Scene A due to the lack of photographs and the more faded nature of this portion of the panel. However, both compositions show a broadly similar narrative that can be relatively easily understood. Each shows an attack by forces on horseback and on foot who overwhelm the opposition, and each includes the targeted killing of an individual defender by multiple attackers. Both scenes are classic Plains Biographic narratives, suggesting they were drawn by Plains artists fully fluent in the intricacies of the Biographic art lexicon. In contrast, at the time these scenes were apparently drawn, local Ute artists typically drew far fewer explicitly narrative scenes, and, instead, concentrated on drawing horses and bison hunts. Only later did Ute Biographic art come to include more fight scenes (Cole 1990:213-235).

That Scene B represents an earlier narrative than Scene A is suggested by the faded appearance of its pigment. While a few guns appear in this scene, a relatively early date is indicated by the depiction of an armored horse. The use of such leather armor rapidly diminished with the proliferation of guns in warfare, to which the armor offered little protection. Scene A, on the other hand, shows many guns used by both attackers and defenders and likely records a later attack, but one essentially involving the same two groups, as evidenced by the incorporation of Scene B elements into Scene A.

We suggest the following scenario. Comanches intruding into Ute territory in the early days of the Comanchería expansion came into conflict with a local Ute population, probably living in one or more villages in the Colorado River valley. Likely, the conflict was due to the Comanches' bringing their extensive horse herds to graze the lush floodplain combined with the intrusive human population's impact on available game resources. The result—commemorated in Scene B—was a relatively large-scale Comanche attack on the Ute village, during which an important local leader was killed. Part of the village population fled to take refuge in more rugged territory nearby—likely the Book Cliffs region just north and northwest of the Loma area.

Returning some years later (as evidenced by more guns, the absence of horse armor, and the less-faded imagery in Scene A) the invading Comanches again engaged in conflict with the locals. Another fight, this one against fortified villagers, possibly in the more rugged Book Cliffs country, resulted in the attacking Comanche force overrunning a defensive position and again killing a prominent man. This was commemorated in Scene A by a second artist who incorporated parts of Scene B into his newly drawn battle scene. The result is a graphic record of the late eighteenth-century expansion of the Comanchería recorded here in the upper reaches of the East Salt Creek drainage for all to see.

Notes

1. Cole (1990:220-221) corrected her error in a subsequent publication, possibly because she had visited the site in the interim. In this source, she indicates that these are fallen combatants.

2. For the entire following discussion, the reader must remember that the difficulty of counting and describing the attacking force—including the exact number of horsemen, the details of the mounted men, and the specifics of their weaponry—is due both to the extreme sketchiness of some figures and the fact that at least one animal—facing away from the fight—may not be a horse.

3. The authors identify two stacked arrays in a battle scene as a tally of arrows shot by the opposing forces (Fowles et al. 2017:177), but by comparison with other Biographic uses of this convention, we suggest they are a generic representation of the opposing forces themselves.

References Cited

Berry, Michael S.
2011 Class I Cultural Resource Overview for the Grand Junction Field Office of the Bureau of Land Management. Bureau of Land Management, Grand Junction Field Office, Grand Junction, Colorado.

Cole, Sally J.
1987 *An Analysis of the Prehistoric and Historic Rock Art of West-Central Colorado.* Cultural Resource Series, 21, Bureau of Land Management, Denver, Colorado.

1990 *Legacy on Stone.* Johnson Books, Boulder, Colorado.

Conner, Carl, and James D. Keyser
2019 *Archaeological Assessment of the Caps Spring Rock Art Sites (5DT2156 and 5DT2157), Delta County, Colorado.* DARG (Dominquez Archaeological Research Group). OAHP Document No. DT.LM.R80, submitted to History Colorado, State Historical Fund, 1200 Broadway, Denver, Colorado 80203 in compliance with State Historical Fund Project #2018-AS-005.

Fowles, Severin, and Jimmy Arterberry
2013 Gesture and Performance in Comanche Rock Art. *World Art* 3(1):67–82.

Fowles, Severin, Jimmy Arterberry, Heather Atherton, and Lindsay Montgomery
2017 Comanche New Mexico: the Eighteenth Century. In *New Mexico and the Pimería Alta: The Colonial Period in the American Southwest,* edited by John G. Douglass and William M. Graves, pp. 157–186. University Press of Colorado, Boulder.

Fowles, Severin, and Lindsay A. Montgomery
2019 Rock Art Counter-Archives of the American West. In *Murals of the Americas: Papers from the 2017 Mayer Center Symposium at the Denver Art Museum,* edited by Victoria I. Lyall, pp. 101–120. Denver Art Museum, Denver, Colorado.

Greer, Mavis, John Greer, and James D. Keyser
2019 Armored Horses in Northwestern Plains Rock Art. *Archaeology in Montana* 60(2):53–99.

Hämäläinen, Pekka
2008 *The Comanche Empire.* Yale University Press, New Haven, Connecticut.

2010 The Politics of Grass: European Expansion, Ecological Change, and Indigenous Power in the Southwest Borderlands. *William and Mary Quarterly* 67(2):173–208.

Hotz, Gottfried
1991 *The Segesser Hide Paintings: Masterpieces Depicting Spanish Colonial New Mexico.* Thomas E. Chavez, editor. Museum of New Mexico Press, Santa Fe.

Kaiser, David A., and James D. Keyser
2020 Hoofprints and Footprints—The Grammar of Biographic Rock Art. In *American Indian Rock Art, Volume 46,* edited by Richard A. Rogers, Evelyn Billo, and Robert Mark, pp. 23–45. American Rock Art Research Association, Cupertino, California.

Keyser, James D.
1987 A Lexicon for Historic Plains Indian Rock Art: Increasing Interpretive Potential. *Plains Anthropologist* 32:43–71.

1996 Painted Bison Robes: The Missing Link in the Biographic Art Style Lexicon. *Plains Anthropologist* 41:29–52.

2008 Craig Sandrocks: Historic Plains Horse Petroglyphs in Northwestern Colorado. *Southwestern Lore* 74(3-4):1–21.

2011 Horse and Rider Rock Art in Western Colorado. In *Class I Cultural Resource Overview for the Grand Junction Field Office of the Bureau of Land Management,* edited by Michael S. Berry, pp. 4.67–4.86. Bureau of Land Management, Grand Junction Field Office, Grand Junction, Colorado.

Keyser, James D., and David A. Kaiser
2010 Getting the Point: Metal Weapons in Plains Rock Art. *Plains Anthropologist* 55:111–132.

2022 *War Stories: Reading Plains Indian Biographic Rock Art.* Berghahn, New York.

Keyser, James D., and Michael A. Klassen
2003 Every Detail Counts: More Additions to the Plains Biographic Rock Art Lexicon. *Plains Anthropologist* 48:7–20.

Keyser, James D., and George R. Poetschat
2005 *Warrior Art of Wyoming's Green River Basin: Biographic Petroglyphs Along the Seedskadee.* Oregon Archaeological Society, Publication No. 15, Portland.

2008 *Ute Horse Raiders on the Powder Rim: Rock Art at Powder Wash, Wyoming.* Oregon Archaeological Society Press, Publication No. 19, Portland.

Loendorf, Lawrence L., and David D. Kuehn
1991 *1989 Rock Art Research, Piñon Canyon Maneuver Site, Southeastern Colorado.* University of North Dakota, Department of Anthropology, Contribution 258.

Mahaney, Nancy
1986 Rock Art. In *Archaeological Survey Along State Highway 139: Loma to Douglas Pass,* by Lori Rhodes, pp. 85–98. Highway Salvage Report No. 58, Colorado Department of Highways, Denver.

McCallister, Alison, James D. Keyser, and David A. Kaiser
2021 "Horse Stealing is an Eminent Art Among Them": Blackfoot Horse-Raiding Imagery at Writing-on-Stone. In *American Indian Rock Art, Volume 47,* edited by David A. Kaiser, Mavis Greer, and James D. Keyser, pp. 25–41. American Rock Art Research Association, Orem, Utah.

Mitchell, Mark D.
2004 Tracing Comanche History: Eighteenth Century Rock Art Depictions of Leather Armoured Horses from the Arkansas River Basin, South-eastern Colorado, USA. *Antiquity* 78(299):115–126.

Moulton, Gary E. (editor)
1988 *The Journals of the Lewis & Clark Expedition, Volume 5, July 28–November 1, 1805.* University of Nebraska Press, Lincoln.

Newton, Cody
2011 Towards a Context for Late Precontact Culture Change: Comanche Movement Prior to Eighteenth Century Spanish Documentation. *Plains Anthropologist* 56(217):53–70.

Parsons, Mark L.
1987 Plains Indian Portable Art as a Key to Two Texas Historic Rock Art Sites. *Plains Anthropologist* 32:257–274.

Petersen, Karen Daniels
1971 *Plains Indian Art from Fort Marion.* Norman: University of Oklahoma Press.

1988 *American Pictographic Images: Historic Works on Paper by Plains Indians.* Alexander Gallery, New York.

Rhodes, Lori
1986 *Archaeological Survey Along State Highway 139: Loma to Douglas Pass.* Highway Salvage Report No. 58, Colorado Department of Highways, Denver.

Secoy, Frank Raymond
1992 *Changing Military Patterns of the Great Plains.* University of Nebraska Press, Lincoln. (Reprint edition, originally published 1953 as *Changing Military Patterns on the Great Plains (17th Century through Early 19th Century),* Monographs of the American Ethnological Society 31.

Cueva Higuerillas (Cucurpe, Sonora): A Ritual Space, a Cohesive Social Space, or Part of a Whole?

Beatriz Menéndez Iglesias, Tomás Pérez-Reyes, César Armando Quijada López, and Alejandro Terrazas Mata

Cucurpe valley, located in the lower foothills of the Sierra Madre Occidental in the state of Sonora, is distinguished by its high concentration of rock art sites. The region is defined within the Pima-Opata border. The Cucurpe rock art assemblages are characterized mainly by paintings, and in some cases engravings, rarely presenting both techniques. The chronology of the area is established around the pre-Hispanic period until the Colonial period. This is a preliminary study of the Cueva Higuerillas rock art site, a significant place because of its iconography. Numerous representations of hands are painted on its walls that, along with the morphology and iconographic interconnection, make this site a representative place in the region. In this sense, we question its functionality, whether it is a symbolic space, a space for social cohesion, or both.

Sonora has one of the highest concentrations of rock art in Mexico. However, it should be pointed out that among the diverse problems posed by the study of Sonora's rock art are the lack of detailed and exhaustive documentation of the sites and the lack of direct dating of both engravings and paintings, all due to the scarcity of projects and the limited budgets for their development. All this determines, in short, a scarcity of research work and a broad future for new generations of archaeologists.

As a result of my research stay at the National Autonomous University of Mexico, specifically at the Institute of Anthropological Research, I decided to initiate a project in Sonora. For this reason, the project "Cave documentation and study of patinas in desert environments: from the Sonoran Desert to the Sierra Madre Occidental" was proposed (in Spanish, DREPNS—Documentación rupestre y estudio de pátinas en el Norte de Sonora: del desierto sonorense a la Sierra Madre Occidental). Within this project, the documentation of rock art in Cucurpe (Figure 1) was contemplated. For this purpose, an exhaustive documentation of each archaeological site was carried out and new technologies were applied to record the rock art, such as photogrammetry and DStretch (Figure 2).

Throughout these pages we will deal with the Cueva Higuerillas, a significant site because of its iconography, including numerous representations of hands. In this sense, we wonder whether it is a symbolic space or a space of social cohesion. We will try to address this question to see its possible functionality, bearing in mind that this is a preliminary study.

Background

Several researchers have been interested in the study of rock art in Cucurpe. As early as the 1920s, Carl Sauer and Donald Brand travelled through different regions of northern Sonora, visiting for the first time some of the

Beatriz Menéndez Iglesias
Postdoctoral Scholarship Program, National Autonomous University of Mexico
Scholar of the Institute of Anthropological Research

Tomás Pérez-Reyes
National Institute of Anthropology and History, INAH-Sonora Center

César Armando Quijada López
National Institute of Anthropology and History, INAH-Sonora Center

Alejandro Terrazas Mata
Institute of Anthropological Research, National Autonomous University of Mexico

American Indian Rock Art, Volume 48. Amy Gilreath, Ken Hedges, and Anne McConnell, Editors. American Rock Art Research Association, 2022, pp. 51–62.

Figure 1. Location map of Cucurpe in the state of Sonora.
Figura 1. Mapa de ubicación de Cucurpe en el estado de Sonora. Image: https://descargarmapas.net.

Figure 2. Color comparison using the Munsell scale in Cueva Higuerillas.
Figura 2. Comparación de colores utilizando la escala Munsell en Cueva Higuerillas. Image: C. A. Quijada.

archaeological sites in Cucurpe and making the first reports (Sauer and Brand 1931:82–87).

Decades later we see the work of Professor Armando Quijada Hernández, who compiled information on 20 rock art sites with engravings and paintings in Cucurpe, which he presented at the XLI International Americanist Congress, held in Mexico City in 1974, and later at the First Symposium on the History of Sonora at the University of Sonora in 1975, where he pointed out:

> In the territory of the Municipality of Cucurpe, one of the largest concentrations of Rock Art in Sonora is found. Canyons and cliffs with numerous caves abound in this place, which were undoubtedly used by the primitive inhabitants... In these natural shelters is where the drawings and engravings representing anthropomorphic and zoomorphic figures are found, the most common of the latter being that of the deer; there are also what may be suns and moons, as well as highly stylized crosses. There are positive hands, and the...labyrinth common at some rock art stations in Arizona. The most common color used is red... Because of its abundance, and because of its characteristics, the Cucurpe Rock Art deserves special attention [Quijada Hernández 1976:443–444, translation by senior author].

In the 1970s, Beatriz Braniff, a researcher at the Northwest Regional Centre of INAH, initiated an archaeological project in the San Miguel river basin, in which she reported 32 archaeological sites. This region was one of the main regions for the development of her doctoral thesis on the Pima-Opata border (Braniff 1992), a border she established in this area.

At the end of 1990, the engravings of the site known as "Los pies del viejo" were recorded, and a few years later, in 1993, the engravings of the outer area of the Cueva Blanca de la Pulsera were located, which became the first cave in which engravings and paintings are documented in the same archaeological site (Quijada López 1996; Quijada López and Contreras Barragán 2006).

Subsequently, in 2004 César A. Quijada in collaboration with Jane Kolber, Daniel Frey, and the help of the American Indian Rock Art group at Cochise College, presented a paper entitled "Cueva de La Pulsera, Cucurpe, Sonora" at the American Rock Art Research Association conference held in Nuevo Casas Grandes, Chihuahua (Frey et al. 2005).

In this same decade, in 2007, and within the project "Prehistoric Research in Northwest Mexico: Baja

California Sur and Sonora," Ramón Viñas of the Catalan Institute of Human Paleoecology and Social Evolution (IPHES), Tarragona, and Albert Rubio of the Prehistoric Research and Studies Seminar (SERP), University of Barcelona, carried out their first visit, accompanied by César A. Quijada of the INAH Sonora Centre in Hermosillo, to some caves with paintings in the Cucurpe region, particularly along the Saracachi and San Miguel rivers. These included the caves Blanca La Pulsera and El Arco (Viñas 2009), which were subsequently documented in 2009, when researcher Beatriz Menéndez joined the project and the project was renamed "Biodiversidad de las sociedades cazadoras-recolectoras del Cuaternario de México" (BSCRCM, Biodiversity of the Hunter-gatherer Societies of the Quaternary of Mexico). On this occasion, Cueva Higuerillas was visited and recorded, although not exhaustively documented. Some results have been presented at the UISPP Congress (2014) and IFRAO Congress (2015), held at the University of Burgos (Spain) and the University of Cáceres (Spain), respectively. These communications were published in the digital journal *Expressions* (Rubio et al. 2014) and in the same proceedings of the IFRAO Congress 2015 (Viñas et al. 2015).

Among the latest research carried out in the region, in 2013 archaeologist Tomás Pérez-Reyes, from the INAH Sonora Centre, presented the Cueva de los Monos at the IFRAO 2013 Congress. In this work, the author gives a general description of the site and mentions the existence of a series of paintings from the Prehispanic to the contact or Colonial times (Pérez-Reyes 2013). That same year and during the celebration of the same congress, César A. Quijada presented the representations of hands in Sonora, detailing the panels of the Cueva de los Monos (Quijada López 2013:496–499).

Documentation of Rock Art and Patina Studies in Northern Sonora Project

The project "Cave Documentation and Patina Study in Northern Sonora" (DREPNS, in Spanish) contemplates the collection of samples for the study of patinas in two different environments: the desert (Sierra de El Álamo, Caborca) and the lower foothills of the Sierra Madre Occidental (Cucurpe) (Figure 3). On the one hand, the project consists of sampling rocks with varnish or patina unmodified by humans, both in the desert environment and in the lower parts of the sierra, in order to compare also the variation of varnishes in both environments. This is mainly focused on seeing,

Figure 3. The study regions (Caborca and Cucurpe) in relation to the ecoregions.

Figura 3. Las regiones de estudio (Caborca y Cucurpe) en relación con las ecorregiones. Based on Mott Lacroix et al. 2017.

in desert environments, the possibility of dating engravings from patinas and making paleoenvironmental reconstructions. Sampling was also done in the lower parts of the sierra at Cucurpe, in order to compare the variation of the varnishes in both environments. Likewise, it was decided to document rock art in the community of Cucurpe, since there are few exhaustive studies of the abundant rock art sites in the region.

Location

The municipality of Cucurpe is located in north-central Sonora, 54 km southeast of the city of Magdalena de Kino. It is located on the parallel 30°19' north latitude and the meridian 110°42' west longitude, bordering to the north with the municipality of Ímuris, to the east with Arizpe, to the south with Opodepe, to the west with Santa Ana, and to the northwest with Magdalena de Kino. The area is located in the H12B71 (Cucurpe) and H12B72 (Saracachi) charts, scale 1:50,000, of INEGI.

It covers an area of 1,778.55 km^2 at an altitude of 858 m above sea level, in the lower part of the Sierra Madre Occidental, an area close to the border with the Sierras and Llanos Sonorenses province. It borders to the west the Cucurpe mountain range and to the east the San Antonio mountain range. Its fluvial network includes the Dolores and Saracachi rivers, which converge to form the San Miguel River, a tributary of the Sonora River. It is a region with an abundance of ravines and cliffs with rockshelters and caves (Figure 4).

Figure 4. The region of Cucurpe in the lower foothills of the Sierra Madre Occidental.
Figura 4. Región de Cucurpe en las estribaciones bajas de la Sierra Madre Occidental. Image: B. Menéndez.

The Sierras and Valles del Norte sub-province, which is part of the larger Sierra Madre Occidental province, occupies the eastern and northern portion of the study area, and is mostly made up of slightly steep high sierra topoforms. This morphology is observed in the La Madera, Magdalena, and La Jojoba mountain ranges, interrupted in the central-northern region by an intermountain valley where the town of Ímuris is located, outside the municipal boundaries. In the Sierra La Madera and specifically on the El Barandal hill, where the borders between the municipalities of Magdalena, Imuris and Cucurpe converge, the highest altitude is 2,020 meters above sea level. In the Magdalena riverbed is the lowest elevation at 800 m above sea level. This makes an elevation differential in the order of 1,220 m. (Hernández Vega 2007).

The territory was occupied by Opatas and high Pimas at the time of the arrival of the Jesuit missionaries. In 1647 the missionary Marcos del Río founded the first population with the category of mission town and gave it the name of "Los Santos Reyes de Cucurpe" (INAH 2019).

Geological Context

The north-central region of Sonora, where Cucurpe is located, corresponds to a terrain composed of Mesozoic and Late Paleozoic rocks that represents a transition zone from continental to oceanic crust. González-León considers it as a block of deep marine sediments of Ordovician to Permian age, found mainly in Baja California Norte and in the central and southeastern portion of Sonora, in relation to the Caborca terrain to the north, supposedly transported and accreted in the Late Permian-Middle Triassic (González-León 2010).

The geological context is very complex with outcropping lithological units represented by igneous (plutonic, hypabyssal and volcanic), volcanosedimentary, sedimentary (terrigenous and carbonate), and metamorphic rocks, ranging in age from Precambrian to Recent with some outcrops of the oldest rocks in the Mexican Republic.

Cucurpe Rock Art Manifestations

The Cucurpe valley is located in the lower foothills of the Sierra Madre Occidental (Sonora), distinguished by its high concentration of rock art sites. It is worth mentioning its fluvial network, which includes the Dolores and Saracachi rivers that converge and form the San Miguel River, a tributary of the Sonora River. This orography characterizes the region for having abundant ravines and cliffs with shelters and caves where the cave paintings are located.

The map (Figure 5) shows the distribution of rock art sites in the region, where more groups of paintings

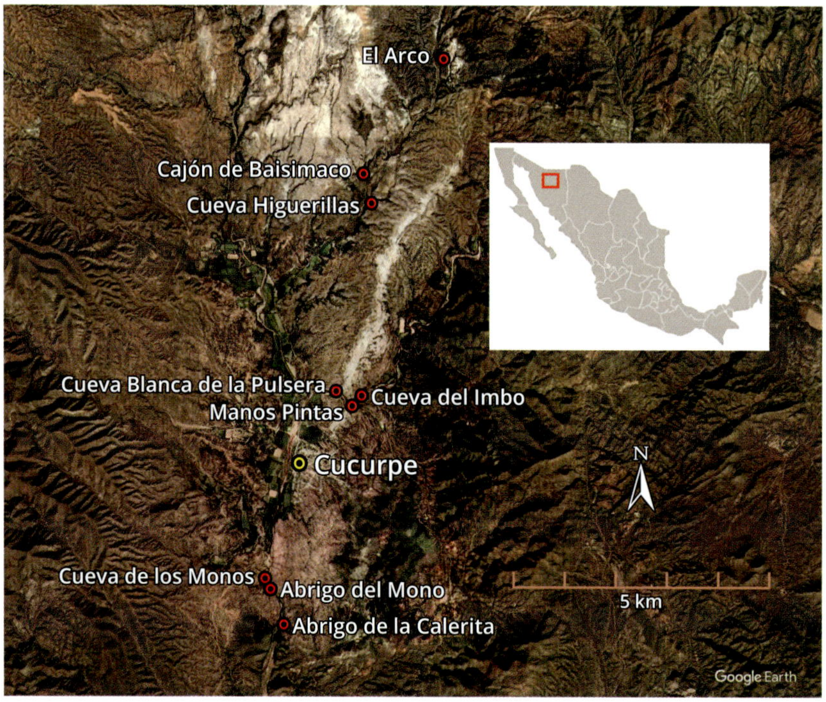

Figure 5. Distribution of rock art sites in the region of Cucurpe.
Figura 5. Distribución de los sitios de arte rupestre en la región de Cucurpe.

than engravings have been documented. This is probably due to the formation of these caves or shelters, which allow the paintings to be better preserved.

The region is defined within the Pima-Opata border, established by Beatriz Braniff in her doctoral thesis (1992). The Cucurpe rock art assemblages are characterized by the fact that they are mainly painted art and in some cases engravings, rarely presenting both techniques. The chronology of the area is established around the Prehispanic period up to the Colonial period. Some of these rock art sites are El Arco, Cueva de las Manos Pintas, Cueva de Los Monos (Figure 6), and Cueva Blanca de La Pulsera (paintings and engravings) (Figure 7).

Figure 6. Cueva de los Monos I.
Figura 6. Cueva de Los Monos I. From Pérez-Reyes 2013:*Figure 9.*

Figure 7. Cueva Blanca de La Pulsera.
Figura 7. Cueva Blanca de La Pulsera. Image: B. Menéndez

The Cueva Higuerillas Rock Art Site

During the fieldwork of the DREPNS project in March 2020, two rock art sites were documented in Cucurpe: first, El Cajón de Baisimaco (Figure 8), which is predominantly engraved with only one painting, and then Cueva Higuerillas, where we found just the opposite.

Both El Cajón de Baisimaco and Cueva Higuerillas were recorded for the first time in 2009, when we participated in the BSCRCM project (Viñas 2009).

Figure 8. El Cajón de Baisimaco, one of the rock sites documented in the DREPNS project.
Figura 8. El Cajón de Baisimaco, uno de los yacimientos rupestres documentados en el proyecto DREPNS. Image: B. Menéndez.

On that occasion it was not possible to carry out an exhaustive documentation of the site, so it was decided to do so in this new project.

Cueva Higuerillas is a rockshelter whose nature is volcanic tuff, like the previous site, and which, like the previous one, is easily degraded by environmental factors. It is located at the southeastern end of the Baisimaco Canyon, about 200 meters from the site of El Cajón de Baisimaco. The orientation of the shelter is southwest, with the sun entering in the afternoon, and it is quite shady. On the other hand, the rock paintings are located in the central part of the shelter, where there is no water runoff or rain seepage. However, there are some fissures, cracks, and flaking due to the nature of the support itself (Figure 9).

Figure 9. Cueva Higuerillas shelter, location of the rock art complex.
Figura 9. Abrigo de Cueva Higuerillas, ubicación del complejo de arte rupestre. Image: C. A. Quijada.

The shelter is currently used by the rancher to store bales of straw, which are placed in front of the painted wall. This, in part, protects most of the paintings, since the bales are not in contact with the wall, but in front of it. The shelter is fenced, so it is also protected from vandalism, although inside the fence there are tools and some rubbish related to the livestock activity that is practiced at the site. In order to record and document the cave paintings, all the straw bales covering them had to be removed (Figure 10), with the prior authorization of Mr. Denton, the owner of the site.

Figure 10. The straw bales are placed in front of the paintings without touching them. The bales had to be moved in order to document the rock paintings. When viewing the wall at its maximum extent, many more figures were observed than on the first visit to the site in 2009.
Figura 10. Las pacas de paja se colocan delante de las pinturas sin tocarlas. Los fardos tuvieron que ser movidos para poder realizar la documentación de las pinturas rupestres. Al ver la pared en su máxima extensión, se observaron muchas más figuras que en la primera visita en 2009. Image: B. Menéndez.

Typology at Cueva Higuerillas

The graphic units are located in two different panels. The main Panel A is located inside the shelter itself and is the concentration with the largest number of representations. It extends over a length of about 11 m and a maximum height of 2.5 m. The lowest ones are almost on the groundline. A total of 166 graphic units were counted.

The inventory consists of red paintings, some in light ochre (orange), and only one engraving, which were compared with the Munsell scale:

- Engraving: between 8/1 2.5YR and 6/1 10R.
- Red paint: between 5R 4/6 and 3/6.
- Orange paint: between 10R 4/5 and 4/8.

Of the total of 166 graphic units, 136 are hands. However, other representations are observed at the typological level. A very thick vertical line, thinner horizontal lines, and another vertical line were recorded, interconnecting with the rows of hands. Other geometric forms such as circles, semicircles, and a unit formed by concentric circles were also documented. In addition, two units have an elongated trunk and two strokes on the lower part similar to some kind of anthropomorphic form, without arms or head (Figures 11 to 13).

Figure 11. A very thick vertical line.
Figura 11. Una línea vertical muy gruesa. Image: B. Menéndez.

Figure 12. Three concentric circles which are connected with the hands, with some of the hands superimposed on the circles.
Figura 12. Tres círculos concéntricos que se conectan con las manos, con algunas de las manos superpuestas a los círculos. Image: B. Menéndez.

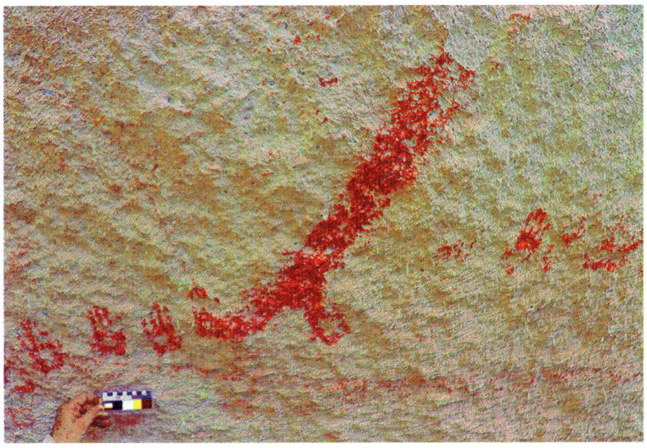

Figure 13. A possible anthropomorph without head or arms. DStretch LRE.
Figura 13. Un posible antropomorfo sin cabeza ni brazos. DStretch LRE. Image: B. Menéndez.

Moreover, on the right side of the panel there is a rather irregular, thickly outlined serpentiform element, which is difficult to see without the use of DStretch (Figure 14). To the right of this serpentiform element and separated from the rest of the representations is the only documented engraving. It is located in the lower right part of the panel and could be representing an atlatl (Figure 15).

Figure 15. Detail of the only engraving documented in Cueva Higuerillas, possibly an atlatl.
Figura 15. Detalle del único grabado documentado en Cueva Higuerillas, posiblemente un átlatl. Image: B. Menéndez.

On the panel it can be seen that the rows of hands are interconnected by lines, one of which crosses the hands at finger level. We can also see that a long staff, the anthropomorphic figures, and the other geometric symbols, such as the concentric circles, have superimposed hands (Figure 16). This superimposition was observed using DStretch, as it could be seen that the

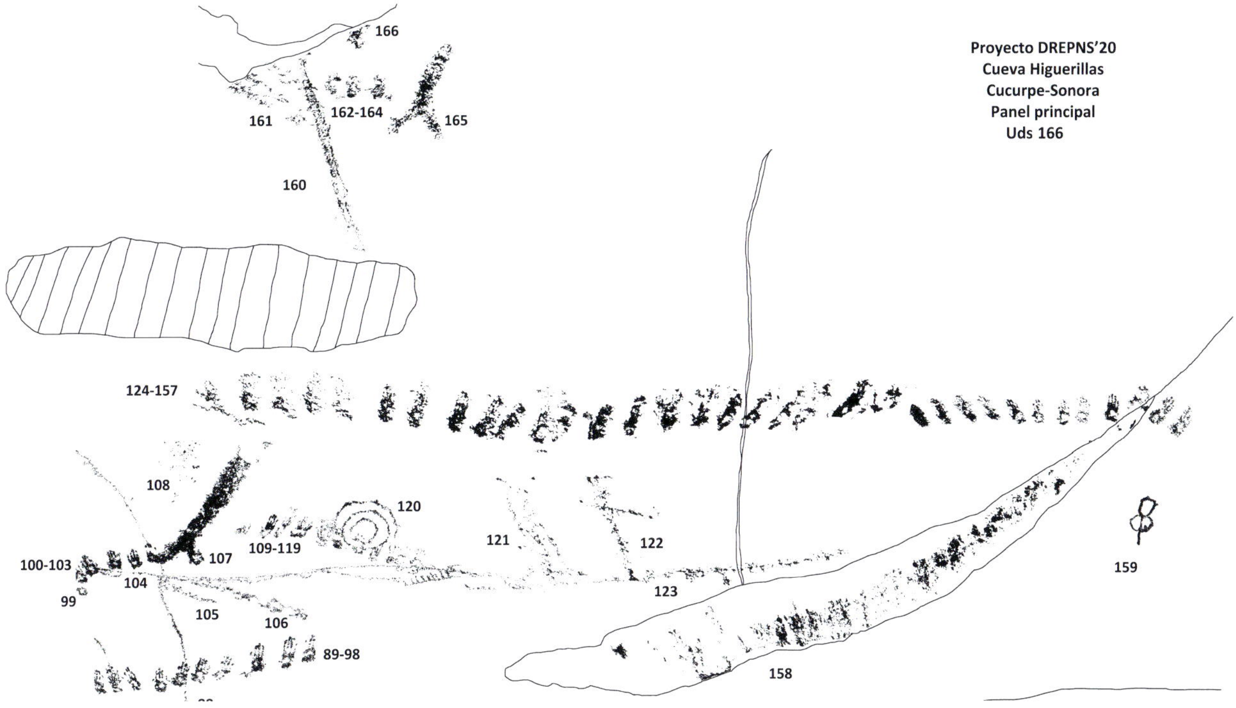

Figure 14. Digital tracing showing elements in Higuerillas Cave. Element 158 is the serpentiform motif, barely visible to the naked eye but revealed with DStretch. Element 159 is the only engraving documented in the site.
Figura 14. Calco digital que muestra los elementos de la cueva de Higuerillas. El elemento 158 es el motivo serpentiforme, apenas visible a simple vista pero revelado con DStretch. El elemento 159 es el único grabado documentado en el yacimiento. Image: B. Menéndez.

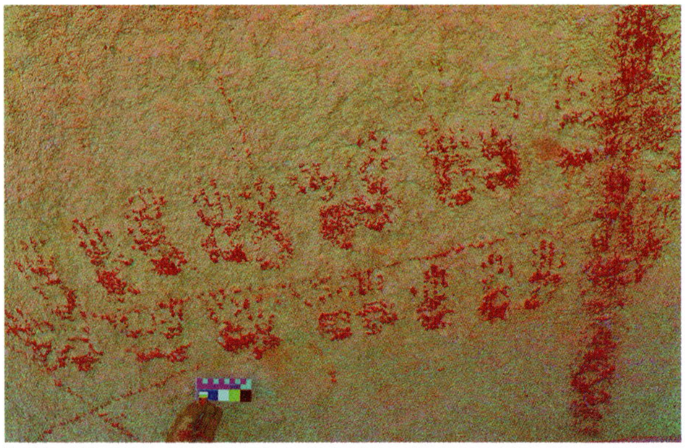

Figure 16. Handprints, showing lines that connect the hands. DStretch color space LRE.
Figura 16. Huellas de manos, mostrando las líneas que conectan las manos. DStretch espacio de color lre. Image: B. Menéndez.

Figure 17. Hands and finger streaks or fingerprints (top left).
Figura 17. Manos y digitaciones o huellas de dedos (arriba a la izquierda). Image: B. Menéndez.

color of the hand left marks of different tonality on the rest of the figures.

The second panel, Panel B, is located on the outside of the shelter, several meters away on a vertical wall. On this panel, the motifs could not be fitted to a specific typology, since they are remnants of pigments of tonalities similar to those found inside the shelter. This is due to the fact that environmental phenomena have a direct impact on the wall, causing it to deteriorate.

Characteristics of the Hand Representations

As mentioned above, the number of hand representations preserved at Cueva Higuerillas is 136. The hands are generally depicted paired, right and left, with the exception of two which are mismatched, both left hands. The fact that the hands are mismatched on only two occasions might be thought to be due to the paint being lost, rather than intentional. However, once analyzed in more detail, there is no doubt that these are individual hands, as no traces of additional paint can be seen, either with the naked eye or with DStretch.

Within this typology of hands, we have also included finger streaks. In this case, there are two groups that represent only the fingers of the authors. They are distributed vertically, probably in descending traces. Each group has rows of finger streaks marked as if they had been dragged across the surface (Figure 17).

With regard to the morphology of the hands, they are between 15 and 19 cm long, with the exception of one hand, which is 24 cm long. The width of the hands is between 10 and 13 cm. Therefore, these are young adult hands, male and/or female, and in no case do the hands appear to be those of infants. The hand of 24 cm was measured in the field and the dimensions were checked on the digital tracings. Since it is not within the normal size range, we think that the author may have distorted it when applying the color to the wall; whether intentionally or unintentionally is difficult to discern, but this could be the explanation for the unusually large size.

Another characteristic that defines them morphologically is that they all have the center of the hand unpainted. At first it seemed to be intentional, but the roughness of the support means that the palm of the hand, due to its convexity, does not completely touch the surface of the canvas and, therefore, the area remains unpigmented (Figure 18).

Figure 18. Image showing the unpainted hollow of the palm of the hand.
Figure 18. Imagen que muestra el hueco de la palma de la mano sin pigmento. Image: B. Menéndez.

Rock with Cupules

Inside the shelter, a rock with small cupules on its upper face (Figure 19) is located outside the straw bale area toward the exterior, but protected from the rain inside

Figure 19. Rock with small cupules located inside the shelter.
Figura 19. Roca situada en el interior del abrigo con pequeñas cúpulas o cazoletas. Image: B. Menéndez.

the dripline. The rock measures 168 cm by 110 cm and is similar in nature to the shelter, i.e., volcanic tuff. Due to its dimensions, although it is free-standing, it does not appear to have been moved, or at least not for a long time. A total of 18 cupules or cups have been counted, which a priori do not show any identifiable pattern.

Discussion: A Ritual Space, a Cohesive Social Space or Part of a Whole?

Representations of hands are among the earliest rock art manifestations worldwide, from the oldest caves of Franco-Cantabrian rock art to the rock art of Australia. The technique is usually similar in all places, either positive handprints made by direct pressure of the hand with paint on the support, or negative, carried out using the stencil technique and distributing the paint with an airbrush or by spitting the paint directly, where the amputation of fingers can be included (Grant 1967:54).

In the case of Sonora, there are several sites with representations of hands. However, the high concentration at Cueva Higuerillas makes it unique in the whole territory. In order to locate examples for comparison to the representations found in this shelter, we have reviewed other sites in the state having the same characteristics (Figure 20). Cave sites with hands in positive and negative and structured in rows are documented (Quijada López 2013), but in no case have we identified the interconnections by lines or the high concentration of hands that we observed in Cueva Higuerillas. The absence of representations with these characteristics has led us to look at other areas farther away from Sonora, such as Arizona or New Mexico, where we also have not been able to observe similarities with the representations of Cueva Higuerillas.

Moreover, the morphology of hands with a hollow

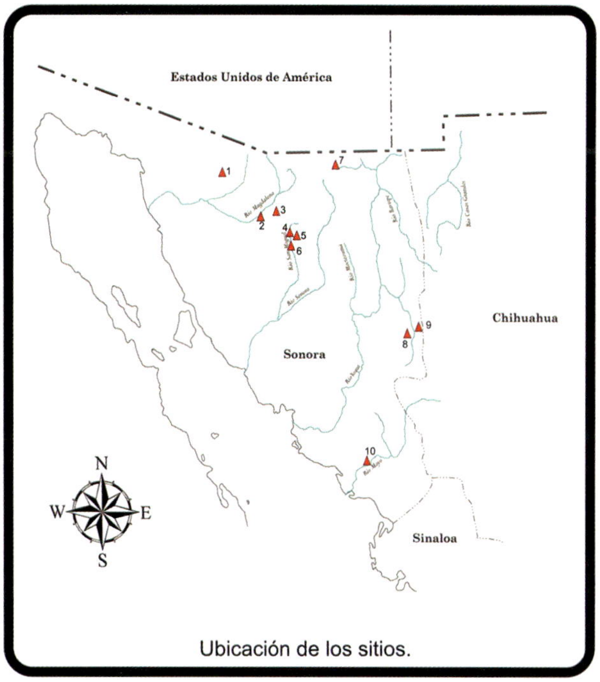

Figure 20. Distribution map of sites with hands in the state of Sonora.
Figura 20. Mapa de distribución de sitios con representaciones de manos en el estado de Sonora. Image: C. A. Quijada.

palm has been found elsewhere in southwestern Arizona and even in Utah (Patterson 1992:107–108). In some cases, some of the paint was removed before the hands were impressed, leaving the palm unpainted or forming lines or geometric figures (Grant 1967:54–55; Patterson 1992:107–1089). In Cucurpe there is at least one other cave site with representations of hands, Cueva de los Monos. However, in this case, the hands are represented in negative and not in positive (Figure 21).

The hollow palm is not always due to the elimination of that part of the paint, as this lack of pigment

Figure 21. Representation of negative hands in Cueva de los Monos (Cucurpe).
Figura 21. Representación de manos en negativo en la Cueva de los Monos (Cucurpe). Image: B. Menéndez.

may be due to chipping or irregularities in the surface of the rock. In the case of Cueva Higuerillas, it is striking that all the hands show this gap. In this specific case, the cause seems to be the morphology of the wall together with the technique of applying the pigment. Consequently, it would not be cultural or symbolic, although it would be technical.

Representations of hands are widespread throughout rock art from the prehistoric to more recent periods. According to Polly Schaafsma (1980:119), the hand, "... an important motif in Pueblo painting even today, has persisted from these earliest beginnings....The idea that these prints, usually made by pressing a paint-covered hand against the rock, served as a means of identification is supported by ethnographic information." Other authors such as Ellis and Hammack (1968:35) also refer to the fact that among the Pueblo Indians currently, they leave handprints at sacred sites where they have prayed to confirm that they have completed their task and that they are identified by the entity to which they have prayed. Therefore, we can understand that these representations have a symbolic and at the same time social character. It is necessary to rely on ethnography to try to understand the reason for these motifs and their possible relationship with the rest of the elements represented on the panels.

The rest of the typological elements of the ensemble are related to the representations of hands. These are, as mentioned above, concentric circles, a long "staff," and representations of what appear to be anthropomorphic figures without heads and feet. The latter may be a way in which the authors represented the anthropomorphic figures, i.e., their own style. References to this typology can be found throughout the Southwest of the United States. In the case of the concentric circles, there have been many proposed interpretations, but among Pueblo Indians this representation often refers to the sun (Figure 22). To cite one specific example, "In Pueblo explanation of this old symbol...the outer circle represents the ring of light around the Sun, the second represents Sun himself, and the inner circle or dot his umbilicus, which opens to provide mankind with game and other sustenance" (Ellis and Hammack 1968:35). Some elements identified as sun symbols have two or more than three circles. In Cueva Higuerillas, the possible solar symbol is formed by three concentric circles, although the most external one is incomplete. Alongside these circles, there are also horizontal lines and below them what appears to be a horizontal staircase or rake (see Figure 12).

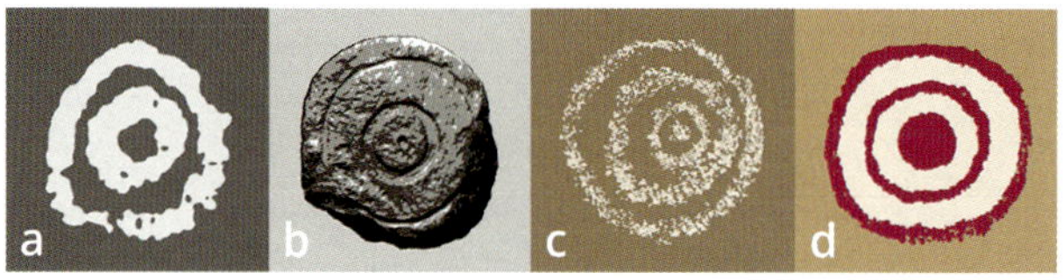

Figure 22. Mogollon (a) and Pueblo (b–d) concentric circle elements identified as sun symbols. (a) Feather Grotto, New Mexico (after Ellis and Hammack 1968:Figure 4), (b) Pueblo stone carving (after Ellis 1975:Figure 2), (c) Holly House, Hovenweep, Colorado (from photo by Ken Hedges), (d) Peñasco Blanco, Chaco Canyon, New Mexico (adapted from Fuller 2020).

Figura 22. Elementos de círculos concéntricos Mogollón (a) y Pueblo (b-d) identificados como símbolos solares. (a) Gruta de las Plumas, Nuevo México (según Ellis y Hammack 1968:Figura 4), (b) Talla de piedra Pueblo (según Ellis 1975:Figura 2), (c) Casa Holly, Hovenweep, Colorado (de una foto de Ken Hedges), (d) Peñasco Blanco, Cañón Chaco, Nuevo México (según Fuller 2020). Illustration by Ken Hedges.

The cupule rock found in this archaeological context should also be noted. Other sites with mortars or cupules have been documented in various assemblages at Cucurpe. An example of this is Cueva Blanca de La Pulsera, which is undoubtedly a place linked to ceremonies or fertility rites, both for its representations and for the context of the cave itself (Viñas et al. 2015:1150). Likewise, in El Cajón de Baisimaco we have also documented these small-sized cupules or mortars (Menéndez Iglesias 2021). This seems to indicate that they could have been used to prepare some kind of concoction related to a ceremony or ritual or to prepare pigments. It remains for now to corroborate this by determining whether uncontaminated material can be extracted from the interior of the cupules in Cueva Higuerillas. This would allow us to evaluate their use or determine what these small mortars or cupules might have contained.

Preliminary Conclusions

We present here a preliminary study of the representations documented at Cueva Higuerillas. This site is characterized by a high concentration of paintings in relation to the Cucurpe region. Among the characteristics observed are paired, adult, interconnected hands, anthropomorphs without arms and head, geometric elements such as concentric circles—also interconnected with the hands—what seems to be an atlatl, and a rock with cupules. What could all these elements be telling us?

In our opinion, it seems to be a place where groups gathered with the need to mark their presence and identity as a community. It would have been a place of social cohesion, where only adults would have participated, based on the size of the hands represented. Perhaps it was some kind of meeting or concentration of the adult population, linked to some ritual of fertility of the land or propitiatory for hunting, as we find representations such as the concentric circles that could represent the Sun or the engraving of an atlatl. In addition, the rock with the cupules must have been used at these times of assembling in the shelter.

Although it is true that Cueva Higuerillas has very interesting elements to analyze, we need to look deeper into this subject. These representations lead us to the ethnographic record, which will be the next step to follow to analyze Cueva Higuerillas in more depth. To do this, we must consider examples such as the Pueblo Indians, where we also see some of the elements present in this place.

Acknowledgments. Thanks to all the collaborators of the DREPNS project, to the Institute of Anthropological Research and the Institute of Geology at the UNAM, as well as to the INAH-Sonora Centre. Thanks to the Coordination of Humanities of the UNAM for their support and confidence in this project through the Postdoctoral Fellowship Program from 2019 to 2021, which I developed at the Institute of Anthropological Research of the UNAM, advised by Dr. Alejandro Terrazas Mata. And finally, thanks to the Gerda Henkel Foundation (Düsseldorf, Germany) and its Patrimonies Funding Initiative programme for its current support with the financing of the project *Rock art in Northern Sonora: Between Stones and Pigments*, which includes the study presented here.

References Cited

Braniff, Beatriz

1992 *La Frontera Protohistórica Pima-Opata en Sonora, México: Proposiciones Arqueológicas Preliminares.* Colección Científica No. 240. Instituto Nacional de Antropologia y Historia, México, D. F.

Ellis, Florence Hawley

1975 A Thousand Years of the Pueblo Sun-Moon-Star Calendar. In *Archaeoastronomy in Pre-Columbian America*, edited by Anthony F. Aveni, pp. 59–88. University of Texas Press, Austin.

Ellis, Florence Hawley, and Laurens Hammack

1968 The Inner Sanctum of Feather Cave, a Mogollon Sun and Earth Shrine Linking Mexico and the Southwest. *American Antiquity* 33(1):25–44.

Frey, Daniel, César Quijada, and Jane Kolber

2004 Los Petrograbados y las Pinturas Rupestres de La Pulsera, Cucurpe, Sonora / The Petroglyphs and Pictographs of La Pulsera, Cucurpe, Sonora. In *American Indian Rock Art, Volume 31*, edited by Marilyn Sklar, pp.136–54. American Rock Art Research Association, Tucson, Arizona.

Fuller, Michael J.

2020 Penasco Blanco (web page). Michael J. Fuller, St. Louis Community College-Florissant Valley, Missouri. Electronic document, http://users.stlcc.edu/mfuller/Penasco.html, accessed April 21, 2022.

González-León, Carlos M.

2010 Evolución geológica y disposición del paisaje actual. In *Diversidad biológica de Sonora*, edited by Francisco E. Molina Freaner and Thomas R. Van Devender, pp.19–49. Universidad Nacional Autónoma de México, Mexico City.

Grant, Campbell

1967 *Rock Art of the American Indian.* Thomas Y. Cronwell Company, New York.

Hernández Vega, Julio César

2007 *Inventario físico de los recursos minerales del municipio Magdalena de Kino estado de Sonora.* Servicio Geológico Mexicano, Fideicomiso de Fomento Minero, Dirección de Minas, Magdalena, Sonora, México.

Instituto Nacional de Antropología e Historia (INAH), México – Coordinación Nacional de Monumentos Históricos

2019 Templo de los Santos Reyes. Ficha del Catálogo Nacional de Monumentos Históricos Inmuebles número I-0012600444. Electronic document, http://catalogonacionalmhi.inah.gob.mx/consulta_publica/detalle/72438,accessed August 28, 2022.

Menéndez Iglesias, Beatriz

2021 Documentación rupestre y estudio de pátinas en el Norte de Sonora: del Desierto sonorense a la Sierra Madre Occidental. Partial technical report, 2020 season. Unpublished.

Mott Lacroix, Kelly E., Elia Tapia, and Abraham Springer

2017 Environmental Flows in the Desert Rivers of the United States and Mexico: Synthesis of Available Data and Gap Analysis. *Journal of Arid Environments* 140:67–78.

Patterson, Alex

1992 *Rock Art Symbols of the Greater Southwest.* Johnson Books, Boulder, Colorado.

Pérez-Reyes, Tomás

2013 The Cave of the Monkeys, an Approach to the Pictorial Representations of the Cucurpe Valley, Sonora, Mexico/La cueva de los Monos. Un acercamiento a las representaciones pictóricas del Valle de Cucurpe, Sonora, México. IFRAO 2013 Proceedings (CD). In *American Indian Rock Art, Volume 40*, edited by Peggy Whitehead, pp. 981–992. American Rock Art Research Association, Glendale, Arizona.

Quijada Hernández, Armando

1976 Arte Rupestre en Sonora. Primer Simposio de Historia de Sonora, pp.433–455. Instituto de Investigaciones Históricas de Sonora, Universidad de Sonora, Hermosillo.

Quijada López, César Armando

1996 Los grabados de Cucurpe, Sonora. In *Crónica y Microhistoria en el noroeste de México*, edited by César Quijada, pp. 17–28. Instituto Sonorense de Cultura y Sociedad Sonorense de Historia, Hermosillo, Sonora, México.

2013 Manifestaciones Gráfico Rupestres de Manos en Sonora, México. IFRAO 2013 Proceedings (CD). In *American Indian Rock Art, Volume 40*, edited by Peggy Whitehead, pp. 489–506. American Rock Art Research Association, Glendale, Arizona.

Quijada López, César Armando, and Eréndira Contreras Barragán

2006 Rock Art in Sonora/El arte rupestre en Sonora. 1994 IRAC Proceedings. In *American Indian Rock Art, Volume 21*, edited by Frank Bock, John Clegg, Edwin Krupp, and Georgia Lee, pp. pp. 79–102. American Rock Art Research Association, Phoenix, Arizona.

Rubio, Albert, Ramón Viñas, César Armando Quijada, Joaquín Arroyo, Beatriz Menéndez, Antonio Hernanz, María Iriarte, and Neemias Santos
2014 The Rock Art of Saracachi River Basin: The El Arco and Blanca de la Pulsera caves, Sonora (México). *Expressions* 6:134–146.

Sauer, Carl, and Donald Brand
1931 Prehispanic Settlements of Sonora with Special Reference to Cerros Trincheras. *University of California Publications in Geography* 5:67–149.

Schaafsma, Polly
1980 *Indian Rock Art of the Southwest.* School of American Research, Santa Fe, and University of New Mexico Press, Albuquerque.

Viñas, Ramón
2009 Biodiversidad de las sociedades cazadoras y recolectoras del Cuaternario de México. 2009. Campaign technical report 2008 Institute of Human Paleoecology and Social Evolution, Tarragona, Spain.

Viñas, Ramón, Albert Rubio, César Armando Quijada, Beatriz Menéndez, Joaquín Arroyo, and Larissa Mendoza
2015 Análisis técnico-temático del conjunto rupestre de Cucurpe (Sonora, México). In *Symbols in the Landscape: Rock Art and its Context,* edited by Hipólito Collado Giraldo and José Julio García Arranz, pp.1145–1162. Proceedings of the XIX International Rock Art Conference, IFRAO 2015. Arkeos No. 37. Instituto Terra e Memória, Mação, Portugal.

The Spanish version of this paper begins on the next page.

La versión en español de este artículo comienza en la página siguiente.

Cueva Higuerillas (Cucurpe, Sonora): ¿espacio ritual, espacio social de cohesión o parte de un todo?

Beatriz Menéndez Iglesias, Tomás Pérez-Reyes, César Armando Quijada López, and Alejandro Terrazas Mata

En las estribaciones bajas de la Sierra Madre Occidental en el estado de Sonora, se localiza el valle de Cucurpe, distinguido por su alta concentración de sitios con arte rupestre. La región se define dentro de la frontera Pima-Ópata. En referencia a los conjuntos de rupestres de Cucurpe, éstos se caracterizan por ser principalmente arte pictórico y en algunos casos grabados, presentando en escasas ocasiones las dos técnicas. La cronología del área se establece en torno al período Prehispánico hasta la época Colonial. Se presenta aquí un estudio preliminar del sitio con arte rupestre de Cueva Higuerillas, un lugar significativo por la iconografía que presenta. En sus paredes se pintaron numerosas representaciones de manos, las cuales aunadas a su morfología e interconexión iconográfica, hace de este sitio un lugar representativo en la región. En este sentido, nos preguntamos su funcionalidad, si se trata de un espacio simbólico, de cohesión social o ambos.

Sonora presenta una de las mayores concentraciones de arte rupestre de México. Sin embargo, hay que señalar que entre los diversos problemas que plantea el estudio del arte rupestre sonorense están la falta de documentación detallada y exhaustiva de los sitios y la falta de datación directa tanto de los grabados como de las pinturas, todo ello debido a la escasez de proyectos y a los limitados presupuestos para su desarrollo. Esto determina, en definitiva, una escasez de trabajos de investigación y un amplio futuro para las nuevas generaciones de arqueólogos.

Como resultado de una estancia de investigación en la Universidad Nacional Autónoma de México de la Dr. Menéndez, concretamente en el Instituto de Investigaciones Antropológicas, se decidió iniciar un proyecto en Sonora. Para ello se propuso el proyecto "Documentación rupestre y estudio de pátinas en el Norte de Sonora: del desierto sonorense a la Sierra Madre Occidental". Dentro de este proyecto se contempló la documentación del arte rupestre en Cucurpe (Figura 1). Para ello, se realizó una documentación exhaustiva de cada sitio arqueológico y se aplicaron nuevas tecnologías al registro rupestre, como la fotogrametría y el DStretch crgb (Figura 2).

A lo largo de estas páginas nos ocuparemos de la Cueva Higuerillas, un yacimiento significativo por su iconografía, que incluye numerosas representaciones de manos. En este sentido, nos preguntamos si se trata de un espacio simbólico o de un espacio de cohesión social. Intentaremos abordar esta cuestión para ver su posible funcionalidad, teniendo en cuenta que se trata de un estudio preliminar.

Antecedentes

Varios han sido los investigadores se han interesado en el estudio del arte rupestre en Cucurpe. Ya en la década de 1920, Carl Sauer y Donald Brand recorrieron diferentes regiones del norte de Sonora, visitando por primera

Beatriz Menéndez Iglesias
Programa de Becas Postdoctorales, Universidad Nacional Autónoma de México
Becario del Instituto de Investigaciones Antropológicas

Tomás Pérez-Reyes
Instituto Nacional de Antropología e Historia, INAH-Sonora Centre

César Armando Quijada López
Instituto Nacional de Antropología e Historia, INAH-Sonora Centre

Alejandro Terrazas Mata
Instituto de Investigaciones Antropológicas, Universidad Nacional Autónoma de México

American Indian Rock Art, Volume 48. Amy Gilreath, Ken Hedges, and Anne McConnell, Editors. American Rock Art Research Association, 2022, pp. 63–70.

vez algunos de los sitios arqueológicos de Cucurpe y realizando los primeros reportes (Sauer y Brand 1931:82–87).

Décadas después tenemos el trabajo del profesor Armando Quijada Hernández, quien recopiló 20 sitios de arte rupestre con grabados y pinturas en Cucurpe, que fue presentado en el XLI Congreso Internacional Americanista, celebrado en la ciudad de México en 1974, y posteriormente en el Primer Simposio de Historia de Sonora en la Universidad de Sonora en 1975. En la publicación de este simposio señaló:

> En el territorio del Municipio de Cucurpe, se encuentra una de las mayores concentraciones de Arte Rupestre de Sonora. Abundan en este lugar los cañones y acantilados con numerosas cuevas, que indudablemente fueron aprovechados por los primitivos habitantes... En estos abrigos naturales es donde se encuentran los dibujos y grabados que representan figuras antropomorfas y zoomorfas, la más común de estas últimas es la del venado; también pueden apreciarse lo que tal vez sean soles y lunas, así como cruces muy estilizadas. Hay manos positivas, y se encuentran el...laberinto común en algunas estaciones rupestres de Arizona. El color más utilizado es el rojo.... Por su abundancia, y por sus características, el Arte Rupestre de Cucurpe merece un trabajo especial...[Quijada Hernández 1976:443–444].

En la década de 1970, Beatriz Braniff, investigadora del Centro Regional Noroeste del INAH, inició un proyecto arqueológico en la cuenca del río San Miguel, en el que reportó 32 sitios arqueológicos. Esta región fue una de las principales para el desarrollo de su tesis doctoral sobre la frontera Pima-Opata (Braniff 1992), frontera que ella estableció en esta región.

A finales de 1990 se registraron los grabados del sitio conocido como "Los pies del viejo", y años más tarde, en 1993, se localizaron los grabados de la zona exterior de la Cueva Blanca de la Pulsera, que se convirtió en la primera cueva en la que se documentan grabados y pinturas en un mismo sitio arqueológico (Quijada López 1996; Quijada López y Contreras Barragán 2006).

Posteriormente, en 2004 César A. Quijada en colaboración con Jane Kolber, Daniel Frey y la ayuda del grupo American Indian Rock Art del Cochise College, presentaron una ponencia titulada "Cueva de La Pulsera, Cucurpe, Sonora" en la conferencia de la American Rock Art Research Association celebrada en Nuevo Casas Grandes, Chihuahua (Frey et al. 2005).

En esta misma década, en 2007, y dentro del proyecto "Investigación Prehistórica en el Noroeste de México: Baja California Sur y Sonora", Ramón Viñas, del Instituto Catalán de Paleoecología Humana y Evolución Social (IPHES), de Tarragona, y Albert Rubio, del Seminario de Investigación y Estudios Prehistóricos (SERP), de la Universidad de Barcelona, realizaron una primera visita, acompañados por César A. Quijada, del Centro INAH Sonora, a algunas cuevas con pinturas en la región de Cucurpe, particularmente en los ríos Saracachi y San Miguel. Entre ellas se encontraban las cuevas Blanca La Pulsera y El Arco (Viñas, 2009), las cuales fueron documentadas posteriormente en 2009, cuando la investigadora Beatriz Menéndez se incorporó al proyecto y éste pasó a llamarse "Biodiversidad de las sociedades cazadoras-recolectoras del Cuaternario de México". En esta ocasión se visitó y registró Cueva Higuerillas, aunque no se documentó exhaustivamente. Algunos resultados han sido presentados en el Congreso de la UISPP (2014) y en el de IFRAO (2015), celebrados en la Universidad de Burgos (España) y en la Universidad de Cáceres (España), respectivamente. Estas comunicaciones fueron publicadas en la revista digital *Expressions* (Rubio et al. 2014) y en las mismas actas del Congreso IFRAO 2015 (Viñas et al. 2015).

Entre las últimas investigaciones realizadas en la región, en 2013 el arqueólogo Tomás Pérez-Reyes, del Centro INAH Sonora, presentó la Cueva de los Monos en el Congreso IFRAO 2013. En este trabajo, el autor hace una descripción general del sitio y menciona la existencia de una serie de pinturas desde la época prehispánica hasta el momento de contacto europeo o colonial (Pérez-Reyes 2013). Ese mismo año y durante la celebración del mismo congreso, César A. Quijada presentó las representaciones de manos en Sonora, detallando los paneles de la Cueva de los Monos (Quijada López 2013:496-499).

Proyecto de Documentación de Arte Rupestre y Estudio de Pátinas en el Norte de Sonora

El proyecto "Documentación rupestre y estudio de pátinas en el Norte de Sonora» (DREPNS) contempla la recolección de muestras para el estudio de pátinas en dos ambientes diferentes: el desierto (Sierra de El Álamo, Caborca) y las estribaciones bajas de la Sierra Madre Occidental (Cucurpe) (Figura 3). El proyecto consiste en muestrear rocas con barniz o pátina no modificada por el ser humano, tanto en el ambiente desértico como en las partes bajas de la sierra, para comparar también la variación de los barnices en ambos contextos ambientales. Esto está enfocado principalmente a ver en ambientes desérticos la posibilidad de fechar grabados a partir de pátinas y hacer reconstrucción paleoambiental. También se realizaron muestreos en las partes bajas de la sierra de Cucurpe, para comparar la variación de los barnices en ambos ambientes. Asimismo, se decidió realizar la documentación del arte rupestre en la comunidad de Cucurpe, ya que existen pocos estudios exhaustivos de los sitios de arte rupestre en la región, los cuales son bastante abundantes.

Localización

El municipio de Cucurpe se encuentra en el centro-norte de Sonora, a 54 km al sureste de la ciudad de Magdalena de Kino. Se encuentra en el paralelo 30°19' de latitud norte y el meridiano 110°42' de longitud oeste, colindando al norte con el municipio de Ímuris, al este con Arizpe, al sur con Opodepe, al oeste con Santa Ana y al noroeste con Magdalena de Kino. La zona se encuentra en las cartas H12B71 (Cucurpe) y H12B72 (Saracachi), escala 1:50.000 del INEGI.

Tiene una superficie de 1,778.55 km2 a una altura de 858 m sobre el nivel del mar, en la parte baja de la Sierra Madre Occidental, zona cercana a los límites con la provincia de las Sierras y Llanos Sonorenses. Limita al oeste con la sierra de Cucurpe y al este con la sierra de San Antonio. Su red fluvial incluye los ríos Dolores y Saracachi, que convergen para formar el río San Miguel, afluente del río Sonora. Es una región en la que abundan las barrancas y los acantilados con abrigos y cuevas (Figura 4).

La subprovincia de las Sierras y Valles del Norte, que forma parte de la provincia más amplia de la Sierra Madre Occidental, ocupa la parte oriental y septentrional de la zona de estudio, y está constituida en su mayor parte por topoformas de sierra alta ligeramente empinadas. Esta morfología se observa en las sierras de La Madera, Magdalena y La Jojoba, interrumpida en la región centro-norte por un valle intermontano donde se encuentra la localidad de Ímuris, fuera del término municipal. En la Sierra de La Madera y concretamente en el cerro de El Barandal, donde confluyen los límites entre los municipios de Magdalena, Imuris y Cucurpe, la mayor altitud es de 2.020 metros sobre el nivel del mar. En el cauce del río Magdalena se encuentra la zona con menor elevación de unos 800 m sobre el nivel del mar. Esto hace una diferencia de elevación del orden de 1.220 m. (Servicio Geológico Mexicano, 2007).

El territorio estaba ocupado por ópatas y pimas altos a la llegada de los misioneros jesuitas. Fue en 1647 cuando el misionero Marcos del Río fundó la primera población con categoría de pueblo de misión y le dio el nombre de "Los Santos Reyes de Cucurpe" (INAH, 2019).

Contexto geológico

La región centro-norte de Sonora, donde se ubica Cucurpe, corresponde a un terreno compuesto por rocas del Mesozoico y del Paleozoico Tardío que representa una zona de transición de la corteza continental a la oceánica. González-León lo considera como un bloque de sedimentos marinos profundos de edad Ordovícica a Pérmica, que se encuentra principalmente en Baja California Norte y en la porción central y sureste de Sonora, en relación con el terreno de Caborca al norte, supuestamente transportado y acrecentado en el Pérmico tardío-Triásico medio (González-León 2010).

El contexto geológico es muy complejo, aflorando unidades litológicas representadas por rocas ígneas (plutónicas, hipabisales y volcánicas), vulcanosedimentarias, sedimentarias (terrígenas y carbonatadas) y metamórficas, con edades que van desde el Precámbrico hasta el Reciente y con algunos afloramientos de las rocas más antiguas de la República Mexicana.

Manifestaciones de arte rupestre de Cucurpe

El valle de Cucurpe se ubica en las estribaciones inferiores de la Sierra Madre Occidental (Sonora), distinguiéndose por su alta concentración de sitios con arte rupestre. Destaca su red fluvial, que incluye los ríos Dolores y Saracachi que convergen y forman el río San Miguel, afluente a su vez del río Sonora. Esta orografía caracteriza a la región por tener abundantes barrancas y acantilados con abrigos y cuevas donde se encuentran las pinturas rupestres.

El mapa que vemos (Figura 5) muestra la distribución de los sitios de arte rupestre en la región, donde se han documentado más grupos de pinturas que de grabados. Esto se debe probablemente a la formación de estas cuevas o abrigos, que permiten una mejor conservación de las pinturas.

La región se define dentro de la frontera Pima-Opata, establecida por Beatriz Braniff en su tesis doctoral publicada en 1992, como se ha mencionado anteriormente. Los conjuntos de arte rupestre de Cucurpe se caracterizan por ser principalmente arte pictórico y, en algunos casos, grabados, presentando raramente ambas técnicas. La cronología de la zona se establece en torno al período Prehispánico hasta la época Colonial. Algunos de estos sitios rupestres son El Arco, Cueva de las Manos Pintas, Cueva de Los Monos (Figura 6), y Cueva Blanca de La Pulsera (pinturas y grabados) (Figura 7).

El sitio de arte rupestre de Cueva Higuerillas

Durante el trabajo de campo del proyecto DREPNS en marzo de 2020, se documentaron dos sitios de arte rupestre en Cucurpe. Primero, El Cajón de Baisimaco (Figura 8), que es predominantemente grabado y tiene una sola pintura, y posteriormente, Cueva Higuerillas donde encontramos todo lo contrario.

Tanto El Cajón de Baisimaco como Cueva Higuerillas fueron registrados por primera vez en 2009, cuando participamos en el proyecto BSCRCM (Viñas, 2009). En aquella ocasión no fue posible realizar una documentación exhaustiva del yacimiento, por lo que se decidió hacerlo en este nuevo proyecto.

Cueva Higuerillas es un abrigo rocoso cuya naturaleza es la toba volcánica, al igual que el yacimiento anterior, y que, al igual que éste, se degrada fácilmente por factores medioambientales. Se encuentra en el extremo sureste del Cañón de Baisimaco, a unos 200 m del yacimiento de El Cajón de Baisimaco. La orientación del abrigo es suroeste, entrando el sol por la tarde, siendo bastante sombreado. Por otro lado, las pinturas rupestres se encuentran en la parte central del abrigo, donde no hay escorrentía de agua ni filtración de lluvia. Sin embargo, existen algunas fisuras, grietas y desconchados debido a la naturaleza del propio soporte (Figura 9).

El refugio es utilizado actualmente por el ganadero para almacenar pacas de paja, que se colocan delante de la pared pintada. Esto ha permitido, en parte, que la mayoría de las pinturas estén protegidas, ya que los fardos no están en contacto con la pared, sino por delante de ella. El abrigo está vallado, por lo que también está protegido del vandalismo, aunque dentro de la valla hay herramientas y algunos restos relacionados con la actividad ganadera que se practica en el lugar. Para poder resgistrar y documentar las pinturas rupestres fue necesario retirar todas las pacas de paja que cubrían las pinturas (Figura 10), previa autorización del Sr. Denton, propietario del lugar.

Tipología en Cueva Higuerillas

Las unidades gráficas se encuentran en dos paneles diferentes. El panel principal o A se encuentra dentro del propio abrigo y es el que concentra el mayor número de representaciones. Se extiende en una longitud de unos 11 m y una altura máxima de 2,5 m. Las más bajas se encuentran casi en la línea del suelo. Se han contabilizado un total de 166 unidades gráficas.

Se trata de pinturas rojas, algunas en ocre más claro (anaranjado), y un solo grabado, que se compararon con la escala Munsell:

- Grabado: entre 8/1 2,5YR y 6/1 10R.
- Pintura roja: entre 5R 4/6 y 3/6.
- Pintura anaranajada: entre 10R 4/5 y 4/8.

Del total de 166 unidades gráficas, 136 son manos. Sin embargo, se observan otras representaciones a nivel tipológico. Se registró una línea vertical muy gruesa, líneas horizontales más finas y otra línea vertical que se interconecta con las filas de manos. Se documentaron otras formas geométricas como círculos, semicírculos y una unidad formada por círculos concéntricos. Además, dos unidades tienen un tronco alargado y dos trazos en la parte inferior similares a algún tipo de forma antropomorfa, sin brazos ni cabeza (Figuras 11 a 13).

Además, en el lado derecho del panel hay un elemento tipo serpentiforme bastante irregular y de trazo grueso, que es difícil de ver sin el uso de DStretch crgb (Figura 14). A la derecha de este elemento serpentiforme y separado del resto de las representaciones se encuentra el único grabado documentado. Se localiza en la parte inferior derecha del panel y podría estar representando un atlatl (Figura 15).

En el panel se puede ver que las filas de manos están interconectadas por líneas, una de las cuales cruza las manos a la altura de los dedos. También se observa un bastón largo, figuras antropomorfas y demás símbolos geométricos, como círculos concéntricos que tienen manos superpuestas (Figura 16). Este solapamiento se observó utilizando el DStretch crgb, ya que se pudo ver que el color de la mano dejaba marcas de diferente tonalidad sobre el resto de las figuras.

El segundo panel o Panel B se encuentra en el exterior del refugio, a varios metros de distancia del mismo y en una pared vertical. En este panel, los motivos no han podido ser identificados a una tipología concreta, ya que son restos de pigmentos de tonalidades similares a los encontrados en el interior del abrigo, pero sin forma aparente. Esto se debe a que al estar expuesto el panel directamente a fenómenos medioambientales, estos inciden directamente en la pared provocando por tanto su deterioro.

Características de las representaciones de manos

Como se ha mencionado anteriormente, el número de representaciones de manos conservadas en Cueva Higuerillas es de 136. Aparecen representadas generalmente emparejadas, derecha e izquierda, a excepción de dos de ellas que están desparejadas y que son manos izquierdas. El hecho de que las manos estén desparejadas sólo en dos ocasiones podría pensarse que se debe a la pérdida de la pintura, más que a una intención. Sin embargo, una vez analizadas con más detalle, no hay duda de que se trata de manos individuales, ya que no se aprecian restos de pintura adicional, ni a simple vista ni con DStretch.

Dentro de esta tipología de manos, también hemos incluido las huellas dactilares. En este caso, hay dos grupos que representan sólo los dedos de los autores, o digitaciones. Están distribuidas verticalmente, probablemente de arriba a abajo, es decir, en trazos descendentes. Cada grupo de digitaciones está distribuido en filas de dedos marcados como si hubieran sido arrastrados por la superficie (Figura 17).

En cuanto a la morfología de las manos, presentan una longitud de entre 15 y 19 cm, con la excepción de una mano, que mide 24 cm. La anchura de las manos oscila entre 10 y 13 cm. Por lo tanto, se trata de manos de adultos jóvenes, hombres y/o mujeres, y en ningún caso las manos parecen ser infantiles. Respecto a la mano de 24 cm, se midió durante el trabajo de campo y las dimensiones se comprobaron posteriormente en los calcos digitales. Podemos pensar que al no estar dentro del rango de tamaño normal, el autor puede haberla distorsionado al aplicar el color al soporte, intencionadamente o no, es algo difícil de discernir. Consideramos que no es un tamaño común y parece que esta distorsión al aplicar el pigmento podría ser la explicación para la dimensión fuera de los parámetros normales.

Otra característica que los define morfológicamente es que todos tienen el centro de la mano sin pigmento. En principio podría ser intencionado, pero la rugosidad del soporte hace que la palma de la mano, debido a su convexidad, no toque completamente la superficie del lienzo y, por tanto, la zona quede sin pigmentar (Figura 18).

Roca con cúpulas

En el interior del refugio, una roca con pequeñas cúpulas en su cara superior (Figura 19) está situada fuera de la zona de pacas de paja hacia el exterior, pero protegida de la lluvia por dentro de la línea de goteo. Se trata de una roca de 168 cm por 110 cm y de naturaleza similar a la del abrigo, es decir, toba volcánica. Debido a sus dimensiones, aunque es independiente, no parece haber sido movida, o al menos no desde hace mucho tiempo. En la cara superior de la misma se han contabilizado un total de 18 cúpulas o pequeñas cazoletas, que "a priori" no presentan ningún patrón identificable.

Discusión: ¿Un espacio ritual, un espacio social cohesionado o parte de un todo?

Las representaciones de manos se encuentran entre las primeras manifestaciones de arte rupestre en todo el mundo, desde las cuevas más antiguas del arte rupestre Franco-Cantábrico hasta el arte rupestre de Australia. La técnica suele ser similar en todos los lugares, por un lado, las manos en positivo por presión directa de la mano con pigmento sobre el soporte, y por otro, en negativo, realizadas con la técnica del esténcil, distribuyendo la pintura con aerógrafo o escupiéndola directamente con la boca, donde se puede ver en ocasiones la falta de algún dedo o falange (Grant 1967:54).

En el caso de Sonora, existen varios sitios con representaciones de manos. Sin embargo, la alta concentración en Cueva Higuerillas lo hace único en todo el territorio. Con el fin de tener referencias en relación a las representaciones encontradas en este abrigo, se ha tratado de ver otros sitios con las mismas características en el estado (Figura 20), documentándose manos en positivo y negativo y estructurados en hileras (Quijada López 2013). Sin embargo, en ningún caso hemos identificado que presenten las interconexiones mediante líneas que observamos en Cueva Higuerillas, ni la alta concentración de manos que contiene este sitio. La ausencia de representaciones con estas características nos ha llevado a buscar en otras zonas más alejadas de Sonora, como Arizona o Nuevo México, donde tampoco hemos podido observar similitudes con las representaciones de Cueva Higuerillas.

En relación a la morfología de las manos que presentan la palma hueca, se han encontrado en otros lugares del suroeste de Arizona e incluso en Utah (Patterson 1992:107-108). En algunos casos, esto se debe a que cuando las manos fueron impresas, se eliminó parte de la pintura, dejando la palma sin pintar, a menudo formando líneas o figuras geométricas en su interior (Grant 1967:54-55; Patterson 1992:107-1089). En

Cucurpe hay al menos otro yacimiento rupestre con representaciones de manos, la Cueva de los Monos. Sin embargo, en este caso, las manos están representadas en negativo y no en positivo (Figura 21).

Esto no siempre se debe a la eliminación de esa parte de la pintura, ya que esta falta de pigmento puede deberse a desconchados o irregularidades en el soporte. En el caso de Cueva Higuerillas, llama la atención que todas las manos presenten esta laguna. En este caso concreto, parece deberse a la morfología del soporte junto con la técnica de aplicación del pigmento. En consecuencia, no sería algo cultural ni simbólico, sino técnico.

Las representaciones de manos están muy extendidas en el arte rupestre, desde la Prehistoria hasta períodos más recientes, como se ha mencionado. Según explica Polly Schaafsma en su obra *American Indian Rock Art*, la mano es "...an important motif in Pueblo painting even today, has persisted from these impressions...The idea that this prints, usually made by pressing a paint-covered hand against the rock, served as a means of identification is supported by ethnographic information" (Schaafsma, 1980:119). Otros autores como Ellis y Hammack se refieren también al hecho de que entre los indios Pueblo actualmente se dejan las huellas de las manos en los lugares sagrados donde ha rezado para confirmar que han cumplido su labor y que sean identificados por la entidad a la que han rezado (Ellis y Hammack 1968:35). Por lo tanto, podemos entender que estas representaciones tienen un carácter simbólico y a la vez social. Será necesario apoyarse en la etnografía para intentar comprender el porqué de estos motivos y su posible relación con el resto de elementos representados en los paneles.

El resto de los elementos tipológicos del conjunto están relacionados con las representaciones de manos. Se trata, como ya se ha mencionado, de círculos concéntricos, un largo "bastón" y representaciones de lo que parecen ser figuras antropomórficas sin cabeza ni pies. Estas últimas pueden ser una forma de representar las figuras antropomorfas por parte de los autores, es decir, su propio estilo. Se pueden encontrar referencias a esta tipología en todo el suroeste de los Estados Unidos. En el caso de los círculos concéntricos, se han propuesto muchas interpretaciones, pero entre los indios Pueblo esta representación suele referirse al Sol (Figura 22). Para citar un ejemplo específico, "In Pueblo explanation of this old symbol...the outer circle represents the ring of light around the Sun, the second represents Sun himself, and the inner circle or dot his umbilicus, which opens to provide mankind with game and other sustenance" (Ellis y Hammack 1968:35). Algunos elementos identificados como símbolos solares tienen dos o más de tres círculos. En Cueva Higuerillas, el posible símbolo solar representado está formado por tres círculos concéntricos, aunque el más externo está incompleto. Junto a estos círculos aparecen también líneas horizontales y debajo de ellas lo que parece ser una escalera o rastrillo horizontal (véase la figura 12).

También hay que destacar la roca con cúpulas encontrada dentro del contexto arqueológico. En Cucurpe se han documentado otros conjuntos rupestre que presentan morteros o cúpulas. Un ejemplo es la Cueva Blanca de La Pulsera, sin duda un lugar vinculado a ceremonias o ritos de fertilidad, tanto por sus representaciones como por el contexto de la propia cueva (Viñas et al. 2015:1150). Asimismo, en El Cajón de Baisimaco también hemos documentado estas cúpulas o morteros de pequeño tamaño en la parte exterior del conjunto (Menéndez Iglesias 2021). Esto parece indicar que pudieron ser utilizados para preparar algún tipo de brebaje relacionado con algún tipo de ceremonia o ritual o en quizá para preparar pigmentos. Queda por ahora corroborar que se pueda extraer material no contaminado del interior de las cúpulas de Cueva Higuerillas. Esto nos permitiría ver si tenían algún tipo de uso y qué podían contener estos pequeños morteros o cúpulas.

Conclusiones preliminares

Presentamos aquí un estudio preliminar de las representaciones documentadas en Cueva Higuerillas. Este yacimiento se caracteriza por una alta concentración de pinturas en relación con la región de Cucurpe. Entre las características observadas se encuentran: manos emparejadas de adultos jóvenes e interconectadas, antropomorfos sin brazos ni cabeza, elementos geométricos como círculos concéntricos -también interconectados con las manos-, lo que parece ser un posible atlatl, y una roca con cúpulas o pequeñas cazoletas. ¿Qué pueden decirnos todos estos elementos?

En nuestra opinión, parece tratarse de un lugar donde se reunían grupos con la necesidad de dejar su presencia como identidad comunitaria. Habría sido un lugar de cohesión social, en el que sólo habrían participado adultos jóvenes, a tenor del tamaño de las manos representadas. Quizás se trate de algún tipo de reunión o concentración de la población, vinculada a algún ritual de fertilidad de la tierra o propiciatorio para la caza, ya que encontramos representaciones como los círculos concéntricos que podrían representar al Sol o el grabado de un atlatl. Además, la roca con las cúpulas debió ser utilizada en estos momentos de ocupación en el abrigo.

Si bien es cierto que Cueva Higuerillas tiene elementos muy interesantes para analizar, es necesario profundizar en este tema. Estas representaciones nos remiten a la etnografía, que será el siguiente paso a seguir para analizar Cueva Higuerillas en profundidad. Para ello, debemos tener en cuenta ejemplos como el de los indios Pueblo, donde también vemos algunos de los elementos presentes en este lugar.

Agradecimientos. Gracias a todos los colaboradores del proyecto DREPNS, al Instituto de Investigaciones Antropológicas y al Instituto de Geología de la UNAM, así como al Centro INAH-Sonora. Gracias a la Coordinación de Humanidades de la UNAM por su apoyo y confianza en este proyecto a través del Programa de Becas Postdoctorales de 2019 a 2021, que desarrollé en el Instituto de Investigaciones Antropológicas de la UNAM, asesorada por el Dr. Alejandro Terrazas Mata. Y finalmente, gracias a la Fundación Gerda Henkel (Düsseldorf, Alemania) y su programa Patrimonies Funding Initiative por su apoyo actual con el financiamiento del proyecto *Arte rupestre en el norte de Sonora: Entre piedras y pigmentos*, que incluye el estudio que aquí se presenta.

Referencias citadas

Braniff, Beatriz
1992 *La Frontera Protohistórica Pima-Opata en Sonora, México: Proposiciones Arqueológicas Preliminares.* Colección Científica No. 240. Instituto Nacional de Antropologia y Historia, México, D. F.

Ellis, Florence Hawley
1975 A Thousand Years of the Pueblo Sun-Moon-Star Calendar. In *Archaeoastronomy in Pre-Columbian America,* edited by Anthony F. Aveni, pp. 59–88. University of Texas Press, Austin.

Ellis, Florence Hawley, and Laurens Hammack
1968 The Inner Sanctum of Feather Cave, a Mogollon Sun and Earth Shrine Linking Mexico and the Southwest. *American Antiquity* 33(1):25–44.

Frey, Daniel, César Quijada, and Jane Kolber
2004 Los Petrograbados y las Pinturas Rupestres de La Pulsera, Cucurpe, Sonora / The Petroglyphs and Pictographs of La Pulsera, Cucurpe, Sonora. In *American Indian Rock Art, Volume 31,* edited by Marilyn Sklar, pp.136–54. American Rock Art Research Association, Tucson, Arizona.

Fuller, Michael J.
2020 Penasco Blanco (web page). Michael J. Fuller, St. Louis Community College-Florissant Valley, Missouri. Electronic document, http://users.stlcc.edu/mfuller/Penasco.html, accessed April 21, 2022.

González-León, Carlos M.
2010 Evolución geológica y disposición del paisaje actual. In *Diversidad biológica de Sonora,* edited by Francisco E. Molina Freaner and Thomas R. Van Devender, pp.19–49. Universidad Nacional Autónoma de México, Mexico City.

Grant, Campbell
1967 *Rock Art of the American Indian.* Thomas Y. Cronwell Company, New York.

Hernández Vega, Julio César
2007 *Inventario físico de los recursos minerales del municipio Magdalena de Kino estado de Sonora.* Servicio Geológico Mexicano, Fideicomiso de Fomento Minero, Dirección de Minas, Magdalena, Sonora, México.

Instituto Nacional de Antropología e Historia (INAH), México – Coordinación Nacional de Monumentos Históricos.
2019 Templo de los Santos Reyes. Ficha del Catálogo Nacional de Monumentos Históricos Inmuebles número I-0012600444. Electronic document, http://catalogonacionalmhi.inah.gob.mx/consulta_publica/detalle/72438,accessed August 28, 2022.

Menéndez Iglesias, Beatriz
2021 Documentación rupestre y estudio de pátinas en el Norte de Sonora: del Desierto sonorense a la Sierra Madre Occidental. Partial technical report, 2020 season. Unpublished.

Mott Lacroix, Kelly E., Elia Tapia, and Abraham Springer
2017 Environmental Flows in the Desert Rivers of the United States and Mexico: Synthesis of Available Data and Gap Analysis. *Journal of Arid Environments* 140:67–78.

Patterson, Alex
1992 *Rock Art Symbols of the Greater Southwest.* Johnson Books, Boulder, Colorado.

Pérez-Reyes, Tomás
2013 The Cave of the Monkeys, an Approach to the Pictorial Representations of the Cucurpe Valley, Sonora, Mexico/La cueva de los Monos. Un acercamiento a las representaciones pictóricas del Valle de Cucurpe, Sonora, México. IFRAO 2013 Proceedings (CD). In *American Indian Rock Art, Volume 40,* edited by Peggy Whitehead, pp. 981–992. American Rock Art Research Association, Glendale, Arizona.

Quijada Hernández, Armando
1976 Arte Rupestre en Sonora. Primer Simposio de Historia de Sonora, pp.433–455. Instituto de Investigaciones Históricas de Sonora, Universidad de Sonora, Hermosillo.

Quijada López, César Armando
1996 Los grabados de Cucurpe, Sonora. In *Crónica y Microhistoria en el noroeste de México,* edited by César Quijada, pp. 17–28. Instituto Sonorense de Cultura y Sociedad Sonorense de Historia, Hermosillo, Sonora, México.

2013 Manifestaciones Gráfico Rupestres de Manos en Sonora, México. IFRAO 2013 Proceedings (CD). In *American Indian Rock Art, Volume 40,* edited by Peggy Whitehead, pp. 489–506. American Rock Art Research Association, Glendale, Arizona.

Quijada López, César Armando, and Eréndira Contreras Barragán
2006 Rock Art in Sonora/El arte rupestre en Sonora. 1994 IRAC Proceedings. In *American Indian Rock Art, Volume 21,* edited by Frank Bock, John Clegg, Edwin Krupp, and Georgia Lee, pp. pp. 79–102. American Rock Art Research Association, Phoenix.

Rubio, Albert, Ramón Viñas, César Armando Quijada, Joaquín Arroyo, Beatriz Menéndez, Antonio Hernanz, María Iriarte, and Neemias Santos
2014. The Rock Art of Saracachi River Basin: The El Arco and Blanca de la Pulsera caves, Sonora (México). *Expressions* 6:134–146.

Sauer, Carl, and Donald Brand
1931 Prehispanic Settlements of Sonora with Special Reference to Cerros Trincheras. *University of California Publications in Geography* 5:67–149.

Schaafsma, Polly
1980 *Indian Rock Art of the Southwest.* School of American Research, Santa Fe, and University of New Mexico Press, Albuquerque.

Viñas, Ramón
2009 Biodiversidad de las sociedades cazadoras y recolectoras del Cuaternario de México. 2009. Campaign technical report 2008 Institute of Human Paleoecology and Social Evolution, Tarragona, Spain.

Viñas, Ramón, Albert Rubio, César Armando Quijada, Beatriz Menéndez, Joaquín Arroyo, and Larissa Mendoza
2015 Análisis técnico-temático del conjunto rupestre de Cucurpe (Sonora, México). In *Symbols in the Landscape: Rock Art and its Context,* edited by Hipólito Collado Giraldo and José Julio García Arranz, pp.1145–1162. Proceedings of the XIX International Rock Art Conference, IFRAO 2015. Arkeos No. 37. Instituto Terra e Memória, Mação, Portugal.

Rings and Roars: Voices of Bell Rocks in Ancestral O'odham (Hohokam) Ritual

Janine Hernbrode

Distributed amidst the petroglyphs at three of the largest Ancestral O'odham (Hohokam archaeological culture) petroglyph sites in southern Arizona are assemblages of boulders that resonate when struck, producing distinct bell-like sounds. The visual traces of sound-making on large bell rocks and adjacent bedrock indicate they were not only chimed with percussion strikers to resonate with sound but also were abraded with a grinding motion to produce volumes of sound. Some of the bell rocks investigated also appear to have been roughly shaped or pecked to resemble animal heads, an indication that the boulders were objects accorded animacy and having a "voice." Many of these boulders have petroglyphs and use-wear evidence consistent with usage during precontact times. Recent investigation of remote smaller petroglyph sites that lack naturally occurring bell rocks has revealed the presence of both bell rock manuports and a ringing striker. A fourth large petroglyph site lacks bell rocks but is associated with a cache of copper bells on a hillside overlooking the site. These discoveries further illuminate the importance of bell-like sounds in the cultural practice of the Hohokam and suggest that the bells were necessary to complete the landscape characteristics of sacred sites. Experiments show abrading makes volumes of sound. This work introduces the concept of high-volume sound generation as part of Hohokam ritual activities. The ethnographic record for the Tohono O'odham reveals that the sounds of bells and the production of volumes of sound are both used in their rituals.

Archaeology has long been focused on the physical properties of the landscape and human-built structures with expansion into discussing viewsheds, proximities to other occupation sites, and the analysis of artifacts. But in reconstructing and understanding the lived experiences of people of the past, the sounds of ritual and the spaces utilized for that purpose are integral parts of those experiences, and of the study of those places. The O'odham consider Hohokam petroglyph imagery and the places where it is concentrated as sacred, where spirits of the ancestors dwell (Ferguson 2008:1). In defining the characteristics of sacred places, Eliade found dramatic landscape features to be breakthrough points where the sacred shows itself to humans and places where its innate power can be recognized in "cosmic signs" (Eliade 1958:11–12,116; Hedges 1993:121). Naturally occurring bell rocks in three of the largest petroglyph sites in southern Arizona—the Picacho Mountains, the Cocoraque Butte area, and another site in the Ironwood Forest National Monument—help define these places as sacred and may have been a primary "cosmic sign" leading to designation and utilization of this landscape for ritual purposes. Previously, we have noted other common characteristics of Ancestral O'odham sacred petroglyph sites as places where *axes mundi* provide openings to the Lower World, where the presence of water testifies to the proximity of the Lower World, and where the petroglyphs illustrate emergence from the Lower World (Hernbrode and Boyle 2018). The imagery accompanying ritual has been a more elusive topic but a few petroglyph sites have shown the time depth of the O'odham ritual costumes adorned with bells worn for the celebration of the Wikita ceremony (Hernbrode 2021:146).

Janine Hernbrode
Independent Researcher

American Indian Rock Art, Volume 48. Amy Gilreath, Ken Hedges, and Anne McConnell, Editors. American Rock Art Research Association, 2022, pp. 71–84.

Sounds of ritual have been noted by ethnographers. We've been informed of the Hohokam descendants' practices of singing, ritual oratory, and the sounds of dance, drum, rasp, bells, bullroarers, and various rattles and tinklers from the earliest ethnographers (Chesky 1942:4; Hayden 1987:278, 280, 283, 286, 300–301, 316; Lumholtz 1912:97; Pendleton and Hayden 1987:Plates I, IV(d), V(c), VI(l), X(e–f); Russell 1908:166–170, 270; Underhill 1946:29–31). And indeed, sound-making artifacts have been described in the archaeological record. For the Ancestral O'odham—the name for the archaeological Hohokam culture (450–1450 C.E.) preferred by the O'odham people (Loendorf and Lewis 2017)—fragile sound-making artifacts that do not survive the ravages of time underground, like flutes, gourd rattles, and cocoon rattles, appear as images on ceramics (Haury 1976:238), in an occasional petroglyph, and within modern photos of the descendent group. Trumpets in the form of *Strombus* shells (commonly called "conches") have been excavated from villages in southern Arizona along the Santa Cruz, Gila, and Agua Fria rivers (Vokes and Gregory 2007:332, 340). Ritual among the Hohokam had the potential of being a cacophony of these sound-making activities blended with human singing voices, the conversation of adults, and the exuberance of children. One early ethnographer of the O'odham found "much noise is made in the evening before the feast is begun" (Lumholtz 1912:96). Later, Lumholtz (1912:122) found the singing so loud he walked home to his camp "enjoying the singing better at the distance of a mile." For the Hohokam in the Tucson area, the sound-making instruments and activities also must have included the sounds of rocks that ring when struck.

Bell rocks are found and used purposefully by Native people worldwide in both ritual and non-ritual contexts. Hedges's work (1993:124) covered many locations in the American West where bell rocks were employed by precontact people, including one of the sites detailed here, Cocoraque Butte near Tucson. Ringing rock use has been reported spanning from the earliest Paleolithic in European caves (Dams 1984) to the recent past in Africa where "rock gongs" were used both in rituals for rainmaking, fertility, and initiation, and in non-ritual contexts for sending signals and entertainment. Hundreds of bell rocks were recorded in an intense effort to study this phenomenon along the Nile River at the Fourth Cataract before the area was flooded by a dam in 2008 (Kleinitz 2006:149).

Of the four large Ancestral O'odham petroglyph sites near Tucson, three have been recorded with petroglyphs numbering greater than 3500 in each (Hernbrode 2019; Hernbrode and Boyle 2013; Wallace and Holmlund 1986). All are gigantic boulder exposures at the foot of larger mountains with Sonoran Desert vegetation dominated by the giant saguaro cactus (Figures 1a, b). All are highly visible from great distances. Each of the sites has a gathering place at the foot of the boulder piles of adequate size to accommodate multiple village groups, an indication that the rituals were more open and participatory during use (Wright 2014: 211–212). Each site has either a current water source or evidence of water availability in the past and is linked to a large habitation site nearby. The recorded sites have use spanning the Archaic through the Hohokam to the O'odham (Hernbrode 2019; Wallace and Holmlund 1986:16–21). All of the recorded sites have unusual sound properties in the form of echoes or other sound phenomena from interaction of sound waves and landscape (Hernbrode 2011a and b, 2017). Three of the four sites have at least one group of huge boulders with

Figure 1. (a) Cocoraque Butte is one of four large petroglyph sites near Tucson. All are inselbergs at the foot of larger mountains with boulder exposures that can be seen from a great distance. (b) A portion of the Ancestral O'odham (Hohokam archaeological culture) petroglyphs on one side of the Cocoraque Butte, Locus A.

the startling capability of chiming like large metallic bells (Hernbrode and Boyle 2016; Madsen 1995; Wallace 2012). Our investigations found that some of these remarkable bell rocks are so sensitive they ring softly when tapped by a finger.

In previous work with Peter Boyle at Cocoraque Butte analyzing 83 bell rocks with use-wear, we estimated the weight of the bell rocks based on their dimensions and the density of granodiorite. Boyle converted the dimensional data to cubic feet to help with visualization of scale and variation in size. The median volume of the bell rocks is 7.1 cubic feet (range 0.8 to 49.2); the median estimated weight is 1009 pounds (range 79 to 5,015) (Hernbrode and Boyle 2016:99). We also analyzed the patina on bell rocks on the same hillside and with the same exposure as the petroglyphs (Hernbrode and Boyle 2016:99). We concluded that the bell rocks had been used around the same time the rock art was made.

This study includes a wider range of bell rock use, encompassing 148 bell rocks at 7 different ritual sites within a 50-mile radius west and north of downtown Tucson.

Why Do They Ring?

Though their physical properties are culturally irrelevant, the first question many people ask is why they ring. Rocks of many compositions are capable of ringing. Emily J. Brown (2014:62) investigated museum collections of elongate stones that ring collected from excavations of kivas in the Rio Grande Valley. She found stones of argillaceous limestone, basalt, phyllite, phonolite, feldspar and similar materials. In the Hohokam sites I have investigated near Tucson, the rock compositions of ringing boulders or ringing strikers is granodiorite, rhyolite, vesicular basalt, bomb tuff, and unidentified others. Judging from my search for noncultural ringing boulders for experiments, the incidence of boulders meeting the physical properties necessary to ring well is fairly small. Density matters. Though both sandstone and basalt can ring, a hard and dense material like basalt will allow the sound wave to move more freely than in sandstone made of small particles held more loosely together. The loose configuration tends to attenuate the movement of the sound wave.

By striking these ringing boulders with force, usually at one end or the other, the strike sets a sound wave of vibration through the boulder. The boulder's homogeneity enables the vibration to pass more easily. Cracks, crystals, and other aberrations in the central areas of the rock will attenuate the movement of the vibration and dampen the sound (Warren B. Davison, personal communication 2021). Though many people ask if the boulders are hollow, a hollow rock would not be expected to ring because the void in the middle of the rock would dampen movement of the sound wave.

What Was Used as a Striker?

In 2014, Peter Boyle and I investigated two pillars, one from inside a community structure at Tumamoc Hill that was said to ring and another similar broken pillar from a structure in the same area. One end of each of the pillars was buried below the floor surface. Our experiments showed that one end buried in dirt muffles the sound of a ringing boulder in a ratio approximately the same as the amount buried. We also found the first pillar did not ring, however the vesicular basalt rock used to strike it in the demonstration rang beautifully. This striking rock was found on the community structure's floor near the pillar and was the first ringing striker to come to our attention (Boyle and Hernbrode 2014).

The instruments used to strike the bell rocks are more portable and thus have been located less often than the bell rocks. Two fist-sized rocks were found underneath bell rocks at separate sites, one with an extensively abraded surface on all sides (Figure 2), the other more angular than the abraded one with use-wear on just one side. Fist-sized strikers form large pecks on the surface of bell rocks suggesting great volume was one goal of the user.

Figure 2. Extensively used striking and abrading stone found at the foot of a large abraded bell rock.

Large pecks are most common, but tiny pecks are the norm at a remote site in Saguaro National Park. There I found two strikers, both pointed rocks that result in very small pecks. One pointed rock has a bulb and point on the end suggestive of a bird head and beak (Figure 3). The ringing rock was found on top of a shelflike angular boulder near the bottom of the boulder pile. Native tobacco was growing at the base of the angular boulder where one would stand to use the object. The rock is small, easily portable, just a rough form that could be birdlike, but it rings and surrounding boulders do not. The use-wear is in the form of small pecks. The ringing rock does not appear to be of the same composition as the petroglyph boulders.

Figure 3. Elongate portable bell rock with a birdlike shape and pecked use-wear located at a small site near Tucson. The ringing rock was found on a shelflike projection at the foot of the petroglyph site. (Identifying numbers redacted from site photos.)

The other pointed rock at this site appears to be another ringing striker. It was located in a niche below the largest petroglyph panel on the largest boulder at the site. In climbing up to help record the petroglyph boulder, I put my foot into a niche to use it as a step. My shoe moved the striker and it rang. The boulder with the petroglyphs does not ring but has medium use-wear along one edge from small pecks, presumably from being struck with the ringing striker stowed below. This artifact is made of volcanic bomb tuff, a densely textured rock made of volcanic fragments and ash that hardens after being thrown from the volcano (Chesterman and Lowe 1978:691–692). We found no other pieces of bomb tuff in the vicinity, and conclude it is a manuport. I was able to collect a non-cultural piece of bomb tuff at a volcanic area in west-central Arizona for experiments of its ringing qualities.

In testing the cultural bell rocks, we used wooden instruments as strikers in order to prevent damage to the patina on the strike zones. Many of the boulders at Cocoraque Butte and Cocoraque Ranch have two levels of repatination: one a darker patina comparable to that on the Hohokam petroglyphs, and one a lighter color comparable to that on the O'odham imagery and on marks from modern-day casual visitation by others. Using a wooden mallet as a striker protects the patina and thus protects the archaeological evidence. In December 2014, while the Rock Band Rock Art Recording Team (a group of trained and experienced volunteers) was recording Cocoraque Butte, we observed a Native American family select an appropriate boulder with use-wear and tell the children how to elicit a ring with a wooden stick.

Use-wear on Bell Rocks

Few people recognize bell rock use-wear. Bell rocks have the possibility of being overlooked both in recordings and also in casual visitation (Wallace 2012:vi–vii). Lack of awareness contributes to the problem but another consideration is that 50% of the bell rocks we have investigated in the Tucson area do not have petroglyphs on their surfaces. In a field of boulders with petroglyphs, it is difficult to focus on the ones with just strike marks and abrading. It appears that the arrays of pecking and abrading caused by bell rock use can be rationalized as "just" random concentrations of pecking and puzzling grinding features or cupules. One tap with a wooden mallet changes that perception.

Examination of use-wear on bell rocks from seven Hohokam petroglyph sites—including the three discussed in this paper—in southern Arizona gives us a broad understanding of some of their purposes and how they were used. There are at least two different striking methods and two abrading methods that appear to have been used to elicit sounds from the boulders.

The first striking method results in dense zones of strike marks where the boulder is struck repeatedly in the same general area but not at exactly the same place (Figure 4a, b). When the individual strikes can be seen, the resulting peck marks tend to be large, indicating the boulder was struck with force to elicit as much sound as possible from the blow. These strike zones are not flat and do not appear to be abraded. Some zones show patina of the same level as that which has reformed on the nearby Hohokam rock art in addition to a brighter patina color at the center of the strike zone. Brighter color indicates less time has elapsed between the usage and today than the darker colors at the periphery of the strike zone. More modern use may have occurred between the close of the Hohokam Classic Period around 1450 C.E. until the time the O'odham moved their ceremonies to churchyards and villages rather than centering on petroglyph sites. Some bell rocks in pub-

Figure 4. (a) This strike zone is the result of random strikes near one end of a bell rock. Large pecks from the strikes indicate the boulder was struck with force to elicit as much sound as possible. Note the two colors of repatination, the darker matching the Hohokam petroglyphs. (b) A loose grouping of small pecks and light strike zones indicate a bell rock was not used extensively and probably not struck for volume.

licly accessible sites have even more modern use-wear caused by people using objects as hard as or harder than the boulder to strike them. If you think you may encounter a need to test a boulder for sound, please include a wooden mallet in your pack. In general, rubber mallets are not hard enough to set the vibration.

The second striking method is more precise. Focusing the strikes at one location leads to shallow circular indentations with widely sloping edges (Kleinitz 2006:149,152). Of fourteen measured indentations on highly used bell rocks at Cocoraque Ranch, the average width was 9.4 cm with a range between 5.8 and 15 cm. One intensely used squarish boulder of comparatively modest dimensions (93 x 67 x 16 cm) has 7 indented marks on all sides of its periphery and rests in a niche with megaphone-like sound properties. This boulder has also been subject to intensive and prolonged abrading of the surface. The result is that all dark patina is removed (Figure 5).

Use-wear from light abrading or from dragging a striker over a boulder with a rough surface is both audibly and visibly different from the striking evidence. Some bell rocks with naturally pockmarked surfaces have use-wear I was able to replicate using non-cultural ringing rocks. The experiments show the long sweeping curves over the surface of the boulder (Figure 6) may be the result of dragging or possibly forcefully sweeping a loosely held striker over the roughness. This results in a "brrrrrring" sound, a variation that could suit any creative musician.

Figure 5. This heavily abraded bell rock with seven strike indentations around the periphery is the most utilized of all of the bell rocks studied.

Figure 6. Bell rocks with uneven surfaces can be played by dragging a striker lightly or forcefully across the surface to elicit a longer brrrrring sound.

At two of three sites with bell rocks in Saguaro National Park, the petroglyphs are situated in areas where there are no naturally occurring bell rocks. In order to have a bell sound, a ringing boulder (Figure 7) was found elsewhere and imported to the site. The imported ringing rocks are not of the same composition as the cultural rocks at the site. We located four ringing rocks that appear to have been imported to the sites. None were used extensively as they all have strike zones showing light to mid-level use.

Figure 7. Imported bell rock at a petroglyph site where the local boulders do not ring.

At the third site, I found one more rock that does not fit into the previous categories (Figure 8). Both the rocky outcrops of bedrock across the site and the bell rock are local mudstones and fine siltstones. In addition to parallel lines, a concentric circle, and a spiral, the bell rock has generalized and random strikes on the face and the back of the small boulder, presumably from being rung with force. This very small rock is triangular in cross-section when viewed from the end. Its upper edge appears on initial observation to be heavily abraded, but on closer examination it looks as if the shape is the result of progressive exfoliation of the upper layer with the oldest loss, at the far right, having patina similar to that of the rock face. Two sections at either side of the remaining raised portion were detached at a later date, the color of their patina indicating that they were exposed at about the time that the petroglyph and strike marks were made. Since parts of the petroglyph are missing, it seems likely that these sections came loose as the stone was struck to make the glyphs and ring the bell. Close examination reveals a hairline crack showing where the remaining section may delaminate at some future time. Striking the rock produces a ring, consistent with the presence of strike marks and possible abrasion, primarily along the upper edges.

Figure 8. Portable bell rock made of local stone with unusual exfoliation and use-wear.

Experiments Making Rings and Roars

In working at Cocoraque Butte and Cocoraque Ranch, the Rock Band helped explore the properties of bell rocks (Hernbrode 2017). These experiments found that the quality of the sound is influenced by the composition and shape of the boulder but there are also other factors. The hardness of the striker is evident in the volume of sound emitted. The harder the striker, the louder the sound. We also found the skill of the user, the force and method of the strike, the perch of the boulder on the substrate, and the direction of the sound wave within the boulder to be critical to the sound.

Our explorations of sounds from bell rocks that are located in clusters resulted in widely disparate tones untuned to a specific tonal range. Unlike the smaller elongate baguette-shaped lithophones and kiva bells reported by other researchers (Brown 2014; Martarano 2021), the size of the boulders at the Cocoraque complex limits the opportunity to tune the selections or organize them to a specific tonal range. However, some large bell rocks appear to have been moved but the purpose apparently was not inspired by tonal harmony. Nonetheless, tones may have been song accompaniment. Song is a primary vehicle of O'odham beliefs, and ethnographic studies record the use of instruments accompanying ceremonial songs (Russell 1908:166–170; Underhill 1946:29).

Even tones that are disparate to our ears could be useful. Ceremonies for the 1930s Tohono O'odham consisted of oratory describing a desired event, singing of songs to describe the same event, and a dance with special materials and costumes (Underhill 1946:18). Songs were passed down but additions of new songs were allowed (Underhill 1946:35). If the Hohokam had a similar practice, then the clusters of tones from adjacent bell rocks could have had a mnemonic function to aid recall during a repeated song and ritual, particularly those from a four-year cycle of celebration like that of some versions of the Wikita ceremony (Galinier 1991:493, 503).

Rings are easy. Strike the boulder and it emits a beautiful tone. Obtaining a roaring sound is another matter. The roar is the result of abrading the boulder, moving the abrader so the vibrations move through the boulder in both directions. The reward for abrading is that it results in continuous sound. Extensive abrading is evident on four bell rocks with exceptional tones at Cocoraque Ranch, one at another of the sites with a large bell (Figure 9), and a small bell rock in Saguaro

Figure 9. Example of an extensively abraded bell rock that also has multiple strike indentations, the characteristic form of cupules found on bell rocks worldwide.

National Park. Jenny Adams (personal communication 2021), an archaeologist focusing on ground stone, inspected one of the boulders. Her opinion was that the extensive use-wear on one end of the boulder would not result from striking multiple times but is the result of abrading the surface. At her suggestion, experiments were conducted using a small non-cultural bell rock and a smooth river-rock abrader. Striking the bell rock with force produced a sound so uncomfortably loud I could not continue without ear protection. Abrading was louder.

Information from the Centers for Disease Control and Prevention gives decibel levels that are capable of damaging hearing under prolonged circumstances. Striking or abrading bell rocks in the experiments on non-cultural rocks produced sound as high as 87 decibels, loud enough to damage hearing.

In the experiments, abrading produced a continuous roar of sound that was consistently slightly louder (by 3dB) and greatly more prolonged than that produced by striking the boulder. It is difficult to say how far the sound might carry. Modern ambient noise and an age difference between the Hohokam people and the modern investigators make assumptions and comparisons difficult. But abrading produced the aura of sound needed for participation in ceremonial activities conducted in gathering places well below the perch of the bell on the mountainside. Softer bell sounds might have been used in more exclusive rituals and initiations.

Without specifying the purpose of the signaling, the literature suggests that bell rocks may have been used for that purpose (Boivin et al. 2007:282; Kleinitz 2006:149). Up until the experiments, I doubted that signaling was a possible use for bell rocks but 87 decibels is slightly louder than a motorcycle and that is loud enough to be heard at a distance. The bells could be effective in signaling to gather for a non-emergency occasion. At the Cocoraque complex, using the boulders for signaling in emergencies seems much less likely. The human voice screaming reaches 100 decibels, a better emergency signal than a bell rock located up a steep boulder-covered slope that reaches 87 decibels. The sound of the bell rock might be less frequently heard than human voices and thus attract more attention than yells of warning, but the difference in decibel levels still makes me think the human voice would issue a more effective alarm, and your voice is with you rather than on the mountainside. In his 1909–1910 visit Lumholtz (1912:120) heard a meeting called to order by the "loud voice of the herald…sounded from the lodge." And later in the same passage, "I have no doubt that his voice carried over the entire rancheria." Underhill (1938:6) mentions that the herald warns of an approaching enemy. And then, apparently, through more practical means the O'odham have found that singing carries even further than speaking and thus is the preferred way to address spirits (Bahr 1975:6). Though metallic cow bells were available in the early 1900s, no bell ringing was mentioned in this regard. In fact, the only mentions of bell ringing are in reference to one ceremony, the Wikita (Hernbrode 2021:147).

Positioning

The position of the boulder is also important. Most bell rocks are naturally perched in positions that barely touch a hard substrate below, maximizing their ability to resonate when struck (Figure 10a). Others appear to have been repositioned on other boulders or bedrock to enhance their tonal qualities (Figure 10b). Some elongate bell rocks (Figure 10c) project from a cluster of boulders so they are held at only one end by other boulders. Regardless of whether they rest in natural positions, appear to have been lifted and repositioned, are imported from another area, are small or gigantic, are sandstone, metamorphic, or volcanic in composition, they have the common qualities of homogeneity and are in an unrestrained position that allows them to transfer vibrations freely enough from one end to the other.

Position on the site can also be critical. Two-thirds of the way to the top of the Cocoraque Ranch petroglyph mountain is a niche behind a broken boulder (Figure 11) with large petroglyph-covered boulders on all sides and open on the side that faces the clearing below. The clearing is across the creek and beyond the corral at the base of the mountain, where it func-

Figure 10. (a) Bell rock positioned to touch the substrate as little as possible to enhance its ability to vibrate. (b) Propping up a bell rock with a small stone enhances its ability to resonate. Note the strike zones on the bottom of the boulder. (c) This bell rock projects from a cluster of boulders that hold one end. It rings well indicating it can still vibrate in this position.

tions now as a parking area for the ranch. Scattered artifacts in this clearing/parking area suggest ancient activity. Words spoken in a normal voice in the niche above can be heard below in the clearing without special effort or special equipment. The sound waves, even from normal speech, are sent without obstruction down the mountain, over the trees at the creek edge, and over the corral fences to anyone standing in the clearing. The bell rock with the most use-wear of all of the 130 bells located at Cocoraque Ranch and Cocoraque Butte rests in this niche. This bell (Figure 5) is completely abraded in addition to having seven strike indentations. Evidence and experiment results suggest

Figure 11. Large boulders surround a niche with special sound properties two-thirds of the way up the mountain. The bell rock with the most use-wear at this site (Figure 5) rests in the niche.

that abrading this boulder in this location would result in a roar that would fill the area below. Whether the purpose was to drive away evil, signal the populace, provide special drama for a special story, replicate the roar of thunder or other natural phenomena, or any other reason, the capabilities of this boulder combined with this niche are impressive.

Making a Site Sacred

The awe-inspiring imperceptible cosmic forces that Eliade and later Hedges found in the physical landscape at ritual sites can be influenced by human modification. During 2018–2021 the Rock Band recorded 28 petroglyph sites in Saguaro National Park. At three sites bell rocks were identified even though two of them are located in areas where the local rocks do not naturally ring and the bell rocks appear to have been imported. All of the bell rock sites have other characteristics common to O'odham sacred sites such as evidence of previous water availability and petroglyphs. The absence of grinding features at the sites indicates a more likely use for ritual than for gathering or processing. The largest of the three has 1040 petroglyphs and two bell rocks of portable size. Another site is quite small with 26 petroglyphs but it also has two portable bell rocks whose composition does not match that of the boulders at the site. The third site has a portable bell rock of local composition. Though all have water sources, two of the sites have experienced enough disturbance before the area was designated a National Park to preclude any certainty about the presence of a natural feature representing an *axis mundi*. However, the presence of the portable bell rocks at these sites suggests that their import was imperative either to perform specific rituals or to complete the site characteristics that make the location appropriate. They are a hint that sites lacking some of the necessary characteristics can be enhanced to increase their sacredness. Surely, portable and naturally present bell rocks join petroglyphs and an inspiring landscape in making a site sacred.

There appears to be one more way the sacredness of a site could have been enhanced. One rare sound-making artifact that must have been deployed strategically are the copper bells that have emerged from archaeological sites. Current thought is that the copper bells were produced in west Mexico and traded into the American Southwest. A tabulation of copper bells found at archaeological sites throughout the Southwest is provided by Vokes and Gregory (2007:325, 327). Far more copper bells (180 bells) have been found at Hohokam sites than within any other prehistoric Southwestern culture area. Half of the Hohokam bells have been found in burial contexts (Rice 2016:196). In their study of Southwestern distribution networks, Vokes and Gregory (2007:323) found a difference between the Hohokam copper bells that occur in multiples and other groups' copper bells that appear either singly or as part of storehouses with other objects. They conclude that, rather than representing storehouses for distribution of elite goods, the Hohokam clusters of bells are likely not part of a regularized exchange system. Instead, they suggest that they could represent the remains of special garments or costumes, a conclusion also reached by Emil Haury about bells found in the earliest excavation at Snaketown in 1937 (Gladwin et al. 1938:163–166). However, Vokes and Gregory also mention the Romo Cache (Figure 12a and b), a Hohokam jar containing more than 24 bells and 100,000 beads (Haury and Gifford 1959), as being a special circumstance. I agree.

The cache was found on a conical hill next to an important ceremonial site with more than 3,250 petroglyphs (Hernbrode and Boyle 2013:44). A large expanse of bedrock facilitates an echo, a megaphone-

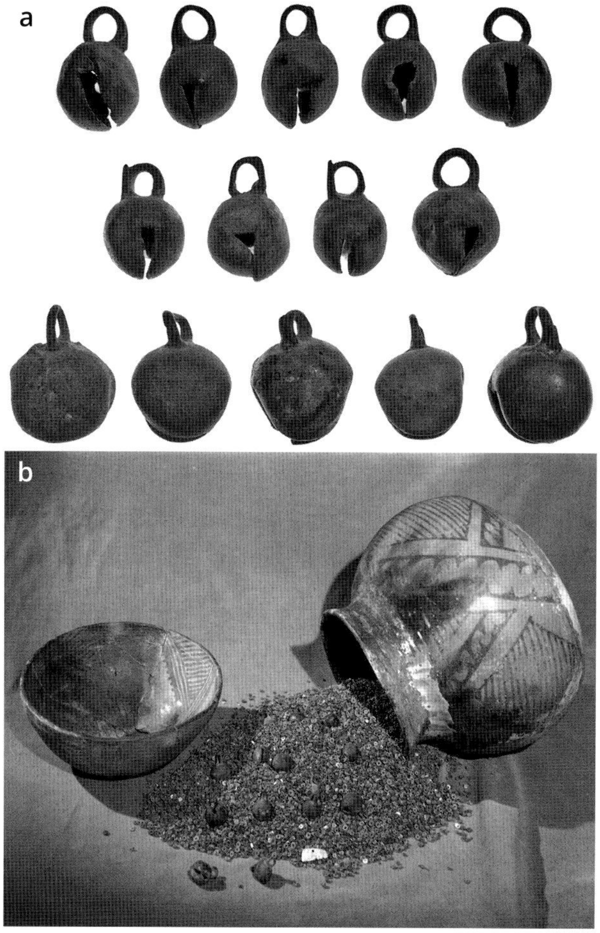

Figure 12. (a) A sample of the copper bells, A-9073, located in the Romo Cache. When Mr. Romo found the Cache, he gave some of the bells to friends before the treasure made its way to Arizona State Museum. The number of copper bells in the original cache is estimated to be 24 to 30. Arizona State Museum, University of Arizona, E.B. Sayles, photographer. ASM 5174. (b) The Romo Cache's ceramic jar, A-9071, and lid, A-9072, that contained the copper bells and beads, A-9074 and A-9075. The estimated 100,000 beads were weighed to determine the number. The cache was located on a conical hill overlooking a petroglyph site. Arizona State Museum, University of Arizona, Douglas Lindsay, photographer. ASM 9104.

like hole in a cluster of seven substantial boulders, and a "surround sound" phenomenon in the canyon bottom (Hernbrode 2011a), all adding to the presence of Eliade's "cosmic signs." The water source flows through the site below a cave-like cavity among the sizeable boulders marked with emergence figures (Hernbrode and Boyle 2018) (Figure 13). Unlike the three other large ceremonial sites near Tucson, this particular site has granitic boulders, a composition that does not ring when struck. That the cache was hidden among boulders on a hillside overlooking the gathering place suggests the copper bells were not used for ringing. They may have been brought to the ceremonies in the jar but possibly not removed and utilized. No threads for connecting the beads and the bells were evident in the jar (Haury and Gifford 1959:10). Perhaps this cache of elite goods that includes an extraordinary number of copper bells would be necessary to complete the characteristics of this sacred site.

Portable bell rocks at petroglyph sites where the boulders do not naturally ring and the cache of 24 or more copper bells at a petroglyph site where the boulders do not naturally ring are evidence that the ringing of bells was not viewed merely as a decorative addition to the rituals as has been suggested. The bells, whether bell rocks or copper bells, were an integral part of defining the sacred landscape and evidently one of the mysterious signs that makes a location suitable for the most sacred of the ceremonies. In making a place sacred, the bells, bell rocks, and bell sounds take on additional importance beyond the pleasant noises of the jingling of shell tinklers and metallic bells on costumes that are part of Native American practice today.

Shaping the Ringing Boulders

Our study area is within Tohono O'odham ancestral lands. In O'odham tradition sacred objects included objects of veneration similar to items found in burials for the Ancestral O'odham (archaeological Hohokam). This continuity between sacred objects of the Tohono O'odham (Underhill 1946:24) and the Hohokam archaeological culture (Bostwick et al. 2010:95–97) includes quartz crystals, seashells, eagle down or wings, projectile points, and unusually shaped or animal-shaped stones or wood. The ethnography indicates these items were kept and honored because they were said to hold power (Underhill 1946:24). Bostwick et al. (2010) suggested that these items could be related to special memberships in groups, clan moieties, and sodality-based ceremonial cults.

Clearly, bell rocks are part of the sacred landscape and, although we do not know specifically how their power was viewed, it follows that an animal-shaped bell rock, similar to the animal-shaped wood and stone items, occupies a very special place. The assignments of animacy to objects other cultures would consider inanimate also appears to be steeped in tradition and passed forward to the O'odham.

Jenny Adams has worked with people internationally who are still using grinding features in their everyday lives. In their world view, human-constructed or -altered things contain an essence of the maker, "it's a sense of being that lives in the object until it is released" (Adams 2008:215). Native Americans apply animacy to things that Euro-American culture would consider inanimate. Speaking about the O'odham worldview, Adams said "If the past was like the present, then mundane and sacred were not as separate as they are in our culture. Almost everything has a life history that needs to be honored" (Jenny Adams, personal communication 2021).

Figure 13. A large expanse of bedrock below a cluster of seven boulders facilitates an auditorium-like trajectory of sound from the cluster.

Four of the bell rocks we have investigated have animal head or head-and-body shapes that are recognizable. Figure 14a shows a bell rock shaped like a bear's head in profile, with two ears, a diamond-shaped impression for an eye, a squarish snout, and pecked nose. Pecking and abrading are evident. Although bears are important, it has been suggested that the pecked line altering the shape of the substantial snout, and now less evident because of use-wear, could make this figure look like Coyote, one of the two most important figures to the O'odham, symbolic of the Coyote moiety. Another bell rock is shaped like an arrow or spear point (Figure 14b). Others may have more culturally based shapes reminiscent of objects not discernible to me (Figure 14c). Some are naturally shaped and some appear to have been altered to more fully represent the intended sacred being. Altering includes shaping by abrading, shaping by breaking off pieces from the edge, adding eyes or other features made from concentric circles or spirals, and emphasizing areas by abrading to make a wing, a beak, or other animal feature. Moreover, bell rocks can be said to have "voice" in the same way ceramics have a voice when they are pinged. They are animate beings to be honored in the same way that the stones in shapes reported by Underhill (1946:24) represent O'odham guardian spirits.

Figure 14. (a) Bell rock shaped like a bear head in profile. Pecking and abrading are evident. (b) Bell rock similar to the shape of an arrow or spear point. One edge appears altered to enhance the desired shape. (c) Puzzling bell rock shape with an upper edge that appears altered. Some of the shapes could reflect more culturally based beings not recognizable by me.

One of the bell rocks resembles a parrot in profile (Figure 15a). The head, eye, basic form of the beak, and suggestion of a wing are natural features of the boulder and abraded areas further define the beak, neck area, the flared tail, and wing. The most utilized areas of the bell are on the lower edge of the boulder where one strike zone is so heavily used it appears to have broken away. At the top of the wing area is a natural rust color on the boulder that could correspond to the small number of red feathers on the top of the thick-billed parrot wing (Figure 15b). Interestingly, there are records of thick-billed parrots in Arizona during wetter periods. In fact, in 1904 they visited in huge flocks to feed on pine nuts and observers variously counted between 700

Figure 15. (a) Bell rock with possible parrot shape including an abraded and pecked beak, natural head and eye, possible abraded wing shape, and small amount of natural red color at the top of the wing area (edited in Photoshop to remove shadow in head area). (b) Thick-billed parrot, Rhynchopsitta pachyrhyncha *(after photo by Tim Lenz, CC BY 2.0 license). (c) Scarlet macaw,* Ara macao *(after photo by Brian Pitcher, CC BY 2.0 license).*

and 1,000 birds (Brown 2009:250). The excavation of the ancient Gila River village of Snaketown (17 miles south of Phoenix) recorded both a thick-billed parrot and a macaw in contexts indicating dates from 1 to 900 C.E. (Haury 1976:115–116; Rea 2007:163). Macaws (Figure 15c) have a greater history in the Tucson area than thick-billed parrots. Rincon Phase (950–1050 C.E.) macaw remains of two birds were recovered at Los Morteros (Gillespie 1995:706–707). In addition, Amadeo Rea (2007:163) cites records from 1701 and 1716 noting that the villagers of San Xavier del Bac, near Tucson, were raising macaws for their red feathers and that macaw red feathers were given to Fr. Eusebio Kino at a village 45 miles to the west of San Xavier. Although the parrot-shaped bell rock does not have a long macaw tail, it is evident that captive macaws relinquished their tail plumage often and a tailless bird must have been its normal condition.

Another bell rock resembles the head of a vulture (Figure 16a), known colloquially as "buzzard." Black vultures were observed roosting at Cocoraque Ranch during the recording period from 2015 to 2018; however, the red head and behavior of the turkey vulture (Figure 16b) and its prominent role in cosmology and oral history make it one of the two most important beings to the O'odham (Rea 2007:95; Russell 1908:225-228). The shape of the boulder has been abraded at the chin area, possibly to alter the shape but also a possible place to generate continuous sound. A large eye in the form of a partially complete concentric circle petroglyph has been added that appears to correspond to the shape of the skin around the vulture's eye, and the uneven surface of the bell rock corresponds to the wrinkled wattle of the bird. Indentations in the boulder correspond to the prominent nostrils on the vulture. The beak area is greatly abraded at the end showing the contrast between the bird's red head and the white end of its hooked beak. Bostwick et al. (2010:95–97) suggested stones and other objects in Hohokam burials may be related to special memberships in groups. This bell rock in the shape of Buzzard could relate to the Tohono O'odham moiety Buzzard (Underhill 1946:5), a present-day division that may reach deeply into the past.

Figure 16. (a) Abrading on the pointed beak-like end of this bell rock, shaping in the chin area, and added pecking to represent an eye enhance the rock's resemblance to the head of a vulture. (b) Turkey vulture, also known as "buzzard." Buzzard is the name of one of the moieties of the Tohono O'odham (photo by Andy Reago & Chrissy McClarren, CC BY 2.0 license).

Other bell rocks that have recognizable shapes give distinct impressions of a snake and, as noted above, a bear and an arrowpoint. Another shows special abrading and has pieces removed from two edges. It also has a prominent natural eye but neither I nor others could decide what it might have represented. If this one is counted in the total, there are six bell rocks that appear to have been altered to represent a cultural being.

When the prehistoric Hohokam way of life faded about 1450 C.E., the people changed their strategies for living in the desert, and archaeologists recognize them as O'odham. The O'odham people continued to use these same landscapes and petroglyph sites (Hernbrode 2019:97) because sacred places are not altered by changing the way of farming and building. However, the arrival of Spanish missionaries in 1690 began to change the O'odham as they embraced Christian practices, started the cultivation of wheat, turned to herding livestock and growing peaches, and celebrated with feast days at the Mission. Accepting the Christian faith brought a focus away from petroglyph sites to church buildings with bells instead. The efforts of Eusebio Kino in 1692, Luis Velarde in 1715, and a succession of other missionaries to make fealty to Spain and its king a primary goal were never accomplished. The O'odham maintain their distinctive cultural practices and have never fully embraced the developments that the Spanish originally hoped to make. They did shift their rituals to churches, but seldom use the church building. Rather, the ceremonies primarily take place outside in the churchyard, where there are processions, dancing, and feast preparations (Fontana 1981:35–44, 47–50, 98).

Conclusion

In southern Arizona near Tucson, there are four large Hohokam archaeological culture petroglyph sites. Three of these have been recorded and have more than 3500 petroglyphs each. In addition to their extensive petroglyph collections they also share a number of other characteristics. They are sited near water on inselbergs at the foot of larger mountains, have Sonoran Desert vegetation, have unusual sound properties, have adjacent flat spaces that can accommodate large numbers of people, and are visible from a distance. Three of the four sites also have clusters of bell rocks, with the fourth in an area that lacks naturally ringing boulders but had a cache of 24 or more copper bells. Portable bell rocks have also been found at three small petroglyph sites in Saguaro National Park. Two of these sites lack naturally ringing rocks; the third has a bell rock of local composition. These facts indicate bell rocks or bell sounds were an integral part of Hohokam sacred sites, one of Eliade's "mysterious signs" leading to selection of the sites for rituals. The evidence that the Hohokam added bell rocks to ritual sites where the local rocks do not ring shows that the sites were enhanced to fit the desired landscape. Researchers have suggested that the Hohokam caches of copper bells were evidence of bell use on special costumes. The observations in this paper add credence to the idea of bells having much greater importance to the site than use as costume decoration.

Comparison of archaeological material culture of the Hohokam and the ethnographic record of the O'odham shows similarities between objects sacred to the O'odham and to their ancestors. A few of the bell rocks have been altered to represent animals or other sacred beings common to both cultures.

Experiments on non-cultural bell rocks established four different methods of striking and abrading to elicit sound from the boulders, with abrading producing a continuous roar of sound. The acoustic characteristics of the sites, the properties of the striker, and positioning of the bell rock on the substrate contribute to the effectiveness of the sound. In all, the experiments resulted in a better understanding of the purposes and capabilities of the nearly 150 cultural bell rocks investigated at these sites over a 10-year period.

Acknowledgments. The Rock Band Rock Art Recording Team, a group of devoted volunteer sketchers, photographers, and data collectors, has scrambled over boulders and shared in the tasks to advance our understanding of bell rocks. They have my eternal gratitude. I also wish to thank Warren B. Davison, Senior Engineer, Steward Observatory, University of Arizona, Tucson, for helping me understand the physics of bell rocks and why they ring. Too, I owe a special thanks to Jenny Adams, whose experience with ground stone among both current users and ancient ones has advanced the knowledge of how ground stone is revered and used worldwide. Thanks to Katherine Cerino and Peter Boyle for their help with editing. I cannot conclude this without thanking Bob Hernbrode, my husband, who bought a truck equal to the task of finding the sites and adds his talents to the research.

Figure Credits: Lance K. Trask—Figures 1a and b, 4a and b, 5, 7, 10a, 11, 14a, 16a; Gordon P. Hanson—Figures 3, 8, 10b, 15a; E.B Sayles—Figure 12a; Douglas Lindsay—Figure 12b; CC BY 2.0 license—Figure 15b and c, 16b; Janine Hernbrode—Figures 2, 6, 9, 10c, 13, 14b and c.

References Cited

Adams, Jenny
2008 Beyond the Broken. In *New Approaches to Old Stones: Recent Studies of Ground Stone Artifacts,* edited by J.R. Ebeling and Y.M. Rowan, pp. 213–229. Equinox Archaeology Books, London.

Bahr, Donald M.
1975 *Pima and Papago Ritual Oratory: A Study of Three Texts.* Indian Historian Press, San Francisco.

Boivin, Nicole, and Adam Brumm, Helen Lewis, Dave Robinson, Ravi Korisettar
2007 Sensual, Material, and Technological Understanding: Exploring Prehistoric Soundscapes in South India. *Journal of the Royal Anthropological Institute* 13(2):267–294.

Bostwick, Todd W., Stephanie M. Whittlesey, and Douglas R. Mitchell
2010 Reconstructing the Sacred in Hohokam Archaeology: Cosmology, Mythology, and Ritual. *Journal of Arizona Archaeology* 1:89–101.

Boyle, Peter, and Janine Hernbrode
2014 Explorations of Sound at Tumamoc. Addendum to *New Perspectives on the Rock Art and Prehistoric Settlement Organization of Tumamoc Hill, Tucson, Arizona,* edited by Gayle Harrison Hartmann and Peter C. Boyle. Arizona State Museum Archaeological Series 208, University of Arizona, Tucson.

Brown, David E.
2009 Troublesome Times and Notable News. In *Arizona Wildlife: The Territorial Years,* edited by David E. Brown, pp. 250–252. Arizona Game and Fish Department, Phoenix, Arizona.

Brown, Emily J.
2014 "A Sound Like That of Bells": Lithophones in the Southwest. In *Enduring Curiosity, Generous Service,* edited by Emily J. Brown, Carol J. Condie, and Helen K. Crotty, pp. 57–68. Papers of the Archaeological Society of New Mexico 40. Albuquerque, New Mexico.

Chesky, Jane
1942 The Wikita. *Kiva* 8(1):1–8.

Chesterman, Charles W., and Kurt E. Lowe
1978 *Audubon Society Field Guide to North American Rocks and Minerals.* Alfred A. Knopf, New York.

Dams, Lya
1984 Preliminary Findings at the "Organ" Sanctuary in the Cave of Nerja, Malaga, Spain. *Oxford Journal of Archaeology* 3:1–14. Electronic document, https://doi.org/10.1111/j.1468-0092.1984.tb00112.x, accessed September 10, 2022.

Eliade, Mircea
1958 *The Sacred and the Profane: The Nature of Religion.* Harcourt, New York.

Ferguson, T. J.
2008 *Cocoraque Butte: Signs of History in the Storied Landscape of the Tohono O'odham.* Unpublished report prepared for Arizona Open Lands Trust, Tucson.

Fontana, Bernard L.
1981 *Of Earth and Little Rain: The Papago Indians.* Northland Press, Flagstaff, Arizona.

Galinier, Jacques
1991 From Montezuma to San Francisco: The Wi:gita Ritual in Papago (Tohono O'odham) Religion. Translated by Adelaide Bahr and Donald Bahr. *Journal of the Southwest* 53(4):486–538.

Gillespie, William B.
1995 Vertebrate Remains from Los Morteros. In *Archaeological Investigations at Los Morteros, a Prehistoric Settlement in the Northern Tucson Basin,* edited by Henry D. Wallace, pp. 673–719. Anthropological Papers No. 17, Center for Desert Archaeology, Tucson, Arizona.

Gladwin, Harold S., Emil W. Haury, E.B. Sayles, and Nora Gladwin
1938 *Excavations at Snaketown: Material Culture.* Medallion Paper 25. Gila Pueblo, Globe, Arizona. Facsimile reprint 1965, University of Arizona Press, Tucson.

Haury, Emil W.
1976 *The Hohokam: Desert Farmers and Craftsmen.* University of Arizona Press, Tucson.

Haury, Emil W., and Carol A. Gifford
1959 A Thirteenth Century "Strongbox." *Kiva* 24(4):1–11.

Hayden, Julian
1987 The Vikita Ceremony of the Papago. *Journal of the Southwest* 29(3):273–324.

Hedges, Ken
1993 Places to See and Places to Hear: Rock Art and Features of the Sacred Landscape. In *Time and Space: Dating and Spatial Considerations in Rock Art,* edited by Jack Steinbring, Alan Watchman, Paul Faulstich, and Paul S. Taçon, pp 121–127. Occasional AURA Publication No. 8. Australian Rock Art Research Association, Melbourne.

Hernbrode, Janine
2011a *Acoustics at Sheep Tanks.* Report to Coronado National Forest Archaeologist, USFS. Experiments: 11/22/2011, Report 12/2/2011, Sutherland Wash Rock Art District Site 117.

2011b *Acoustics at Plaza.* Report to Coronado National Forest Archaeologist, USFS. Experiments: 12/27/2011, Sutherland Wash Rock Art District Site 23.

2017 Notes from Sound Experiments at Cocoraque Ranch, November 17, 2017, in possession of the author.

2019 Rock Art After the Hohokam: Elements, Style, and Continuity of the Tohono O'odham at Cocoraque Butte. *American Indian Rock Art, Volume 45,* edited by Ken Hedges and Anne McConnell, pp. 89–101. American Rock Art Research Association, San Jose, California.

2021 Messages from the Ancestors: Hohokam Ritual Imagery and O'odham Ethnography. *American Indian Rock Art, Volume 47,* edited by David A. Kaiser, Mavis Greer, and James D. Keyser. pp. 139–150. American Rock Art Research Association, Cupertino, California.

Hernbrode, Janine, and Peter Boyle
2013 Gender in Hohokam Imagery and Landscape: Sutherland Wash Rock Art District, Coronado National Forest, Arizona. In *American Indian Rock Art, Volume 39,* edited by William D. Hyder. pp. 43–54. American Rock Art Research Association, Glendale, Arizona.

2016 Petroglyphs and Bell Rocks at Cocoraque Butte: Further Evidence of the Flower World Belief Among the Hohokam. In *American Indian Rock Art, Volume 42,* edited by Ken Hedges pp. 91–105. American Rock Art Research Association, San Jose, California.

2018 Becoming Human: Rock Art Depictions of Transformation in Landscapes of Emergence. In *American Indian Rock Art, Volume 44,* edited by David A. Kaiser and James D. Keyser, pp. 97–110. American Rock Art Research Association, San Jose, California.

Kleinitz, Cornelia
2006 Acoustic Elements of (Pre)Historic Rock Art Landscapes at the Fourth Nile Cataract. In *Between the Cataracts,* edited by Wlodzimierz Godlewski and Adam Lajtar, pp. 149–160. Proceedings of the 11th Conference of Nubian Studies, Part 2, Fascicule 1, Session papers. Warsaw University Press, Warsaw, Poland.

Loendorf, Chris, and Barnaby V. Lewis
2017 Ancestral O'odham: Akimel O'odham Cultural Traditions and the Archaeological Record. *American Antiquity* 82(1):123–139.

Lumholtz, Carl
1912 *New Trails in Mexico: An Account of One Year's Exploration in North-Western Sonora, Mexico, and South-Western Arizona, 1909–1910.* Charles Scribner's Sons, New York.

Madsen, John
1995 Cocoraque Butte Bell Rock recording 8/18/1993, Arizona State Museum Accession Number ACC 95-40-1.

Martarano, Marilyn
2021 Lithophones of the Great Sand Dunes National Park (video). 2021 Stephen H. Hart Awards. History Colorado YouTube Channel. Electronic document, https://www.youtube.com/watch?v=GNWDLLl9y6Y, accessed September 10, 2022.

Pendleton, Isabelle, and Julian Hayden
1987 Vikita Portfolio: Plates 1–11. *Journal of the Southwest* 29(3):unpaginated.

Rea, Amadeo M.
2007 *Wings in the Desert: A Folk Ornithology of the Northern Pimans.* University of Arizona Press, Tucson.

Rice, Glen E.
2016 *Sending the Spirits Home: The Archaeology of Hohokam Mortuary Practices.* University of Utah Press, Salt Lake City.

Russell, Frank
1908 *The Pima Indians.* Twenty-sixth Annual Report of the Bureau of American Ethnology 1904-1905, pp. 3–389. Facsimile reprint 1975 with a new Introduction, Citation Sources, and Bibliography by Bernard L. Fontana, University of Arizona Press, Tucson.

Underhill, Ruth M.
1938 *Singing for Power: The Song Magic of the Papago Indians of Southern Arizona.* University of California Press, Berkeley. Facsimile reprint 1993 with forward by Ofelia Zepeda, University of Arizona Press, Tucson.

1946 *Papago Indian Religion.* AMS Press, New York.

Vokes, Arthur W., and David A. Gregory
2007 Exchange Networks for Exotic Goods in the Southwest and Zuni's Place in Them. In *Zuni Origins,* edited by David A. Gregory and David R. Wilcox, pp 318–357. University of Arizona Press, Tucson.

Wallace, Henry D.
2012 Foreword to the Reissue. In *Petroglyphs of the Picacho Mountains, South Central Arizona,* by Henry D., and James P. Holmlund, pp. v-x. Anthropological Papers 6 (reissue edition). Institute for American Research, Tucson, Arizona.

Wallace, Henry D., and James P. Holmlund
1986 *Petroglyphs of the Picacho Mountains, South Central Arizona.* Anthropological Papers 6. Institute for American Research, Tucson, Arizona. Reissued 2012 with new introduction by Henry D. Wallace, Archaeology Southwest, Tucson.

Wright, Aaron
2014 *Religion on the Rocks: Hohokam Rock Art, Ritual Practice, and Social Transformation.* University of Utah Press, Salt Lake City.

A Close Look at the Fine-line Engravings at Palatki Heritage Site

Peter Anick, Spence Gustav, and Walter van Roggen

The Palatki Heritage Site lies within a box canyon in the Verde Valley of central Arizona. Inhabited for perhaps as long as the past 13,000 years by Paleoindian, Archaic, Sinagua, Yavapai, Apache, and European settlers, its natural alcoves have preserved hundreds of pictographs and petroglyphs. Intermixed among the pictographs, and often barely visible, are finely cut incisions forming parallel lines, snakelike designs, checkerboards, cross-hatching, and other geometric patterns. We describe an ongoing effort, in conjunction with volunteers from the Sedona Friends of the Forest, to document and study what may be one of the richest troves of such abstract incised art in the Southwest. Using 3D modeling, high-resolution photography with raked lighting, and a software application developed to support the recording and interpretation of linear engravings, we present findings for several cliffside panels which contain thousands of line segments. We also attempt to place the incised figures within a relative chronology based on stylistic analysis of superimposed pictographs and petroglyphs.

Compared to painted and pecked designs, faint fine-line geometric petroglyphs are rarely featured in coffee table books about rock art, let alone in archaeological journals. Yet, given their wide distribution in both space and time throughout the western United States, they represent a cultural phenomenon that deserves more scientific attention. The best-known examples may be the so-called Great Basin Scratched Style, reported by Heizer and Baumhoff in the 1960s (Heizer and Baumhoff 1962:94, 208). This style is composed primarily of straight lines, sometimes organized into parallel groups, checkerboards, diamonds, or other geometric patterns. As Hambelton (2011:25) laments, "Because scratched petroglyphs are often faint, less elaborate, and resemble graffiti they were often ignored or misunderstood and as a result have not been sufficiently recorded or researched."

A few examples that have been studied in detail include scratched rock art complexes in Nevada (Ritter 1994), Little Lake Ranch in California (Reed 2012), and the Bennett Hills of southern Idaho (Hambelton 2011). Based on the superimposition of lines over pecked petroglyphs as well as experimental dating of varnish, much Desert West scratched art is thought to be relatively recent, from about 1,500 years ago into historic times (Gilreath and Hildebrandt 2008:12; Hambelton 2011:23).

However, similar designs have also been found on small stone slabs within archaeologically datable contexts. These indicate a very long timeline for producing incised rectilinear art. At the Gault site in Texas, for example, chert and limestone slabs bearing both random lines as well as very intricate geometric patterns (Figure 1) were found in Paleoindian and Archaic contexts (Lemke et al. 2015, Wernecke and Collins 2012).

Inspired by such ancient dates, Loendorf (2012) searched for rock art panels containing fine-line incisions superimposed by known Archaic-style petroglyphs, and he located several such examples on the High Plains along

Peter Anick
Brandeis University, Waltham, Massachusetts

Spence Gustav
Sedona Friends of the Forest, Sedona, Arizona

Walter van Roggen
Northwoods Software Corporation, Nashua, New Hampshire

Figure 1. Example of stone decorated with fine cross-hatching, found in Dalton (late Paleoindian) context at the Gault site, Texas. Photo by Peter Anick.

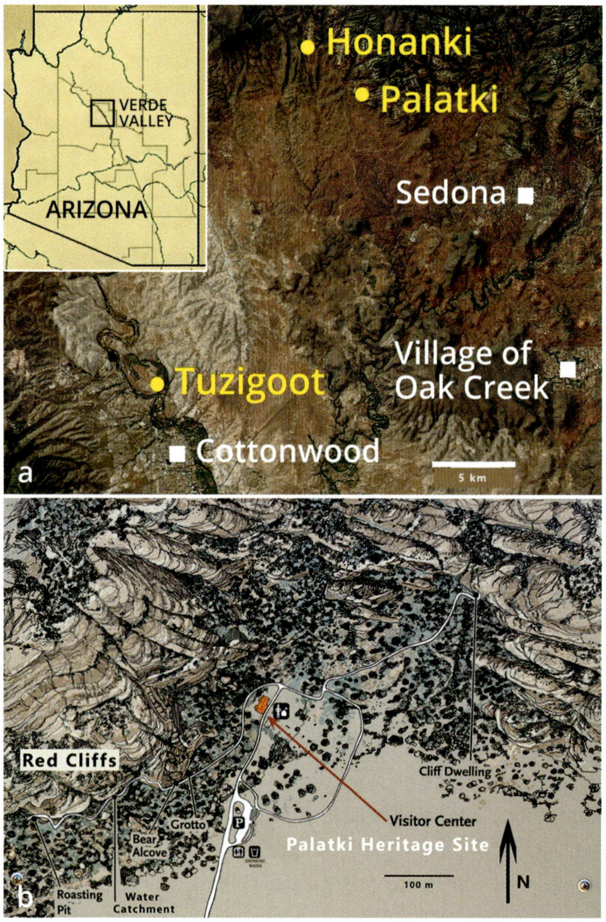

Figure 2. (a) Location of Verde Valley within Arizona, along with major archaeological sites and modern towns. (b) The trails and main archaeological areas at Palatki Heritage Site. Based on a map courtesy of the U.S. Forest Service.

the Colorado/New Mexico border. Noting the greater degree of repatination of the fine-line motifs, along with a lack of early-to-middle Archaic sites nearby, he raised the possibility that the earlier incisions might actually represent Paleoindian art.

A similar observation was made by Peter Pilles, archaeologist for the Coconino National Forest in central Arizona. He speculated that weathered linear patterns found at the Honanki and Palatki Heritage sites near Sedona might date back to the Clovis period (Pilles 2014:15). A photo Pilles presented during his keynote address at the 2019 conference of the American Rock Art Research Association piqued the curiosity of one of the authors, Peter Anick, who had examined a number of incised stones while working at the Gault site in 2013. Peter Pilles arranged a tour of the two Heritage sites with retired geoscientist Spence Gustav, who was involved in an effort to document the region's rock art using photogrammetry. Joined by another colleague, Walter van Roggen, the three of us spent the better part of the day focused on the least visible cultural artifacts on the cliff walls. Subsequent discussions about what we saw and photographed led to a collaboration resulting in the research described here. A number of volunteers from the Sedona Friends of the Forest also assisted in our documentation efforts.

Palatki Heritage Site

The Palatki Heritage Site is located in Red Canyon, just northwest of the town of Sedona in north-central Arizona (Figure 2a). It lies within an ecotone between the Colorado Plateau's forests to the north and the Sonoran Desert to the south, hosting a mix of plant and animal species that, along with reliable water sources, would have long attracted human exploitation. Clovis and Archaic projectile points attest to the presence of hunter-gatherers from Paleoindian times up to the initiation of farming around A.D. 600 (Pilles 2014; Spurr and Deats 2015). The Southern Sinagua occupied the area for about 700 years, abandoning their cliff dwellings around A.D. 1300–1400. Yavapai and Apache continued to use the valley through historic times and into the present.

Today, the Palatki Heritage Site is managed by the U.S. Forest Service. It consists of three distinct sections: an historic ranch, a Sinagua cliff dwelling, and a 700-meter-long stretch of cliff wall known as the Red Cliffs, which contains numerous pictograph and petroglyph panels. Figure 2b points out some of the most important archaeological sites along this trail.

The Grotto (site AR-03-04-06-0284) includes a

large semicircular recess under a protective overhang. Its 17 primary panels contain many Archaic and Sinagua painted figures, some in conjunction with incised lines. Further to the south along the cliff face are a number of other alcoves with rock art. Some panels display complex incised designs with little evidence of painted images. Well preserved, they offer an opportunity to identify not only distinct motifs and superimpositions within them but also holistic characteristics of what may be larger compositions. For example, in the 1.4-meter-long panel at the Water Catchment alcove, part of which is shown in Figure 3, lines from one pattern appear to merge into another.

At the west end of the trail is the Roasting Pit site (AR-03-04-06-0287), so named because of a fire pit used by Sinagua and Yavapai to prepare agave, a major food source. Close by, there is a large vertical open fracture in the cliff face. Several long ghostlike figures reminiscent of Utah's Archaic Barrier Canyon Style (Schaafsma 1980:61–72) are painted on adjacent panels.

Roughly four kilometers to the northwest, the Honanki Heritage Site sits along the west face of Loy Butte. It shares many features with Palatki, including incised geometric petroglyphs, pictographs, and cliff dwellings. Although some of the weathered line art cited by Pilles is found here, we chose to confine our initial study to Palatki, as it offered several advantages for investigating incised-line art. Specifically:

- There are dozens of incised subpanels likely totaling tens of thousands of lines, some in a relatively good state of preservation.
- Prior documentation efforts by Loendorf (1994) and Pilles (1994) provide a tentative cultural timeline for many of the pictographs, which span the Archaic through historic periods.
- Since a number of panels contain both incised lines and pictographs, superimpositions between lines and paint could allow for bracketing of time frames within which various incised figures were carved.

Documentation Goals and Methods

Our primary goal was to determine the temporal relationships between stylistically Archaic pictographs and incised lines to identify which motifs, if any, could be attributed to the Archaic period or earlier. Out of approximately 100 panels at Palatki, for this initial study we selected two that contain stylistically Archaic pictographs sharing wall space with linear incisions.

From the two panels, we designated three areas, each of roughly a meter square or less, for detailed analysis. Each area was photographed in its entirety using ambient light and containing a scale. Then, a sequence of detailed photographs was taken which together covered the same area but at much higher resolution (roughly 6x9 cm on average). Each subarea was photographed at least three times, with raked lighting sourced from the side, 45 degrees below, and directly below. Multiple photos were found to be essential in order to bring extremely fine lines into relief via shadows created on at least one of the detail photos, depending on their angles on the panel.

Once the various digital images had been captured, much subsequent analysis could proceed online. DStretch versions (Harman 2008) of some photos were created to help interpret the extent and character of the paint. In a few cases, 3D photogrammetric models were created to help visualize wall surfaces, which, as shown in Figure 4, are geologically complex.

Geological Observations

The native rock of the Red Cliffs is a light red Permian sandstone. Many of the panels are coated with

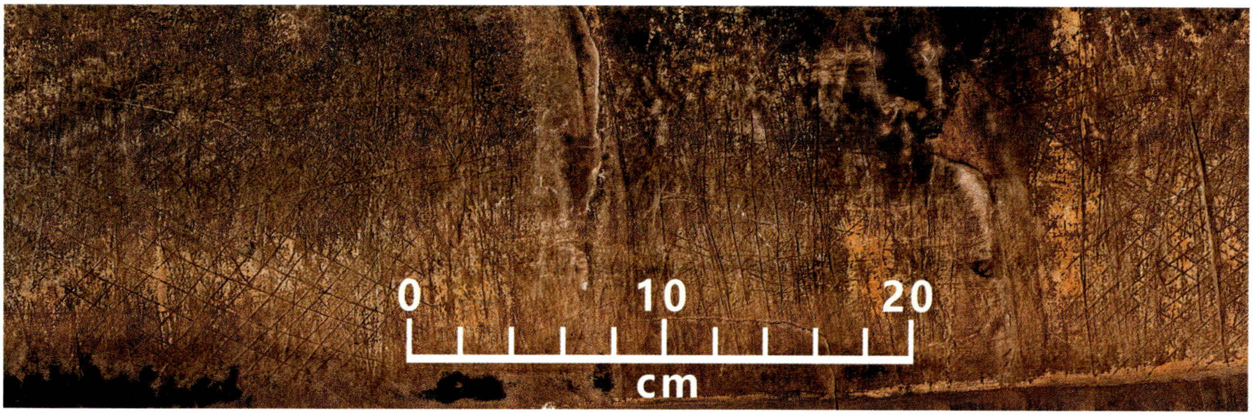

Figure 3. Portion of panel in the Water Catchment alcove exhibiting many clearly visible geometric patterns. Photo by Spence Gustav.

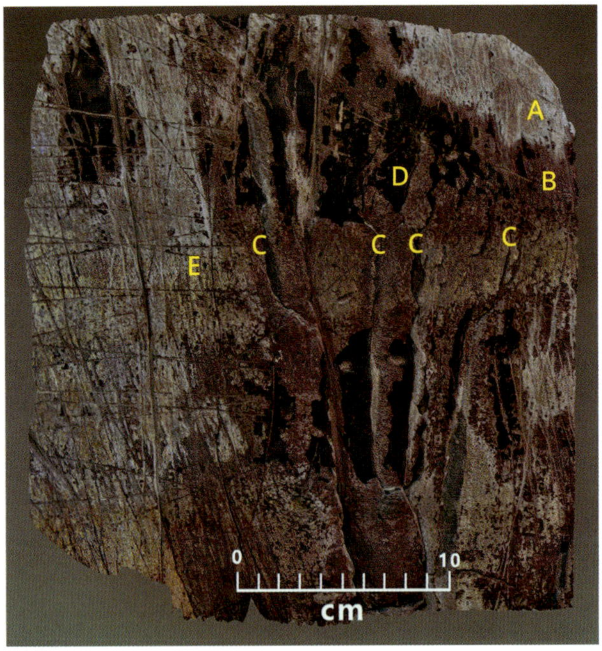

Figure 4. 3D model of a Red Cliffs panel showing layers of fracture fill over dark red iron-rich zones. (a) Topmost fracture-fill layer visible on this surface with thickness of approximately 1 mm composed of primarily silt and clay-sized particles. (b) Underlying fracture-fill layer with thickness of approximately 1–2 mm composed of more silt and possibly very-fine sand and clay. (c) Multiple en échelon fracture sections with rock sections closer to the camera eroded or sloughed off the cliff face deeper on the right side. Each vertical fracture section varies from approximately 2 to 6+ mm. (d) Iron-enriched zone below the fracture fill and directly present between the fracture fill and the native sandstone. In this photo, no actual native Schnebly Hill Sandstone is visible other than possibly in the lower right-hand corner. (e) Example area of fine incised lines. Model by Spence Gustav.

a thin (1–3 mm) layer of fracture fill. This claylike clastic material had seeped into thin planar fractures within the sandstone which were produced by shear and tensional stresses while the rock was still deep underground (Nelson 2001). Several areas also have carbonate or sulphate fracture-fill surfaces, presumably due to variations of composition and the migration path of the ground water. Given such variations in their formation, it is not surprising that Loendorf (1994:1.2) reported a lot of variability in the hardness of the cliff faces.

Just beneath the fracture-fill layer, we often observe a dark red, iron-rich layer formed when iron precipitating out from the sandstone was trapped by the less-permeable clay of the fracture fill (Figure 4). Most of the fine incised lines did not penetrate beyond the outer layer of fracture fill. At some locations, the incisions structurally weakened the surface, allowing fill to flake off over time and expose patches of the iron-rich layer below. Occasionally, the faint impression of an incised line can be observed on this lower layer, presumably the vestige of a deeper incision made into the now-missing fracture fill. Compression of the fracture-fill material around a groove during incising sometimes helped to preserve the fill material within a line while the weakened surfaces on either side of the line had eroded away.

Software Developed for Documentation and Interpretation

To aid in documenting the thousands of lines, Walter van Roggen developed a web application called the Fine Line Analyzer (FLA). The tool provides a visual workspace for drawing line segments, using the reference photo and detailed photos as guides. Among its features are:

- computing statistics about line counts and angles
- automated and manual joining of adjacent line fragments
- tags for capturing attributes of lines
- tools for annotating superimpositions at intersection points and for showing transitive relationships among lines
- color and thickness options for visualizing lines
- outputting a shareable ".lines" file, which allows multiple people to work independently on subareas and merge their work later

One advantage of using a digital documentation tool like this is that potentially subjective decisions about lines and superimpositions can be revisited and, if necessary, revised based on reviewing the underlying photos or eyeballing the panel of interest at the site. Given the high volume of line data, the development of a specialized tool was deemed a necessity.

Roasting Pit, Panel 27

Our first study area was a section of Panel 27 in the Roasting Pit. The panel is dominated by a pair of circular painted designs thought to represent shields (Figure 5). A partially detached black pigment sample from the 81-centimeter-wide shield on the left has previously provided an AMS calibrated radiocarbon date between A.D. 700 and 1200, consistent with a Sinagua interpretation (Armitage et al. 2000). This date provides one point of reference for relatively dating lines carved within the scope of the shield. However, our primary motivation for choosing this panel was the presence of ghostlike figures resembling Utah's Ar-

Figure 5. Panel 27 at the Roasting Pit, dominated by two large painted shields. In the upper right the red outline of a Barrier Canyon-style figure is painted over a series of alternating light and dark wavy lines. Friends of the Forest volunteer, Ed Hodges, points to the top of a finely carved "snake." Nearly all incised lines are carved below this level within the fracture-bounded subpanel. Photo by Spence Gustav.

chaic Barrier Canyon Style (Schaafsma 1980:61–72). In his provisional chronology for the Red Cliffs sites, Loendorf (1994:2.6) proposed that these figures may be 3,000–5,000 years old. Figure 5 shows the full Panel 27, with a volunteer standing in front for scale. As the photo indicates, most of the pictographs could have been painted by someone standing at ground level. The obvious exception is the Barrier Canyon-like outline in the upper right. The lower portion of this faded red outline is painted directly over alternating light and dark wavy lines. By virtue of the superimposition, this cluster of wavy lines is likely the oldest painted motif on the panel and potentially among the oldest on the Red Cliffs. Unfortunately, we could not detect any incised lines sharing this upper section of the panel, eliminating the possibility of relative dating.

However, a nearly identical Barrier Canyon-style outline appears below and to the left. DStretch reveals the top of it just above the edge of the left shield (Figure 6). The elongated form traverses the right hemisphere of the shield and terminates in short legs at the base of the panel. Inspection of the lower half of this shield area revealed the presence of weathered lines, some of which intersect the faded red paint of the tall Archaic figure.

Figure 6. DStretch (LDS) version of Panel 27 at the Roasting Pit. The magenta outline of a Barrier Canyon-style figure traverses the right hemisphere of the left shield-like painting. Photo by Peter Anick.

We selected this lower section of the panel as our study area. Traces of the one-centimeter-wide dull red outline of the Barrier Canyon-style figure can be seen on the reference photo to the right of a brown anthropomorph believed to be Sinagua (Figure 7). White stripes of the shield run over both the brown anthropomorph and the red outline. Detailed photos with raked lighting revealed the presence of many incised lines that were practically invisible to the naked eye in the field. Inspection of lines intersecting the red outline showed evidence of red paint over the lines in nearly all cases (Figure 8). The one exception was a group of long, haphazard scratch marks which cut into paint and left light-colored scars. Visible in the center of Figure 7, these slightly arching and zigzagging lines are assumed to be relatively recent additions. Likely scratched with a blunt stone, they look distinctly different from the carefully incised lines of less than 0.5 mm width that are found here under the red paint.

The study area is extremely weathered, with some sections of fracture fill missing altogether, leaving the darker iron-rich layer below exposed. Weathering has left discontinuities in what were likely long, continuous lines, complicating documentation with the FLA. With so many line segments present, it is not always clear which of several adjacent incisions is the most

Figure 7. Study area A1 at the Roasting Pit (65x44 cm). White stripes and "rays" are part of a Sinagua shield design. A brown anthropomorph under the white paint is likely also Sinagua. To its right, the faded red vertical lines are the outline of an Archaic ghostlike figure. Vestiges of incised "snake" forms can be seen on the left, descending into an area where the fracture fill has peeled off to reveal an iron-rich layer below. Some relatively recent light, zigzagging scratch marks can be seen across the center of the shield, particularly over the brown anthropomorph. Photo by Spence Gustav.

Figure 8. Detailed photo from area A1 at the Roasting Pit, DStretch using the LDS *setting. A section of the faded red ghost-like outline (rendered a dark magenta color in DStretch) runs vertically down within the right side of the photo. Incised lines transecting the outline show evidence of being covered by paint. Spaced parallel lines suggest underlying motifs such as grids and cross hatching. Some lines, such as the long vertical one second from the right, show a second parallel line drawn nearly over the first, as if the carver was trying to reinforce or extend a line with a second incision. Photo by Spence Gustav.*

likely continuation of a line segment with a similar orientation. Figure 9 shows 4,982 lines (composed from 8,265 segments) captured with the FLA. The graph on the right provides a histogram of line angles, indicating a predominance of near vertical lines (at the center of the graph), followed by horizontal lines (top and bottom). These suggest the presence of checkerboard patterns, although the density of lines at many different angles tends to obscure the detection of multi-line motifs such as checkerboard grids and angled cross-hatching.

Looking closely at detailed photos, systematic relationships among lines can be used to identify possible motifs within the chaos. For example, the detailed photo in Figure 8 shows a number of roughly equally spaced vertical lines and at least two sets of spaced diagonals at different angles. Spaced horizontal lines, nearly invisible with this light angle, can be detected in the equivalent photo with light angled from below. Thus, the majority of lines in this small section may represent portions of two larger diamond patterns and a checkerboard. Short "random" line segments that appear unrelated to others occur as well. Superimposition analysis for groups of lines could potentially tease motifs apart. Unfortunately, the weathering on this panel has left many of the line intersections too difficult to analyze with confidence.

Further to the left within our study area of Panel 27, Loendorf (1994:1.29) had noted several distinct incised motifs comprised of long, thin, bounded areas, tapered on both ends, with diamond cross hatching within the outlines. Because the fine cross-hatching

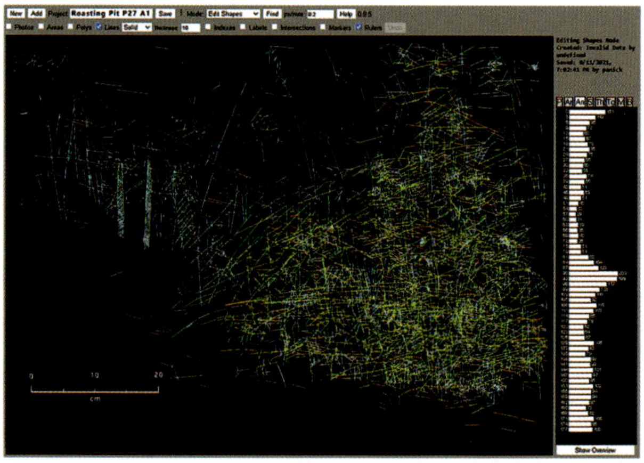

Figure 9. Screenshot of line segments recorded in Fine Line Analyzer for area A1, Panel 27, at the Roasting Pit A histogram of line angles (from 0 to 180 degrees) is shown on the right.

resembles the pattern on a diamondback rattlesnake, he conjectured that these represented snakes. We will continue to refer to such motifs as "snakes," although this designation is purely speculative. Figures 10 and 11 show several examples clustered in the lower left hemisphere of the Sinaguan shield. Differences in weathering and execution suggest that they were made by different artists at different times. The second snake from the left, 15 cm long and a mere 1.5 cm wide, is very precisely carved, with little of the internal cross hatching extending beyond its boundaries. By contrast, the wider snake to the right has uneven sides and more cross-hatching extending beyond its bounds. Bits of white and dark paint over the snakes indicate that they predate the painting of the shield, but their relation to the Archaic red paint on the right side of the panel is unclear. To establish that the snakes themselves date to the Archaic, one would have to find a sequence of superimposed lines that can be traced back to some line directly superimposed by the red paint of the Barrier Canyon-style figure. Several faint, evenly spaced horizontal lines can be seen running behind the snakes, but weathering makes it difficult to ascertain whether any of the other lines intersecting the snakes superimpose the snakes or not. The best we can say at this point is that the width and depth of the lines comprising the snakes resemble the lines presumed to be Archaic on the right side of the panel.

Figure 10. Four snake figures with different dimensions and style of execution on the left side of study area A1, Panel 27, at the Roasting Pit. Photo by Peter Anick.

Grotto, Panel 15

The second panel chosen for this study is within a highly decorated section of the Grotto. As shown in Figure 12, Panel 15 consists of two sections separated by a long, vertical fracture. We focused on the left side of the fracture, dividing the vertical space into two subareas (A1 above, A3 below) starting from roughly one meter above the base (Figure 13) up to a highly eroded section just below the ceiling. As on Panel 27 in the Roasting Pit, some of the paintings are higher than can be reached by someone standing at the base of the wall. At the top of the panel (Figure 14) is a cluster of vertical wavy light and dark lines that closely resembles in paint and style the Archaic zigzags we encountered at the Roasting Pit.

Figure 11. Detail showing the care of execution, particularly on the well-defined snake in the center of the photo. Several horizontal and diagonal lines can barely be seen running behind the snakes, hinting at a checkerboard pattern with relatively widely spaced lines. Photo by Spence Gustav.

Figure 12. View of Panel 15 at the Grotto. Ed Hodges stands at the base with a 2-meter pole, pointing at the location of an incised snake. A buff-white rake symbol is painted to its right at the same level. Painted wavy lines descend from above, starting just below a dark red, highly eroded section near the ceiling. White carbonate precipitate surrounding the eroded section indicates that water occasionally seeps through the cliff face here. Photo by Spence Gustav.

Figure 13. Reference photo for the lower study area within Grotto Panel 15. Area A3 has additional buff-white wavy lines, deep vertical grooves, and a rake symbol. Note the white painted zigzag superimposed over the wavy lines to the left of the fracture, and white highlights added over the rake on the right. Photo by Spence Gustav.

Many more wavy lines in the same buff-white paint extend over other portions of the panel. Loendorf (1994:4.11) suggests that the profusion of vertical wavy lines on this panel may be related to the water that sometimes flows over the lip of the overhang protecting the alcove. Coauthor Spence Gustav has observed water pouring down from above, like a waterfall, after a heavy rain.

A rake symbol appears midway down the panel, with more wavy lines below it. Its style and buff-white paint suggest that it is also Archaic and likely contemporaneous with the other wavy-lined features on the panel. A lighter white paint appears over parts of this image. This lighter white paint is associated with Sinagua imagery found elsewhere along the cliff face. Here, within Panel 15, a stick-figure anthropomorph (Figure 14 inset) and a descending zigzag are both painted in lighter white on top of earlier paintings of wavy lines.

Along with the presumed Archaic pictographs, the large quantity and variety of incised lines make this panel particularly interesting. Unlike at the Roasting Pit panel, where engraving does not extend beyond the reach of a person standing at the base, incised lines here continue to the very top of the panel, nearly a meter higher up on the wall than can be accessed while standing on the current floor. The overwhelming majority are fine lines between 0.2 and 0.4 cm wide, like those in the Roasting Pit. However, we also encounter wider V-shaped and U-shaped grooves, as well as some splayed effects in which a mass of tightly packed fine lines run roughly in parallel for a few centimeters before splaying apart at the ends. A snakelike motif (pointed at by Ed Hodges in Figure 12) appears in direct association with buff-white wavy lines.

Figure 14. Reference photo for the upper study area within Grotto Panel 15. Area A1, comprising the upper left side of the panel, displays clusters of vertical wavy lines similar to those at the Roasting Pit (Figure 5). Inset shows DStretch (LAB) detail of Sinagua-style stick figure painted over vertical zigzags. Photo by Spence Gustav.

As at the Roasting Pit, the detailed photos bring out a surprising degree of complexity which is difficult to detect in person in ambient light, especially in the painted sections. Figure 15 illustrates the density of lines within area A3, as captured in the FLA. Our documentation is likely incomplete, since experience has shown that reviewing a detailed photo can reveal lines missed during earlier passes. It currently contains 12,955 line segments, which, after likely continuations are merged, provides an estimate of 8,825 lines drawn within the roughly 62x92-cm region. The upper area of A1 is more weathered but also shows a high density of lines, many of which are arranged into consistently spaced, parallel configurations implying intentional grids and cross-hatching. Incisions fill the space up to the large vertical fracture that divides Panel 15 into two vertical sections. While painted motifs in differ-

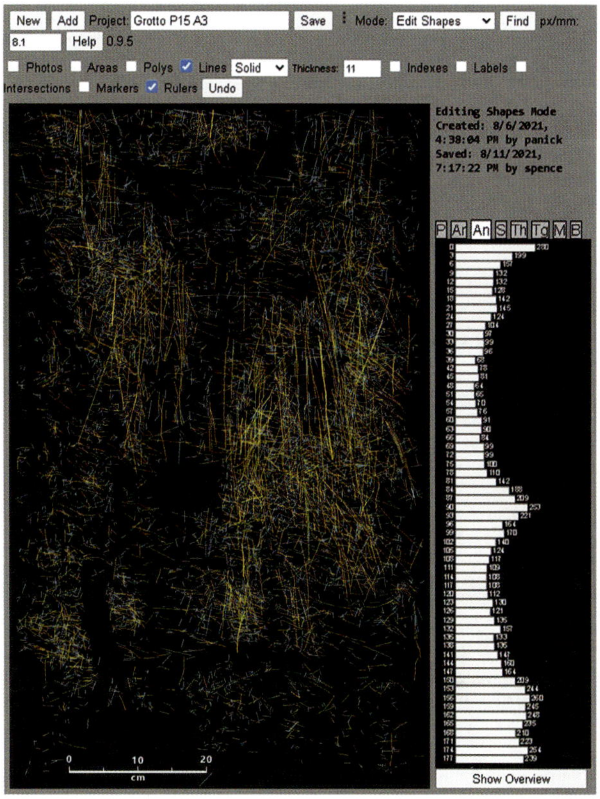

Figure 15. Screen capture showing the line segments recorded within area A3, Panel 15, at the Grotto. Histogram of line orientations on the right.

ent pigment and style decorate the wall to the right of the fracture, no incised lines could be detected in this region of the panel.

Where paint and lines do overlap within areas A1 and A3 on the left side of the fracture dividing Panel 15, it is nearly always evident that the paint is over the lines. Figure 16a shows several examples of incisions covered over by painted zigzags. In Figure 16b, a section of bounded cross-hatching resembling the snakes from Panel 27 at the Roasting Pit is clearly superimposed by presumably Archaic buff-white paint.

At first glance, a cluster of wide vertical grooves in the vicinity of the rake symbol appear to be cutting through the paint, which would be consistent with an interpretation of similar grooves elsewhere as "Verde incised," a style associated with protohistoric Apaches (Pilles 2014:17). However, closer inspection of the photos tells a more complicated story (Figure 17). Many of the deep grooves contain traces of buff-white paint, even though other sections of the same grooves show no trace of paint where they again intersect painted lines. To account for this discrepancy, we speculated that paint may have skipped over parts of the grooves or adhered poorly and flaked off. We asked a local artist who has experi-

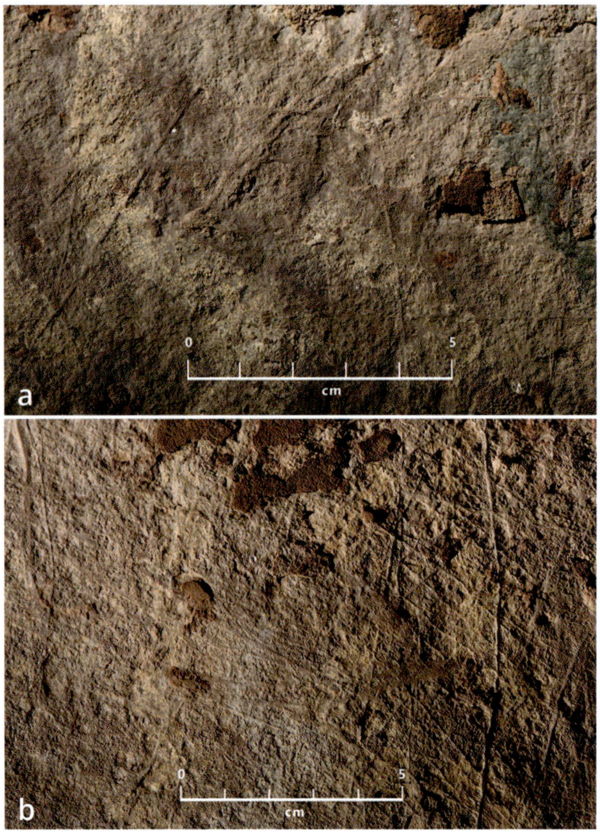

Figure 16. Examples of paint superimposed over incised lines in Panel 15 at the Grotto. (a) Detail from the top of area A1 showing buff-white and black zigzags transected by many faint lines. (b) Detail showing portion of the "snake" motif in area A3, with cross-hatching overlain by buff-white zigzags. Photos by Spence Gustav.

mented with pre- and protohistoric Native American pigments whether paint might be expected to skip over grooves in some cases, leaving the impression that the paint was instead cut by the groove later. She confirmed that viscous paint applied with a finger or brush could skip over deeper grooves, or just catch their edges, while completely covering over shallower incisions (Nori Thorne, personal communication 2021).

Further evidence that the wide grooves were cut prior to the application of paint comes from fine lines which can be seen impacting the grooves. Following along some of these fine lines, we come across sections that are clearly under paint. Since the grooves must have preceded these lines, we can deduce that the grooves must also have preceded the paint.

Experimentation

Unlike scratch marks produced by lightly abrading a surface with a hard object, the linear incisions at Palatki penetrate the surface, resulting in fine continuous

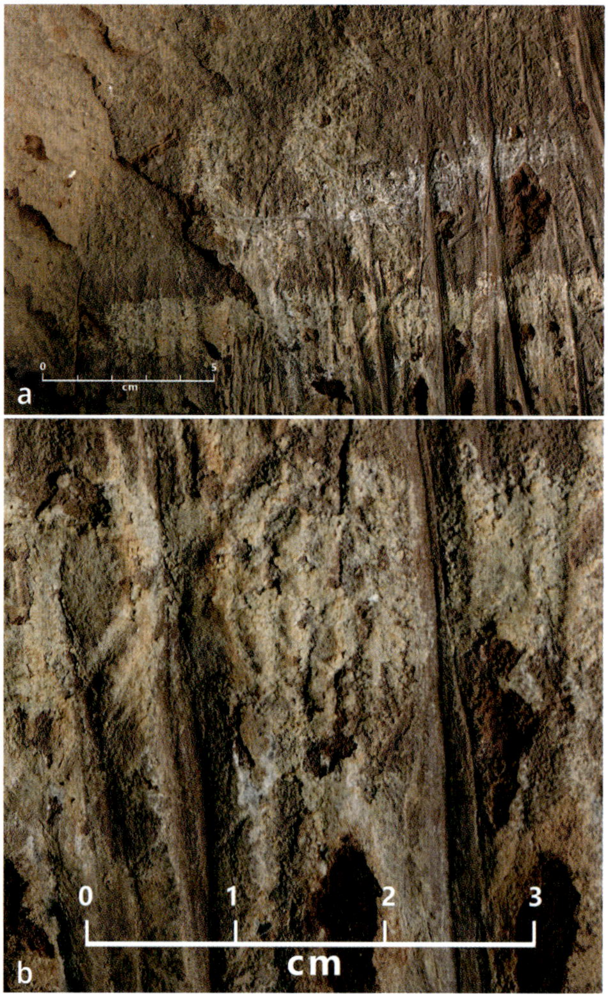

Figure 17. (a) Top of rake symbol in area A3, Panel 15, at the Grotto, showing wide grooves and fine lines superimposed by Archaic (buff-white) paint. (b) Detail showing fine vertical lines running within some grooves. Diagonal lines both cut and are cut by wide grooves. Photos by Spence Gustav.

lines and deeply abraded grooves. To simulate such incising on a fracture-fill surface, we experimented with a flattened layer of dried modeling clay. By pressing hard with the sharp edge of an obsidian flake, we could incise a shallow line roughly a millimeter in width. With less pressure, we could reduce the width slightly while sacrificing depth. Dampening the clay allowed for thinner and deeper cuts, although too much dampening allowed the clay to be distorted when one line crossed another.

Similar experimentation on very-fine- to fine-grained sandstone samples from the Palatki area using sharp chert and obsidian points resulted in lines that vary from 0.4 to 0.7 mm wide, with the variation in line width appearing to correlate with the grain size of the rock sample. Several samples were found that had an incomplete partial covering of fine clastic fracture fill (primarily silt-sized) and several siltstone to very-fine sandstone samples did result in incised lines that were in the range of 0.2 to 0.4 mm, as seen on the areas of interest in the study. The majority of tests on (horizontally positioned) sandstone samples did not appear to easily approximate the depth of incised lines seen in the areas of interest, even though strong pressure was placed on the sample when the tool was held in the hand. A further experiment was carried out with a very fine, modern, steel flat-bladed screwdriver. It was found that greater pressure could more easily be put on the test surface, with somewhat deeper lines being achieved.

Based on this experience, it seems likely that some parts of the cliff surface were more amenable to fine incising than others. Preferred areas would have been known and reused. It was also clear from our experiments that straight lines were much easier to incise than curves, which could explain, for purely practical reasons, why curved, incised figures rarely appeared. We also found it easier to apply pressure when making vertical lines than horizontal ones, which might account not only for the predominance of vertical lines but also for our observation that horizontal lines, on the whole, tended to be shallower and thus harder to see in our detail photos than vertical lines. Similar practical considerations might explain the prevalence of grids and cross-hatching within the densely incised regions. If the intent of the artist was to symbolically "cover" a section of cliff face, such designs might have been seen as the most effective way to achieve that goal.

A cursory survey of other panels along the cliff face showed that fracture fill was present at all panels where complex incising was observed, although many panels covered with fracture fill did not show evidence of such incising. We found little correlation between densely incised subpanels and the presence of pictographs. Complex incised drawings similar to those encountered in our study areas were noted within six additional panels (out of 17) at the Grotto and two additional panels (out of 36) at the Roasting Pit. Particularly well-preserved examples were found in the Water Catchment and Bear Alcove sites at Palatki. Complex designs tend to completely fill well-defined regions within a panel, terminating at natural features such as fractures, edges, and angle changes. Smaller isolated clusters of incised lines also occur on some panels. These often consist of small groups of vertical lines with occasional diagonals. They may have been produced by a different culture or for a different purpose, perhaps even by artists testing a panel's suitability for incising.

Discussion

When exploring the nooks and crannies of highly magnified photos on a computer screen, it is easy to forget that the thousands of line segments in the two panels we have been documenting occupy less than two square meters of surface area. The lines form a chaotic jumble when viewed en masse but, as we have noted, various subsets of lines appear to form patterns such as grids and cross-hatching when their features and relationships are examined closely, taking into account distances between lines and similarities/differences in line width, depth, weathering, and orientation. Simonis (1986) has proposed that what appear to be haphazard scratches at a site near Kingman, Arizona, are actually remnants of many superimposed grid-like designs. We suspect that the same is true of the areas we chose for this study.

When sandstone or fracture fill is freshly cut, the pulverized stone remaining in the incision is highly reflective, creating a bright mark that is easy to see. Over time, wind, water, and physical contact can remove the fine "rock flour," leaving behind an incision which is the color of the working surface and, therefore, much harder to see. The color contrast can be seen in Figure 18 which shows some recent graffiti carved over older incised lines at the Water Catchment site (AR-03-04-06-0286) in the Red Cliffs. How long it takes for the rock flour to dissipate is a matter of how exposed the panel is, but it is likely to be on the scale of years to hundreds of years, rather than the thousands that might be required to repatinate desert varnish. The relatively quick dulling of images might account in part for the repeated reuse of the same areas at Palatki. The resulting complexity of these reused panels suggests that art-

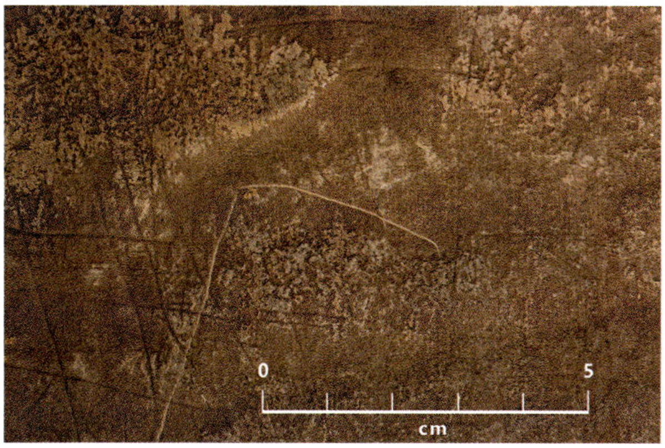

Figure 18. Example showing the color of recent graffiti vs. older incised lines at the Water Catchment site, between the Roasting Pit and the Grotto. Photo by Spence Gustav.

ists made a point of creating new lines and grids at different orientations, rather than simply re-carving the previous designs.

Within the complex panels, many of the lines are remarkably straight, requiring care taken by the artist. As exemplified by the snakes in Figure 11, cross-hatching may be composed of parallel lines just a few millimeters apart. Some lines start and end precisely on other lines. While precision varies from figure to figure, it is evident that these are not casual drawings. The density of lines at the very top of Panel 15 at the Grotto suggests that this section, like the area below, was worked on multiple times. The upper area, above the reach of someone standing at the base, would presumably have required some effort to access, a further testament to the significance of the engraving activity.

Regarding the antiquity of the incised imagery, our superimposition findings relative to presumably Archaic paint strengthen the case for an Archaic or older origin for the designs found in our study areas, and, by inference, for similar panels found elsewhere on the Red Cliffs. One explanation for the dearth of incisions cutting through paint is that the pictographs and incisions were products of different cultures who occupied the region at different times. Alternatively, the same culture may have practiced both styles but refrained from using panels for incising once they were painted on, for practical or religious reasons. We are aware of several instances on the Red Cliffs where incised lines do appear to cut through Sinagua paint, indicating that some incising was practiced here in the post-Archaic period, but these cases may be stylistically distinct.

Conclusions and Future Directions

The incised rock art at Red Cliffs represents a significant cultural manifestation that merits further investigation. While it shares some motifs with more recently dated scratched designs found throughout the western United States, our detection of superimposition by stylistically Archaic pictographs suggests that much of the fine-line engraving at Palatki is Archaic or older. Designs are overwhelmingly rectilinear; they exhibit care in execution and tend to fill all of the workable area within a subpanel. Similarities with a small but growing number of Southwest sites bearing complex geometric incisions suggest that our findings here may contribute to the understanding of a regional tradition of "Early Incised" parietal art that could date as far back as the Paleoindian period (Loendorf 2012; Malotki and Dissanayake 2018; Pilles 2014; Vance 2020).

This project, from the start, was considered a long-term, multifaceted effort that would progress from this initial study to more-detailed analyses of additional areas of interest in the Red Rock District of the Verde Valley. Multiple areas of interest with similar geological characteristics and comparable rock art panels have been identified at several sites located at and between Palatki and Honanki Heritage Sites. We are hopeful that some of these panels, with less weathering and less overlying paint than at our current study areas, will be more amenable to detailed interline superimposition analysis, giving us a better picture of how the complex incised panels evolved over time.

Our cursory comparison of panel areas as to surface material, distribution of pictographs and petroglyphs, and erosion components will be elevated to a more-detailed level for comparison and evaluation. Examples of incisions intersecting with painted figures will be sought out for eventual comparison of motifs and other characteristics which might serve to distinguish incised designs which appear above vs. below Archaic, Sinagua, and Yavapai paint.

Due to the belief that clastic fracture-fill layers may be a key component of the presence and nature of the fine lines, X-Ray Diffraction (XRD) of mineral components of the rock face would be desirable to determine and compare clay, carbonate, sulphate, and silicate components. This may help identify new locations where examples of incised art are likely to be found. As Lemke et al. (2015:113) have reported for early portable art, "an expectation to find such artifacts plays a key role in their identification and recovery." Our increased sensitivity to the possibility of faint incisions has already led to the discovery of new areas where incised art had not been previously noted.

Radiocarbon analysis of pictograph paint components would also be desirable to provide confirmation of age relationships which, except for two cases (Armitage et al. 2000), are currently based solely on style. Since sampling for C-14 dating is typically not an option at these protected sites, a potential alternative is to employ portable X-Ray Fluorescence (XRF) to identify comparative, nonorganic mineral components of the paint to test the hypothesis that comparable pictograph styles share comparable ingredients which vary across styles and cultures.

Acknowledgments. This project could not have been achieved without the abundant assistance of volunteers from the Sedona Friends of the Forest and the United

States Forest Service Coconino Forest staff.

Peter Pilles (Coconino Forest Archaeologist), Dr. Anne Dowd (Coconino Forest Red Rock District Archaeologist), and Bruce Carlson (Coconino Forest Red Rock District Heritage Site Manager) were instrumental in providing information and access to the site during the Covid pandemic shutdown and allowing work to continue during periods when the site was open to the public.

Forest Service Site Resident Host volunteers Barbara Kennedy, Thomas Iraci, and Carol Davis provided numerous hours of support for the project on site during their "off duty" days.

Professor Kennard Bork provided confirmation and additional interpretation of the nature of the cliff face rock surface and fracture-fill issues, plus the identification of the iron-enriched zone described. Alan Cornell provided various examples of prehistoric style stone tools and methods of their employment to potentially create the incised lines studied.

Nori Thorne provided insight and examples of pictograph and petroglyph methods to assist in the interpretation of how such methods might be identified in the archaeological record.

Dr. Bonnie Gustav-Golub provided information and input as to archaeological and anthropological concepts, methods, and practices.

The following Sedona Friends of the Forest volunteers were instrumental in doing much of the data acquisition and interpretation for this study:

Cultural Heritage Photo Documentation Team volunteers: Jon Petrescu, Terri Petrescu, Ed Hodges, Brian Painchaud, Marilyn Painchaud, Vicky Garrard, Tim Anderson, Michelle Prostrollo, Peg Kern, David Irvine, Robert Elliott, and Kerri Simonian spent many hours acquiring photo coverage of the various areas of study.

Cultural Heritage volunteers Jennifer Young, Annie Glickstein, Rosalie O'Donnell, April Heinrich, and Kerri Simonian put in many hours of computer-based line interpretation via the Fine Line Analyzer software described in the article. Tony Hendey and Wendell Waybright provided onsite analysis of superimposed incised lines and paint as control and confirmation of the software and photo imagery interpretation.

References Cited

Armitage, Ruth Ann, Marian Hyman, Marvin W. Rowe, Lawrence L. Loendorf, and John R. Southon
2000 Dated Rock Paintings at Red Cliffs, Arizona. *Kiva* 65(3):253–266.

Gilreath, Amy J., and William R. Hildebrandt
2008 Coso Rock Art Within Its Archaeological Context. *Journal of California and Great Basin Anthropology* 28(1):1–22.

Hambelton, Karla Lucille
2011 *Scratched Petroglyphs in the Bennett Hills, Idaho.* Ph.D. Dissertation, Portland State University.

Harman, Jon
2008 *Using Decorrelation Stretch to Enhance Rock Art Images.* Electronic document, https://dstretch.com/AlgorithmDescription.html, accessed August 12, 2021.

Heizer, Robert F., and Martin A. Baumhoff
1962 *Prehistoric Rock Art of Nevada and Eastern California.* University of California Press, Berkeley.

Lemke, Ashley K., Daniel C. Wernicke, and Michael B. Collins
2015 Early Art in North America: Clovis and Later Paleoindian Incised Artifacts from the Gault Site, Texas. *American Antiquity* 80(1):113–133.

Loendorf, Lawrence L.
1994 *Rock Art at Red Cliffs.* Report #43-8167-3-0501 prepared for USDA Forest Service, Coconino National Forest.
2012 Old Petroglyphs on the North American High Plains. In *L'art pléistocène dans le monde / Pleistocene art of the world / Arte pleistoceno en el mundo,* edited by Jean Clottes, pp. 607–619. Actes du Congrès IFRAO 2010, Tarascon-sur-Ariège, France.

Malotki, Ekkehart, and Ellen Dissanayake
2018 *Early Rock Art of the American West: The Geometric Enigma.* University of Washington Press, Seattle.

Nelson, Ronald
2001 *Geologic Analysis of Naturally Fractured Reservoirs.* 2nd Edition. Gulf Professional Publishing, Houston.

Pilles Jr., Peter J.
1994 Rock Art of the Red Rock Canyons, Sedona, Arizona. Paper presented at the 1994 International Rock Art Congress, Flagstaff, Arizona.
2014 Ancient Rock Art of the Verde Valley. *Archaeology Southwest Magazine* 28(2):15–17.

Reed, Rebekah M.
2012 Scratched Rock Art at Little Lake Ranch. In *Rock Art at Little Lake: An Ancient Crossroads in the California Desert,* edited by Jo Anne Van Tilburg, Gordon E. Hull, and John C. Bretney, pp. 106–117. Cotsen Institute of Archaeology, University of California, Los Angeles.

Ritter, Eric W.
1994 Scratched Rock Art Complexes in the Desert West: Symbols for Socio-Religious Communication. In *New Light on Old Art: Recent Advances in Hunter Gatherer Rock Art Research,* edited by David S. Whitley, and Lawrence L. Loendorf, pp. 51–66. Institute of Archaeology Monograph 36. University of California, Los Angeles.

Schaafsma, Polly
1980 *Indian Rock Art of the Southwest.* School of American Research, Santa Fe, and Museum of New Mexico Press, Albuquerque.

Simonis, Don
1986 Scratched Style Petroglyphs near Kingman, Arizona. Paper presented at the Thirteenth Annual American Rock Art Research Association Symposium, Flagstaff, Arizona.

Spurr, Kimberly, and Stewart Deats
2015 A Summary of Prehistoric Mortuary Patterns in the Middle Verde Valley of Arizona. *Journal of Arizona Archaeology* 3(1 and 2):22–42.

Vance, Meghann M.
2020 *Pleistocene Rock Art? Early Incised on the Tonto National Forest, Payson District, Arizona.* Poster presented at the Southwest Symposium, Tempe, Arizona. Electronic document, https://www.academia.edu/41887202/The_Payson_Panel, accessed August 12, 2021.

Wernecke, D. Clark, and Michael B. Collins
2012 Patterns and Process: Some Thoughts on the Incised Stones from the Gault Site, Central Texas, United States. In *L'art pléistocène dans le monde / Pleistocene art of the world / Arte pleistoceno en el mundo,* edited by Jean Clottes, pp. 669–681. Actes du Congrès IFRAO 2010, Tarascon-sur-Ariège, France.

Mesoamerica, Macaws, and More: Exploring the Geospatial Relationships and Cultural Significance of Parrot, Raptor, and Related Bird Iconography at Mesa Prieta, New Mexico

Chester R. Liwosz

As early as the Pueblo II Period (900 to 1150 C.E.), high-value trade goods in archaeological contexts demonstrate strong social ties between the American Southwest and Mesoamerica. While early scholarship explained these connections through political economy, the last quarter century of research has turned toward ideological connections such as Jane Hill's concept of the Flower World Complex exemplified in Turner and Mathiowetz's (2021) recent volume. Cosmological concepts such as the Flower World directly inform our approaches to iconography of Puebloan pottery, murals, and of course rock art. Macaws embody these inter-regional socioeconomic ties and the Flower World's colorful religious symbolism. "Knifewing" motifs also manifest Mesoamerican mythology. This report explores the landscape contexts of Northern Rio Grande Classic Period (1300 to 1598 C.E.) parrot/macaw petroglyphs and related motifs at one of North America's most prolific rock art landmarks—Mesa Prieta, New Mexico—to elucidate new insights into the birds' enduring significance through centuries of dramatic social change. As the scholarly successor to a virtual reality (VR) tours project, this parrots paper utilizes those 3D and VR representations to contextualize petroglyph panels and the surrounding landscape. Featured loci (sensu lato) provide a colorful backdrop familiar to die-hard fans of Schaafsma, Slifer, and Fowles.

Chester R. Liwosz
Mesa Prieta Petroglyph Project,
Velarde, New Mexico

Macaws (*Ara* sp., especially *Ara macao*) served important social and religious roles in Pueblo life and, in fact, across the greater region of the U.S. Southwest and Northwest Mexico (alternatively "Southwest/Northwest") since at least 700 C.E. and continuing into contemporary Pueblo culture today (Crown 2016:331). While the earliest evidence of macaws in the Southwest/Northwest dates to a Hohokam site between 600 and 700 C.E. (Mathiowetz 2021:180), Ancestral Pueblos appear not to have imported these birds until 900–975 C.E. (George et al. 2018). In the following I will use the words "parrot" and "macaw" interchangeably; however, they are not entirely synonymous. Multiple species of parrots have been identified in zooarchaeological and iconographic contexts in the Southwest/Northwest, largely dominated by the genus *Ara* and in particular the scarlet macaw *Ara macao* (George et al. 2018; Schwartz 2020, Schwartz et al. 2021, 2022) but also including the military macaw (*Ara militaris*) and thick-billed parrot (*Rhynchopsitta pachyrhyncha*) (Crown 2016; Crown and Lyons 2021; Weiner 2015).

Study Locations

Mesa Prieta and its smaller twin, La Mesita, are literally cut from the same rock, both formed from a low-viscosity basaltic lava flow originating near present-day Pilar, New Mexico, and the subsequent erosional cutting of the

American Indian Rock Art, Volume 48. Amy Gilreath, Ken Hedges, and Anne McConnell, Editors. American Rock Art Research Association, 2022, pp. 99–112.

This study addresses colonized lands within the traditional territory of Tewa-speaking pueblos, and on the margins of Northern Tiwa farmland. Specifically, the colonial toponyms "Mesa Prieta" and "Black Mesa" refer to a place and landform traditionally called *Tsįkwajè*. As an effort to recognize and address the impacts of colonization on indigenous communities, this study integrates information from ethnography, consultation, and indigenous-authored primary accounts. I and the Mesa Prieta Petroglyph Project recognize the vitality of living indigenous cultures whose cultural heritage we study, including Tewa, Northern Tiwa, Jicarilla Apache, and Comanche.

Rio Grande, Rio Chama, and Rio Ojo Caliente. Sometime in the Middle Pleistocene, possibly after 440,000 B.P., movement along the Embudo Fault System (a part of the Rio Grande Rift Zone) fractured this basaltic capstone and its underlying strata, inducing a roughly 10-kilometer-long westward meander in the course of the Rio Grande that cut off La Mesita from Mesa Prieta (see Grauch et al. 2017). Subsequent river-driven erosion of unconsolidated Miocene and Pliocene sediments underlying the basalt capstone has produced an extensive series of relatively large "Toreva-block" benches (per Reiche 1937) along Mesa Prieta's eastern escarpment (Kendall 2020), and to a lesser extent parts of La Mesita's escarpments. Toreva benches host numerous archaeological activity areas, as well as the stratigraphic arrangement exposing petroglyph-friendly patinated basalt. At present, the basalt-capped mesa encompasses an area of roughly 32,000 acres (50 square miles), including the spans of the two curving escarpments that give it a "canoe" shape when seen from above.

Archaeological recovery of fluted points (e.g., Futch 1999:2.1) and other components of the Paleoindian toolkit indicate initial human occupation of the mesa and its immediate surroundings began during the earliest peopling of the American Southwest (Liwosz 2021). Petroglyphs, artifacts, and trail features indicate continuous occupation by diffuse nomadic populations throughout the Archaic (MacKenzie and Borduin 2019), as well as Post's (2002) facetiously named "Latest Archaic" of the Ancestral Pueblo Developmental (600 to 1100 C.E.) and Coalition (1100 to 1300 C.E.) periods (Fowles 2018; Steen 1983:169; cf. Schaasfma 1980:18-19, 160 for stylistically related motifs). This report, however, focuses exclusively on a narrow suite of iconography related to cultural practices believed to have been introduced, at least in part, to the area when Tewa ancestors migrated into the Chama and soon thereafter Española basins from the Galisteo Basin and Colorado Plateau, an event which marks the onset of the Pueblo Classic Period (1300 to 1598 C.E.) for the Northern Rio Grande (Duwe 2019; Naranjo 2006; Ortiz 1969; Ortman and Davis 2019; Steen 1983:169-170).

During the Classic Period, several pueblos dotted the landscape around the foot of Mesa Prieta. It appears that the earlier of these were founded along the Rio Chama and its tributary Rio Ojo Caliente (Ortman and Davis 2019), with Ancestral Tewa settlement of the Rio Grande beginning a few decades later. Pueblos (both Tewa and possibly Northern Tiwa) from Late Precontact through modern times known to be associated with Mesa Prieta include Kuu, Posi Owingeh, Sæ Shu Oŋwįkeji, Ponsipa-akeri, Te'ewi, and Tunuypa, with Ohkay Owingeh (also known as San Juan from the eighteenth through twentieth centuries) and Santa Clara the closest still occupied (Camilli et al. 2019; Harrington 1916:156, 170, 224). Rather than isolated middle-range polities, these pueblos represented a somewhat diverse range of multi-settlement community structures and mutual alliances (Cruz and Ortman 2019).

Petroglyph recording in the area of Mesa Prieta began sporadically as a part of regional and interregional studies. Schaafsma (1980:Figure 199), for example, includes among many illustrated design motifs the so-called "monsoon panel" (discussed below) from Mesa Prieta, and Figures 167, 168, and 169 in her 1992 overview of New Mexico provide examples of petroglyphs near Velarde, New Mexico. Slifer and Duffield (1994) include a color plate and several other figures of flute player variants from the Mesa Prieta vicinity, and Slifer (2000) also features five figures (21a, 44t, 92, 122a, and 220) and a plate (11) of petroglyphs in the Mesa Prieta area. Systematic recording of the petroglyphs at Mesa Prieta, though, began in 1993 and 1994 when Helen and Jay Crotty, at the behest of Katherine Wells, started working on a 188-acre parcel that became The Archaeological Conservancy's (TAC) Wells Petroglyph Preserve (Wells et al. 2008). Founded under the name Vecinos del Rio in 1999, the Mesa Prieta Petroglyph Project (MPPP, or MP3) is a community-based, volunteer-driven effort inspired by the 1993 through 1994 field school, and its members continue to record the cultural heritage (also including archaeological artifacts and features) of the mesa. Although MP3 has since expanded its service area to include about 18,000 acres of public and private lands, fully half of the study loci described in the next section are within this initial 188-acre unit now known as the Wells Petroglyph Preserve.

Featured Content

This report represents a humanities-focused study of the presence of macaw imagery within the MP3's service area, focusing on loci *sensu lato* recorded mostly by volunteers and student interns, and largely between 2004 and 2021. Most of the examples provided here initially became the focus of a virtual reality (VR) tours project begun in 2020 in response to MP3's need to maintain public engagement while abiding by public health and safety restrictions during the Covid-19 pandemic. As such, this paper is effectively a scholarly complement to a less-verbose "Macaws/Parrots" VR tour that is currently publicly available on a web-based platform (see Acknowledgments).

I selected study loci (not to be confused with the Archaeological Society of New Mexico Rock Art Council's [ASNM RAC] use of the term) from MP3's over 60,000 petroglyph records using simple SQL query statements to search a database of approximately 25,000 elements across 7,000 panels. The ASNM RAC's classification (Berrier 2018) for parrot motifs, 5j, is also inclusive of raptor images, so those too are included in the results. For a small number of featured category 5j petroglyphs, their host panels have been recorded but are not yet digitized into the geodatabase, requiring prior knowledge of the location on the mesa to locate the record. Aware that not all parrot images may have been recognized as such at the time of initial recording, I incorporated categories 5h ("unidentified bird") and 10z ("thunderbird/knifewing") in the query statements. Turkey images and bird tracks were excluded. With raptors encompassed by 5j, and the role of eagles and Eagle Dancers analogous to the Great Plains Thunderbird (Kurath and Garcia 1970:219), including 10z with 5j is a natural step. While it seems odd to lump the knifewing motif with the distinctly different raptor variants that bridge category 5j with 10z, knifewings, too, take on a non-trivial role in the discussion that follows.

It bears mentioning that while ASNM RAC uses "locus" as loosely synonymous with "panel," I distinguish within this text between "loci" as small, bounded areas that contain one or more panels of interest regardless of the actual boulder count, and "panel" for the rock face with the petroglyphs in question. From the combined results of the SQL query and knowledge of undigitized records, I defined six study loci on which to focus, five of which I introduce in brief below.

The first study locus, survey and recording designation 001_20Z01_A, is a single large boulder bearing 20 petroglyph panels and approximately 100 cupules (Figure 1). This exceptional stand-alone location includes a prominent 5j image with outstretched wings and a triangular, forward-facing body with its head rendered in profile. Other nearby bird imagery is on private property that is excluded from the study at hand. Study locus 001_20Z01_A is located low on the slope near the Rio Grande, just above the transition from bosque to scrubland vegetation communities. As a note for later consideration, prior to the American Period channelization of this section of the Rio Grande, the Rio and the bosque together formed a broad corridor of braided channels and floodplain wetlands—in short, ideal farmland.

The second study locus straddles MP3's survey blocks 012 and 015 (complicating the naming regimen) on the Wells Petroglyph Preserve. Located in one of the densest concentrations of petroglyphs on the mesa, this location is a 200 m long by 100 m wide ellipse that encompasses three category 5j images, six category 10z, and at least a dozen 5h. Based on observations made for this study in the spring of 2021,

Figure 1. The aptly named "cupule rock," with artificially brightened 5j raptor motif (inset). Note the inverted-triangle-shaped body, distinguishing this raptor from parrot renderings.

several of these records will be updated to match what is reported here. Like the previous area, this too is located low on the mesa.

The next three loci are in relatively close proximity to each other but worth considering independently. Panel 001_07B01_J (Figure 2) contains a 5j image adjacent to two other birds (one typical of a turkey) among other images. Nearby, a tight clustering of panels deserves recognition as its own locus, "ABC" (for panels A, B, C1, and C2). The ABC cluster (Figures 3a–e) features three related variations on the parrot/macaw motif and includes another well-known panel that will be discussed later as a component of its context. Also nearby, Panel 001-_07Z03_V sports a "cloudblower" accompanied by a 5j parrot (Figure 4a). While recorded as the same category as flute players (4j if anthropomorphic), cloudblowers also encapsulate cloud-making actions such as smoking tobacco (Harrington 1916:53), and iconographically pipe smoke and "flute breath" can be difficult to distinguish from each other.

Figure 2. "Mounted macaw" panel, aka the "parrot-on-a-stick" (far right).

Figure 3. (a) Detail of Panel A macaws in naturalistic (left) and abstracted (right) styles. (b) Wide view of Panel A showing spaced but extensive ritual pecking. (c) Two views of the 3D model of the overall cluster, showing relationships of the panels and boulders from the front (left), and a tilted view (right) with all three panels visible. (d) Detail of Panel B, animal flute player, equinox marker, and suspected constellation. (e) Detail of Panel C, macaw mirroring the forms of the macaws in Panel A.

In 2011, the late BLM archaeologist Paul Williams headed up the MP3 Summer Youth Intern Program (SYIP) to systematically document the 269 recorded petroglyph panels at site LA 78951, aka the "Dancing Buffalo Site." Nine of these panels are reported to contain images categorized as parrots, raptors, thunderbirds, knifewings, and/or unidentified birds, including examples shared in some of the figures below. The myriad of iconographic variability here combined with its liminal position at literal crossroads has attracted other researchers including Fowles (2021), whose research complements the many stories to be told of this location.

Discussion

Iconographic Use of Feathers

The classification of motifs as macaws or other parrots is predicated not upon a uniform design but upon certain cues within the execution of the bird. The middle-range theory used to define these cues is derived in part from decorated pottery sherds and painted kiva murals (e.g., Crotty 1992, 1995, 2007; Patterson 1992:152;

Figure 4. Variations on bird images, with other frequently associated motifs and attributes. (a) Example showing a 5j parrot with a flute player/cloud blower motif. (b, c) Similar images of raked-wing birds recorded variously as (b) 5j parrot/raptor and (c) 10z thunderbird/knifewing. Note the flute player (b) and the associations of a cupule infixed in a grinding surface on the upward-facing panel (c).

Smith 1952:185). While still debated, these theoretical identifications are foundational to the petroglyph recording process and their scholarly origins are beyond the scope of this paper. Most commonly parrots are distinguished from raptors with the former being rendered in profile and the latter with a front-facing body and only the head in profile, however there are exceptions for both. Notably parrot beaks are portrayed with a characteristic curved or hooked end, although this alone is not a surefire tell. Perhaps one of the most telling features of a parrot image would be long, extensive tail features.

In my first set of examples, the tail feathers appear to be emphasized. Atypically, a presumed parrot image in the second study locus (Figure 5a) is depicted with the body front-on and wings spread. It is unlikely that a macaws' wings would have been kept clipped, and

Figure 5. (a) Parrot in flight, one of several 5j images in the 012/015 location. (b) Elaborate parrot with patterns indicating chromaticism; knifewing at top of panel.

because of how strongly they bond with their keepers, the practice would be largely unnecessary (Schwartz 2020:48). Instead, it is believed they would be allowed to accompany their keepers, delivering a visible and audible presence (Crown and Lyons 2021; Schwartz et al. 2022). In other instances (see Figure 2), the apparent extension of the tail feathers qualifies the image as a variant of the motif casually known as "parrot-on-a-stick." The viewer's initial inclination may be to interpret the image as a stuffed or taxidermied bird mounted onto a stick, staff, or scepter. While some pueblos are historically known to have used stuffed birds in religious contexts including but not limited to mounting on prayer sticks (Crown 2016:336), this was not universally the case (Schwartz 2020:5–6). Zooarchaeological evidence of processing marks on macaw bones from Pueblo Bonito in Chaco Canyon show no indications of processing birds for taxidermy during the Pueblo I and Pueblo II Periods (Bishop 2021; Bishop and Fladd 2018). This forces an alternative consideration that the "parrot-on-a-stick" motif could be an iconographic shorthand for the use of only macaw *feathers* on a prayer stick.

Other iconographic treatments of parrot feathers cleverly use different marking/infill patterns to indicate areas of varying color, as in Figure 5b. This example interestingly communicates macaw chromaticism even in the inherently monochromatic medium of petroglyph pecking, distinguishing the colors of the primary feathers, neck, and body from the densely infilled pecking that makes the tail feathers prominent. The earlier mentioned use of feathers on prayer sticks was likely largely for ideological chromatic associations, as opposed to a direct invocation of a particular bird species (Smith 1952:189–193). Nonetheless, macaws conveyed certain religious connotations—a topic I will return to later after laying the socioeconomic frameworks within which these associations evolved and operated.

Macaws in the Southwest: Exchange and Breeding Colonies

Not all macaw images—such as the example in Figure 6—sport impressive tail feathers. Images without extended tail feathers may be plucked birds, or the lack of tail feathers might indicate nestling or juvenile age stages, but these ages are not represented in the archaeological record (Hargrave 1970:53, Table 10). Watson et al. (2015:8239) use the term "juvenile" in a generic way to include Hargrave's immature, newfledged, and adolescent stages, all of which exhibit tail feathers (Schwartz 2020:52) and collectively make up the majority of recovered remains in the zooarchaeological record.

Figure 6. Image recorded as a 5j parrot, possibly a juvenile macaw.

Aside from the aforementioned very small number of earlier macaw remains recovered from Hohokam settlements, the earliest clear evidence of a sustained presence of macaws in the Southwest occurs around the turn of the tenth century C.E. (George et al. 2018). This largely corresponds with an intensification of socioeconomic connections between the Southwest and Mesoamerica around 850 to 900 C.E., as evidenced by prestige goods such as cacao, copper bells, and, of course, macaws, as well as shared iconographic influences (Mathiowetz 2021). Macaw imports by Chaco and other Ancestral Pueblo polities appear to be commensal to the vibrant chromaticism of Jane Hill's (1992) Flower World Complex of religious expression (Hays-Gilpin and Hill 1999; Weiner 2015). Chaco also maintained trade in high-value goods with other regions such as the Gulf of California or the Pacific coast (e.g., Mathien 1984); while Mathien does not expressly mention California's Channel Coast and Islands, it would be prudent to consider this culturally and economically influential region as a potential source of shell as well. It is important to dispel the antiquated notion that polities such as Chaco Canyon and its "outliers" Aztec and Salmon Ruins were outposts or colonies of Mesoamerican societies. Instead, prestige goods from distant regions accrued new local meanings, and during the Pueblo I and II periods are believed to have reinforced status and social inequality (Watson et al. 2015).

Discounting precontact colonization, the next most tempting explanation for the sake of simplicity is down-the-line trade (Mathien 2005:121, 271), perhaps in exchange for turquoise, hides, or other goods (Roediger 1941:71). This model proposes that macaws moved along the same networks as copper bells and cacao, the latter of which shares remarkable overlap in natural habitat. Recent studies, however, refute this model. In captive settings young macaws must be separated from the nest around the age of seven weeks, yet they are notoriously difficult to raise and temperamental before training (Crown 2016:333). The taming process also involves preventing them from finding a mate, leading to them bonding with their keepers; this makes exchanging juvenile macaws exceedingly difficult (and adults nearly prohibitive), and requires keepers with specialized knowledge (McKusick 2001; Watson et al. 2015). As an alternative, recent evidence (Schwartz et al. 2021; Somerville et al. 2010; Watson et al. 2015) suggests that some of Chaco's macaws may have come from intermediaries such as the breeding colony at Paquimé proposed by Minnis and others (1993); however, the picture is more complicated. At least some of the nonlocal macaws from Chaco began their lives as far away as southern Mexico, as indicated by strontium isotope analysis (Schwartz et al. 2021), implying the possibility of direct trade for some specimens along many possible routes (Whalen 2022:230-232).

Birdkeeping and Gender Roles

Intermediary breeding colonies, while answering some questions, do not resolve the sourcing of macaws with strontium isotope signatures characteristic of southern Mexico (Oaxaca, Chiapas, Yucatán). Furthermore, the Casas Grandes and Classic Mimbres trade networks declined with their atrophying population centers prior to Euroamerican contact. Yet, ethnographic and historical reports (e.g., Crown 2016; Harrington 1916:43, 224; Schroeder 1968:95) indicate their presence in Pueblo society persisted well into Postcontact times, potentially even the present day. With intermediaries unlikely in the Late Precontact times of the Rio Grande Classic Period, and the dramatic shift from ranked societies of Pueblo I and II to the effectively egalitarian societies of extant and Classic Period Pueblos, any exchange system predicated upon the personal/familial acquisition of prestige goods is unsuited for describing Northern Rio Grande parrot keeping. In light of these dramatic shifts in Puebloan socioeconomic structures (and those of their cultural neighbors) the persistent importance of parrots is a testament to their innate symbolic and ideological value.

The first matter to be reconciled is that of the exchange system. Small local breeding populations throughout the Southwest/Northwest may have endured, but not on the scale previously seen at Paquimé (the success of which is debated and undermined by aforementioned isotopic evidence). Nonetheless, throughout this transition into the ever-ill-defined "ethnographic present," parrots retained their association with the sun, the south, and the summer monsoons (Crown 2016; Smith 1952:173, 180, 189). In the next section I will elaborate on the religious significance of this association, but under the current concern it demonstrates that into Classic Pueblo and the ongoing "Pueblo V" of today, macaws are not just sources of colorful feathers but the embodiment of the qualities of their native range. Without strong intermediaries this symbolism lends evidence to the notion of direct trade in which Pueblo persons trained in parrot husbandry undertook a periodic pilgrimage to acquire and return with live birds. This pilgrimage to Mexico for macaws has been attested to by Tewa persons (Roediger 1941:71). Given the knowledge necessary to keep and raise non-native birds that can live up to five decades in a climate likely to kill them during winter months, it is no accident that many Rio Grande Pueblos have, or are suspected to have had, some derivation of a parrot clan (Schroeder 1968:109–110).

As Rogers (2007) argues, addressing gender is requisite in petroglyph studies, and must not be done uncritically. To that end it is important to answer exactly who is undertaking these journeys to acquire birds, and who is responsible for their care. In all likelihood, given the evidence against down-the-line trade presented above, the person making the journey and the person responsible for caring for the bird were often one and the same. Creel and McKusick (1994:520) infer from pottery depictions and mortuary associations that women were responsible for keeping macaws and other parrots, playing active roles in ceremonies involving them as well. Women, therefore, not only provided care for the birds on behalf of their clan or community, but also at least some of these women are likely to have made the journey to Mesoamerica to trade for them. This contrasts with turkey husbandry, which was typically the domain of men (Dolan 2021).

By contrast to the situation with macaws, the acquisition of raptor feathers was a relatively more local affair. Although until now I have largely ignored the raptor component of this study, this is an appropriate point to reintroduce the matter to lay groundwork for the next sections. Both the Tewa and Northern Tiwa Pueblos were known to keep raptors, mostly eagles and hawks, in cages or pens (Schroeder 1968:109). At Ohkay Owingeh, Schroeder (1968:110) notes, "Eagles were plentiful in the mountains so they did not keep any in cages" (cf. Harrington 1916:43, 205). This does not mean getting the feathers was easy, yet they are ubiquitous in the ethnographic record (e.g., Colton 1949; Kurath and Garcia 1970; Roediger 1941) and the iconographic record (Figures 4b, c). Eagle feathers were gathered from the wild from Mesa Prieta (one of the "mountains" referred to above) by Tewa of Ohkay Owingeh, Santa Clara, and likely other area settlements such as the presently depopulated nearby pueblos of Phioge and Sae Shu. This was achieved through the use of eagle trap features (Figures 7a, b) (Harrington 1916:205). These are often located on very steep slopes or bluffs, using the terrain and a stacked stone wall or excavated cavity to create an enclosed hide for a person, much like those reported in other parts of the western United States by Murray and team (2009:70–75). Covered with brush, these structures shrouded a person from view while they held bait through the roof, waiting for the eagle to strike so they could grab its legs and pluck feathers. Needless to say, this task comes with some risk of lacerations. While I am not aware of direct reports for this immediate area of exactly whose task this was, anecdotal reports indicate this was predominantly a pursuit of young men.

Figure 7. (a, b) Probable eagle trap features on Mesa Prieta located in close proximity, in an area that also includes several bird motifs. (c, d) Bird images near the locations of Figures 4a and 4b.

Rain and Religion (Macaws and Monsoons)

It seems that regardless of time period, the association of macaws with the south and its climate endured among the Pueblos (Schaafsma 2022:241). Emblematic of the sun and the tropical track it takes across the sky year-round in its homeland further south, and in the summers of the Southwest/Northwest (Crown 2016; Smith 1952; Tyler 1991:13), macaws balance against their diametrically opposed raptor cousins—hawks and especially eagles. For the Tewa pueblos, "The Eagle, *tse,* associated with the northern zenith, is mimed in a famous dance..." Kurath and Garcia (1970:19), while Roediger (1941:71) also reports that eagles are always associated with the zenith. As far as seasonal associations, while macaws may struggle outdoors in New Mexico winters, I have personally witnessed bald eagles *(Haliaeetus leucocephalus)* active in the immediate area around the time of the winter solstice. This is reminiscent of an account in which Santa Clara hosted an Eagle Dance on Christmas Day 1927 (Kurath and Garcia 1970:221). Summarily category 5j birds are a complementary cohort in directionality and seasonality. Together, macaws and eagles invoke rain. When buried in newly sown fields, feathers from macaws, eagles, and hawks reinforced agricultural success (Creel and McKusick 1994:521; Roediger 1941:70–71).

Summer brings with it the monsoon season, during which the colorful coats of scarlet macaws invoke rainbows such as those so often following afternoon thundershowers (Crown 2016; Schaafsma 2022:241). Rainbow symbolism is an association for macaws shared by Pueblos and Mesoamerica. Nahuatl speakers connect rainbows, flowers, and macaws with the deity Xochipilli (Crown 2016:334; Hays-Gilpin and Hill 1999). The shared Flower World Complex to which these images belong goes beyond chromaticism to include aspects of masculinity, including warfare. Knifewing, a bird said to accompany warriors onto the battlefield and to scalp enemies (e.g. Schaafsma 2000:127, 143), is perhaps included in the 10z category not only as a "mythical bird" but also because it is easily confused with Thunderbird by the lay person (Marchaza 2007). Both the Pueblos and many Mesoamerican cultures understand knifewing as emblematic of military action and conflict (Gilman et al. 2014:101; Schaafsma 2007), the conjunction of knifewings and parrots on the same panels (e.g., Figures 5b and 9) reinforces socioeconomic and ideological connections between these disparate regions.

Coming from the south, the direction where summerlike sun is constant and rain is frequent, macaws not only follow the south-to-north track of the Southwest/Northwest summer monsoons but assume a causal role for this motion in Pueblo cosmology. Recent indigenous consultants at Mesa Prieta identified macaw feathers among the adornments of masked figures (e.g., Figure 8a) whose headwear strongly resembles that of renderings of ASNM RAC Design Element Inventory (DEI) category 10x, cloud terrace beings (Figure 8b), the latter of which is recognizable by its stepped/terraced body (Berrier 2018; Harrington 1916:56; Seltzer 2017:60). These and category 9f cloud terrace motifs (Figure 8c), while together not the most common images overall, exhibit a strong affinity for locations that have nearby panels with 5j parrots like the small and roughly pecked image that depicts a probable parrot (Figure 8d), or share the same panel with them (Figure 9).

In public ceremonialism, the presence of macaws and raptors was manifested in the use of their feathers, possibly stuffed birds, and other ritual implements derived from their parts. Macaw feathers have been associated with particular katsinas and are integral symbolic components of certain types of prayer sticks, dance poles, and wands, as well as regalia including masks and tablitas (Crown 2016:336; Schaafsma 2022:247; Smith 1952:130–131). Much the same can be said about eagles and their feathers (Kurath and Garcia 1970:20, 264; Roediger 1941:162, 164, 167-169, 174); however, as previously mentioned the specific associations are complementary and at times occupy opposing positions in certain dualities (cf. Ortiz 1969).

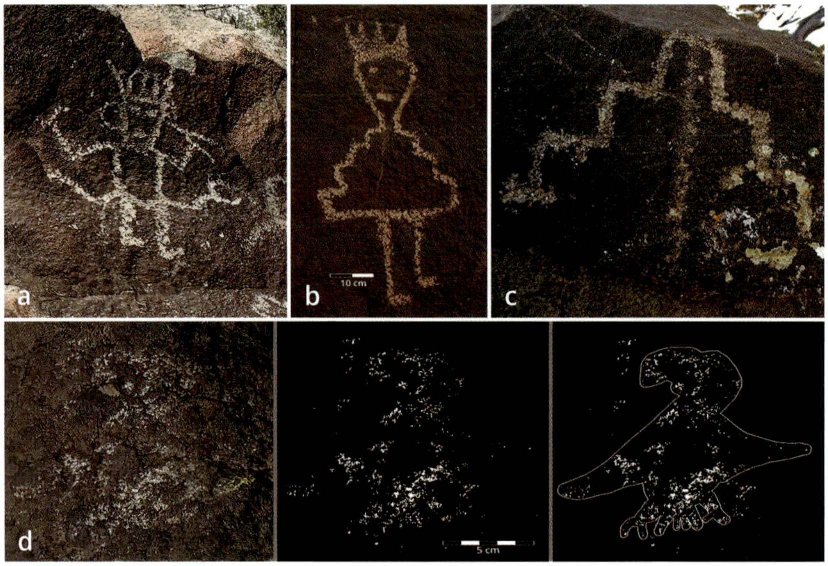

Figure 8. (a) Masked figure described by Tewa consultants as having macaw feathers; note the two-horned serpent, associated with flowing watercourses. (b) Cloud terrace being with mask/regalia similar to (a). (c) Cloud terrace motif next to (d). (d) Small glyph identified by the author as a probable 5j parrot motif near (c), shown with graphic rendering and suggested bird outline.

Macaws may have overflown feasts and other such events; however, they were not always let free. Depositional evidence of juveniles corroborates reports such as by Harrington (1916:224) who, when describing the social significance of *Tsįkwajè*, indicated "there are rents and clefts in its eastern side that I have reason to believe are used to-day by the Indians of San Juan [sic] for sacrificial purposes." Similarly, McKusick (2001) determined that many of the juvenile macaw remains represent sacrifices made during vernal equinox ceremonies. While not celebrated at all Tewa pueblos, vernal equinox events are reported from Ohkay Owingeh and Nambé (Harrington 1916:61-63; Kurath and Garcia 1970:132; cf. Ortiz 1969:95, 169). These events may align in part with the burying of feathers in freshly sown fields, although birds have been known to be kept alive and merely plucked (e.g., Gilman et al. 2014).

Parrot iconography overlooking fields, including at least half of the study loci as confirmed by archaeological evidence, may thus have two seasonal associations, both of which are linked with ceremonies that reinforce the agricultural cycle (Creel and McKusick 1994:521). In the spring, parrot images may play similar roles to buried feathers, while in the summer they may operate as harbingers of (or prayers for) a good rainy season (Schaafsma 2022:250-253). No panel better summarizes this significance than does the "monsoon panel" (Figure 9). This outstanding panel features cloud terraces, iconographic lightning, a cornstalk, and multiple bird images including at least one category 5j parrot, and one or two possible 10z knifewings (note: one was recorded as a category 5h "unidentified bird"). The unambiguous parrot (Figure 9a), rendered in profile, overflies a cornstalk growing above a stylized lightning bolt (either double-ended, or split terminus if it is continuous with an intersecting zigzag line). An upright, forward-facing bird central above the more prominent cloud terrace (Figure 9b) is framed by lightning bolts; its position could conjecturally relate to the scarlet macaw's association with rainbows. Alternatively, it may instead be an instance of either a thunderbird or knifewing motif, as it shares some stylistic attributes with the diving bird recorded as a 10z "thunderbird/knifewing" (Figure 9c). Regardless, all three birds contextually express connections to rain and agricultural fertility.

Archaeoacoustic Associations

Pueblo religious celebrations are inherently musical events, so the sonic associations and vocalizations of parrots and raptors naturally follow from their symbolic and physical roles described in the prior section. Nonetheless their musical roles are not constrained merely to bird calls and ornaments on instruments. Kurath and Garcia (1970:218–232) relate details of the Tewa Eagle Dance, in which two dancers embody a pair of eagles. By dancing, performers produce a number of sounds with body-work and handheld instruments, and the characters they play are integral to sung lyrics. It is no accident that many 5j images share a panel with or are on a panel adjacent to one of several variations on flute player motifs (e.g., Figures 4a, b). I will elaborate on this momentarily. Less obviously, acoustic associations may be implicit in the co-occurrence of 5j parrot/raptor and 10z thunderbird/knifewing motifs with cupules on the same rock since cupules are frequently (though not universally) associated with lithophones, aka ringing rocks. Similarly, Waller (2016) posits that associations such as these indicate that parrot images mark locations with particularly good echoes.

Figure 9. High-resolution 3D model of the "monsoon panel." (a) Enhanced detail of parrot, cornstalk, and lightning arrow; note intersection of lightning with zigzag line. (b) Enhanced detail of bird central above cloud terrace; note visual punning of the diverging lightning bolts mirroring the shape of the cloud terrace, inverted (the infilled disc was superimposed later). (c) Enhanced detail of diving bird, and smaller cloud motif added later.

Interestingly, most of the study loci feature at least one instance (often multiple instances) of flute player images occurring in close proximity to a 5j parrot/raptor or closely related design. Brown (2005:186) observes "Many of the flute players in association with animals are with birds," and goes on to specify that some of these birds "are clearly macaws" (e.g., Figure 4a). Material culture reinforces the iconographic relationship. Raptor and parrot feathers were affixed to flutes, whistles, rattles, and other musical instruments (Smith 1952:173). Ancestral Puebloans sometimes made flutes and whistles out of bird bones in a way that is technologically distinct from those made of wood or reeds (Brown 2019; Van Dyke 2019). Three of five such whistles reported by Judd (1954:304–305) from the same context at Pueblo Bonito were made out of golden eagle ulnae (Brown 2014:19). These traditions are not merely relegated to the past. In 2017, Patrick Shendo Mirabel (Tiwa, Taos Pueblo) performed at a fundraising event for the Mesa Prieta Petroglyph Project, using (among other instruments) a multi-stop flute/whistle made of eagle bone, effectively a modern Pueblo reproduction of these earlier Ancestral Pueblo iterations.

Brown (2005, 2014) has argued that some (not necessarily all) flutes had personhood, as evidenced by depositional practices. Whistles and flutes such as those played by Mirabel often invoke the sounds of bird calls. For birds such as macaws and certain corvids who can be trained to speak phrases and connect names to individuals (Smith 1952:180), vocalizations reinforce the living animal's personhood. Not entirely unlike the case of the Yugüe bone flute recovered from a Terminal Formative Period mortuary context in coastal Oaxaca (Barber and Sánchez 2012), music from Ancestral Pueblo bird bone instruments may have been understood as giving agency and animacy to both object and animal in what Joyce and Barber (2015) term "ensoulment." Category 5j petroglyphs may contribute to such posthumous invocations, especially when present alongside signs of musical expression or other acoustical evidence.

Synthesis

With the above evidence of the previous subsections established, I turn to this study's final example, the "ABC" cluster (Figure 3). This location, like others, sits immediately above the transition from irrigable bosque to semiarid scrubland slopes; like the examples in Figures 1, 2, 4a–c, 5a and b, 7c and d, and 8d, it overlooks known or suspected precontact agricultural fields. Beginning with the upward facing Panel A (Figure 3a), a naturalistic macaw image is adjacent to a highly stylized abstracted macaw, the latter of which is iconographically recognizable both by the diagnostic hooked beak and by its mimicry of the overall form of the former. The latter of these also forms a palimpsest with an earlier image inferred to be from the Late Archaic Period. This panel is replete with sparse but extensive ritual pecking (Figure 3b), some of which appears to postdate the macaw images based on repatination. This unstructured pecking subtly suggests that the boulder may have acoustical qualities. In fact, I experimentally verified this lithophone's bell-like resonant ringing using a noninvasive soft hammer technique (my own knuckles, to be precise). This boulder sits atop and overhangs Panel B (Figure 3c), allowing it both to ring more clearly in its partially suspended position, and to cast a celestially significant shadow onto Panel B's animal flute player (Figure 3d). Recognizable as an MP3's adoptive logo, this prominent petroglyph very closely traces the same shape of the stars in and immediately around Ursa Major, leading to the suspicion that it depicts the dog Harrington (1916:50) reported Tewa identifying in this constellation. Kincheloe observes that during the equinox at solar noon, Panel A's shadow traces the curves of Panel B's animal flute player's tail and back (Wells and Kincheloe 2018:22–23). Small but not forgotten, Panel C sits nestled up against Panels A and B (truthfully C1, as another face of the cobble-sized stone, C2, also has some pecking). Panel C's minimalist macaw (Figure 3e) mirrors the shapes of the macaws on Panel A, and in its own distinctive way distinguishes between types of plumage with the head, body, and legs rendered in dense pecking, and the long feathers of the wings and tail executed as medium-to-sparse pecking.

Here, the myriad of earlier associations with category 5j designs and macaws in particular are consolidated. The duo on Panel A immediately overlook prime farmland, much of which is still used for that very purpose today. This fits well with the spatial associations listed in the prior paragraph, and the iconographic convergence of macaws and a cornstalk in Figure 9a. Tenuous associations between the 5j parrot/raptor category and ringing rocks as mediated by cupules on prior examples (Figures 1 and 4c) are explicit and demonstrable at cluster ABC through the ritual pecking and my own experimental verification. Musical connections continue with convergence of three macaws and a flute player, akin to the examples in Figures 4a and 4b. Even Kincheloe's equinox observation gains credence with one of the macaw's seasonal associations being the vernal equinox, a celebration (as noted above) observed by Ohkay Owingeh. Cluster ABC, to coin a phrase, "has it all."

Concluding Remarks

With rigorous review of ethnographic accounts, and the invaluable assistance of indigenous consultation, it is possible to tease out a supportable theoretical platform for discussing particular iconographic themes. In the case of macaws, and indeed for all figurative and abstract design sets, systematic archaeological contextualization is part and parcel of the process. For the topic at hand, these contexts include constructed features, associated artifacts, ecological information, and recurring iconographic associations. Through the post-positivist model of the best fit for many lines of evidence, this study subtly employs a semiotics-inspired way of constructing a supportable scholarly narrative without transgressing into the academically taboo territory of subjective interpretations.

For the case of macaws and their category 5j flatmates the raptors, this narrative is a compelling story that at once delineates the regional, ethnolinguistic, and diachronic distinctiveness of the birds' religious symbolism to Eastern and Ancestral Pueblos, while simultaneously situating said connotations in an expansive and diverse "worldwide web" (so to speak) of interconnected and enduring cultural traditions spanning thousands of miles and easily over a thousand years. Although an uninitiated iconographer might reflexively find that the colorful imported macaw and the muted but majestic eagle may make strange bedfellows, their companionship encompassed by 5j surpasses superficial similarities, continuing through deeper shared connections to rain, agricultural fertility, and music. Music and especially song-poems are a hallmark of Jane Hill's (1992) notion of the Flower World Complex, a suite of visual, oral/aural, and ideological concepts connecting the macaw's Mesoamerican homeland to the Pueblo Southwest (Turner and Mathiowetz 2021). As colorful as monsoon rainbows, macaws embody Hill's chromaticism criterion. Even eagles, whose feathers became Eagle Dancers and whose bones became flutes and whistles, share just as integral of a role as macaws in the Pueblo rendition of this religious suite. Largely ignored but not wholly forgotten, other raptors including hawks and turkey vultures (or buzzards as they are sometimes known), and in antiquity possibly also ospreys and even condors, shared the Southwestern skies. Variations on the 5j and 10z motifs with aberrant features such as elongated necks (e.g., Figures 4b, c) may hint at some of these birds not only sharing a DEI category but an actual similar cultural role; others have begun to broach this topic (e.g., Cordero 2021; LaZar and Dombrosky 2021). Of course, the knifewing should not be forgotten, having followed the same route as the macaw, although in which direction seems yet undecided.

As much as I have endeavored to relate a comprehensive analysis, this report is yet limited in several ways. My study areas were only a sample of this already somewhat uncommon image, at least uncommon when considered as a percentage of the overall element count recorded by MP3 so far. At times I was pleasantly surprised by my observations, and at other times the reverse was true, and a couple of the already small tally of parrots/raptors had to be stricken from the record upon review. As I expressed at the onset in the land recognition statement, it is important that this and any archaeological research in the Southwest examines the cultural patrimony of living cultures whose enduring presence is often made invisible by the processes of colonization. Out of respect for the sensitivity of certain matters to these communities, I have omitted cultural information that, while supportive of my arguments, seemed irresponsible to share in publication. Nonetheless, I hope this report has given some life and vibrancy to parrot petroglyphs, placing them among the clouds, overlooking fields, amidst the thunderclaps of lightning bolts, vocalizing and bringing song to the dramatic Southwest landscapes, as integral and iconic parts of seasonal Pueblo festivities (both in spring and summer), and even intimately into the household.

Acknowledgments. This study of parrot, raptor, and related images at Mesa Prieta was initiated as part of a virtual reality tours project supported by the New Mexico Humanities Council and the National Endowment for the Humanities. This and other VR tours, each of specific petroglyph themes, can be found on the Mesa Prieta Petroglyph Project's website, https://www.mesaprietapetroglyphs.org/virtualtours.html.

I want to extend my gratitude to the participants of the 2021 Summer Youth Intern Program. Interns Ariana, Hayden, Joaquin, Josh, and Keenan recorded (and/or updated records of) petroglyph panels and other archaeological evidence I shared in this report. I also wish to thank the late Paul Williams for his initiative leading SYIP teams in the past, and especially those prior interns who, under his direction, recorded other loci that I've also reported here.

References Cited

Barber, Sarah B., and Mireya Olvera Sánchez
2012 A Divine Wind: The Arts of Death and Music in Terminal Formative Oaxaca. *Ancient Mesoamerica* 23:9–24.

Berrier, Margaret
2018 Design Element Inventory (DEI). Archaeological Society of New Mexico Rock Art Council (ASNM RAC). Online reference copy: https://www.mesaprietapetroglyphs.org/uploads/4/2/3/9/42390305/2019_design_element_inventory_illustrated_5pp.pdf

Bishop, Katelyn
2021 A Zooarchaeological Reassessment of the Parrots of Chaco Canyon. Presentation given at the annual meeting of the Society for American Archaeology virtual conference, April–July 2021.

Bishop, Katelyn J., and Samantha G. Fladd
2018 Ritual Fauna and Social Organization at Pueblo Bonito, Chaco Canyon. *Kiva* 84(3): 293–316.

Brown, Emily
2005 Instruments of Power: Musical Performance in Rituals of the Ancestral Puebloans of the American Southwest. Ph.D. dissertation, Columbia University.

2014 Music of the Center Place: The Instrument of Chaco Canyon. In *Flower World: Music Archaeology of the Americas*, edited by Matthias Stöckli and Mark Howell, Volume 3, pp. 11– 31.

2019 Musical Instruments of the Prehistoric Southwest. Mesa Talks public lecture series.

Camilli, Eileen L., Kurt F. Anschuetz, Susan J. Smith, and Christopher D. Banet
2019 Prehispanic Pueblo Cotton Cultivation with Gravel-Mulch Technology in the Northern Rio Grande Region. In *Reframing the Northern Rio Grande Pueblo Economy*, edited by Scott G. Ortman, pp. 31–48. Anthropological Papers of the University of Arizona 80. University of Arizona Press, Tucson.

Colton, Harold S.
1949 *Hopi Kachina Dolls with a Key to Their Identification*. University of New Mexico Press, Albuquerque.

Cordero, Robin
2021 Winter Garden Hunting Along the Rio Grande Flyway: A Case Study in the Procurement of Migratory Birds by Puebloans along the Rio Grande. Presentation given at the annual meeting of the Society for American Archaeology virtual conference, April–July 2021.

Creel, Darrell, and Charmion McKusick
1994 Prehistoric Macaws and Parrots in the Mimbres Area, New Mexico. *American Antiquity* 59(3):510-524.

Crotty, Helen K.
1992 The Archaeological Society of New Mexico's Rock Art Recording Field School at Three Rivers Petroglyph Site. In *Interpreting the Past: Research with Public Participation*, edited by LouAnn Jacobson and June-El Piper, pp. 31–44. New Mexico Bureau of Land Management Cultural Resources Series, Santa Fe.

1995 Anasazi Mural Art of the Pueblo IV Period, A.D. 1300–1600: Influences, Selective Adaptation, and Cultural Diversity in the Prehistoric Southwest. Ph.D. dissertation, University of California Los Angeles.

2007 Western Pueblo Influences and Integration in the Pottery Mound Painted Kivas. In *New Perspectives on Pottery Mound Pueblo*, edited by Polly Schaafsma, pp. 85–108. University of New Mexico Press, Albuquerque.

Crown, Patricia L.
2016 Just Macaws: A Review for the U.S. Southwest/Mexican Northwest. *Kiva* 82(4):331–363.

Crown, Patricia, and Patrick D. Lyons
2021 Macaws and Parrots of the Arizona Mountains. Presentation given at the annual meeting of the Society for American Archaeology, April 2021.

Cruz, Patrick, and Scott G. Ortman
2019 Revisiting Settlement Cluster: Political Organization and Economic Cooperation. In *Reframing the Northern Rio Grande Pueblo Economy*, edited by Scott G. Ortman, pp. 61–74. Anthropological Papers of the University of Arizona, Number 80. University of Arizona Press, Tucson.

Dolan, Sean
2021 Turkeys in the Mimbres Valley, New Mexico: Pottery Iconography, Genetics, and Diet. Presentation given at the annual meeting of the Society for American Archaeology virtual conference, April–July 2021.

Duwe, Samuel
2019 The Economics of Becoming: Population Coalescence and the Production and Distribution of Ancestral Tewa Pottery. In *Reframing the Northern Rio Grande Pueblo Economy*, edited by Scott G. Ortman, pp. 104–118. Anthropological Papers of the University of Arizona, Number 80. University of Arizona Press, Tucson.

Fowles, Severin
2018 Pueblo Emergence on the Taos Frontier. In *Life Beyond the Boundaries: Constructing Identity in Edge Regions of the North American Southwest*, edited by Karen G. Harry and Sarah A. Herr, pp. 57–88. University of Colorado Press, Boulder.

2021 The Biographical Revolution in Plains Visual Culture, 1680–1880 CE. Webinar, Crow Canyon Archaeological Center, January 14, 2021. Electronic resource, https://youtu.be/NUdzpxx0_A4

Futch, T. G.
1999 An Archaeological Assessment and Cultural Properties Inventory of The El Guique Gravel Mine For Espanola Transit Mix. On file at the Laboratory of Anthropology, Santa Fe, New Mexico.

George, Richard J., Stephen Plog, Adam S. Watson, Kari L. Schmidt, Brendan J. Culleton, Thomas K. Harper, Patricia A. Gilman, Steven A. LeBlanc, George Amato, Peter Whiteley, Logan Kistler, and Douglas J. Kennett
2018 Archaeogenomic Evidence from the Southwestern U.S. Points to a pre-Hispanic Scarlet Macaw Breeding Colony. *Proceedings of the National Academy of Sciences* 115(35):8740–8745.

Gilman, Patricia A., Marc Thompson, and Kristina C. Wyckoff
2014 Ritual Change and the Distant: Mesoamerican Iconography, Scarlet Macaws, and the Great Kivas in the Mimbres Region of Southwestern New Mexico. *American Antiquity* 79(1):90–107.

Grauch, V. J. S., Paul W. Bauer, Benjamin J. Dreneth, and Keith I. Kelson.
2017 A Shifting Rift—Geophysical Insights into the Evolution of Rio Grande Rift Margins and the Embudo Transfer Zone near Taos, New Mexico. *Geosphere* 13(3):870–910.

Hargrave, L. L.
1970 Mexican Macaws, Comparative Osteology and Survey of Remains from the Southwest. *Anthropological Papers Number 20*. University of Arizona Press, Tucson.

Harrington, John Peabody
1916 *The Ethnography of the Tewa Indians*. Twenty-Ninth Annual Report of the Bureau of American Ethnology to the Secretary of the Smithsonian Institution.

Hays-Gilpin, Kelley, and Jane H. Hill
1999 The Flower World in Material Culture: An Iconographic Complex in the Southwest and Mesoamerica. *Journal of Anthropological Research* 55(1):1–37.

Hill, Jane
1992 The Flower World of Old Uto-Aztecan. *Journal of Anthropological Research* 48:117-144.

Joyce, Arthur A., and Sarah B. Barber
2015 Ensoulment, Entrapment, and Political Centralization: A Comparative Study of Religion and Politics in Later Formative Oaxaca. *Current Anthropology* 56(6):819–847.

Judd, Neil M.
1954 The Material Culture of Pueblo Bonito. *Smithsonian Miscellaneous Collections* 124. Smithsonian Institution, Washington, D.C.

Kendall, Jerome
2020 Mesa Prieta Geology and Petroglyphs Recon. Project proposal submitted to the Mesa Prieta Petroglyph Project, accepted September 24, 2020. Report on file at the Laboratory of Anthropology, Santa Fe.

Kurath, Gertrude Prokosch, and Antonio Garci
1970 Music and Dance of the Tewa Pueblos. *Museum of New Mexico Research Records Number* 8. Museum of New Mexico Press, Santa Fe.

LaZar, Miranda, and Jonathan Dombrosky
2021 Tracking Individual Raptors in the Archaeological Record Using Stable Isotopes: Limitations, Possibilities, and Causes of Intraskeletal Value Variation. Presentation given at the annual meeting of the Society for American Archaeology virtual conference, April–July 2021.

Liwosz, Chester R.
2021 A Briefing on the Chronology and Iconography of the Mesa Prieta Petroglyph Landscape in North-Central New Mexico. In *ASNM Collected Papers in Honor of James Condor, Volume* 47, edited by Matthew Barbour and Emily Brown, pp. 61–75. Museum of New Mexico Press, Santa Fe.

MacKenzie, Janet, and Candace Borduin
2019 *Archaic Petroglyphs of Mesa Prieta, Northern New Mexico.* New Mexico Archaeological Council, Albuquerque.

Marchaza, Lauren M.
2007 Selling Authenticity: The Role of Zuni Knifewings and Rainbow Gods in Tourism of the American Southwest. Master's thesis, Ohio University.

Mathien, Frances Joan
1984 Social and Economic Implications of Jewelry Items of the Chaco Anasazi. In *Recent Research on Chaco Prehistory*, edited by W. James Judge and John D. Schelberg, pp. 173–186. Division of Cultural Research, U.S. Department of the Interior, National Park Service, Albuquerque.

2005 *Culture and Ecology of Chaco Canyon and the San Juan Basin.* Division of Cultural Research, U.S. Department of the Interior, National Park Service, Albuquerque.

Mathiowetz, Michael D.
2021 Life in Bloom: The Casas Grandes Flower World and Its Antecedents in Northwest Mesoamerica, Northern Mexico, and the American Southwest. In *Flower Worlds: Religion, Aesthetics, and Ideology in Mesoamerica and the American Southwest,* edited by Michael D. Mathiowetz and Andrew D. Turner, pp. 174–200. University of Arizona Press, Tucson.

Mathiowetz, Michael D., and Andrew D. Turner (editors)
2021 *Flower Worlds: Religion, Aesthetics, and Ideology in Mesoamerica and the American Southwest.* University of Arizona Press, Tucson.

McKusick, Charmion
2001 Southwest Birds of Sacrifice. *The Arizona Archaeologist* 31. Phoenix, Arizona Archaeological Society.

Minnis, Paul E., Michael E. Whalen, Jane H. Kelley, and Joe D. Stewart
1993 Prehistoric Macaw Breeding in the North American Southwest. *American Antiquity* 58(2):270–276.

Murray, Wendi Field, Nicholas C. Laluk, Barbara J. Mills, and T. J. Ferguson
2009 Archaeological Collaboration with American Indians: Case Studies from the Western United States. Collaborative Anthropologies 2(1): 65–86.

Naranjo, Tessie
2006 We Came from the South, We Came from the North: Some Tewa Origin Stories. In *The Mesa Verde World*, edited by David Grant Noble, pp. 49–58. School of American Research Press, Santa Fe.

Ortiz, Alfonso
1969 *The Tewa World: Space, Time, Being, and Becoming in a Pueblo Society*. University of Chicago Press.

Ortman, Scott, and Kaitlyn E. Davis
2019 Economic Growth in the Pueblos? In *Reframing the Northern Rio Grande Pueblo Economy*, edited by Scott G. Ortman, pp. 1–16. Anthropological Papers of the University of Arizona, Number 80. University of Arizona Press, Tucson.

Patterson, Alex
1992 *A Field Guide to Rock Art Symbols of the Greater Southwest.* Johnson Books, Boulder.

Post, Steven
2002 Emerging from the Shadows: The Archaic Period in the Northern Rio Grande. In *Traditions, Transitions, and Technologies*, edited by Sarah J. Schlanger, pp. 33–48. University Press of Colorado, Boulder.

Reiche, Parry
1937 The Toreva-Block: A Distinctive Landslide Type. *The Journal of Geology* 45(5):538–548.

Roediger, Virginia More
1941 *Ceremonial Costumes of the Pueblo Indians: Their Evolution, Fabrication, and Significance in the Prayer Drama.* University of California Press, Berkeley.

Rogers, Richard A.
2007 From Hunting Magic to Shamanism: Interpretations of Native American Rock Art and the Contemporary Crisis in Masculinity. *Women's Studies in Communication* 30(1):78–110.

Schaafsma, Polly
1980 *Indian Rock Art of the Southwest.* School of American Research, Santa Fe, and University of New Mexico Press, Albuquerque.

1992 *Rock Art in New Mexico.* Museum of New Mexico Press, Albuquerque.

2000 *Warrior, Shield, and Star: Imagery and Ideology of Pueblo Warfare.* Western Edge Press, Santa Fe.

2007 Documenting Conflict in the Prehistoric Pueblo Southwest. In *North American Indigenous Warfare and Ritual Violence*, edited by Richard J. Chacon and Rubén G. Mendoza, pp. 114–128. University of Arizona Press, Tucson.

2022 Riders of the Rainbow. In *Birds of the Sun: Macaws and People in the U.S. Southwest and Mexican Northwest,* edited by Christopher W. Schwartz, Stephen Plog, and Patricia A. Gilman, pp. 241–262. University of Arizona Press, Tucson.

Schroeder, Albert H.
1968 Birds and Feathers in Documents Relating to Indians of the Southwest. In *Collected Papers in Honor of Lyndon Lane Hargrave,* edited by Albert H. Schroeder, pp. 95–114. Papers of the Archaeological Society of New Mexico No. 1. Museum of New Mexico Press, Santa Fe.

Schwartz, Christopher W.
2020 Scarlet Macaws, Long-Distance Exchange, and Placemaking in the U.S. Southwest and Mexican Northwest, ca. 900–1450 CE. Ph.D. dissertation, Arizona State University, Tempe.

Schwartz, Christopher W., Andrew D. Somerville, Ben A. Nelson, and Kelly J. Knudson
2021 Investigating pre-Hispanic Scarlet Macaw Origins through Radiogenic Strontium Isotope Analysis at Paquimé in Chihuahua, Mexico. *Journal of Anthropological Archaeology* 61, Article 101256.

Schwartz, Christopher W., Kelley L. M. Taylor, and Michelle Hegmon
2022 The Human Experience of Transporting and Raising Scarlet Macaws at Paquimé in Northern Chihuahua, Mexico. In *Birds of the Sun: Macaws and People in the U.S. Southwest and Mexican Northwest,* edited by Christopher W. Schwartz, Stephen Plog, and Patricia A. Gilman. pp. 297–320. University of Arizona Press, Tucson.

Seltzer, Heather Lynn
2017 Signs and Symbols: Exploring Changes in Iconography in the Contact Era Rio Grande Pueblo World. Master's thesis, University of Colorado, Boulder.

Slifer, Dennis
2000 *The Serpent and the Sacred Fire: Fertility Images in Southwest Rock Art.* Museum of New Mexico Press, Santa Fe.

Slifer, Dennis, and James Duffield
1994 *Kokopelli: Fluteplayer Images in Rock Art.* Ancient City Press, Santa Fe, New Mexico.

Smith, Watson
1952 Kiva Mural Decorations at Awatovi and Kawaika-a, With a Survey of Other Wall Paintings in the Pueblo Southwest. *Papers of the Peabody Museum of Archaeology and Ethnology,* Volume 37. Harvard University.

Somerville, Andrew D., Ben A. Nelson, and Kelly J. Knudson
2010 Isotopic Investigation of Pre-Hispanic Macaw Breeding in Northwest Mexico. *Journal of Anthropological Archaeology* 29:125–135.

Steen, Charlie R.
1983 The San Juan Anasazi in the 13th Century. *Proceedings of the Anasazi Symposium 1981,* edited by Jack E. Smith, pp. 169-173. Cortez Printing/Mesa Verde Museum Association, Colorado.

Turner, Andrew, D., and Michael D. Mathiowetz
2021 Introduction. Flower Worlds: A Synthesis and Critical History. In *Flower Worlds: Religion, Aesthetics, and Ideology in Mesoamerica and the American Southwest,* edited by Michael D. Mathiowetz and Andrew D. Turner, pp. 3–32. University of Arizona Press, Tucson.

Tyler, Hamilton A.
1991 *Pueblo Birds and Myths.* Northland Publishing, Flagstaff.

Van Dyke, Ruth M.
2019 Sensory Archaeology in the Pueblo Southwest. In *The Routledge Handbook of Sensory Archaeology,* edited by Robin Skeates and Joanna Days, pp. 498–519. Routledge, Taylor and Francis Group, London.

Waller, Steven J.
2016 Macaws in Rock Art as a Possible Symbol of Sound Reflection. Presentation given at the San Diego Rock Art Symposium, San Diego, California.

Watson, Adam S., Stephen Plog, Brendan J. Culleton, Patricia A. Gilman, Steven A. LeBlanc, Peter M. Whiteley, Santiago Claramunt, and Douglas J. Kennett
2015 Early Procurement of Scarlet Macaws and the Emergence of Social Complexity in Chaco Canyon, NM. *Proceedings of the National Academy of Sciences* 112(27):8238–8243.

Weiner, Robert S.
2015 A Sensory Approach to Exotica, Ritual Practice, and Cosmology at Chaco Canyon. *Kiva* 81(3–4): 220–246.

Wells, Katherine, Candie Borduin, and Suzie Frazier
2008 Vecinos del Rio Mesa Prieta Petroglyph Project. In *Proceedings of Set in Stone: A Binational Workshop on Petroglyph Management in the United States and Mexico,* Workshop Proceedings, Petroglyph National Monument, National Park Service, compiled by Joseph P. Sánchez, Angelica Sánchez-Clark, and Edwina L. Abreu, pp. 127–140. National Park Service.

Wells, Katherine, and John Kincheloe
2018 *Silent Music: The Animal Flute Players on the Wells Petroglyph Preserve in Northern New Mexico.* Mesa Prieta Petroglyph Books, Velarde, New Mexico.

Whalen, Michael E.
2022 Obtaining Macaws. In *Birds of the Sun: Macaws and People in the U.S. Southwest and Mexican Northwest,* edited by Christopher W. Schwartz, Stephen Plog, and Patricia A. Gilman. pp. 221-240. University of Arizona Press, Tucson.

The Rock Engravings of the Atlantic Axis: A Common Link in Recent European Prehistory

Estrela C. García García

Through a formal and stylistic study, rock engravings made during recent prehistory in the European Atlantic axis are analyzed as a means to discover a common culture that flourished in the period of the Metal Ages, and that unites countries that today seem as different as Portugal, Spain, the United Kingdom, Ireland, and France. These carvings show a prehistoric culture marked by schematic art and the abstraction of sacred and religious imagery, as well as a clear cult of war hierarchies through the representation of weapons and other motifs, indicating a commercial and cultural exchange in this territory during the Metal Ages.

In recent decades the study and research of rock engravings of recent prehistory in Europe has experienced a strong expansion as interest has grown from the academic and scientific, as well as social, sphere. This translates into a greater influx of research work related to this topic. In this period of time, local and international study and dissemination initiatives have also grown exponentially, from amateur associations to research groups with members in numerous European countries in which international cooperation is key. All this opens the door to new proposals for the protection, research, and dissemination of archaeological heritage in a broader scope, at the same time encouraged by significant international organizations such as UNESCO, ICOMOS, or the CARP initiative of the European Union.

The main focus of this article is the context of Atlantic Europe, in which a multitude of rock engravings corresponding to recent prehistory are present—from the Megalithic phenomenon to the beginning of the Roman Empire, which is normally known as the Metal Ages or the pre-Roman period. The formal and morphological differences and similarities of these representations have been studied for years, and thanks to the enormous effort and work of researchers from numerous universities, we can establish a common cross-territorial typology which demonstrates a common prehistoric culture based on cultural and commercial exchange and the existence of a shared language of signs.

Estrela C. García García
Doctorate Researcher,
Universidade de Santiago de Compostela (Galicia, Spain),
Member of the research group GEPN-AAT

Chronology

Recent Prehistory in Europe: Setting the Context

The term recent prehistory extends from the beginning of the Neolithic in Europe (around 6000 B.C.) to the end of the Iron Age (A.D. 1–3, or earlier in some cases), framing a very important transition period in European prehistoric societies in which the nomadic lifestyle that characterized the Paleolithic is abandoned and, with the introduction of agriculture and livestock, the first settlements are produced, leading to the first populations of the European Atlantic with small nuclei of inhabitants.

It is important to keep in mind that this chronological context applies only to this geographical setting since, although almost all societies experience a similar development, chronologies vary from one area to another depending on social development, the degree of isolation from other geographical areas, and the amount of resources to which they have access.

But before delving into the Neolithic, it is important to briefly understand the previous period, which is the transition from the Paleolithic to the Neolithic, also known as the Mesolithic. This time frame is around 6000 or 7000 years depending on the region, from approximately 12,000 to 6000 B.C. (Torres Goberna 2012b). We know that the Neolithic transition is delayed in Atlantic Europe, and that this is due—among other factors—to the geographical distance from the Anatolian peninsula and the Middle East, where this explosion takes place, and to the existence of enormous climatic differences, since in Europe the last glaciation was still being abandoned, which caused a much colder and more humid environment. Gradually, the agricultural communities of Anatolia penetrated into Europe, and around 8000 to 6500 B.C. they had already established themselves in Atlantic regions such as the northwest of the Iberian Peninsula or the south of the British Isles (Torres Goberna 2012b).

Figure 1 shows how this staggered transition to the Neolithic takes place, in which the farther a territory is from the region of Anatolia and the Arabian Peninsula—the nerve center of the development and appearance of the first Neolithic societies in Eurasia—the later this change from the old to the new Stone Age takes place. This explains the different relative dating of the engravings, which we will see hereafter.

Material remains from the Mesolithic and Neolithic periods have been found that reveal these cultural encounters between different groups of people, who exchanged not only material elements such as ceramics, but also cultivation techniques to take better advantage of the crops and the land (Fabregas Valcarce and Suárez Otero 1999:544).

However, the management of agriculture was not yet perfected, and evidence has been found of a combination of sedentary and nomadic life: they mixed hunting with cultivation, and as soon as an area had been exploited and no longer provided a harvest, the groups moved to other areas where they could continue cultivating, as Torres Goberna (2012b) affirms.

It is during this time frame, which spans the Atlantic area between 6000 and 3000 B.C.—always allowing for chronological variability between different geographical areas—that the first engravings of the Atlantic Style, or motifs that would be the precursors of this style if you prefer, are produced (Figure 2). They are found inside megalithic monuments, which were huge stone funerary structures in which these societies buried their dead in common graves, together with grave goods and belongings that they decorated with paintings and engravings.

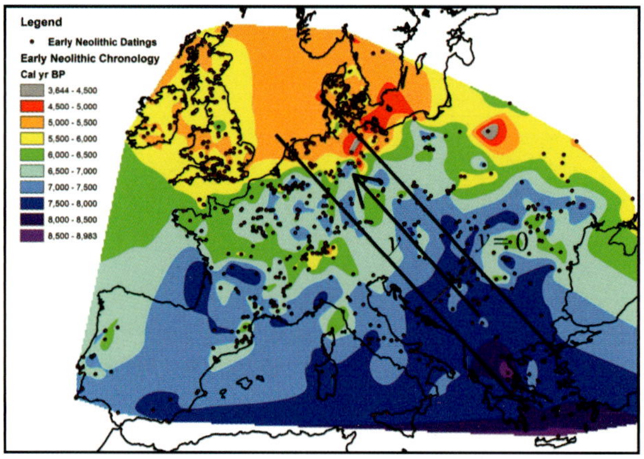

Figure 1. Map illustrating chronology of the Neolithic arrival and transition in Europe.

Figura 1. Mapa que ilustra la cronología de la llegada y transición del Neolítico en Europa (Isern et al. 2012:Figure 1, open access).

Figure 2. Two orthostats taken from the Silleda Mamora, Braña (Galicia), exhibited in the Museum of Pontevedra, Spain.

Figura 2. Dos ortostatos extraídos de la Silleda Mamora, Braña (Galicia), expuestos en el Museo de Pontevedra, España (Lameira 2015, CC BY-SA 4.0 license).

Gradually, through exchanges linked to transhumance and contacts between different regions, farming methods were perfected and techniques such as fallow rotation were introduced, which made it possible to exploit agricultural land over the course of a whole year. This, together with the burning of forests, which produced large amounts of grass for agriculture, settled the populations and the nomadic lifestyle disappeared little by little to become more and more sedentary, entering fully into the Chalcolithic, or the Metal Age.

The beginning of this period marks, as its name indicates, the start of the practice of metallurgy. The first metal to be smelted was copper, soft and easy to handle, which allowed the manufacture of the first metal utensils. This undoubtedly improved the quality of life of these populations, and increased the amount of resources available thanks to a key factor: the production of more resistant weapons, which allowed them not only to carry out commercial exchanges, but also to attack enemies and defend their resources. This is when, on the one hand, they began to settle in fortified settlements, and on the other hand, they made the first tools with which they would make the Atlantic Style stone engravings.

The next period is the Bronze Age based on a metal, even more resistant and harder than copper, that comes from the amalgamation of that metal with tin. This begins approximately in 2500 B.C. and continues until 600 B.C. This period marks a peak in the production of the Atlantic Style engravings, coinciding with a great social development.

In this period, burials in stone monuments of megalithic nature continue, but these are reduced in size, housing a smaller number of individuals, which indicates a major change marked by the emergence of social classes—now that there are greater material and cultural exchanges, it is also essential to protect and defend these resources, so that the production of weapons increases, and individuals who handle, manufacture, and control these weapons are those who are placed at the head of a social hierarchy (English Heritage 2021).

The habitational settlements are now more defined, with settlements of circular houses usually built in a strategic location in the territory that allowed 360° visualization of a very wide area, usually fortified with a wall and moats. In the region of Galicia, this type of settlement is called *castros* (Figure 3), but they are also common in other areas such as the British Isles (English Heritage 2021).

The final stage of the Metal Ages is the Iron Age, in which these societies experience a very great expansion, with very complex and developed customs, rituals, structures, and cultures. But it is at this time that the production of the Atlantic Style engravings declines, partly due to the Romanization that occurs at the end of the millennium, around 50 B.C. (Johnson 2021).

Figure 3. The archaeological site of Castro de Borneiro, Cabana de Bergantiños, A Coruña, Galicia, Spain.
Figura 3. El yacimiento arqueológico de Castro de Borneiro, Cabana de Bergantiños, A Coruña, Galicia, España. Photo by Estrela C. García García, 2021.

The arrival of the Romans marks the end of prehistory in Europe, and therefore of the Atlantic Style engravings, although not of the practice of creating petroglyphs, which continues throughout the ages as archaeological evidence shows us, with engravings with Latin letters from Roman times, or crosses from medieval times with the arrival of Christianity to these territories—sometimes on the same panels from prehistoric periods, which show us the enormous importance that the symbolic gesture of engraving something on stone has always had.

Chronology for the Atlantic Style Rock Engravings

As we have just mentioned, the chronologies vary depending on the region we are talking about due to the factors of the Neolithic expansion and the availability of resources. That is why the appearance of these engravings is disparate between different regions, as we can see in Figure 4.

It is evident that there is not only chronological variability, but also a common range between 4000 and 1000 B.C. (with the exception of Ireland) in which the greatest peak of the Atlantic Style petroglyphs occurs, and which corresponds to the social development caused by the management of metallurgy.

Of course, in addition to the stylistic correspondence, the sharing of this temporal space is a fundamental aspect of the thesis of this paper, since this common chronological band is a further indication of the existence of an Atlantic culture.

Nevertheless, it is also vital to underline that in terms of chronology it is very difficult to establish a clear period when it comes to rock engravings, since in the absence of pigments in the grooves—at least not in those located in the open air—it is not possible to establish a direct dating of them. To date prehistoric

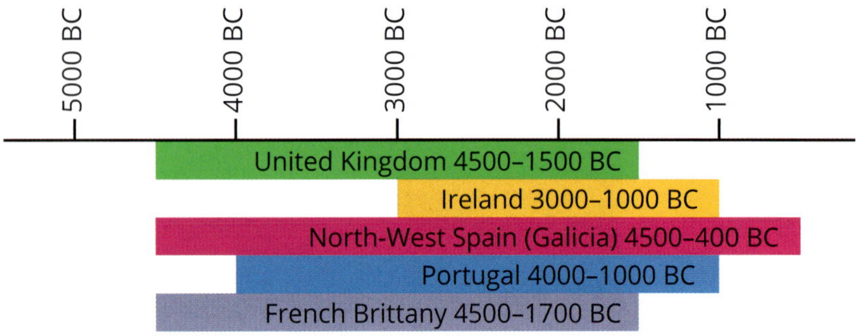

Figure 4. Chronology of the development of Atlantic Style engravings in the distribution areas.
Figura 4. Cronología del desarrollo de los grabados de estilo atlántico en las áreas de distribución. Chart by Estrela C. García García, 2021.

petroglyphs, an indirect dating method is almost always employed using nearby sites or representative correspondences, as in the case of engravings of weapons such as swords in the northwest of the Iberian Peninsula, which by their nature can only be later than the Copper Age since metallic weapons did not exist before that time. Regarding comparisons with material remains, in this same region there have been cases in which archaeological evidence includes objects represented in these engravings, such as the aforementioned weapons, or even anthropomorphic idols.

The Atlantic Style

Description and Characteristics

The Atlantic Style includes all those prehistoric engravings made from the Megalithic or Chalcolithic period through the Bronze Age in the regions near the Atlantic Ocean in western Europe. Although cases of panels have been documented in places farther away from the coast, it is certain that they are still geographically related to other inland enclaves (Figure 5).

Of course, the term Atlantic Style rock art is used due to the majority of this art being located in the Atlantic Ocean coastal countries, but recently there have been discoveries of engravings framed in this type of style in places such as Granada (Spain, in the southwest of the Iberian Peninsula) or Norway, as we will see below.

Most of these engravings are found in open-air deposits or sites, usually on granitic stone surfaces, in a generally horizontal position, and in such a way that they are fully integrated into the landscape, located in strategic places or related to other nearby sites through material and archaeological evidence (Fábregas Valcarce 2010:43–56). They can be presented as isolated elements, small in size, or as part of large assemblages scattered over an extensive area (Valdez-Tullett 2017:50). They were made by marking an outline and pecking with a metallic or stone tool, depending on the chronological moment.

It is not known exactly what the reason was for the realization of these engravings; the only thing we can be sure of is that these carvings had symbolic importance, since this style is distributed and repeated across great geographical distances.

As it happens with the movable art of the European Paleolithic, it is possible that these motifs could appear in other objects, clothes, tattoos, and paintings that, by the passage of time and the deterioration of these types of materials, have been lost.

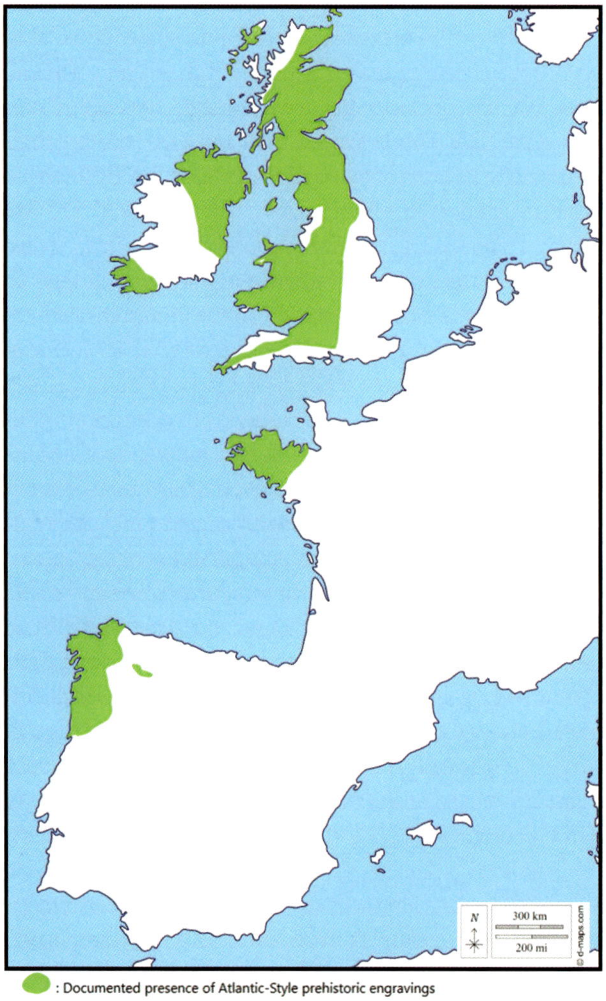

Figure 5. Map of the distribution of Atlantic Style engravings.
Figura 5. Mapa de la distribución de los grabados de estilo atlántico. Map by Estrela C. García García, 2021.

The most representative motifs of this type of engravings comprise the style of cups and rings, which is the combination of these two motifs to compose panels of various sizes, showing the abstract or geometric nature that characterizes the engravings. There are also naturalistic elements representing zoomorphs, anthropomorphs, or weapons.

Another key element that is part of these sculptures is the environment in which they are found, mainly in the open air. There are theories about the direct relationship that petroglyphs would have with other elements of a geographical context, such as natural passages, access to resources, the location of sites that were once settlements, or even astronomical calendars to measure the pace of time for activities such as harvests. Therefore, their location in space is as important as what they represent, but once again, the temporal distance prevents us from being able to determine the exact connection they had.

Another environment in which this type of engraving is present is inside megalithic monuments of funerary nature, usually corresponding to the Neolithic or the period known as Megalithic, due to the appearance and spread of this type of structure throughout the European continent. This type of monument had an enormous social importance, since they were burial places in which numerous individuals, sometimes even entire families, were buried together with their personal belongings and paraphernalia. In these monuments a main chamber was created, which was surrounded by large stones, usually of granitic nature, on top of which a huge stone slab was placed to cover the interior (Figure 6). Joining this chamber with the exterior was a corridor, through which natural light entered. These monuments were aligned with the sun's path, from east to west, so that at the times of the summer or winter solstice, the sun illuminated the entrance and the interior completely, which could be indicative of a rite of passage from life to death.

Of course, these constructions were decorated, and these graphic embellishments are found inside the entrance corridors and also in the funerary chambers where the burials took place. These engravings, due to the protection afforded by being indoors, have retained traces of pigments that also adorned these walls. The motifs represented in this type of monument are practically unique, since they can rarely be seen in open-air sites (Historic Environment Scotland :2021).

Figure 6. The dolmen of Pedra da Arca, Vimianzo, A Coruña, Galicia, Spain.
Figura 6. El dolmen de Pedra da Arca, Vimianzo, A Coruña, Galicia, España. Photo by Estrela C. García García, 2021.

A very clear example of this combination of paintings and engravings is from the dolmen of Dombate in Bergantiños (A Coruña, Galicia, northwest Spain), which contains red and black paintings made of iron oxide and charcoal, forming linear, zigzag, and grid motifs, superimposed on a white primer base made with kaolin on the granitic surface (Figure 7a).

As can be seen in these figures, the paintings are present throughout the interior of the monument, from the corridor to the burial chamber, accompanied by very elaborate motifs in the form of engravings, in particular an undefined element that has been called "the thing" (Figure 7b).

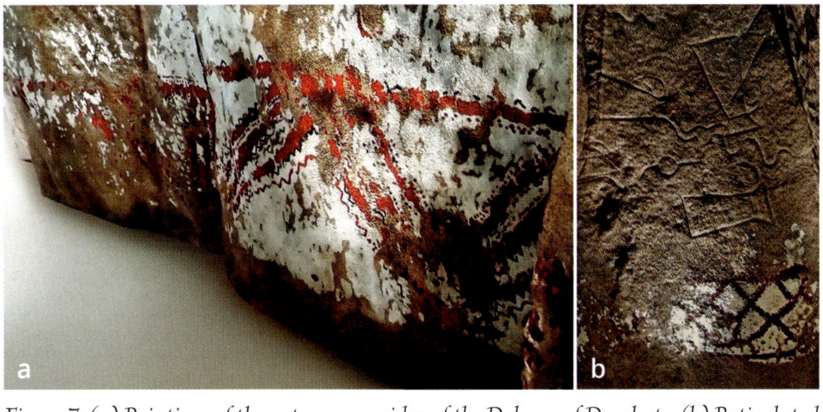

Figure 7. (a) Paintings of the entrance corridor of the Dolmen of Dombate. (b) Reticulated paintings and engravings in the interior of the burial chamber of the Dolmen of Dombate. Replicas in the Interpretation Center of the Dolmen of Dombate, A Coruña, Galicia, Spain.
Figura 7. (a) Pinturas del corredor de entrada del Dolmen de Dombate. (b) Pinturas reticuladas y grabados en el interior de la cámara funeraria del Dolmen de Dombate. Réplicas en el Centro de Interpretación del Dolmen de Dombate, A Coruña, Galicia, España. Photos by Estrela C. García García, 2021.

Within the area of distribution of these engravings we also find many other notable examples incorporated into megalithic monuments, such as Newgrange, in County Meath, Ireland, a huge burial mound built 5200 years ago, which places it chronologically in the Neolithic (Knowth.com n.d.). Its structure is similar to that of any megalithic monument, but stands out for its size of 85 meters in diameter. In this monument are the remarkable magnificent engravings in spiral form (Figure 8) located on enormous orthostats in the interior and exterior of the monument, highlighting the famous triple spiral motifs on orthostat C10 (Figure 8b). There are also other elements such as zigzag lines, reticules, semicircles, serpentiforms, or cups.

Figure 8. (a) One of the orthostats at the entrance of the Newgrange monument, decorated with spiral engravings. (b) The famous triple spiral on orthostat C10, illuminated by the rising sun on winter solstice.

Figura 8. (a) Uno de los ortostatos de la entrada del monumento de Newgrange, decorado con grabados en espiral. (b) La famosa triple espiral del ortostato C10, iluminada por el sol naciente en el solsticio de invierno. (a, Schulze 2017, CC BY 2.0 license; b, Holt 2014, CC BY 2.0 license).

Closely related to the Newgrange megalith is the Gavrinis tomb in Brittany, dating from 5500 years ago, with a chronology similar to its Irish "relative." In its interior are engravings of concentric semicircles, forming images that resemble waves, accompanied by others such as serpentiform or radial motifs (Figure 9).

It has already been mentioned that this historical period is the prelude to the whole phenomenon that occurs from the Chalcolithic, with the exponential increase of engravings in the open air. The exact reason for this increase in this type of representations is not known, although it is most likely that it was an accumulation of causes related to the social development that produces the control of the territory through resources such as agriculture, livestock, and metallurgy. If one thing is certain, it is that art, or the graphic imagery, is born of the society that creates it, and, therefore, is intimately related and connected to conventions and social structures that today we can only imagine across the temporal distance that separates us from recent European prehistory.

Distribution

The distribution of these engravings occurs along the axis of the countries bordering the Atlantic Ocean, usually in coastal areas, although stations and sites have been found in places far from the shores.

From the north of Portugal, through the northwest of the Iberian Peninsula—including the regions of Galicia and El Bierzo—to Brittany, Ireland, and the United Kingdom, we see a natural corridor, following an arc that unites such separated territories. That, of course, would give a clear sign of a communicative circuit between these regions, with a clear cultural exchange and the existence of a shared collective imagery (see Figure 5).

Within these regions, the density of panels is different in each, with the region with the highest number of panels or stations being Galicia in the northwest of the Iberian Peninsula, in what is now Spain, with around 4000 in total (as of 2018) in an area of 30,000 km^2 (Rodríguez Rellán et al. 2018:113), a number that has continued to increase since then. This density is much greater compared to other areas, such as England, with 5000 stations counted up to that same year spread over 130,000 km^2 (Historic England 2018:1).

Figure 9. Replicas of decorated orthostats from the entrance corridor of Gavrinis in the Tumulus de Bougon Museum, Bougon, France.

Figura 9. Réplicas de ortostatos decorados del corredor de entrada de Gavrinis en el Museo Tumulus de Bougon, Bougon, Francia (Jahnke 2007, CC BY-SA 3.0 license).

Recent research has even found panels with these engravings in areas further away from this corridor, such as in the province of Granada, Spain (Redondo Ortega and Martínez Rodríguez 2021:124), or other even more distant regions such as Norway (Lødøen 2017:9–10). Also notable are the engravings in the region of El Bierzo, in the community of Castilla y León (Spain), with a typology and a style identical to those found in the northwest of the peninsula, and which are rarely mentioned or included in scientific classifications (Campos Gómez 2018:10).

It should be noted that, despite the occurrence of these relationships with the Atlantic Ocean as the centralizing axis, it is likely that the number of stations in other areas will increase as new discoveries occur, and given the locations of these new finds, it may be necessary to rethink the nomenclature of this typology of engravings in favor of a more generic one.

Therefore, and after this brief note, we find in this territorial strip the engravings have enormous formal and symbolic similarities, made by a common culture within a similar chronological period. All the typologies and the similarities between them will be described later. It is also important to note the similarities of their location in the landscape, since it is identical in all these cases, and brings to light the importance of the distribution in space and the very important role that these enclaves play in the landscape and vice-versa—they should be understood as a unit, or perhaps as two elements in a symbiotic relationship. It is likely that they were located in strategic areas, indicating some kind of spatial communication with other members of a group, such as a location of resources or territorial markers. Therefore, their relationship with the landscape is evident.

In this regard, clear connections have been found between the locations of some panels and strategic areas of this type, such as those investigated by Richard Bradley, Felipe Criado Boado, and Ramón Fábregas Valcárce (1994:166–167). However, these formal similarities are not equivalent in all areas, often varying from one to another, sometimes showing great correspondences between different areas even if they are far from each other. Dr. Joana Valdez-Tullett (2017:227–230) proposes some pathways of communication and formal similarity connecting five widely separated sites distributed among the aforementioned countries, which could indicate these interterritorial connections and reinforce the thesis of a shared graphic-cultural imagery.

Valdez-Tullett (2017:222–233) discusses formal correlations and the attributes of each of these enclaves through study of the deposits using existing databases. Among connections that demonstrate interconnection of these societies despite geographical distance, the ocean itself would serve as a corridor or pathway providing the way for communication, although there are stronger regional correlations.

It is worth mentioning in this section the panels of Auga dos Cebros 1 and O Vivieiro 4, engravings located on the coast of Oia, in Pontevedra (Galicia), which represent Mediterranean-type boats (Figure 10). This enclave is especially interesting since it is right on the coast, which once again indicates a clear relationship with the landscape, but it is the motifs themselves that strengthen this relationship with the territory, even with waters beyond the Atlantic, and clearly indicate the commercial and cultural relations with other areas and cultures (Costas Goberna and De La Peña Santos 2005:278).

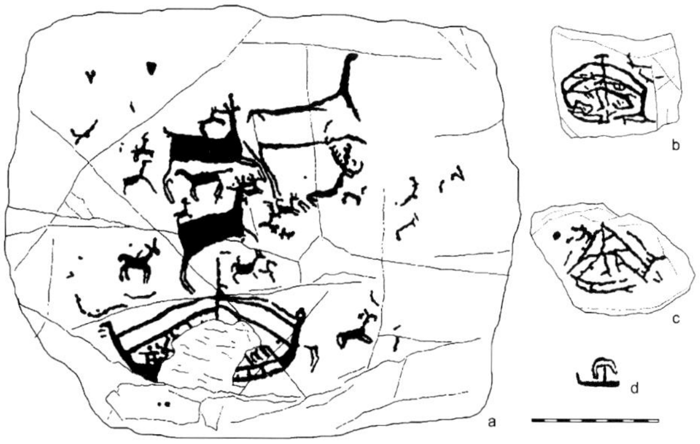

Figure 10. Tracings of the Auga dos Cebros I and O Viveiro IV petroglyphs showing Mediterranean ships.

Figura 10. Trazados de los petroglifos Auga dos Cebros I y O Viveiro IV que muestran barcos mediterráneos (Mederos Martin 2019:Figure 3, CC BY-NC-SA 3.0 license).

This relationship of the engravings with respect to their spatial distribution is therefore demonstrated, and not only formally as we will see below. The environment of the Atlantic coast plays a fundamental role in the foundation of interterritorial relations that give rise to the expansion of this style throughout the Atlantic region, and perhaps beyond.

Typologies

If we analyze the corpus of prehistoric engravings from Atlantic Europe, we find many similarities, which show enormous stylistic similarities between them. That is why these engravings are associated within the same group called "Atlantic Art" or "Atlantic Style Prehistoric Engravings."

The motifs that mainly characterize this style are abstract, composed of cups, concentric circles, spirals, labyrinths, or a mixture of several of them, although other geometric, zoomorphic, or even other representations such as idols or weapons, are also included, which vary according to the region, and in some cases only appear in certain areas (Valdez-Tullett 2013:549).

It is important to mention that in this classification only those motifs belonging to prehistoric times have been included; therefore, other motifs such as crosses or Latin letters, from historical times, have been discarded.

Numerous classifications have been made in this regard over time, increasing or modifying as new discoveries are made, which we will mention later. We will now focus on the general classification, common to all these regions, of our own elaboration, in which the following forms are distinguished.

As can be seen (Figure 11), the corpus of petroglyphs has been divided into two general categories differentiated by their nature, or by what they represent: geometric motifs, which is the majority group; and naturalistic motifs, which is a minority group and is still being studied.

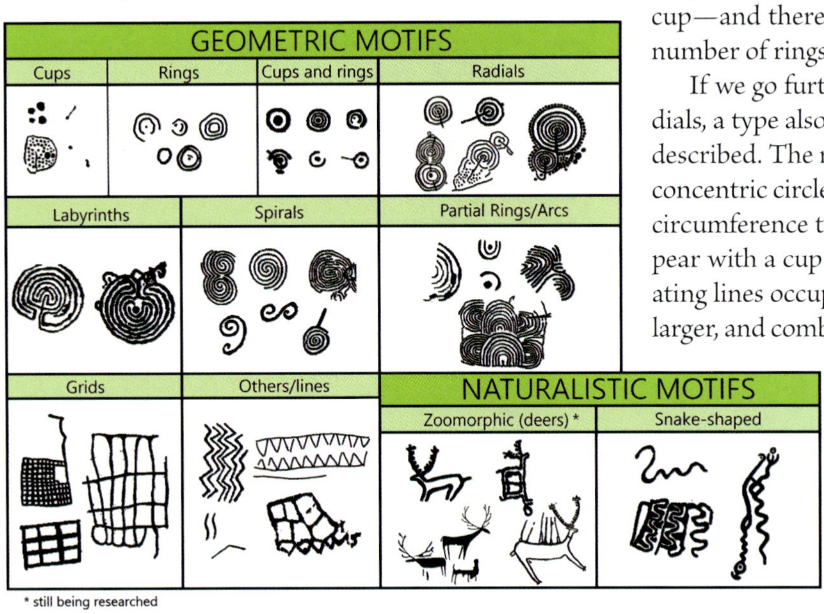

Figure 11. Classification table with the engraved motifs common to all the conforming areas of the Atlantic Style.
Figura 11. Cuadro de clasificación con los motivos grabados comunes a todas las zonas conformadas del Estilo Atlántico. Table by Estrela C. García García, 2021.

As for the first category, the geometric, we find numerous types of engravings that are of an "abstract" or geometric nature—to use current nomenclatures to refer to representations thousands of years old.

The first type is the *cazoletas* (cups, or cupules), which is undoubtedly the most repeated and abundant in the corpus of petroglyphs of the Atlantic arc, appearing in practically all the existing panels, normally in combination with other figures. They are circular depressions in the surface of the rock in which they are found, whose sizes vary, but rarely are they more than 5 cm in diameter, so it is sometimes difficult to distinguish them from natural formations. Sometimes they are joined together by lines (Valdez-Tullett 2017:8; Vázquez Varela 1983:44).

To give an example, we can cite the work of Rodríguez Rellán et al. (2018:113–114), who quantify elements present in the entire corpus of rock art stations *(estaciones rupestres)* recorded up to that time within the region of Galicia in the northwest Iberian Peninsula. Cupules are the most abundant element, found on 61.97% of the engraved rocks, a clear sign of the enormous presence of this motif.

The second most abundant is circular combinations at 33.14%, which in most cases appear in combination with the cups, so we can relate them directly to the third type, called cup-and-ring combinations. These are arranged concentrically around a center—marked with a cup—and there can be between one and an unlimited number of rings of variable size (RAPP 2000:32).

If we go further in our classification we find the radials, a type also closely linked to the three we have just described. The radials (Figure 12) are a variation of the concentric circles or rings that are missing parts of their circumference to form one or more gaps. They can appear with a cup in the center and frequently have radiating lines occupying the gaps. Often their size is much larger, and combinations of numerous radials and other figures, such as cups or lines, may appear. Sometimes these arrangements seem to suggest that they might have some specific social significance or use as, for example, the engravings of Laxe das Rodas in Muros, in Galicia, one of the best-known cases of the use of these engravings as a calendar to mark the passage of time (García Quintela and Santos-Estévez 2015:1215).

The next type framed within these geometric motifs are the labyrinths (Figure 13), which, unlike the previous cases, is a much smaller group—the panels in which labyrinths are seen are rare. These are representations that, as their name indicates, represent circles and lines shaped in such a way

Figure 12. Radial form, Weetwood Moor, Northumberland, United Kingdom.
Figura 12. Forma radial, Weetwood Moor, Northumberland, Reino Unido. Photo by Ken Hedges, 2013.

Figure 13. The labyrinth of Outeiro do Cribo, A Armenteira, Meis, Pontevedra, Galicia, Spain.
Figura 13. El laberinto de Outeiro do Cribo, A Armenteira, Meis, Pontevedra, Galicia, España (Froaringus 2006, CC BY-SA 3.0 license).

as to create a round labyrinth. Most of them are found in the Iberian Peninsula (Valdez-Tullett 2017:10); in total no more than 30 have been counted.

Spirals are one of the scarcest representations, although present in practically all regions of the Atlantic arc. They are curvilinear motifs that rotate in a single line around a center, which present variable sizes and directions—clockwise and counterclockwise—and, as in the previous cases, they frequently appear accompanied by other motifs with which they are directly related (Vázquez Varela 1983:47). Sometimes their design is variable, and they can form complex, more intricate forms (Figure 14).

Figure 14. Complex spiral motif, Laxe das Cruces, área Arqueológica de Tourón, Ponte Caldelas, Galicia.
Figura 14. Motivo complejo en espiral, Laxe das Cruces, área Arqueológica de Tourón, Ponte Caldelas, Galicia. Photo by Ken Hedges, 2013.

The next type of the geometric group are the grids or rectangular reticulated motifs. They are another of the motifs that are present in all the territories of the Atlantic arc, being present in megalithic monuments belonging to the Neolithic as well as in later engraved panels from the Bronze Age. Sometimes they are considered "game boards," especially those located in *castros*—the Metal Age fortifications in the northwestern peninsula—and those that could be associated with sites of later date, after the Roman invasion of the area (Fernández Pintos 2017:201), although these motifs have been found in sites placed in many different periods, from the Neolithic at the Outeiro dos Lameiros station in Baiona, Spain (CarmenLago 2014), to the Bronze Age at Ballynahow Beg (Figure 15) in County Kerry, Ireland (MacWhite 1946:49).

The last type of this first classificatory group brings together various types of lines arranged in numerous ways: rectilinear, zigzag, angular, or combinations of several types. This type of representation is presented in panels of many chronologies, although their presence is common in the passages and walls of the chambers of megalithic monuments of funerary character. The Northumberland engravings in England and the Gavrinis engravings in France stand out, framed between the end of the Neolithic period and the beginning of the Bronze Age (Johnston 1993:259–266).

The other main group in the corpus of Atlantic Style engravings is the naturalistic, in which the zoo-

Figure 15. Ballynahow Beg, County Kerry, Ireland.
Figura 15. Ballynahow Beg, Condado de Kerry, Irlanda (Fáilte Ireland 1977, CC BY-NC-ND 4.0 license).

morphs, which include mainly deer, and serpentiforms, are framed.

This is clearly the least common set, since the main characterization of this style is abstract or geometric engravings. Until recently the only group with naturalistic or zoomorphic features were the serpentiforms, due to their enormous symbolism and their association with myths and legends among the populations of Atlantic Europe from the Bronze Age until not so long ago, but now numerous panels with zoomorphic representations have been documented in Galicia and some in northern Portugal, mainly with motifs of deer, horses, and other undetermined animals.

Especially noteworthy are those of Laxe dos Carballos in Campo Lameiro, a large hunting scene (Figure 16) with a huge deer (Figure 17) as the most prominent figure, having numerous spears stuck in it, accompanied by other more schematic figures of deer and other animals, along with some concentric circles and large cupules or basins. It is one of the best representations of both zoomorphic and hunting scenes in northwestern Spain.

Finally, it is necessary to mention another of the most outstanding panels of the Atlantic Style: the large vertical panel of Outeiro dos Lameiros (Figure 18), 15 meters high, portrays some 78 equids, along with other figures such as a ladderlike form, sun signs, and a huge central figure with an appendage at the bottom whose nature is undetermined (Torres Goberna 2012c).

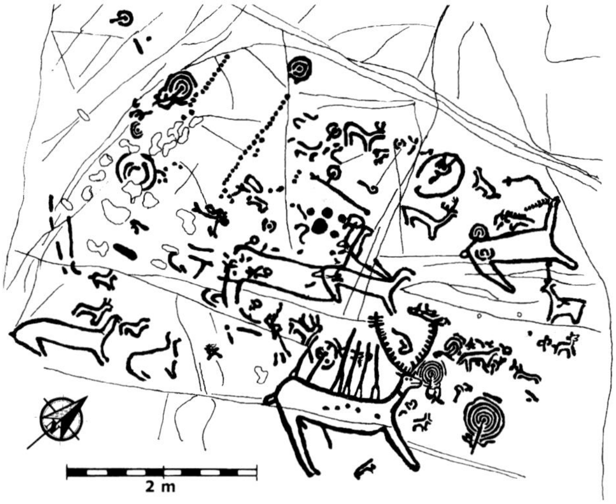

Figure 16. Petroglyph tracing from Laxe dos Carballos, in the Parque Arqueológico del Arte Rupestre de Campo Lameiro.
Figura 16. Rastreo de petroglifos de Laxe dos Carballos, en el Parque Arqueológico del Arte Rupestre de Campo Lameiro (Fernández Pintos 2015:Figure 134, CC BY-NC-ND 4.0 license).

Figure 17. The large deer at Laxe dos Carballos.
Figura 17. El gran ciervo de Laxe dos Carballos. Photo by Ken Hedges, 2015.

Outside the area of Galicia and northern Portugal this type of engraving with zoomorphs had never been documented. However, the year 2021 saw publication of the discovery of the first examples of cervids in Scotland, which are still under an exhaustive study. This is the Dunchraigaig panel, in the Kilmartin Glen area (Figure 19). The deer would date to the late Neolithic or early Bronze Age, i.e., between 4000 and 5000 years old (Barnett et al. 2021:2). About five deer, male and female, are depicted on the underside of a half-buried rock inside a stone cist, made by pecking the surface, probably with a stone tool (Barnett et al. 2021:3–4). These engravings have already set a precedent in our understanding of the prehistoric art of the time.

Figure 18. (a) The large panel of Outeiro dos Lameiros. (b) DStretch processed as grayscale to enhance the figures.
Figura 18. (a) El gran panel de Outeiro dos Lameiros. (b) DStretch procesado como escala de grises para mejorar las figuras (Leclere 2010, CC BY-SA 2.0 license).

Figure 19. Tracing of the deer engravings at Dunchraigaig Cairn, Kilmartin, Scotland.
Figura 19. Rastreo de los grabados de ciervos en Dunchraigaig Cairn, Kilmartin, Escocia. Illustration by Ken Hedges (adapted from Valdez-Tullett and Barnett 2021:13).

The last subgroup belonging to the zoomorphs are the serpentiforms, which, as we have already mentioned, have a special mythological importance. This type of engraving appears associated with or even framed in a populated area or within megalithic monuments; that is, unlike the others, they are created in an environment of habitation or frequent visitation, while the other engravings appear in the middle of the natural environment relatively far from habitational sites, or at least not within their perimeter. This implies that serpentiforms were made with a different intention; legends and myths speak of the relationship of snakes with fertility and fertilization. Let us take the case of A Pedra da Serpe, in Campo Lameiro (Figure 20), located inside the *castro* of Penalba, which was a special altar, since, on the night of San Juan, those couples who wished to have offspring had to have intercourse on top of the stone and carry a bowl of milk as an offering to the snakes to drink, so that fertilization would be successful (Terras de Pontevedra 2019).

Figure 20. The Pedra da Serpe at the castro of Penalba, Campo Lameiro, Pontevedra, Spain.
Figura 20. La Pedra da Serpe en el castro de Penalba, Campo Lameiro, Pontevedra, España (Terras de Pontevedra 2021).

Although we have made a detailed description of these engravings, it is essential to understand that the engravings present in the panels appear combined, forming very complex compositions, from which it is also impossible to determine the exact chronology of each element, as discussed above.

Most of the elements appear related to each other, and it is precisely this combination that, on the one hand, makes it difficult to distinguish singular elements and, on the other hand, provides the enormous graphic and visual quality of these panels. It is important to note that the placement of these motifs was clearly intentional, and that these combinations seem to have been planned from the very beginning (Valdez-Tullett 2017:15) (Figure 21). In the field of archaeology, or in science in general, there is a tendency to make classifications to better understand the elements we study; however, we must understand that at that time these panels were not made with respect to classifications, but to other different motivations, and that what we

Figure 21. Circular forms with radials, combined with grooved geometric and serpentine forms, Pedra da Serpe, Valga, Pontevedra, Galicia.

Figura 21. Formas circulares con radiales, combinadas con formas geométricas acanaladas y serpentinas, Pedra da Serpe, Valga, Pontevedra, Galicia (Negreira 2021, CC BY-SA 4.0 license).

see today is the result of the combination of the work of artists who, over the years, were adding their contribution to the previous work.

Motifs common to all these areas have been discussed, i.e., those appearing in at least two separate regions or countries, and thus forming part of an iconography common to the Atlantic axis. However, the corpus of petroglyphs belonging to this style is not complete, since there are numerous other typologies that have not been included in this classification because they are unique to a specific region, such as weapons, typical of the northwest of the peninsula, specifically Galicia, where numerous examples of daggers, halberds, axes, and arrows can be found, sometimes wielded by anthropomorphs. The panel of Pedra das Ferraduras, in Fentáns, Pontevedra, which shows enormous 2-meter-long swords, stands out in particular.

This on the one hand provides us with a chronological context belonging to the Metal Age, when metallurgy begins to be practiced and becomes another resource for these societies along with agriculture and livestock; and on the other hand, it also portrays other changes in the societies of recent prehistory in Europe, which are the new social and power classes that are generated by managing these weapon resources and the control over the territories providing these resources—they now have a stronger resource, not only for defense against attack from enemies, but also as an important source of economic gain through commercial exchange (Vázquez Varela 1990:50).

Finally, we mention another type of engravings which are the *idoliforms,* engravings portraying cylindrical objects that sometimes have anthropomorphizing features such as eyes or a mouth, which also echoes the rich religious or sacred culture of these objects (Figure 22). In turn, material remains of sculptures with similar shapes have been found in what is now known as Portugal and in Brittany, which once again strengthens these interregional cultural relations and exchanges (Alonso Romero 2007:33).

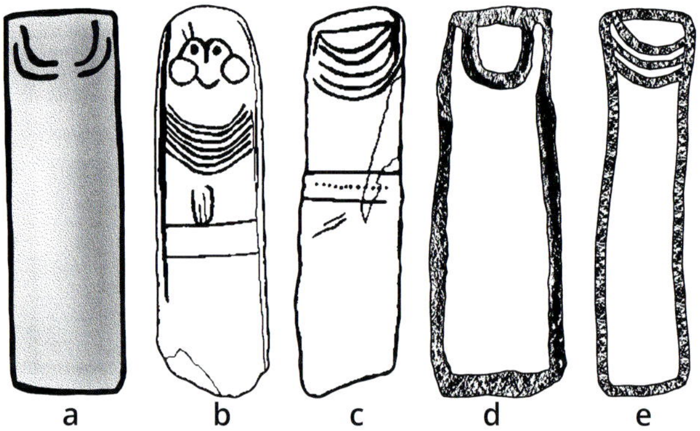

Figure 22. Comparison of decorated idol-cylinders from (a) Sintra and (b) Quinta de Vila Maior, Portugal, and (c) Alto da Escrita, Galicia, with idoliform petroglyphs (d, e) at Pedras das Ferraduras, Galicia.

Figure 22. Comparación de los cilindros-idolillos decorados de (a) Sintra, (b) Quinta de Vila Maior, Portugal, y (c) Alto da Escrita, Galicia, con los petroglifos idoliformes (d, e) de Pedras das Ferraduras, Galicia (a after Torres Goberna 2012a; b, c, and e after Fernández Pintos 2015:Figure 143; d after Valdez 2010:Figure 13).

Of course, many more typologies and subgroups of engravings could be studied and commented on: squares, lines, swastikas, deer tracks, boats, etc. But as already mentioned, in this paper we focus only on the typologies that form a common corpus within this style; however, it is important to note that the Iberian regions of Galicia and northern Portugal have the greatest variety of motifs due to the enormous diversity of elements represented, and which so far have not been found elsewhere (Valdez-Tullett 2017:8).

Similarities and Differences Between Regions

In this detailed study it can be verified that these engravings correspond to a common style in Bronze Age Europe, with the Atlantic Ocean as the backbone and as a corridor of interterritorial and cultural communications in this period of time. It is important to understand these engravings as a unit, despite the small differences they may have, since at that time there were none of the borders or concepts of country or nationality that today mark our relations with our neighbors. It was most likely an open territory that allowed the passage between different places.

Of course there are differences, but we find that the similarities are even greater among the rock engravings of Atlantic Europe:

- Similar geographical environment: The contexts in which we find the presence of these types of representations are very similar. On the one hand, they occur in open air places, with large extensions of land, and in places marked or considered special, such as roads or historical landmarks, near habitation sites, or on summits or areas with sacred characteristics, normally associated with social gatherings or from which an enormous amount of territory can be perceived at a single glance. Sometimes these places are related to astronomical events (such as the solstices), and there are even engraved calendars to mark the passage of time, probably for cycles such as harvests. These engravings could be related not only to abstract, sacred, or religious concepts existing only in the imagination, but also to occurrences related to everyday life.
- Funerary contexts: On the other hand, they are also found inside megalithic monuments of funerary character, both in the entrance corridors and in the main chambers, which emphasizes the sacred character of these engravings and marks a prelude to the later development of the Atlantic Style during the Bronze Age.
- Typologies common to several regions: The same motifs have been documented over the years, even from the beginning to the middle of the last century, throughout the geographical distribution area in which these enclaves are located. Not only that, but the motifs are mainly of an abstract nature, indicating a clear common symbolic imagery, and supporting the idea of an Atlantic culture.
- Interterritorial contacts: The distribution of this style, research on the similarities and correspondences of features and attributes in different sites, and the material and archaeological evidence found with respect to the engravings all speak of clear interterritorial contacts. At the same time, evidence is being found of panels or sites in other areas with engravings that could be ascribed to the Atlantic Style, which could expand the territory of distribution of these engravings, or reaffirm the hypothesis of interterritorial communication of cultures.
- Common chronology: In spite of the chronological variables, due to factors such as social development and access to resources in different areas, we find a common period of approximately 2000 years, corresponding to the Bronze Age, in which there is a boom in the appearance and production of engravings framed in the Atlantic Style, which, once again, confirms the existence of this shared culture.

As for the differences, although small, they should be taken into account when approaching the study of this style:

- Difference in motifs: Although, as we have said, there are motifs common to all territories, it is true that certain typologies of this extensive corpus are specific to a particular region. This is the case of most zoomorphs, anthropomorphs, weapons, or idoliforms present in the northwest of the Iberian Peninsula, although these differences may disappear as new finds are made, as in the case of the Dunchraigaig deer in Scotland.
- Different levels of clustering: Another major discrepancy, which is perhaps the most notable, is the enormous level of clustering of panel stations and sites in some areas, such as Galicia, compared to other places such as the United Kingdom, Ireland, or France. This difference could have numerous factors: the climatological difference, the number of inhabitants, the dispersion of habitational nuclei, or others. However, it is true that this gap could decrease over time if new discoveries are made and the number increases, something that always happens.

Conclusions

In short, we are faced with a clear style, which has been established as its own for years in Europe, and which has an enormous archaeological, symbolic, cultural, and even natural value, which is important to protect, preserve, and publicize, since its intrinsic characteristics and the condition of being located outdoors make it extremely fragile to deterioration or to being a victim of destruction or neglect. The archaeological evidence and findings are conclusive, and it is increasingly obvious that during recent prehistory in Europe its inhabitants communicated, exchanged, and made marks that lasted over time and have survived until today. It is therefore important that this style should be recognized and valued as a common language, as signs of a culture that, in reality, are the direct fruits of the society that made them, and that, despite having lost meaning along the way due to temporal distance, are still as important now as they were then.

It is our duty to watch over this invaluable heritage, and to continue to carry out the enormous efforts and work that, for years, academics, societies, and social groups have been doing to fulfil this mission.

References Cited

Alonso Romero, Alfonso
2007 Análisis etnográfico y arqueológico de una Diosa Madre en el petroglifo de Outeiro de Filladuiro en Mallou (Carnota, A Coruña): coviñas y círculos. *Anuario Brigantino* 30: 21–56.

Barnett, Tertia, Joana Valdez-Tullett, and Lyn Wilson
2021 The Dunchraigaig Deer: Discovery of Scotland's Earliest Animal Carvings. Historic Environment Scotland Information Sheet. Electronic document, https://www.academia.edu/49087921/Information_Sheet_The_Dunchraigaig_Deer_discovery_of_Scotlands_earliest_animal_carvings, accessed October 9, 2021. DOI 10.13140/RG.2.2.24845.26087.

Bradley, Richard. Felipe Criado Boado, and Ramón Fábregas Valcárce,
1994 Los petroglifos como forma de apropiación del espacio: algunos ejemplos gallegos. *Trabajos de prehistoria* 51(2):159–168

Campos Gómez, Juan Carlos
2018 *Grabados rupestres de la provincia de León.* Gráficas Eujoa, Meres, Spain.

CarmenLago
2014 Outeiro dos Lameiros I. Patrimonio Galego (website). Electronic document, http://patrimoniogalego.net/index.php/65624/2014/11/outeiro-dos-lameiros-i-2/, accessed May 15, 2021.

Costas Goberna, Fernando Javier, and Antonio De La Peña Santos
2005 Los barcos de los petroglifos de Oia: Los tesoros de un hechicero y una nueva embarcación. *Glaucopis: Boletín del Instituto de Estudios Vigueses* 12:277–292.

English Heritage
2021 An Introduction to Prehistoric England (Before AD 43). Prehistory (web page). Electronic document, https://www.english-heritage.org.uk/learn/story-of-england/prehistory/, accessed July 13, 2021.

Fábregas Valcarce, Ramón
2010 *Os petróglifos e o seu contexto: un exemplo da Galicia meridional.* Instituto de Estudios Vigueses, Vigo, Spain.

Fábregas Valcarce, Ramón, and José Suárez Otero
1999 El proceso de neolitización en Galicia. In *II Congrés del Neolitic a la Península Ibérica SAGVMTVM-PLAV Extra 2*, pp. 541–548.

Fáilte Ireland
1977 Engraved Rock, Ballynahow Beg, east of Cahersiveen, County Kerry. Dublin City Library and Archive (photo). Electronic docujment, https://www.europeana.eu/en/item/438/_f188f265x, accessed May 2, 2022.

Fernández Pintos, Julio
2015 *Concurrencia, Emulación y Tradición. La dinámica artística de los Grabados Rupestres Gallegos.* Self published. Electronic document, https://www.academia.edu/11533134/Petroglifos_de_Galicia_01, accessed April 24, 2022.

2017 *Tableros de juego rupestres del S.O de Galicia.* Self published. Electronic document, https://www.researchgate.net/publication/330090931_Tableros_de_Juego_Rupestres_en_el_SO_de_Galicia, accessed April 27, 2021.

Froaringus
2006 Labirinto do Outeiro do Cribo. Wikimedia Commons (photo). Electronic document, https://commons.wikimedia.org/wiki/File:Labirinto_do_Outeiro_do_Cribo.JPG, accessed July 31, 2022.

García Quintela, Marco V., and Manuel Santos-Estévez
2015 Astronomical Symbolism in Bronze-Age and Iron-Age Rock Art. In *Handbook of Archaeoastronomy and Ethnoastronomy*, edited by C.L.N Ruggles, pp. 1213–1222. Springer Science + Business Media, New York.

Historic England
2018 *Prehistoric Rock Art: Introductions to Heritage Assets.* Historic England, Swindon, United Kingdom.

Historic Environment Scotland
2021 Rock art of Britain and Ireland. Scotland's Rock Art (website). Electronic document, https://www.rockart.scot/about-rock-art/rock-art-of-britain-and-ireland/, accessed August 5, 2021.

Holt, Christopher
2014 Newgrange Triple Spiral. Wikimedia Commons (photo). Electronic document, https://commons.wikimedia.org/wiki/File:Newgrange_Triple_Spiral.jpg, accessed July 31, 2022.

Isern, Neus, Joaquim Fort, and Marc Vander Linden
2012 Space Competition and Time Delays in Human Range Expansions: Application to the Neolithic Transition. *PLOS ONE* 7(12):e51106 (online). Electronic document, https://journals.plos.org/plosone/article?id=10.1371/journal.pone.0051106, accessed August 27, 2021.

Jahnke, Jochen
2007 NOR1523. Wikimedia Commons (photo). Electronic document, https://commons.wikimedia.org/wiki/File:NOR1523.JPG, accessed August 27, 2021.

Johnson, Ben
2021 Prehistoric Britain. Historic UK (website). Electronic document, https://www.historic-uk.com/HistoryUK/HistoryofEngland/Prehistoric-Britain/, accessed July 16, 2021.

Johnston, Susan
1993 The Relationship Between Irish Rock Art and Irish Passage Tomb Art. *Oxford Journal of Archaeology* 12(3):257–279.

Knowth.com
n.d. Newgrange Megalithic Passage Tomb. Knowth.com (website). Electronic document, https://www.knowth.com/newgrange.htm, accessed August 5, 2021.

Lameira
2015 Museo Pontevedra, Ed. Sarmiento 04-01a San Paio de Refoxos, Silleda. Wikimedia Commons (photo). Electronic document, https://commons.wikimedia.org/wiki/File:Museo_Pontevedra,_Ed._Sarmiento_04-01a_San_Paio_de_Refoxos,_Silleda.JPG, accessed August 11, 2022.

Leclere, Luis
2010 Panorámica do panel vertical do Outeiro dos Lameiros–Os Campos–Baiona. Wikimedia Commons (photo). Electronic document, https://commons.wikimedia.org/wiki/File:Panor%C3%A1mica_do_panel_vertical_do_Outeiro_dos_Lameiros_-_Os_Campos_-_Baiona.jpg, accessed October 8, 2021.

Lødøen, Trond
2017 The Meaning and Use(-Fulness) of Traditions in Scandinavian Rock Art Research. In *North meets South: Theoretical Aspects on the Northern and Southern Rock Art Traditions in Scandinavia*, edited by Peter Skoglund, Johan Ling, and Ulf Bertilsson, pp 1–34. Oxbow Books, Oxford.

MacWhite, Eoin
1946 A New View on Irish Bronze-Age Rock Scribings. *The Journal of the Royal Society of Antiquaries of Ireland* 76(2):59–80.

Maderos Martin, Alfredo
2019 Auga dos Cebros (Pontevedra, Galicia): Un barco del Bronce Final II en la fachada atlántica de la Península Ibérica (1325–1050 a. C.). *SAGVNTVM Papeles del Laboratorio de Arqueología de Valencia* 51:23–39.

Negreira, Alex
2021 Pedra da Serpe. obaixoulla.gal (blog). Electronic document, https://www.obaixoulla.gal/elementos/valga/arqueoloxia/pedra-da-serpe, accessed April 25, 2022.

RAPP
2000 *Rock Art Pilot Project: Main Report.* English Heritage, Bournemouth and London.

Redondo Ortega, Jose Juan, and Federico Martínez Rodríguez
2021 Primeros datos sobre un petroglifo prehistórico de Estilo Atlántico hallado en Peña Madura, cuenca alta del Río Dílar, Sierra Nevada (Granada). *Cuadernos de Arte Prehistórico* 11:124–160.

Rodríguez Rellán, Carlos, Alia Vázquez Martínez, and Ramón Fábregas Valcarce
2018 Cifras e imágenes: una aproximación cuantitativa a los petroglifos gallegos. *Trabajos de Prehistoria* 75(1):109–127.

Schulze, John W.
2017 Newgrange–34949126593. Wikimedia Commons (photo). Electronic document, https://commons.wikimedia.org/wiki/File:Newgrange_-_34949126593.jpg, accessed July 31, 2022.

Terras de Pontevedra
2019 Castro de Penalba e Pedra da Serpe. Terras de Pontevedra Tourist Association (website). Electronic document, https://terrasdepontevedra.org/arte-rupestre/castro-de-penalba-e-pedra-da-serpe/, accessed July 23, 2021.

Torres Goberna, Francisco Javier
2012a Edad de Cobre o Calcolítico en Galicia. Historia y arqueología, Naturaleza: Flora y fauna, Rutas e itinerarios (blog). Electronic document, http://oestrymnio.blogspot.com/2012/01/historia-de-galicia-iii-edad-del-cobre.html, accessed May 1, 2022.

2012b Neolítico en Galicia. Electronic document, http://oestrymnio.blogspot.com/2012/03/historia-de-galicia-ii-el-neolitico.html, accessed July 12, 2021.

2012c Petroglifos de Outeiro dos Lameiros (Baiona). Historia y arqueología, Naturaleza: Flora y fauna, Rutas e itinerarios (blog). Electronic document, http://oestrymnio.blogspot.com/2012/10/petroglifos-de-outeiro-dos-lameiros.html, accessed July 6, 2021

Valdez, Joana
2010 *A Gravura na Arte Esquemática do Noroeste Peninsular: O caso do Monte de Góios (Lanhelas, Caminha).* Master's dissertation, Faculdade de Letras da Universidade do Porto, Portugal.

Valdez-Tullett, Joana
2013 A Arte Rupestre Atlântica: passado, presente e futuro. In *Arqueologia em Portugal, 150 anos,* edited by José Morais Arnaud, Andrea Martins, and César Neves, pp. 547–556. Dpi Cromotipo–Oficina de Artes Gráficas, Lda., Lisbon.

2017 Design and Connectivity: *The Case of Atlantic Rock Art.* Volume 1. Ph.D. Dissertation, Department of Archaeology, University of Southampton, Southampton, United Kingdom.

Valdez-Tullett, Joana, and Tertia Barnett
2021 New Light on Scotland's Prehistoric Rock Art: The Recent Discovery of Animal Carvings at Dunchraigaig Cairn (Kilmartin, Scotland). *PAST—The Newsletter of the Prehistoric Society* 98:12–13.

Vázquez Varela, Jose Manuel
1983 Los petroglifos gallegos. *Zephyrus* 36:43–51.

1990 *Los Petroglifos de Galicia.* Universidade de Santiago de Compostela. Ed. Biblioteca de Divulgación, Santiago de Compostela, Spain.

The Spanish version of this paper begins on the next page.

La versión en español de este artículo comienza en la página siguiente.

Los grabados rupestres del eje atlántico: un nexo común en la prehistoria reciente en Europa

Estrela C. García García

A través de un estudio formal y estilístico, se analizan los grabados rupestres hechos durante la prehistoria reciente en el eje atlántico europeo, como un medio para descubrir una cultura común que florece en el periodo de la Edad de los Metales, y que aúna países que hoy en día parecen tan diferentes como Portugal, España, Reino Unido, Irlanda y Francia. Estos grabados muestran una cultura en la prehistoria marcada por el arte esquemático, la abstracción del imaginario sagrado y religioso, así como un claro culto a las jerarquías bélicas a través de la representación de armas, y otros motivos, que indican un intercambio comercial y cultural en este territorio durante la Edad de los Metales..

En las últimas décadas el estudio y la investigación de los grabados rupestres de la prehistoria reciente en Europa ha experimentado una fuerte expansión al crecer el interés desde el ámbito académico y científico, a la vez que social, lo que se traduce en una mayor afluencia de trabajos de investigación relacionados con este tema. En este periodo de tiempo también han crecido exponencialmente las iniciativas locales e internacionales de estudio y difusión, desde asociaciones de aficionados, a grupos de investigación con miembros en numerosos países europeos en los cuales la cooperación internacional es clave. Todo esto abre las puertas a nuevas propuestas de protección, investigación y difusión del patrimonio arqueológico en un ámbito más amplio, a la vez incentivados por importantes organismos a nivel internacional como la UNESCO, ICOMOS o la iniciativa CARP de la Unión Europea.

El foco principal de este artículo es el contexto de la Europa Atlántica, en la cual se localizan multitud de grabados rupestres correspondientes a la prehistoria reciente—desde el fenómeno megalítico, hasta la entrada del Imperio Romano—que normalmente se conoce como la Edad de los Metales o el periodo prerromano. Durante años se han estudiado las diferencias y similitudes formales y morfológicas de estas representaciones, y gracias al enorme esfuerzo y trabajo de investigadores de numerosas universidades podemos establecer una tipología común interterritorial, lo que demuestra una cultura común prehistórica basada en el intercambio cultural, comercial, y la existencia de un lenguaje de signos común.

Estrela C. García García
Investigadora de doctorado en la Universidade de Santiago de Compostela (Galicia, España), Miembro del grupo de investigación GEPN-AAT

Cronología

La prehistoria reciente en Europa: estableciendo un contexto

El término de prehistoria reciente abarca desde el inicio del Neolítico en Europa (alrededor del 6000 a.C) y finales de la Edad del Hierro (1–3 d.C, o anterior en algunos casos), enmarcando un periodo de transición muy importante en las sociedades prehistóricas europeas, ya que se abandona el estilo de vida nómada que caracterizaba el Paleolítico, y con el

American Indian Rock Art, Volume 48. Amy Gilreath, Ken Hedges, and Anne McConnell, Editors. American Rock Art Research Association, 2022, pp. 128–138.

manejo de la agricultura y la ganadería se producen los primeros asentamientos, que darán lugar a las primeras poblaciones del Atlántico Europeo con pequeños núcleos de habitantes.

Es importante tener en cuenta que este contexto cronológico se aplica solamente a este entorno geográfico, ya que, a pesar de que casi todas las sociedades experimentan un desarrollo similar, las cronologías varían de una zona a otra en función del desarrollo social, el grado de aislamiento con respecto a otras áreas geográficas, y de la cantidad de recursos a los que se tuvieran acceso.

Pero antes de adentrarnos en el Neolítico, es importante entender de forma breve el periodo anterior, que es la transición del Paleolítico al Neolítico, también conocido como Mesolítico. Esta franja de tiempo enmarca alrededor de 6000 o 7000 años dependiendo de la región, entre el 12.000 al 6000 a.C aproximadamente (Torres Goberna 2012). Sabemos que la transición neolítica se retrasa en la Europa Atlántica, y esto es debido—entre otros factores—a la distancia geográfica desde la península de Anatolia y el Medio Oriente donde se produce esta explosión, y a la enorme diferencia climática existente, ya que en Europa se estaba abandonando todavía la última glaciación, lo que provocaba un ambiente mucho más frío y húmedo. De forma paulatina, las comunidades agrícolas de Anatolia van penetrando en Europa, y alrededor del 8000 y el 6500 a.C ya se habían establecido en regiones atlánticas como el noroeste de la península ibérica o el sur de las islas británicas (Torres Goberna 2012).

En la Figura 1 se puede observar cómo se produce esta transición escalonada hacia el Neolítico, en la cual, según el territorio se encuentre más alejado de la región de Anatolia y de la península arábiga, centro neurálgico del desarrollo y de la aparición de las primeras sociedades neolíticas de Eurasia, más tarde se produce este cambio de la antigua a la nueva Edad de Piedra. Esto explica las diferentes dataciones relativas de los grabados, que a continuación veremos.

Se han encontrado restos materiales de época Mesolítica y Neolítica que indican este encuentro cultural de distintos grupos de gente, que intercambiaban no solamente elementos materiales como cerámicas, sino técnicas de cultivo para aprovechar mejor las plantaciones y el terreno (Fabregas Valcarce y Suárez Otero 1999:544).

No obstante, el manejo de la agricultura no estaba todavía perfeccionado, y se han hallado evidencias de combinación de vida sedentaria y nómada: combinaban la caza junto con los cultivos, y en cuanto un área había sido explotada y no ofrecía más cosecha, los grupos se trasladaban a otras áreas en las que poder continuar cultivando, como afirma Torres Goberna (2012).

Es durante esta franja temporal, que abarca en el área atlántica entre el 6000 y el 3000 a.C—permitiendo siempre una variabilidad cronológica entre diferentes áreas geográficas—cuando se producen los primeros grabados del Estilo Atlántico, o motivos que serían los precursores de este estilo si se prefiere (Figura 2). Se hallan dentro de monumentos megalíticos, que eran enormes estructuras pétreas funerarias, en las que estas sociedades enterraban a sus muertos en fosas comunes, junto con ajuares y pertenencias, que decoraban con pinturas y grabados, que describiremos con más detalle más adelante.

Poco a poco, a través del intercambio vinculado a la trashumancia y los contactos entre diversas regiones, se van perfeccionando los métodos de cultivo y se introducen técnicas como la rotación de barbecho, que permite explotar un terreno agrario a lo largo de todo un año. Esto, junto a la quema de bosques, que proporcionaban grandes cantidades de pasto para cultivo, fue asentando las poblaciones y el estilo de vida nómada desaparece poco a poco para hacerse más y más sedentario, entrando ya de lleno en el Calcolítico, o la Edad de los Metales.

El inicio de esta época la marca, como su propio nombre indica, el comienzo de la práctica de la metalurgia. El primer metal que se funde es el cobre, un material blando y de fácil manejo que permitió la fabricación de los primeros utensilios metálicos, que sin duda mejoraron la calidad de vida de estas poblaciones, y aumentaron la cantidad de recursos disponibles gracias a un factor clave: la fabricación de armas más resistentes, que les permitía no solamente realizar intercambios comerciales, sino atacar y defender sus recursos. Es entonces cuando por un lado se comienzan a asentar en poblados fortificados, y por otro se fabrican los primeros útiles de con los que realizarán los grabados en piedra de estilo atlántico.

El siguiente periodo es la Edad del Bronce, un metal todavía más resistente y duro que el cobre, que viene de la alienación de este último con el estaño, que se inicia aproximadamente en el 2500 a.C hasta el 600 a.C. Es entonces cuando se produce un pico en la producción de estos grabados, coincidiendo con un gran desarrollo social.

En esta época continúan los enterramientos en monumentos pétreos de naturaleza megalítica, pero estos se reducen en tamaño, albergando un menor número de individuos, lo cual indica de un gran cambio, que es la aparición de las clases sociales: ahora que se producen mayores intercambios materiales y culturales, es fundamental también proteger y defender estos recursos, con lo que la producción de armas aumenta, y los individuos que manejas, fabrica y controlan estas armas son los que se colocan a la cabeza social (English Heritage 2021).

Los asentamientos habitacionales ahora son más definidos, con poblados de casas circulares construidos normalmente en una localización estratégica del territorio que permitía la visualización en 360º de un área muy amplia, habitualmente fortificados con una muralla y fosos. En la región de Galicia, este tipo de poblaciones se las llamaba "castros" (Figura 3), pero también son comunes a otras zonas como en las islas británicas (English Heritage 2021).

La etapa final de la Edad de los Metales es la Edad del Hierro, en la cual estas sociedades viven un auge muy grande, con costumbres, rituales, estructuras y culturas muy complejas y desarrolladas. Mas es en este momento cuando decae la producción de los grabados de estilo atlántico, en parte por la romanización que se produce a finales del milenio, alrededor del 50 a.C (Johnson 2021).

La llegada de los romanos marca el final de la prehistoria en Europa, y por lo tanto de los grabados de Estilo Atlántico, aunque no de la práctica de la creación de petroglifos, que continúa a lo largo de las eras como las evidencias arqueológicas nos muestran, con grabados con letras latinas de época romana, o cruces de época medieval con la llegada del cristianismo a estos territorios, en ocasiones en los mismos paneles de época prehistórica, y que nos muestran la enorme importancia que ha tenido siempre el gesto simbólico de grabar algo sobre una piedra.

Cronología para los grabados rupestres de Estilo Atlántico

Como acabamos de mencionar, las cronologías varían en función de la región que estemos hablando debido a los factores de la expansión neolítica, y la disponibilidad de recursos. Es por eso que la aparición de estos grabados es dispar entre diferentes regiones, como podemos comprobar en Figura 4.

Se evidencia no solamente la variabilidad cronológica, sino que también se puede apreciar una franja común entre el 4000 y el 1000 a.C (a excepción de Irlanda), en la cual se produce el mayor auge de los petroglifos de Estilo Atlántico, y que corresponde con el desarrollo social causado por el manejo de la metalurgia.

Por supuesto, además de la correspondencia estilística, el compartir este espacio temporal es un aspecto fundamental sobre la tesis de este trabajo, ya que esta franja cronológica común es un indicativo más de la existencia de una cultura atlántica.

A pesar de todo, también es primordial subrayar que en cuanto a la cuestión cronológica es muy difícil establecer un periodo claro cuando de grabados rupestres se trata, ya que al no haber presencia de pigmentos en los surcos—al menos no en los situados al aire libre—no es posible establecer una datación directa de los mismos. Para datar los petroglifos prehistóricos casi siempre se utiliza un método de datación indirecta, usando yacimientos cercanos o bien por correspondencias representativas, como es en el caso de los grabados de armas tales como espadas en el noroeste de la península ibérica, que por su naturaleza solamente pueden ser posteriores a la Edad del Cobre, puesto que antes no existían las armas metálicas; o bien por comparación de restos materiales, se han dado casos en los que se han hallado evidencias arqueológicas de objetos representados en estos grabados, como las ya mencionadas armas, o incluso ídolos antropomórficos en esta misma región.

El estilo atlántico

Definición y características

Se enmarcan dentro del Estilo Atlántico todos aquellos grabados prehistóricos realizados entre el megalitismo o Calcolítico y la Edad del Bronce en las regiones cercanas al Océano Atlántico del oeste europeo. Aunque se han documentado casos de paneles en lugares más apartados de la costa, es cierto que siguen guardando relación geográfica con otros enclaves del interior (Figura 5).

Por supuesto, se utiliza el término arte rupestre de estilo atlántico, por la mayoritaria localización de este arte en los países del litoral del océano atlántico, pero recientemente se han realizado descubrimientos de grabados enmarcados en este tipo de estilo en lugares como Granada (España, suroeste de la península ibérica), o Noruega, como veremos más adelante.

La mayor parte de estos grabados se encuentra en yacimientos o sitios al aire libre, normalmente sobre superficies pétreas de naturaleza granítica, en posición generalmente horizontal, y de tal forma que se encuentran totalmente integrados en el paisaje, localizados en lugares estratégicos o relacionados con otros yacimientos cercanos a través de evidencias materiales y arqueológicas (Fábregas Valcarce 2010:43–56). Pueden presentarse como elementos aislados, de tamaño pequeño, o bien como parte de grandes conjuntos esparcidos en una extensa área (Valdez-Tullett 2017:50). Se realizaban marcando un trazado y piqueteando con una herramienta metálica o pétrea dependiendo del momento cronológico.

No se sabe de forma exacta cuál era el motivo de la realización de estos grabados, lo único de lo que podemos cerciorarnos es de la importancia simbólica ya que estos grabados tenían, ya que este estilo se distribuye y se repiten por áreas con mucha distancia geográfica.

Como ocurre con el arte mueble del Paleolítico europeo, es posible que estos motivos pudieran aparecer en otros objetos, ropa, tatuajes, pinturas, que, por el paso del tiempo y el deterioro de este tipo de materiales, se hayan perdido.

Los motivos más representativos de este tipo de grabados es el estilo de anillos y cazoletas, que se trata de la combinación de estos dos motivos para componer paneles de diversos tamaños, lo que nos habla de la naturaleza abstracta o geométrica que caracteriza a estos grabados. Existen también elementos naturalistas que representan zoomorfos, antropomorfos o armas.

Otro elemento principal que forma parte de estas insculturas es el entorno en el cual se encuentran, principalmente al aire libre. Existen teorías acerca de la relación directa que habría de los petroglifos con otros elementos de un contexto geográfico, como son los pasos naturales, el acceso a recursos, la localización de yacimientos que en otro momento fueron poblaciones, o incluso calendarios astronómicos que permitieran medir el paso del tiempo para actividades como las cosechas. Por tanto, su ubicación en el espacio es tan importante como aquello que representan, pero una vez más, la distancia temporal nos impide poder cerciorar cuál era la conexión exacta que tenían.

Otro de los entornos en los cuales este tipo de grabados se presenta es en el interior de monumentos megalíticos de carácter funerario, normalmente correspondiente con el Neolítico o con el periodo denominado Megalitismo, debido a la aparición y propagación de este tipo de estructuras a lo largo del continente europeo. Este tipo de monumentos albergaban una enorme importancia social, ya que era lugares de enterramiento, en los cuales podían albergar numerosos individuos, incluso a veces familias enteras, que se enterraban junto con sus pertenencias personales, y ajuares. En estos monumentos se creaba una cámara principal que se rodeaba con grandes piedras, normalmente de naturaleza granítica, sobre la cual se disponía una enorme placa pétrea que tapaba el interior (Figura 6). Uniendo esta cámara con el exterior había un pasillo, por el cual entraba la luz natural. Estos monumentos se alineaban con el recorrido solar, de este a oeste, haciendo que, en los momentos del solsticio de verano o invierno, el sol iluminara la entrada y el interior completamente, lo que podría ser indicativo de un rito de paso de la vida a la muerte.

Por supuesto, estas construcciones se decoraban, y estos adornos gráficos se encuentran dentro de los pasillos de entrada y también en las cámaras funerarias donde se producían los enterramientos. Dichos grabados, debido a las condiciones de conservación por estar en interior, han conservado restos de pigmentos que también adornaban estas paredes. Los motivos representados en este tipo de monumentos son prácticamente únicos, ya que raramente se pueden ver en enclaves al aire libre (Historic Environment Scotland:2021).

Un ejemplo muy claro de esta combinación de pinturas y grabados es del dolmen de Dombate, en Bergantiños—A Coruña, Galicia, noroeste de España—que contiene pinturas rojas y negras hechas de carbón y óxido de hierro, formando motivos lineales, de zigzag y retículas, superpuestos sobre una base blanca de imprimación sobre la superficie granítica hecha con caolín (Figura 7a).

Como se puede apreciar en estas figuras, las pinturas están presentes dentro de todo el interior del monumento, desde el pasillo hasta la cámara mortuoria, con motivos muy elaborados acompañándolas grabados, en concreto destaca un elemento indefinido que se ha denominado como "la cosa" (Figura 7b).

Dentro del área de distribución de estos grabados también encontramos muchos otros notables ejemplos de grabados dentro de monumentos megalíticos, como es Newgrange, en el condado de Meath, Irlanda, un enorme túmulo funerario construido hace 5200 años, lo que lo sitúa cronológicamente en el Neolítico (Knowth.com n.d.). Su estructura es similar a la de cualquier monumento megalítico, mas destaca por su tamaño, con 89 metros de diámetro. En este monumento son notables los magníficos grabados en forma de espiral (Figura 8), localizados en enormes ortostratos en el interior y el exterior del monumento, destacando uno de los motivos de la triple espiral en el ortostrato C10 (Figura 8b)). También hay otros elementos como líneas en zigzag, retículas, semicírculos, serpentiformes o cazoletas.

Muy relacionado con el megalito de Newgrange es la tumba de Gavrinis en la Bretaña, que data de hace 5500 años, con una cronología similar a su "pariente" irlandés. En su interior cuenta con grabados de semicírculos concéntricos, formando imágenes que asemejan a ondas, y que se acompañan de otras como serpentiformes, o radiales (Figura 9).

Ya se ha mencionado que este periodo histórico es la antesala de todo el fenómeno que se produce a partir del calcolítico, con el exponencial aumento de grabados al aire libre. No se sabe la razón exacta de este aumento de este tipo de representaciones, aunque lo más probable es que fuera una acumulación de causas relacionadas con el desarrollo social que produce el control del territorio a través de los recursos como la agricultura, la ganadería y la metalurgia. Si algo es cierto es que el arte, o el imaginario gráfico, nace de la sociedad que lo crea, y, por lo tanto, está íntimamente relacionado y conectado con convenciones y estructuras sociales que, hoy en día desde la distancia temporal que nos separa de la prehistoria reciente europea, sólo podemos imaginar.

Distribución

La distribución de estos grabados se produce a lo largo del eje de los países lindantes con el Océano Atlántico, normalmente en zonas costeras, aunque se han encontrado estaciones y yacimientos en lugares alejados de las costas.

Desde el norte de Portugal, pasando por el noroeste de la Península Ibérica—incluyendo las regiones de Galicia y El Bierzo—hasta Bretaña, Irlanda y el Reino Unido, vemos un corredor natural, siguiendo un arco que une territorios tan separados, y que, por supuesto daría una clara muestra de un circuito comunicativo entre estas regiones, con un claro intercambio cultural y la existencia de un imaginario colectivo compartido (ver Figura 5).

Dentro de cada una de estas regiones, la densidad de paneles es diferente en cada uno, siendo la región con mayor número de paneles o estaciones Galicia, en el noroeste de la península ibérica, en lo que hoy es España, con alrededor de 4000 en total en el año 2018 en una superficie de 30.000km^2 (Rodríguez Rellán et al. 2018:113), número que ha seguido aumentando desde entonces. Es mucho mayor en comparación a otras zonas como en Inglaterra, con 5000 estaciones contabilizadas hasta ese mismo año repartidas en 130.000km^2 (Historic England 2018:1).

En recientes investigaciones se han hallado incluso paneles con estos grabados en zonas más alejadas de este corredor, como en la provincia de Granada, España (Redondo Ortega y Martínez Rodríguez 2021:124), o incluso otras regiones todavía más distantes como Noruega (Lødøen 2017:9-10). También son notables los grabados en la región de El Bierzo, en la comunidad de Castilla y León (España), cuya tipología y estilo es idéntica a los encontrados en el noroeste de la península, y que pocas veces son mencionados o incluidos en las clasificaciones científicas (Campos Gómez 2017:10).

Cabe apuntar que, a pesar de que se produzcan estas relaciones con el Océano Atlántico como eje centralizador, es probable que el número de estaciones aumente a medida que se produzcan nuevos descubrimientos, y dados los emplazamientos de estos nuevos hallazgos, quizá sea necesario replantearse la nomenclatura de esta tipología de grabados a una más general.

Por tanto, y tras este breve apunte, encontramos en esta franja territorial los grabados cuenta con enormes semejanzas formales y simbólicas, realizados por una cultura común dentro de un periodo cronológico similar. Más adelante se describirán todas las tipologías y las semejanzas entre ellas. Es importante también anotar las similaridades de su localización en el paisaje, ya que es idéntica en todos estos casos, y saca a la luz la importancia de la distribución en el espacio y el importantísimo papel que juegan estos enclaves en el paisaje y viceversa, deben entenderse como una unidad, o quizás como dos elementos en una relación simbiótica. Es probable que se situaran en zonas estratégicas, que indicaran algún tipo de comunicación espacial a otros miembros de un grupo, o bien como localización de recursos, como marcadores territoriales, etc. Por tanto, su relación con el paisaje es patente.

A este respecto se han encontrado conexiones claras de la ubicación de algunos paneles con áreas estratégicas de este tipo, como los realizados por Richard Bradley, Felipe Criado Boado y Ramón Fábregas Valcarce (1994:166–167).

Ahora bien, esta semejanza formal no es equivalente en todas las zonas, ya que varía de unas a otras, existiendo mayores correspondencias entre diferentes áreas, incluso aunque estén alejadas entre sí. La doctora Joana Valdez-Tullett (2017:227–230) propone unas vías de comunicación y semejanza formal entre cinco yacimientos repartidos entre los países anteriormente mencionados, que podrían indicar estas conexiones interterritoriales, y que reforzarían la tesis de un imaginario gráfico-cultural compartido.

En los trabajos de la Dra. Valdez-Tullett (2017:222–233) se habla de correlaciones formales y de los atributos de cada uno de estos enclaves a través del estudio de los yacimientos a través de bases de datos. Las conexiones resultantes entre distintos enclaves que demostrarían la interconexión de estas sociedades a pesar de la distancia geográfica: el propio océano serviría de corredor o de vía que proporcionaría el camino para la comunicación, aunque existan correlaciones regionales más fuertes.

Cabe destacar dentro de esta sección el caso de unos grabados localizados en la costa de Oia, en Pontevedra (Galicia), que representan unos barcos de tipo mediterráneo (Figura 10), denominados los paneles de Auga dos Cebros 1 y O Vivieiro 4. Este enclave es especialmente interesante, puesto que se haya justo en la costa, lo que indica una vez más una clara relación con el paisaje, pero son los propios motivos representados lo que afianza esta relación con el territorio, incluso con aguas más allá del atlántico, y que indican de forma clara las relaciones comerciales y culturales con otras zonas y culturas (Costas Goberna y De La Peña Santos 2005:278).

Queda por tanto demostrada esta relación de los grabados con respecto a su distribución espacial, y no solo formal como comprobaremos a continuación. El entorno de la costa atlántica juega un papel fundamental en la cimentación de relaciones interterritoriales que dan pie a la expansión de este estilo por toda la región atlántica, y quizás más allá de ella.

Tipologías

Si analizamos el corpus de grabados prehistóricos de la Europa atlántica, encontramos muchísimas similitudes, que demuestran enormes semejanzas estilísticas entre sí. Es por eso que estos grabados se asocian dentro de un mismo grupo llamado "Arte Atlántico" o "Grabados prehistóricos de Estilo Atlántico".

Los motivos que caracterizan principalmente este estilo son los abstractos, compuestos de cazoletas, círculos concéntricos, espirales, laberintos, o una mezcla de varios de ellos, aunque se incluyen también otras representaciones geométricas, zoomórficas o incluso otras como ídolos o armas, que van variando según la región, y que en algunos casos sólo aparecen en determinadas áreas (Valdez-Tullett 2013:549).

Es importante mencionar que en esta clasificación solamente se han incluido aquellos motivos pertenecientes a época prehistórica, por tanto, otros motivos como cruces o letras latinas, de época histórica, se han descartado.

Se han hecho numerosas clasificaciones al respecto a lo largo del tiempo, aumentando o modificándose a medida que se producen nuevos descubrimientos, que más adelante mencionaremos. Ahora nos centraremos en la clasificación general, común a todas estas regiones, de elaboración propia, en la que se distinguen las siguientes formas.

Como se puede comprobar (Figura 11), se ha dividido el corpus de petroglifos en dos tipos generales diferenciados por su naturaleza, o por lo que representan: motivos geométricos, que es el grupo mayoritario; y motivos naturalistas, que es minoritario y todavía sigue siendo objeto de estudio.

En cuanto al primer grupo, el geométrico, encontramos numerosos tipos de grabados que son de naturaleza "abstracta" o geométrica, utilizando nomenclaturas actuales para referirnos a representaciones de miles de años de antigüedad.

El primer grupo son las cazoletas (copas, o cúpulas), que sin duda se trata del más repetido y abundante de todo el corpus de petroglifos del arco atlántico, apareciendo en la práctica totalidad de paneles existentes, normalmente en combinación con otras figuras. Son incisiones circulares en la superficie de la roca en la que se halla, cuyo tamaño varía, mas pocas veces se encuentran cazoletas de más de 5cm de diámetro, por lo que en ocasiones es difícil distinguirlas de formaciones naturales (Vázquez Varela 1983:44). En ocasiones aparecen unidas entre sí por líneas (Valdez-Tullett 2017:8).

Por poner un ejemplo, podemos citar el trabajo de Rodríguez Rellán et al. (2018:113–114), que cuantifican los elementos presentes en todo el corpus de estaciones rupestres registradas hasta ese momento dentro de la región de Galicia, en el noroeste de la Península Ibérica. Las cazoletas son el elemento más abundante, encontradas en el 61,97% de las rocas grabadas, una clara muestra de la enorme presencia de este motivo.

El segundo más abundante son las combinaciones circulares, con un 33,14%, que en la mayoría de los casos aparecen en combinación con las cazoletas, por lo que podemos relacionarlas directamente con el tercer tipo, denominado combinaciones de cazoletas-anillos. Éstas están dispuestas concéntricamente alrededor de un centro—marcado con una cazoleta—y puede haber entre uno y un número ilimitado de anillos de tamaño variable

Si vamos más lejos en nuestra clasificación encontramos los radiales, un tipo también estrechamente relacionado con los tres que acabamos de describir. Los radiales (Figura 12) son una variación de los círculos o anillos concéntricos a los que les faltan partes de su circunferencia para formar uno o varios huecos. Pueden aparecer con una copa en el centro y con frecuencia tienen líneas radiales que ocupan los huecos. A menudo su tamaño es mucho mayor y pueden aparecer combinaciones de numerosos radiales y otras figuras, como copas o líneas. A veces estas disposiciones parecen sugerir que podrían tener algún significado o uso social específico como, por ejemplo, los grabados de Laxe das Rodas en Muros, en Galicia, uno de los casos más conocidos de uso de estos grabados como calendario para marcar el paso del tiempo (García Quintela y Santos-Estévez 2015:1215).

La siguiente tipología enmarcada dentro de estos motivos geométricos son los laberintos (Figura 13), que, al contrario de los anteriores casos, se trata de un grupo mucho menos abundante, siendo incluso raros los paneles en los cuales se ven laberintos. Se trata de representaciones que, como su nombre indica, representan círculos y líneas conformados de tal forma que crean un laberinto de tipo redondo. La mayor parte de ellos se encuentran en la península ibérica (Valdez-Tullett 2017:10), en total no se han contabilizado un número mayor a 30.

Las espirales son una de las representaciones más escasas, aunque presentes en prácticamente todas las regiones del arco atlántico. Son motivos curvilíneos que giran en una única línea alrededor de un centro, que presentan tamaños y sentidos variables—en el sentido de las agujas del reloj y en sentido contrario—y, como en los casos anteriores, aparece frecuentemente acompañada de otros motivos con lo que se encuentra directamente relacionada (Vázquez Varela 1983:47). En ocasiones su diseño es variable, y pueden formar complejas formas más intrincadas (Figura 14).

Los radiales son una variación de los círculos concéntricos o anillos, a los cuales les falta parte de su circunferencia, ya sea de forma intencionada o bien por daños que haya podido sufrir la superficie de la roca en la que se hallan. Pueden aparecer con una cazoleta en su centro o sin ella, y normalmente se han encontrado más este tipo de grafismos en los pasillos de entrada a monumentos funerarios, como es el caso de Newgrange en Irlanda o Gravinis en la Bretaña Francesa.

La siguiente tipología del grupo geométrico son las cuadrículas o motivos reticulados rectangulares. Son otro de los motivos que se presentan en la totalidad de los territorios del arco atlántico, estando presentes tanto en monumentos megalíticos pertenecientes al Neolítico, como en paneles de grabados posteriores de la Edad del Bronce. En ocasiones se las considera "tableros de juego", sobre todo aquellos que se sitúan en castros—fortificaciones de la Edad de los Metales en el noroeste peninsular—y que se podrían asociar con unas dataciones más tardías, posteriores a la invasión romana de la zona (Fernández Pintos 2017:201), aunque se han hallado estos motivos a lo largo de numerosas cronologías del Neolítico en la estación de Outeiro dos Lameiros en Baiona, España (CarmenLago 2014) o de la Edad del Bronce en Ballynahow Beg (Figura 15) en el condado de Kerry, Irlanda (MacWhite 1946:49).

La última tipología de este primer grupo clasificatorio aúna varios tipos de líneas dispuestos de numerosas maneras: rectilíneas, en zigzag, angulosas, o combinaciones de varios tipos, este tipo de representaciones se presenta en paneles de numerosas cronologías, aunque es común su presencia en los pasadizos y paredes de las cámaras de monumentos megalíticos de carácter funerario. Destacan los grabados de Northumberland en Irlanda, y los de Gravinis en Francia, enmarcados entre finales de época neolítica y principios de la Edad del Bronce (Johnston 1993:259–266).

El otro gran grupo del corpus de los grabados de Estilo Atlántico son los naturalistas, en los cuales se enmarcan los zoomorfos, que incluyen principalmente ciervos, y serpentiformes.

Este es claramente el conjunto menos común, ya que la caracterización principal de este estilo son los grabados abstractos o geométricos. Hasta hace poco el único grupo de características naturalistas o zoomórficas eran los serpentiformes, debido a su enorme simbolismo y su asociación con mitos y leyendas entre las poblaciones de la Europa Atlántica desde la Edad del Bronce hasta no hace mucho tiempo. Se han documentado numerosos paneles con representaciones zoomórficas en Galicia y algunas en el norte de Portugal, principalmente con motivos de ciervos, caballos y otros animales sin determinar.

Destacan especialmente los de Laxe dos Carballos en Campo Lameiro, una gran escena de caza (Figura 16) con un enorme cérvido (Figura 17) como figura central con numerosas lanzas clavadas, al que acompañan otras figuras más esquemáticas de cérvidos y otros animales, junto con algunos círculos concéntricos, y cazoletas. Es una de las mejores representaciones tanto zoomórficas como de escenas de caza del noroeste peninsular.

Por último, es necesario mencionar otro de los paneles más destacados del Estilo Atlántico: el gran panel de Outeiro dos Lameiros (Figura 18), con 15 metros de longitud y en vertical, retrata unos 78 équidos, junto con otras figuras como un escaleriforme, signos solares y una enorme figura central con un apéndice en la parte inferior cuya naturaleza es indeterminada (Costas Goberna:2012).

Fuera de la zona de Galicia y del norte de Portugal nunca se había documentado este tipo de grabados con zoomorfos. Sin embargo, en el año 2021 se publicó el descubrimiento de los primeros ejemplares de cérvidos en Escocia, que todavía están siendo objeto de un estudio exhaustivo. Se trata del panel de Dunchraigaig, en el área de Kilmartin Glen (Figura 19). Los ciervos datarían de finales del Neolítico o principios de la Edad del Bronce, es decir, entre 4000 y 5000 años de antigüedad (Barnett et al. 2021:3–4). Aparecen unos cinco ciervos, machos y hembras, realizados en la parte inferior de una roca semienterrada, dentro de una cista de piedra, punzando la superficie con una herramienta probablemente pétrea (Barnett et al. 2021:3–4). Estos grabados ya han sentado un precedente en nuestra comprensión del arte prehistórico de la época.

El último subgrupo perteneciente a los zoomorfos son los serpentiformes, que como ya hemos mencionado, tienen una importancia mitológica especial. Este tipo de grabados aparecen asociados, o incluso enmarcados en un área poblada o dentro de monumentos megalíticos, es decir, que a diferencia de los demás, se crean en un entorno de habitación o de visita frecuente, mientras que los otros grabados aparecen en medio del entorno natural relativamente alejados de yacimientos habitacionales, o al menos no dentro de su perímetro. Esto implica que se hacían con una intención diferente, las leyendas y mitos hablan de la relación de las serpientes con la fertilidad y la fecundación. Pongamos el caso de A Pedra da Serpe, en Campo Lameiro (Figura 20), situada dentro del castro de Penalba, que era un altar especial, ya que, en la noche de San Juan, aquellas parejas que desearan tener descendencia debían mantener relaciones encima de la piedra y llevar un cuenco de leche como ofrecimiento a las serpientes para que bebieran, para que la fecundación fuera exitosa (Terras de Pontevedra 2019).

A pesar de que hemos hecho una descripción detallada de estos grabados, es fundamental comprender que los grabados presentes en los paneles aparecen combinados formando complejísimas composiciones, de las cuales tampoco se puede determinar la cronología exacta de cada elemento, como se ha comentado anteriormente.

La mayor parte de elementos aparecen relacionados los unos con los otros, y es precisamente esta combinación lo que por un lado dificulta el trabajo de distinción de elementos singulares, y por otro aporta esta enorme calidad gráfica y visual de estos paneles. Es importante apuntar que el emplazamiento de estos motivos era claramente intencionado, y que estas combinaciones parecen estar planeadas desde un primer momento (Valdez-Tullett 2017:15) (Figura 21). En el campo de la arqueología, o en la ciencia en general, se tiende a realizar clasificaciones para entender mejor los elementos que estudiamos, sin embargo, hay que comprender que en aquel momento estos paneles no se hacían respecto a clasificaciones, sino a otras motivaciones diferentes, y que lo que vemos hoy en día es el resultado de la combinación del trabajo de artistas que, a lo largo de los años, fueron añadiendo su aportación al trabajo anterior.

Se han hablado de los motivos comunes a todas estas áreas, es decir, que aparecen en por al menos dos regiones o países separados, y que por tanto forman parte de una iconografía común al eje atlántico. No obstante, el corpus de petroglifos pertenecientes a este estilo no está completo, ya que existen numerosas otras tipologías que no se han incluido dentro de esta clasificación por ser únicas a una región concreta, como son las armas, propias del noroeste peninsular, en concreto de Galicia, donde se pueden encontrar numerosos ejemplos de puñales, alabardas, hachas y flechas, en ocasiones empuñadas por antropomorfos. Destaca especialmente el panel de Pedra das Ferraduras, en Fentáns, Pontevedra, que muestra unas enormes espadas de 2m de largo.

Esto por un lado nos aporta un contexto cronológico perteneciente a la Edad de los Metales, donde se empieza a practicar la metalurgia, y se convierte en un recurso más para estas sociedades junto con la agricultura y la ganadería; y por otro nos retratan también un cambio más en las sociedades de la prehistoria reciente en Europa, que son las nuevas clases sociales y de poder que se generan al manejar estos recursos armamentísticos, y el control sobre el territorio que estas proporcionan: ahora se cuenta con un recurso más fuerte con el que no solamente se pueden proteger, defender o atacar de enemigos, sino que también son una importante fuente de ganancias económicas a través del intercambio comercial (Vázquez Varela 1990:50).

Por último, mencionaremos otro tipo de grabados que son los idoliformes, unos grabados cilíndricos que en ocasiones cuentan con rasgos antropomorfizantes como ojos o boca, que también hacen eco de la rica cultura religiosa o sagrada de estos objetos (Figura 22). A su vez, se han encontrado restos materiales de esculturas con formas similares procedentes de lo que ahora es conocido como Portugal o Bretaña, lo que una vez más afianza estas relaciones e intercambios culturales interregionales (Alonso Romero 2007:33).

Por supuesto, se podrían estudiar y comentar muchas más tipologías y subgrupos de grabados: cuadrados, líneas, esvásticas, huellas de ciervos, barcos etc. Mas como ya se ha mencionado, en este trabajo nos centramos solamente en las tipologías que forman un corpus común dentro de este estilo, sin embargo, es importante anotar que las regiones íberas de Galicia y el norte de Portugal son las contenedoras de la mayor variedad de motivos debido a la enorme diversidad de elementos representados, y que hasta ahora no se han encontrado en otros lugares (Valdez-Tullett 2017:8).

Semejanzas y diferencias entre diferentes regiones

Por lo tanto, en este estudio detallado se puede comprobar que, estos grabados, corresponden a un estilo común a la Europa de la Edad del Bronce, con el Océano Atlántico como eje vertebrador y como corredor de comunicaciones interterritoriales y culturales en este periodo de tiempo. Es sustancial entender estos grabados como una unidad, a pesar de las pequeñas diferencias que puedan tener, ya que por aquel entonces no existían las mismas fronteras ni conceptos de país o nacionalidad que hoy en día marcan nuestras relaciones con nuestros vecinos, sino que lo más probable es que fuer aun territorio abierto que permitiera el paso entre distintos lugares.

Por supuesto que existen diferencias, encontramos todavía mayores similitudes entre los grabados rupestres de la Europa atlántica:

- Entorno geográfico similar: los contextos en los cuales encontramos presencia de este tipo de representaciones son muy similares. Por un lado en lugares al aire libre, con grandes extensiones de terreno, y en lugares marcados o considerados especiales, como caminos o hitos históricos, cerca de yacimientos habitacionales, o en cumbres o zonas con características sagradas, normalmente asociadas a encuentros sociales o desde los cuales se puede percibir una enorme cantidad de territorio de un solo vistazo, en ocasiones estos lugares se relacionan con eventos astronómicos (como los solsticios), existiendo incluso calendarios grabados sobre los que contar el paso del tiempo, probablemente para marcar ciclos como las cosechas, de tal forma que se podrían relacionar estos grabados no solamente con un imaginario abstracto, sagrado o de carácter religioso, sino que también tienen relación con ocurrencias relacionadas con la vida cotidiana.
- Contextos funerarios: Por otro lado, también se encuentran dentro de monumentos megalíticos de carácter funerario, tanto en los pasillos de entrada como en las cámaras principales, lo que por un lado incide en el carácter sagrado de estos grabados, y por otro marcan una antesala para el desarrollo posterior del estilo atlántico durante la Edad del Bronce.
- Tipologías comunes a varias regiones: se han documentado a lo largo de años, desde incluso principios y mediados del siglo pasado, los mismos motivos en toda el área de distribución geográfica en la que se localizan estos enclaves. No solo eso, sino que los motivos son principalmente de naturaleza abstracta, lo que indica un claro imaginario simbólico común, y afianza la idea de una cultura atlántica.
- Contactos interterritoriales: La distribución de este estilo, así como los trabajos que estudian las similitudes y correspondencias de rasgos y atributos en diferentes yacimientos; y adicionalmente, las evidencias materiales y arqueológicas encontradas con respecto a los grabados nos hablan de claros contactos interterritoriales. A su vez, se están hallando evidencias de paneles o yacimientos con grabados que se podrían adscribir dentro del Estilo Atlántico, lo que podría por un lado expandir el territorio de distribución de estos grabados, o bien reafirmar la hipótesis de la comunicación interterritorial de culturas.
- Cronología común: A pesar de las variables cronológicas, debido a factores como el desarrollo social y el acceso a recursos de zonas diferenciadas, encontramos una franja común de aproximadamente unos 2000 años, correspondiente a la Edad del Bronce, en la que se produce un auge de aparición y realización de grabados enmarcados en el Estilo Atlántico, lo que una vez más, reincide en la existencia de esta cultura compartida.

En cuanto a las diferencias, que, a pesar de ser pequeñas, se deben tener en cuenta a la hora de abordar el estudio de este estilo:

- La diferencia de motivos: si bien como hemos dicho existen motivos comunes a todos los territorios, si es cierto que ciertas tipologías de este corpus tan extenso son propias de una región en concreto, como es el caso de la mayor parte de zoomorfos, los antropomorfos, armas o los idoliformes presentes en el noroeste de la península ibérica. Aunque estas diferencias pueden ir desapareciendo a medida que se produzcan nuevos hallazgos, como es el caso de los ciervos de Dunchraigaig en Escocia.

- Diferentes niveles de concentración: otra de las grandes discordancias, que quizás sea la más notable, es el enorme nivel de concentración de estaciones de paneles y yacimientos en algunas áreas como en Galicia, frente a otros lugares como Reino Unido, Irlanda o Francia. Esta diferencia podría tener numerosos factores: la diferencia climatológica, el número de habitantes, la dispersión de núcleos habitacionales, u otros. Si bien es cierto que esta brecha podría disminuir con el tiempo si se producen nuevos descubrimientos y aumente el número, algo que siempre sucede.

Conclusiones

En resumen, nos encontramos ante un claro estilo, que ya lleva afianzándose como propio desde hace años en Europa, y que alberga un enorme valor arqueológico, simbólico, cultural, e incluso natural, que es importante proteger, conservar y difundir, dado que sus características intrínsecas y la condición de estar localizado al aire libre, lo hacen extremadamente frágil al deterioro o a ser víctima de la destrucción o al abandono. Las pruebas y hallazgos arqueológicos son concluyentes, y cada vez es más obvio que durante la prehistoria reciente en Europa sus habitantes se comunicaban, intercambiaban y realizaban marcas que perduraron en el tiempo y han llegado hasta ahora. Es por tanto que este estilo debe ser reconocido y valorado como tal, como un lenguaje común, como signos de una cultura que, en realidad, son los frutos directos de la sociedad que los fabricó, y que, a pesar de haber perdido el significado por el camino debido a la distancia temporal, siguen siendo tan importantes ahora como lo eran entonces.

Es nuestro deber velar por este valiosísimo patrimonio, y seguir llevando a cabo los enormes esfuerzos y trabajo que, desde hace años académicos, sociedad y grupos sociales llevan haciendo para cumplir esta misión.

Referencias citadas

Alonso Romero, Alfonso
2007 Análisis etnográfico y arqueológico de una Diosa Madre en el petroglifo de Outeiro de Filladuiro en Mallou (Carnota, A Coruña): coviñas y círculos. *Anuario Brigantino* 30: 21–56.

Barnett, Tertia, Joana Valdez-Tullett, and Lyn Wilson
2021 The Dunchraigaig Deer: Discovery of Scotland's Earliest Animal Carvings. Historic Environment Scotland Information Sheet. Electronic document, https://www.academia.edu/49087921/Information_Sheet_The_Dunchraigaig_Deer_discovery_of_Scotlands_earliest_animal_carvings, accessed October 9, 2021.

Bradley, Richard. Felipe Criado Boado, and Ramón Fábregas Valcárce
1994 Los petroglifos como forma de apropiación del espacio: algunos ejemplos gallegos. *Trabajos de prehistoria* 51(2):159–168

Campos Gómez, Juan Carlos
2018 *Grabados rupestres de la provincia de León*. Gráficas Eujoa, Meres, Spain.

CarmenLago
2014 Outeiro dos Lameiros I. Patrimonio Galego (website). Electronic document, http://patrimoniogalego.net/index.php/65624/2014/11/outeiro-dos-lameiros-i-2/, accessed May 15, 2021.

Costas Goberna, Fernando Javier, and Antonio De La Peña Santos
2005 Los barcos de los petroglifos de Oia: Los tesoros de un hechicero y una nueva embarcación. *Glaucopis: Boletín del Instituto de Estudios Vigueses* 12:277–292.

English Heritage
2021 An Introduction to Prehistoric England (Before AD 43). Prehistory (web page). Electronic document, https://www.english-heritage.org.uk/learn/story-of-england/prehistory/, accessed July 13, 2021.

Fábregas Valcarce, Ramón
2010 *Os petróglifos e o seu contexto: un exemplo da Galicia meridional*. Instituto de Estudios Vigueses, Vigo, Spain.

Fábregas Valcarce, Ramón, and José Suárez Otero
1999 El proceso de neolitización en Galicia. In *II Congrés del Neolitic a la Península Ibérica SAGVMTVM-PLAV Extra 2*, pp. 541–548.

Fáilte Ireland
1977 Engraved Rock, Ballynahow Beg, east of Cahersiveen, County Kerry. Dublin City Library and Archive (photo). Electronic docujment, https://www.europeana.eu/en/item/438/_f188f265x, accessed May 2, 2022.

Fernández Pintos, Julio
2015 *Concurrencia, Emulación y Tradición. La dinámica artística de los Grabados Rupestres Gallegos*. Self published. Electronic document, https://www.academia.edu/11533134/Petroglifos_de_Galicia_01, accessed April 24, 2022.

2017 *Tableros de juego rupestres del S.O de Galicia*. Self published. Electronic document, https://www.researchgate.net/publication/330090931_Tableros_de_Juego_Rupestres_en_el_SO_de_Galicia, accessed April 27, 2021.

Froaringus
2006 Labirinto do Outeiro do Cribo. Wikimedia Commons (photo). Electronic document, https://commons.wikimedia.org/wiki/File:Labirinto_do_Outeiro_do_Cribo.JPG, accessed July 31, 2022.

García Quintela, Marco V., and Manuel Santos-Estévez
2015 Astronomical Symbolism in Bronze-Age and Iron-Age Rock Art. In *Handbook of Archaeoastronomy and Ethnoastronomy*, edited by C.L.N Ruggles, pp. 1213–1222. Springer Science + Business Media, New York.

Historic England
2018 *Prehistoric Rock Art: Introductions to Heritage Assets*. Historic England, Swindon, United Kingdom.

Historic Environment Scotland
2021 Rock art of Britain and Ireland. Scotland's Rock Art (website). Electronic document, https://www.rockart.scot/about-rock-art/rock-art-of-britain-and-ireland/, accessed August 5, 2021.

Holt, Christopher
2014 Newgrange Triple Spiral. Wikimedia Commons (photo). Electronic document, https://commons.wikimedia.org/wiki/File:Newgrange_Triple_Spiral.jpg, accessed July 31, 2022.

Isern, Neus, Joaquim Fort, and Marc Vander Linden
2012 Space Competition and Time Delays in Human Range Expansions: Application to the Neolithic Transition. *PLOS ONE* 7(12):e51106 (online). Electronic document, https://journals.plos.org/plosone/article?id=10.1371/journal.pone.0051106, accessed August 27, 2021.

Jahnke, Jochen
2007 NOR1523. Wikimedia Commons (photo). Electronic document, https://commons.wikimedia.org/wiki/File:NOR1523.JPG, accessed August 27, 2021.

Johnson, Ben
2021 Prehistoric Britain. Historic UK (website). Electronic document, https://www.historic-uk.com/HistoryUK/HistoryofEngland/Prehistoric-Britain/, accessed July 16, 2021.

Johnston, Susan
1993 The Relationship Between Irish Rock Art and Irish Passage Tomb Art. *Oxford Journal of Archaeology* 12(3):257–279.

Knowth.com
n.d. Newgrange Megalithic Passage Tomb. Knowth.com (website). Electronic document, https://www.knowth.com/newgrange.htm, accessed August 5, 2021.

Lameira
2015 Museo Pontevedra, Ed. Sarmiento 04-01a San Paio de Refoxos, Silleda. Wikimedia Commons (photo). Electronic document, https://commons.wikimedia.org/wiki/File:Museo_Pontevedra,_Ed._Sarmiento_04-01a_San_Paio_de_Refoxos,_Silleda.JPG, accessed August 11, 2022.

Leclere, Luis
2010 Panorámica do panel vertical do Outeiro dos Lameiros–Os Campos–Baiona. Wikimedia Commons (photo). Electronic document, https://commons.wikimedia.org/wiki/File:Panor%C3%A1mica_do_panel_vertical_do_Outeiro_dos_Lameiros_-_Os_Campos_-_Baiona.jpg, accessed October 8, 2021.

Lødøen, Trond
2017 The Meaning and Use(-Fulness) of Traditions in Scandinavian Rock Art Research. In *North meets South: Theoretical Aspects on the Northern and Southern Rock Art Traditions in Scandinavia,* edited by Peter Skoglund, Johan Ling, and Ulf Bertilsson, pp 1–34. Oxbow Books, Oxford.

MacWhite, Eoin
1946 A New View on Irish Bronze-Age Rock Scribings. *The Journal of the Royal Society of Antiquaries of Ireland* 76(2):59–80.

Maderos Martin, Alfredo
2019 Auga dos Cebros (Pontevedra, Galicia): Un barco del Bronce Final II en la fachada atlántica de la Peníncula Ibérica (1325–1050 a. C.). *SAGVNTVM Papeles del Laboratorio de Arqueología de Valencia* 51:23–39.

Negreira, Alex
2021 Pedra da Serpe. obaixoulla.gal (blog). Electronic document, https://www.obaixoulla.gal/elementos/valga/arqueoloxia/pedra-da-serpe, accessed April 25, 2022.

RAPP
2000 *Rock Art Pilot Project: Main Report.* English Heritage, Bournemouth and London.

Redondo Ortega, Jose Juan, and Federico Martínez Rodríguez
2021 Primeros datos sobre un petroglifo prehistórico de Estilo Atlántico hallado en Peña Madura, cuenca alta del Río Dílar, Sierra Nevada (Granada). *Cuadernos de Arte Prehistórico* 11:124–160.

Rodríguez Rellán, Carlos, Alia Vázquez Martínez, and Ramón Fábregas Valcarce
2018 Cifras e imágenes: una aproximación cuantitativa a los petroglifos gallegos. *Trabajos de Prehistoria* 75(1):109–127.

Schulze, John W.
2017 Newgrange–34949126593. Wikimedia Commons (photo). Electronic document, https://commons.wikimedia.org/wiki/File:Newgrange_-_34949126593.jpg, accessed July 31, 2022.

Terras de Pontevedra
2019 Castro de Penalba e Pedra da Serpe. Terras de Pontevedra Tourist Association (website). Electronic document, https://terrasdepontevedra.org/arte-rupestre/castro-de-penalba-e-pedra-da-serpe/, accessed July 23, 2021.

Torres Goberna, Francisco Javier
2012a Edad de Cobre o Calcolítico en Galicia. Historia y arqueología, Naturaleza: Flora y fauna, Rutas e itinerarios (blog). Electronic document, http://oestrymnio.blogspot.com/2012/01/historia-de-galicia-iii-edad-del-cobre.html, accessed May 1, 2022.

2012b Neolítico en Galicia. Electronic document, http://oestrymnio.blogspot.com/2012/03/historia-de-galicia-ii-el-neolitico.html, accessed July 12, 2021.

2012c Petroglifos de Outeiro dos Lameiros (Baiona). Historia y arqueología, Naturaleza: Flora y fauna, Rutas e itinerarios (blog). Electronic document, http://oestrymnio.blogspot.com/2012/10/petroglifos-de-outeiro-dos-lameiros.html, accessed July 6, 2021

Valdez, Joana
2010 *A Gravura na Arte Esquemática do Noroeste Peninsular: O caso do Monte de Góios (Lanhelas, Caminha).* Master's dissertation, Faculdade de Letras da Universidade do Porto, Portugal.

Valdez-Tullett, Joana
2013 A Arte Rupestre Atlântica: passado, presente e futuro. In *Arqueologia em Portugal, 150 anos,* edited by José Morais Arnaud, Andrea Martins, and César Neves, pp. 547–556. Dpi Cromotipo–Oficina de Artes Gráficas, Lda., Lisbon.

2017 Design and Connectivity: *The Case of Atlantic Rock Art.* Volume 1. Ph.D. Dissertation, Department of Archaeology, University of Southampton, Southampton, United Kingdom.

Valdez-Tullett, Joana, and Tertia Barnett
2021 New Light on Scotland's Prehistoric Rock Art: The Recent Discovery of Animal Carvings at Dunchraigaig Cairn (Kilmartin, Scotland). *PAST—The Newsletter of the Prehistoric Society* 98:12–13.

Vázquez Varela, Jose Manuel
1983 Los petroglifos gallegos. *Zephyrus* 36:43–51.

1990 *Los Petroglifos de Galicia.* Universidade de Santiago de Compostela. Ed. Biblioteca de Divulgación, Santiago de Compostela, Spain.

Your Guess Is Not as Good as Any: Guidelines for the Public Interpretation of Rock Drawings

Richard A. Rogers

A follow-up to "'Your Guess Is as Good as Any': Rock Art, Public Interpretation, and Ownership" (Rogers 2020), this paper examines more recent efforts at the public interpretation of rock art from the Painted Rock Petroglyph Site in southern Arizona, Picture Canyon Natural and Cultural Preserve in northern Arizona, and two sites in the Great Basin in order to identify examples that counter the "your guess is as good as any" approach that dominated many late twentieth-century efforts at public interpretation. With that basis, this paper advances some general principles for negotiating the cultural politics of public interpretation, which include highlighting rather than erasing the relationships between contemporary indigenous peoples and ancient images on rock, portraying contemporary indigenous perspectives as a valid form of knowledge about indigenous pasts, relativizing archaeological knowledge as one of many forms of knowledge about indigenous pasts, avoiding the encouragement of visitors' guesses, and exercising restraint in assigning meanings to specific images.

On Nevada Highway 376, just south of its intersection with U.S. Highway 50, is a Nevada State Historical Marker for Toquima Cave, a pictograph and habitation site located several miles to the southeast on the Humboldt-Toiyabe National Forest, easily accessible by a dirt forest road and a short trail. The version of the sign present from January 1971 (based on marks on the sign itself) until at least 2012 (Figure 1) explained that petroglyphs and pictographs "are associated with the food gathering localities of Nevada's prehistoric inhabitants." In terms of the pictographs at this particular site, "Presumably, these people created the designs as ritual devices to insure success in the hunt." While vague and reliant on outdated understandings of Great Basin rock art—the hunting-magic hypothesis specifically (Whitley 2011) and processual archaeology's foregrounding of subsistence as the driving force behind symbolic forms (Francis 2005; Whitley and Clottes 2005)—the sign established a relationship between the pictographs and "Nevada's prehistoric inhabitants," though those inhabitants were unnamed and there was no reference to Nevada's contemporary indigenous communities.

Sometime between May 2002 and September 2005, an unofficial addition was made to the sign, and sometime before 2012 was removed. The following message was written in black marker at the bottom of the sign: "These petroglyphs make [sic] have been make [as] early as 1958 when local high school kid painted these designs no [sic] the walls of the cave as [a] prank. The Forest Service soon desided [sic] that they could make hay out of these drawings and used them to withdraw more land from use of the general public." This statement was followed by the acronyms USFS (U.S. Forest Service), BLM (Bureau of Land Management), and EPA (Environmental Protection Agency), each in its own circle with a line through the acronym. This is clearly a statement against federal control of public lands, a common sentiment in rural

Richard A. Rogers
Professor of Communication, Northern Arizona University, Flagstaff, Arizona

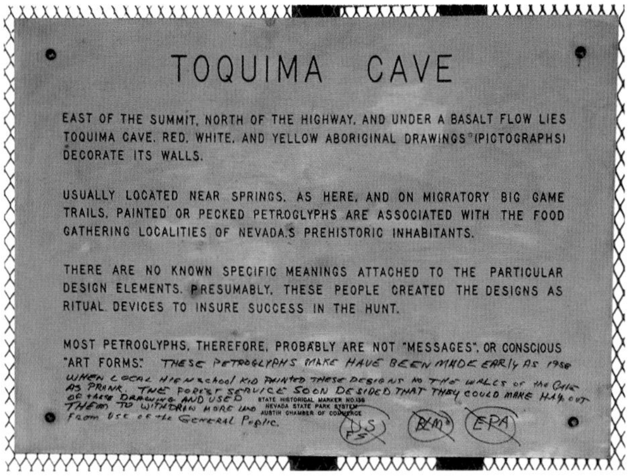

Figure 1. Nevada State Historical Marker No. 136, Nevada Highway 376, Lander County, Nevada. This interpretive sign installed in the 1970s for Toquima Cave was vandalized sometime between May 2002 and September 2005, and replaced in the 2010s.

Nevada, where hostility toward federal land management agency employees has a long history and is linked to right-wing, antifederal, antigovernment ideologies and movements (such as the Sagebrush rebellion of the 1980s and 1990s and the 2014 standoff involving Clark County rancher Cliven Bundy). Perhaps not coincidentally, this act of vandalism occurred right around or soon after the listing of Toquima Cave on the National Register of Historic Places in 2002.

This statement (technically, an act of vandalism) symbolically appropriated the pictographs in Toquima Cave by claiming they are the creation of a (presumably White) teenager, expropriating the rock art from living Native peoples with affiliations to it in order to argue for free and unregulated access, use, and exploitation of public lands in the western U.S., including traditional cultural properties. In contrast to this claim, the National Register of Historic Places Registration Form for Toquima Cave (Kumiega and Walter 2001) clearly indicates the cave's long-term habitation, the continuity between this and other pictograph sites in the region, and direct affiliations with living Native peoples, specifically the Western Shoshone, who regard it as a sacred site.

This unofficial twenty-first-century expropriation of the pictographs in Toquima Cave from all indigenous communities in the Great Basin, past or present, extends the region-wide expropriation of virtually all Great Basin rock art from all living indigenous communities in the twentieth century. In those cases, however, the expropriation was not enacted by local inhabitants and antigovernment activists, but by credentialed anthropologists such as Julian Steward (1929) and Bettinger and Baumhoff (1982), who assigned authorship of most Great Basin rock art to pre-Numic populations as opposed to the Numic peoples (Shoshone and Paiute) who still lived (and live) in the region. The alienation of the region's rock art from its living indigenous communities was motivated by two beliefs. The first one (expressed by Steward) was that the Numic peoples inhabiting the Great Basin in the early twentieth century were too "gastric" or "practical" in orientation to produce high quality rock art (Whitley and Clottes 2005:169). The second was that Numic informants, when asked who made the rock art, consistently stated that it was made by spirits of some kind, statements that were interpreted to mean that they did not know who made it and, therefore it must have been made by cultures who inhabited the region prior to the arrival of the Numic peoples (Whitley 2011:110–111).

From Vandalism Prevention to Indigenous Affiliations

As I have argued previously (Rogers 2020:174), a review of the literature on the public interpretation and education about rock art makes evident a central theme: the primary value or goal of public education about indigenous rock art is the reduction of vandalism and other types of human-caused degradation of rock art sites (e.g., Sanger 1992; Whitley 2011). Ironically, in this case, the public interpretation offered on the Toquima Cave sign was the instigation for vandalism—thankfully, of the sign, not the rock art (which is well protected, previously by a metal fence, now by a more substantial metal cage). However, the illicit additions to the Toquima Cave sign make clear that reducing vandalism is not the only matter of consequence in the public interpretation of rock art. What the vandalism on the sign highlights are issues of ownership, authorship, and cultural affiliation. Public education and interpretation inevitably involve an engagement in cultural politics, specifically, the determination of authority in the management of cultural resources. If one goal of public education and interpretation is to assign value to rock art so that people are less likely to vandalize it, then it is crucial that we critically examine how and which values are assigned to rock art: whose values, from what perspectives, and with what implications for the authority to manage and interpret rock art sites.

The practices and paradigms of archaeology, cultural resource management (CRM), and public interpretation of indigenous heritage have shifted dramatically since the passage of the Native American Graves Protection and Repatriation Act (NAGPRA) in 1990 (Francis 2005), as has, to some degree, broader public consciousness about the importance of Native lands and heritage to contemporary Native peoples. In archaeology and CRM, consultation with affiliated indigenous communities is becoming more of a norm rather than the exception, and archaeological knowledge is often relativized—presented as one perspective, alongside indigenous oral histories, traditional narratives, and cosmologies—as opposed to being the only voice in the room. Attitudes about and management of cultural resources on public lands in particular are no longer governed solely by a falsely universalized notion of the "public" and, more specifically, the notion that cultural resources are part of "our American heritage," needing to be protected "for the benefit of all Americans" (see, e.g., Treuer 2021).

In the 1970s, when the Toquima Cave sign was initially developed, the primary goal of interpretive materials was to enhance the public's appreciation of cultural resources and promote their preservation. Concerns over contemporary indigenous communities affiliated with archaeological sites and consultation with such communities concerning site management are largely post-NAGPRA phenomena. Also paralleling the rise of post-processualism in archaeology, mandatory consultations have become standard practice for land management agencies such as the BLM, Forest Service, and National Park Service (see, e.g., Francis 2005).

Another key factor in efforts to improve public interpretation is limited resources. Once an interpretive sign is installed, its life may be long. The all-metal roadside historical marker for Toquima Cave described above remained in place for well over 40 years. The wooden "your guess is as good as any" sign at Klare Spring in Death Valley National Park that was the inspiration for my earlier paper on public interpretation (Rogers 2020) likely dates to the 1970s or 1980s, and in 2017 at least was still broadcasting Steward's 1929 claim that "Indians living today deny any knowledge of their meaning." Both the Toquima Cave and Klare Spring signs were cleaned or otherwise refreshed after damage from human activity or natural forces. As described later in this paper, the Toquima Cave sign was updated sometime in the last ten years (Nevada State Historic Preservation Office 2021), after nearly 50 years of service. Clearly, one barrier to improving the content of interpretive materials at rock art sites is limited funding for the development and installation of new signs and other materials.

Purpose

In previous work on the public interpretation of rock art (Rogers 2018, 2020), my primary focus was identifying problems with the common themes present in interpretive materials. The most persistent and problematic theme I identified was the intertwining of two ideas: (1) contemporary Native Americans do not possess meaningful information about the rock art of their ancestors, (2) thereby leaving us with only our capacity to guess as to its meanings. The echoes of Julian Steward's (1929:224) claim that "the Indians disclaim all knowledge of their meaning or origin" has been used to encourage visitors' uninformed speculations, implicitly if not explicitly divorcing indigenous rock art from descendant communities. The implication of this common interpretive approach is that ownership and authority over indigenous rock art resides with Westerners as much as (if not more than) it does with contemporary indigenous communities.

For this paper, I shift my focus in two ways. First, I examine more recent examples of the public interpretation of rock art, especially those that counter the "your guess is as good as any" approach. Second, my primary purpose is to identify better examples of public interpretation and to articulate general principles that delineate not only what to avoid (the mistakes of the past) but what to include and how to frame public interpretations of rock art. In the following section, I analyze several relatively recent interpretive texts from the western U.S. to identify interpretive techniques and strategies that improve on those of the late twentieth century. Based on those analyses and my previous work on the cultural politics of the public interpretation of indigenous rock drawings, I present a set of principles and guidelines for more effectively managing the cultural politics of public interpretation. To be clear, this paper does not present guidelines for all aspects of the public interpretation of indigenous rock drawings; my focus is on the cultural politics of interpretation, specifically the implications of public educational messages for perceptions of who has authority over the past meanings and present functions of indigenous rock art.

Assessing Trends in Public Interpretation

Toquima Cave

While researching the Nevada State Historical Marker for Toquima Cave discussed above (Figure 1),

I discovered that the Nevada State Historic Preservation Office (SHPO) developed new language for the sign, which is available on the section of their website listing all Nevada State Historical Markers, and the roadside sign itself was updated with this new language sometime between 2013 and 2021. The original sign stated, "Red, white, and yellow aboriginal drawings (pictographs) decorate [the cave's] walls." It explains that rock drawings are "usually located near springs... and on migratory big game trails" and "are associated with the food gathering localities of Nevada's prehistoric inhabitants." In terms of the specific images in Toquima Cave, the sign states, "There are no known specific meanings attached to the particular design elements. Presumably, these people created the designs as ritual devices to insure success in the hunt. Most petroglyphs, therefore, probably are not 'messages,' or conscious 'art forms.'" Unsurprisingly, this 50-year-old attempt at interpretation had a number of familiar problems (Rogers 2018, 2020). First, it emphasized the lack of known meanings. Second, it did not name "these people" (the makers of the petroglyphs) beyond calling them "Nevada's prehistoric inhabitants" and made no reference to Nevada's contemporary indigenous communities. Third, it reinforced dominant Western notions of "primitive" peoples by linking the rock paintings only to subsistence activities and by denying "Nevada's prehistoric inhabitants" the capacity to engage in the conscious production of art or even messages (symbolic communication).

The new language for the Toquima Cave Historical Marker (Nevada State Historic Preservation Office 2021) begins with a statement, "Toquima Cave is an extraordinary Great Basin Native American archaeological site," that immediately assigns more value to the site than the old text as well as explicitly linking it to Native Americans, albeit those of the past, right up front. In direct contrast to the old text, the new content explains, "The meanings of these ancient designs may be as ceremonial markers, depictions of hallucinations, and art." In this new content, indigenous peoples of the past are granted the capacity to make "art" and engage in rituals other than "hunting magic"—including a cryptic reference to shamanism ("depictions of hallucinations"). Perhaps most significantly—especially given the vandalism to the previous version of the sign discussed above, which claimed that the pictographs were made as a prank by a local teenager—the new content concludes by stating, "Western Shoshone Indians historically occupied this region, and their ancestors most likely painted the Toquima Cave pictographs" (Nevada State Historic Preservation Office 2021).

Grimes Point

At the BLM-managed Grimes Point Archaeological Area just off U.S. Highway 50 in the Carson Desert east of Fallon, Nevada, there are two sets of interpretive signs. Several small signs are positioned along the trail that winds through the petroglyphs, and a larger sign is in the parking lot. Sometime between 2012 and 2019, the parking lot sign was replaced with a new one with a different design, text, and images. On the old sign, a section titled "Ancient Artists—What Were They Saying?" replicated the "your guess" theme by stating, "Nobody knows for sure.... The meaning of the rock art is still debated by scholars. What stories do you see etched on the rock?" In addition to inviting visitors to claim interpretive authority (and hence a sense of ownership) over the site's images, the sign mentioned only "scholars" as relevant authorities, not indigenous peoples. The sign did have a separate section on the "Cattail Eater People," identified as a Northern Paiute group living in Stillwater Marsh to the northwest of Grimes Point when the first non-Native explorers arrived, but contains no references to contemporary indigenous communities affiliated with the site (see Rogers 2018 and 2020 for a more in-depth examination of the pre-2012 signs at the site).

The new parking lot sign (Figure 2) has been improved in at least two important ways. First, it further highlights indigenous communities and their affiliations with the site. The first sentence in the body of the sign states, "The Fallon Paiute-Shoshone Tribe named this area *Su-u* (basalt) for the type of volcanic

Figure 2. New Bureau of Land Management interpretive sign in the parking lot of the Grimes Point Archaeological Area, Churchill County, Nevada.

rock found here." Another section of the sign highlights the Toi Ticutta (Cattail Eaters), similar to the old sign. Archaeologists are only mentioned in relation to the excavation of nearby Hidden Cave, not as authorities on the petroglyphs. Second, the new sign abandons the "what stories do you see etched on the rock?" approach, opting instead for minimalist but useful guides for visitors: "Some petroglyphs show animals and humans, others form unique designs with lines. Visitors can also find petroglyphs in the 'pit and groove' style, featuring groups of circular pits and long, narrow grooves. This technique is the oldest known style of rock art." This approach provides something for visitors to look for and identify in the petroglyphs along the trail while avoiding the tricky issue of meaning and the invitation to guess.

Painted Rock

Also managed by the BLM, the Painted Rock Petroglyph Site is located near Gila Bend, Arizona, in the Sonoran Desert. There are several interpretive signs at the site installed by the BLM around 2005 (Wright 2019), as well as a graphically engaging and textually rich pamphlet, developed by Archaeology Southwest (2018), which is available both in hard copy at the site and online. Two sets of interpretive signs about the petroglyphs are arranged in semicircles on the main trail from the parking lot to the petroglyphs, encouraging visitors to read them before approaching the site (Figure 3). When I last visited the site in early June 2021, workers were installing a steel two-rail fence around the entire site, apparently indicating that the "please stay on trail" sign has not worked well enough.

One sign is titled "Rules of the Road: A Respectful Approach," with the full text in both English and

Figure 3. Two groups of interpretive signs on the path to the Painted Rock Petroglyph Site, Maricopa County, Arizona.

Spanish (Figure 4). This site etiquette sign starts off with a rather unusual approach compared to those at many rock art sites: "Before entering this site, take a moment to consider its deep cultural and spiritual significance. Please be respectful of the site's importance

Figure 4. "Rules of the Road: A Respectful Approach," bilingual interpretive sign at the Painted Rock Petroglyph Site, Maricopa County, Arizona.

to native people, past and present. This site and others like it are a part of our shared American heritage." What is unusual about this statement is the specific call to consider the site's cultural and spiritual significance before entering it, something roughly akin to Western etiquette for entering a (Western) church or (Western) cemetery. In addition, this sign's strategy for establishing the site's value is focused differently than the generic site etiquette signs found at many BLM and other federally managed sites. First, it highlights cultural and spiritual significance as opposed to characterizing the site as a valuable repository of knowledge about the past (i.e., an archaeological resource). Second, it emphasizes the site as part of "our *shared* American heritage;" given the previous sentence's focus on the site's importance to "native people, past and present," the use of "shared" in this sentence connotes both indigenous and non-indigenous peoples. Significantly, this is one of the rare instances I have seen where the pronouns "our" or "we" are used on these kinds of signs in a clearly inclusive manner (Native and non-Native people) as opposed to an implicitly non-Native or Western "we" addressing an implicitly non-Native or Western reader about "them" (indigenous peoples). Another manifestation of this move away from a Western interpretive voice and the presumption of a Western audience is the general "Welcome to the Painted Rock Petroglyph Site" sign (not pictured), which presents its text in Spanish, English, and Tohono O'odham, the latter being descendants of those who made some of the petroglyphs at the site (Archaeology Southwest 2018; Wright 2017). However, there is no explanation on this sign as to why it is presented in Tohono O'odham alongside Spanish and English.

The sign titled "Petroglyphs and their Meanings: What Does It All Mean?" (Figure 5) asks the question that everyone wants to know the answer to, then proceeds with a balancing act between providing meaningful information on the one hand and acknowledging the inherent limitations to outsiders interpreting the images on the other. The answer to the question posed by the

Figure 5. "Petroglyphs and their Meanings: What Does It All Mean?" interpretive sign at the Painted Rock Petroglyph Site, Maricopa County, Arizona.

sign's title is blunt: "As modern visitors, we do not have the knowledge to easily interpret petroglyph meanings." In contrast to the popular "we don't know, so what do you think?" approach, this sign acknowledges the difficulties with interpretation and does not encourage visitors to symbolically colonize the imagery by guessing. It quickly follows this statement, however, with a clarification: "What we do know is that these pictures on boulders and rock panels are filled with mystery, and may have meanings on different levels." This clarification is important because if no one knows what they mean, then the petroglyphs are effectively "empty," not "full," and hence of less value in providing insight into the past (Rogers 2018). There are meanings, but they are multiple, complex, and not easily accessible to outsiders.

The second paragraph on the sign uses the familiar pattern of presenting several possible interpretations—vision quests, rites of passage, spirit helpers, hunting magic, travel information, cultural narratives—with consistent qualifications indicating these are possibilities, not confirmed meanings. It does not encourage guessing, but emphasizes that only "the people that made the designs...knew the meanings of these symbols." No specific archaeological cultures are named, and contemporary indigenous communities are not mentioned on this particular sign.

Surrounding the text on this sign is another potentially effective strategy: reproductions of some common petroglyph images, each with a short linguistic identification of their referent (the actual "thing" they depict), such as sun, moon, snake, scorpion, lizard, turtle, deer, and "man with interlocking hands" (Figure 5). These identifications (a kind of "shallow" interpretation) provide visitors with information that can enhance their experience of observing the petroglyphs while avoiding problematic presentations of symbolic, metaphoric, or narrative meanings that require particular cultural knowledge, although the gendering of the anthropomorph as male seems unwarranted. The sign encourages visitors to use these identifications of the petroglyphs' subject matter during their visit: "While walking along the trail look for some of these petroglyphs."

The sign titled "Archaeologist's Perspective: The Scientific Evidence" (Figure 6) focuses on "recent scientific studies by archaeologists" that have identified two styles of petroglyphs at Painted Rock: the Western Archaic and the Gila. Each of these styles is briefly described, assigned a date range and general cultural

Figure 6. "Archaeologist's Perspective: The Scientific Evidence," interpretive sign at the Painted Rock Petroglyph Site, Maricopa County, Arizona.

affiliation, and illustrated through photographs and named drawings of petroglyphs (e.g., grids, atlatls, ladders, animals, people). As with the previous sign, this one does not identify symbolic meanings, but provides visitors with information that they can use as they explore the petroglyphs; the sign challenges visitors to see if they can identify examples of each style as they view the petroglyphs.

The primary significance of this sign in terms of the cultural politics of public interpretation is that the archaeologist's perspective is named as a perspective, not just implicitly presented as "the facts"—the singular, objective truth. That in itself is a major advance over many interpretive signs at rock art sites, but is unfortunately counteracted by the lack of focus on contemporary indigenous communities and their perspectives on the other signs at the site (with one exception, discussed below). Another limitation of this sign is that most of the drawings of petroglyphs presented to illustrate the two styles (those in the boxes at the bottom of the sign) are not from the Painted Rock site, but from South Mountain in Phoenix (Wright 2019; see Bostwick and Krocek 2002:37, 41, 77, 195). According to Wright (2019), there are no identifiable Western Archaic petroglyphs at the site, an error that could perhaps have been avoided if the sign's creators had endeavored to find more examples of that style at this site to illustrate on the sign. While there are far worse examples of the "copy and paste" tendency in some interpretive signs at rock art sites, this case provides yet another reason to avoid such practices with both text and graphics. If images or information from other sites or regions is used, they ought to be identified as such. To be fair, however, land management agencies such as the BLM are chronically underfunded, especially in relation to unmandated aspects of CRM, and the Painted Rock site had not yet been fully documented when these signs were made (Wright 2019).

Other than the presentation of the text of the "welcome" sign in Tohono O'odham as well as Spanish and English (as described above), only one sign, titled "Who Made These Designs?" (not pictured), highlights the relationship between the Painted Rock site and contemporary indigenous communities: "The O'odham people have called this area home for thousands of years. They believe they are descended from the people known as the Hohokam." However, this connection between past and present indigenous groups is subtly undermined by the sign as a whole, which clearly advances the petroglyphs' affiliation with the Hohokam as established fact while the O'odham people's affiliation with the Hohokam is characterized as a *belief* of the O'odham, a clear contrast to the linking of Western perspectives to "scientific evidence" in the "Archaeologist's Perspective" sign (above).

The site brochure for the Painted Rock Petroglyph Site produced by Archaeology Southwest (2018) corrects for some of the limitations of the interpretive signs, which is somewhat unsurprising given that it is more than a dozen years newer than the signs. This "guest's guide" characterizes the site as "a sacred traditional place." It explains, "descendants of the petroglyph authors continue to visit Painted Rocks.... It remains especially meaningful to descendant communities," including the O'odham, Piipaash, and Yavapai. A highlighted statement in the brochure links the site to contemporary indigenous communities: "The Painted Rocks are vital to descendant communities. Their continued endurance and integrity depend on respectful viewing and adherence to the posted rules of conduct." The focus here is less on "our American heritage" than the heritage and survival of "descendant communities" (contemporary Native peoples). More detailed discussions in the brochure identify the Hohokam and Patayan communities who lived nearby as the authors of many of the petroglyphs, which are then linked to contemporary indigenous groups:

> Today, we know them by their own names: Akimel O'Odham, Tohono O'Odham, Hia C'ed O'Odham, and Piipash. Several other contemporary Native American tribes in Arizona, New Mexico, California, Sonora, and Baja California recognize ancestral connections to Hohokam and Patayan traditions and cultural properties. These include Quechan, Cocopah, Yavapai, and Mojave, among others [Archaeology Southwest 2018].

In short, unlike the BLM signs, the brochure leaves no doubt as to the affiliations between the petroglyphs, their ancient creators, and contemporary indigenous communities, affiliations that are reinforced by the brochure's discussion of meaning.

In the section "What Do These Petroglyphs Mean?" the brochure states:

> While many of the figures are recognizable, such as humans, lizards, and deer, interpreting petroglyphs is never straightforward. Archaeologists, anthropologists, and historians may sometimes attempt to interpret the designs using scant evi-

dence and in ways that reflect their own worldviews and cultural backgrounds. However, the stories and literal meanings of the petroglyphs are unknown to non-Native people. Indeed, where the petroglyphs are and how they are being used by descendent communities today—their context—is necessary for a more complete understanding [Archaeology Southwest 2018].

Like the site's interpretive sign on meaning, but more forcefully, the brochure makes clear that the interpretations of outsiders—even relatively shallow identifications of the "literal" referents of specific images—should be approached with caution, which would seem to discourage guessing on the part of visitors. The only authority that this brochure grants is to contemporary indigenous communities affiliated with the site, as only they have a relevant context for interpreting the images. The petroglyphs' meanings are not unknown, they are "unknown to non-Native people," enhancing a sense of specifically indigenous authority, affiliation, and ownership. Even the interpretations of "archaeologists, anthropologists, and historians" (probably the very types of people who authored the brochure!) should be approached with caution because, despite their expertise, they are still outsiders. The brochure does not just relativize Western scholarly knowledge as one type of knowing among many, but explicitly marginalizes it in favor of the knowledge of descendant communities.

Picture Canyon

The Picture Canyon Natural and Cultural Preserve was established by the City of Flagstaff, Arizona, in 2012. A set of four interpretive signs installed in 2016 at the Waterbird Site discuss the canyon's namesake: a large number of petroglyphs associated with the northern Sinagua archaeological culture (Figures 7–10). All four signs are titled "Images on Stone," presumably an intentional choice over "rock art," which some indigenous communities, such as the Hopi, criticize as an inappropriate label for the purpose and function of these images (see, e.g., Rogers 2018).

Each of the four signs contain this message: "Please show respect for the people who created these images nearly 1,000 years ago by not touching the petroglyphs or climbing on the rocks." Note that this call for respect is not based in appeals to protect "our American heritage" or to preserve it "for the benefit of all Americans," both common phrases used on site etiquette and interpretive signs at many archaeological sites (Rogers 2018,

Figure 7. "Images on Stone," interpretive sign at the Waterbird Petroglyph Site, Picture Canyon Natural and Cultural Preserve, Flagstaff, Arizona.

Figure 8. "Images on Stone," interpretive sign at the Waterbird Petroglyph Site, Picture Canyon Natural and Cultural Preserve, Flagstaff, Arizona.

Figure 9. "Images on Stone," interpretive sign at the Waterbird Petroglyph Site, Picture Canyon Natural and Cultural Preserve, Flagstaff, Arizona.

Figure 10. "Images on Stone," interpretive sign at the Waterbird Petroglyph Site, Picture Canyon Natural and Cultural Preserve, Flagstaff, Arizona.

2020). Instead, the appeal is to respect the indigenous peoples who created the images a millennium ago.

More importantly, however, there is also a repeated emphasis on the connection of contemporary indigenous communities to the site. Three of the four signs have a statement from a contemporary indigenous person explaining the significance of petroglyphs in their respective culture (Hopi, Yavapai, and Zuni), and each statement is distinguished from the rest of the content on the signs by its blue typeface (Figures 8, 9, and 10). On one sign, Zuni Tribal Consultant Octavius Seowtewa is quoted as saying, "Petroglyphs are the library for Zuni—it's how we know we were here" (Figure 8). This statement, while not linked to any particular petroglyph, advances a direct claim about the Zuni's affiliation with the site—"we were here"—based on indigenous, not archaeological, knowledge. On another sign, Yavapai Culture Director Gertrude Smith is quoted as saying, "It is accepted that we, the Yavapai People, were known around the region as the People of the Sun" (Figure 9). This statement relies on traditional indigenous knowledge ("It is accepted that we...were known around the region...") and is linked to the section of the same sign that discusses petroglyphs depicting the sun. As that section of the sign states, "Given that the Yavapai are the People of the Sun, these images [petroglyphs depicting the sun] may indicate their presence" (Figure 9). This statement, from the perspective not of indigenous peoples but of the anonymous (and implicitly Western) authors of the sign, legitimizes contemporary Yavapai perspectives, albeit in a qualified manner ("*may* indicate their presence"). On another sign, a statement from Leigh Kuwanwisiwma, then Director of the Hopi Cultural Preservation Office, explains the importance of petroglyphs in general from a Hopi perspective, and also implicitly affiliates the site with the Hopi through the idea that petroglyphs are "footprints" of Hopi ancestors who "searched for the center of the universe, the Hopi Mesas" (Figure 10). More directly, the sign explains that a specific anthropomorphic petroglyph at the site "with the large round head may represent Ma'saw, the Hopi Earth Guardian'" and the importance of Ma'saw is explained in Kuwanwisiwma's statement on the sign. The sign's Western voice explains that Ma'saw's "location on this boulder, near what some would interpret as a migration symbol, may indicate the migration of some Hopi and Zuni clans from the underworld to this world" (Figure 10), again reinforcing both Hopi and Zuni claims of affiliation with the site.

In its "Protect This Site" section, this same sign (Figure 10) again reinforces the ongoing affiliation of the site with contemporary indigenous communities: "The Waterbird Site is sacred to seven different tribal groups, who continue to visit this area to connect with their culture and ancestors." This is reiterated and further specified on another sign, which explains that the Northern Sinagua created the petroglyphs between 700 and 1300 C.E., but also states, "Many modern native people also lived in or traveled through the Picture Canyon area, including: Apache, Havasupai, Hopi, Hualapai, Navajo, Yavapai, Zuni" (Figure 7).

The emphasis on contemporary indigenous affiliations with Picture Canyon's petroglyphs carries through into the elements of each sign that discuss the meaning of petroglyphs. The first sign (Figure 7) has a section titled "What do they mean?":

> Interpreting the meaning of these images is difficult. Native people who trace their ancestry and cultural traditions to this site offer insightful interpretations, but these interpretations can vary greatly. Petroglyphs can be symbolic like a language, functional like a map, or have spiritual meanings. They can represent clan symbols, communicate stories, or signify cultural territories. Rock art interpretations are based on many lines of evidence, which include oral histories, pattern distributions, dating techniques, and associations with artifacts.

In this general introduction to the issue of meaning, the relevance of affiliated indigenous peoples is again highlighted, but in a way that allows for the legitimacy of different interpretations by indigenous groups. Both the specific meanings and the types of meanings that can be assigned to any petroglyph are multiple, implying that any single meaning for any single petroglyph is unlikely. While the statement highlights Native perspectives early on, it ends with a list of types of mostly archaeological evidence, granting validity to both indigenous (traditional) and Western (scientific) knowledge.

The other three signs each have multiple sections devoted to a particular type of image, many of which reference contemporary indigenous groups. These sections provide some meaningful information to visitors about some of the petroglyphs while also avoiding unqualified, singular interpretations. The section on spirals, for example, explains that they "may represent a migration route, the location of a water hole, a coiled snake, or a whirlwind. Some even interpret spirals to be symbolic of the path of the sun" (Figure 8). The section does not just present a list of options, however, but identifies a common theme in all the identified possibilities: "No matter what interpretation you look at, spirals often indicate movement of some kind." The section on the "waterbird" similarly states that the "petroglyph is commonly referred to as a waterbird, although it could be either a crane or a great blue heron.... Either way, the crane is a clan symbol for the Hopi and Zuni peoples" (Figure 9). Similarly, the section on the same sign titled "Celestial Images" explains, "Sun images are often depicted with rays while images of the moon may have points or be depicted as a crescent or semi-circle." This guide helps visitors to know what to look for while also avoiding being definitive by using qualifiers like "often" and "may." In addition, this sign also contains the material (discussed above) that links the Yavapai to the sun. This approach continues to link the petroglyphs to indigenous cultures past and present, highlights ambiguities and/or multiple perspectives, and provides visitors with much more than the previously dominant approach of "they could be x, y, or z, but who knows for sure" or the even more blunt "their meaning is lost" (Rogers 2020).

Overall, the four signs at the Waterbird site in Picture Canyon present information that can enhance visitors' experience and understanding while not being exclusionary or misleadingly definitive in advancing potential interpretations. In addition, the signs link the site and its petroglyphs to various contemporary indigenous communities and foreground indigenous knowledge more than archaeological and other Western systems of knowing. Despite often presenting multiple possible interpretations without offering any final resolution as to which one is "correct," the signs never revert to inviting visitors to guess as to their meanings.

Guidelines for Public Interpretation

Based on the criticisms of older interpretive signs presented in previous work (Rogers 2018, 2020) and the improved strategies identified in the interpretive materials associated with the four sites discussed above, this section presents two main principles and a variety of specific suggestions for developing interpretive materials for indigenous rock art sites with a sensitivity to cultural politics and authority.

Principle 1: Foreground Indigenous Cultural Affiliations

Interpretive materials for rock art sites should highlight the relationships between indigenous images on rock and contemporary indigenous communities, not only the relatively abstract "archaeological cultures" of the past. This assumes, of course, that cultural affiliations between contemporary indigenous communities and the rock art sites in question exist and are known. The knowledge that justifies portraying affiliations between ancient rock drawings and contemporary indigenous communities, however, should not be exclusively archaeological (or, more broadly, Western).

This principle's impact, however, would be compromised if two subprinciples are not also followed:

- Subprinciple 1.1 Indigenous Authority: Characterize contemporary indigenous perspectives as a valid form of knowledge about indigenous pasts and cultural heritage.
- Subprinciple 1.2 Relativize archaeological/Western perspectives: Present archaeological knowledge as one, not the only or best, form of knowledge about indigenous pasts (this also applies more broadly to knowledge rooted in Western ways of knowing, such as empiricism and the scientific method).

Combining these two principles, it may also be productive, when applicable, to highlight convergences between traditional and archaeological knowledge. When feasible, it may also be valuable to name key divergences between archaeological and traditional perspectives, although in some cases such an approach may overly complicate the core messages of what are often relatively short interpretive texts.

One specific issue to attend to in constructing interpretive materials is the potential ambiguities and exclusivity involved in the use of first-person plural pronouns ("we," "us," "our"). "We" and "our" in interpretive materials often imply those without affiliations to the imagery, specifically non-Natives. When interpretive material is presented from an implied or stated outsider voice (e.g., when "we" means not "them," those who made the drawings or are affiliated with them), it marginalizes indigenous visitors and indigenous perspectives, and perpetuates the shift of ownership and authority away from indigenous communities. Given the slipperiness of exactly whom "we" refers to, identify when possible what specific perspective(s) the information being presented is coming from (e.g., archaeologists and anthropologists, affiliated indigenous communities, or non-Natives).

An important corollary of this principle is to avoid characterizing the meaning, function, or purpose of rock drawings as unknown. Highlighting a lack of knowledge specific to a particular group—like non-Natives or indigenous groups without clear affiliations to the rock drawings—can be an important part of interpreting a site. However, since a universal lack of knowledge or an overall indigenous lack of knowledge can easily be used to justify non-indigenous claims of authority over indigenous cultural heritage (Rogers 2018, 2020), an apparent lack of knowledge (or an unwillingness to share or publicize it) by some groups should not be used to claim that such knowledge does not exist. Based on this corollary, interpretive materials should also avoid characterizing visitors' guesses as a legitimate approach to understanding indigenous rock drawings. While encouraging guessing can be an effective strategy to get visitors (especially, perhaps, children) actively engaged with the imagery, encouraging uninformed speculation by people unaffiliated with the site risks creating a colonialist sense of both authority and ownership over the cultural heritage of indigenous peoples (Rogers 2018).

Because multiple indigenous groups may have affiliations with a single site, because indigenous communities are not monolithically homogenous, because of very real cultural discontinuities created by colonization, and because symbols often have multiple meanings, it is also important to avoid stating or implying that there is only one correct interpretation or understanding of rock drawings. While acknowledging complexities, uncertainties, and/or differences in perception can create a muddled effort at public interpretation, erasing such complexities and ambiguities risks not only oversimplifying people's understanding of the rock art, but alienating some indigenous groups from their cultural heritage.

Principle 2: Exercise Interpretive Restraint

Many visitors to rock art sites want to know, above all, what it means, and plenty of people have made claims about what it means, which can lead to excesses in public interpretation that can potentially misconstrue images on rock, reinforce misconceptions about indigenous peoples, and/or serve to alienate rock drawings from descendant communities (Rogers 2018, 2020). At the same time, one purpose of public interpretation is to enhance visitors' experience and understanding of indigenous images on rock, in part so that they perceive the images as something of value, something to be respected and to avoid damaging. Despite visitors' desire for information about meaning and despite the need to assign positive value to rock art in order to reduce vandalism and unintentional damage, restraint is necessary in order to avoid creating problematic perceptions of rock art and their relationship to descendant communities, as well as misunderstandings of rock drawings due to unconscious projections of Western systems of meaning. While interpretive signs and pamphlets do sometimes push the line here, I have found excesses in relatively ungrounded interpretations to be particularly problematic in the context of volunteer docents who are present at some well-visited sites.

While striving to provide information about rock drawings that can enhance visitors' experience and/or understanding of the rock drawings, it is important to do the following:

- Avoid specific interpretations of specific images when there is insufficient credible knowledge (e.g., calling an embellished anthropomorph a "shaman," or an apparent flute player "Kokopelli").
- Do not list interpretive possibilities for the sake of listing possibilities or to make the point that it is all a mystery; list possibilities because there is some basis for them (e.g., based on tribal consultations, historic ethnography, ethnographic analogies, or archaeological hypotheses grounded in some kind of data).
- Acknowledge limitations such as what those without affiliations to the imagery and sites do not know, or an unwillingness by indigenous communities to share their knowledge publicly.
- Resist the temptation to "copy and paste" from interpretive materials at other sites, especially those with different cultural affiliations; develop site-, region-, and/or culture-specific information for each site to be interpreted in order to avoid falsely

homogenizing distinct rock art traditions and replicating the mistakes of the past (e.g., virtually every interpreted site in the Great Basin portrayed as having been created for hunting magic).

Interpretation of rock drawings can occur on a variety of levels, ranging from identifying the thing that the image visually represents (e.g., a lizard, snake, atlatl, human, rain) to deeper levels involving symbolic meanings, metaphors, and narratives, as well as the specific purposes behind the production of certain images (e.g., vision quests, rites of passage, hunting magic, and clan symbols). Obviously, the move from shallower to deeper levels of interpretation often requires perspectives grounded in the knowledge of affiliated communities and more careful qualifications. However, even the "literal" identification of an image as an image of something (e.g., a lizard) should rarely be presented without qualification (Smith 1998), and ethnographic data or contemporary consultations should guide such identifications when available. For example, across much of the Southwest one can find images that look a lot like a stick-figure lizard. However, some Zuni consultants suggest that some of these figures may be representations of the human form in the previous world, which included a tail (Wright and Hopkins 2016), and some Hopi consultants interpret the "tail" on a human form to be an umbilical cord connecting the person to the earth (Kuwanwisiwma and Koyiyumptewa 2018).

In other cases, visual ambiguities create difficulties in "naming" an image: a zigzag may be a zigzag (a design element), a snake, a rattlesnake specifically, lightning, mountains, or something else. While in some cases additional details may strengthen one identification over another (e.g., an indication of a head at one end and a tapered tail on the other making a zigzag a likely snake), the safest approach might be to call it a zigzag—that is, a descriptive name for the image, not a claim as to what it represents. The "gaze and guess" trap holds true at almost any rock art site (Lewis-Williams 2006), and interpretive signs are an opportunity to model the kind of careful qualifications necessary to navigate the morass of even "simple," "literal" identifications of the subject matter of particular images.

As the zigzag example illustrates, a useful approach taken by the signs at both Picture Canyon and Painted Rock is to provide some simple identifications to enhance visitors' engagement with the images, but the Picture Canyon signs do a much better job than those at Painted Rock at consistently qualifying such identifications, often grounding them in the perspectives of affiliated cultures, and often presenting multiple possibilities, not just one. In general, when providing basic identifications of some images, interpretive materials should do the following:

- Use names that lean toward being more descriptive (e.g., zigzag) as opposed to more interpretive (e.g., snake or lightning), especially if ambiguity is high.
- When appropriate, explain why a particular identification may be more likely than another due to details in the imagery (e.g., a depiction of cloven hoofs, plantigrade feet, or a long upward-oriented tail might make a quadruped more likely to be one species rather than another), an approach that also offers visitors guidance in what to look for while viewing rock drawings.
- Try to avoid using metaphors or comparisons to contemporary objects or cultures alien to those who made the rock drawings (e.g., the "zipper" at Parowan Gap, Utah); while useful, such "innocent" comparisons can affect how people perceive the imagery (e.g., the "Holy Ghost" in Horseshoe Canyon, Utah).
- Try to avoid using names or labels that are loaded—often in misleading ways—in the contemporary cultural frameworks of visitors (e.g., "shaman," whose anthropological meanings are overshadowed by those circulated by the New Age industry; "ritual specialist" or "ritual practitioner" are possible alternatives, if the imagery and/or affiliated consultants justify such an interpretation).
- Avoid using indigenous names (or Anglicizations of indigenous names) without strong insider, ethnographic support for doing so (e.g., don't describe a flute player as "Kokopelli" because the Hopi katsina Kokopelli does not play a flute and members of the Hopi Flute Clan explicitly deny that flute players are "Kokopelli" [Rogers 2018:177–180]).
- Avoid making assumptions about the gender of animals (including humans) depicted in the imagery without adequate gender markers in the imagery itself and/or credible interpretations by indigenous consultants; when a figure is identified as male or female, explain why.
- Avoid using terms such as "geometric," "abstract," and "pure design" to characterize some images simply because they appear to be nonrepresentational from a Western/non-indigenous point of view; to do so is ethnocentric and not grounded in indigenous perspectives (note that describing an image with geometric or design terms such as

zigzag, spiral, or grid may be a good way to avoid ungrounded identifications of the image's subject; the concern here is with describing images as being "abstract" or "pure" designs without relevant knowledge supporting such a characterization).

Everyone may want to know what it means, but the intended meanings and purposes of rock drawings are not the only kinds of information that can enhance visitors' experience and/or understanding. Many other types of information about the images on rock at a particular site can help visitors more actively engage with the imagery, appreciate its value, and learn about rock drawings and the indigenous cultures that produced them:

- Cultural affiliations and information about affiliated cultures
- Relative or absolute time periods for the imagery
- Relationships with other cultural resources (e.g., habitation sites, quarries, trails, artifacts, springs)
- Manufacturing techniques and materials (e.g., direct vs. indirect percussion, pigment sources, binders, materials used for applying paint)
- Terminology (e.g., petroglyphs versus pictographs, specific styles of rock drawings)
- Suggestions for viewing (e.g., at different times of the day or year, attending to the position of panels on the landscape)

Challenges

Developing interpretive materials for cultural sites such as drawings on rock is difficult and challenging work, and such materials inevitably reflect the times and contexts in which they were produced. The difficulties range from the financial to the pedagogical and rhetorical, from the ethical to the regulatory, legal, and bureaucratic. Despite the wide range of challenges, many recent attempts at public interpretation (such as those examined in this paper) demonstrate the progress that has been made since the pre-NAGPRA era exemplified by the Klare Spring "your guess is as good as any" sign in Death Valley or the original Toquima Cave Nevada historical marker that denied the indigenous inhabitants of the Great Basin the ability to make art. While even those outdated signs were well-intentioned, guided by a desire to protect cultural resources, NAGPRA and other social and regulatory changes have thankfully normalized consultation with affiliated indigenous communities. Despite that progress, however, budget-related barriers—personnel, expertise, time, resource barriers to effective consultation with indigenous communities, the money for the materials themselves—result in signs remaining in place despite their not merely outdated, but ethically, politically, and/or empirically problematic content. More thoughtful and less ethnocentric approaches are by themselves of limited effectiveness unless they are accompanied by the resources necessary to retire and replace interpretive signs that, in some cases, could now be regarded as historical resources in themselves.

Promoting Resistance: "There Are Some Indians Still Around"

To understand the stakes of public interpretation, try this exercise: Go to Google in your favorite web browser. Search for "White people," and select the "images" tab. Review the first page of results. How many of the images are more "historic" versus relatively "contemporary" (e.g., less than 75 years old)? Now search for "African Americans" and make the same kind of assessment. Then search for "Asian Americans" and do the same. Then try "Mexican Americans" and take another tally of historical versus contemporary time frames.

Now, try one final search: "Native Americans." How are these image results different than those for the previous U.S. ethnic groups? It is almost guaranteed that the results of your searches for White people, African Americans, Asian Americans, and Mexican Americans returned mostly images of contemporary people from those groups. When I did this exercise on May 24, 2021, all the people in the first 27 images for White people were contemporary (even if they weren't all white!). For African Americans, only two of the 24 images were "historic." For Asian Americans, none of the 24 images was "historic," the same as the "White people" sample. For Mexican Americans, seven of the 23 images were "historic," making the representation of this group the most "historic" in nature, but still far under half. In my search for "Native Americans," in contrast, 18 of the first 26 images of Native Americans were historic; of the eight contemporary images, five of them showed contemporary people dressed very similarly to the people in the historic photos (e.g., fringed buckskin, eagle feather headdresses).

Since at least the late nineteenth century, the dominant image of Native Americans has been that they are the "vanishing race." James Frasier's 1915 statue "The End of the Trail" remains a popular image, visually concretizing the "vanishing race" narrative, a narrative spawned by the idea that primitive savages will inevitably fade away in the face of the inevitable progress of Western civilization (Rogers 2018). Film and television have largely avoided portraying contemporary native peoples, perpetuating the perception of their absence in today's world (Rogers 2018). And in too many cases, interpretive materials at rock art sites have perpetuated this dangerous myth by ignoring contemporary indigenous communities. Since the peoples and cultures who made these images are long gone, then the images on rock really are part of "our [i.e., *my*] American heritage," not that of living descendant communities. Public interpretation needs to track with the changes that have occurred within archaeology and CRM since the passage of NAGPRA in 1990. As Taçon and Brady (2016:5) argue in the introduction to their groundbreaking volume *The Place of Rock Art in the Contemporary World*, we need "to shift the focus of rock art discourse from one that is primarily archaeologically driven to one that considers how rock art, as a distinctive symbolic marker surviving in the modern world, is used to negotiate contemporary relationships between people, places, and identity."

This project began over twenty years ago with my encounter with the infamous "your guess is as good as any" interpretive sign at Klare Spring in Death Valley National Park (Rogers 2018, 2020). After giving the obligatory list of some interpretive possibilities, the sign repeats Steward's 1929 claim that "Indians living today deny any knowledge of their meaning," concluding by telling visitors that "your guess is as good as any." In 2017, I made a pilgrimage back to the sign, where I found it not only intact and unchanged, but refreshed with a new coat of paint. After I had been at the site for a few hours, two black sport utility vehicles pulled up, disgorging four adults and six children, Anglo and seemingly middle class, apparently comprising an extended family. As the doors opened, I picked up a conversation already in progress between a father and (I presume) his son:

"Why did they make them only here?" asks the son.

"We don't know—no one is around to ask," replies the father.

I presumed that the father's answer has been provided by the sign, readily visible and readable from where they parked, but also, or instead, from the broader cultural narrative that the "real Indians" are all dead or degraded, either absent or living without meaningful connection to their cultural heritage.

Almost without pause, the son emphatically retorted, "there are *some* Indians around still." I was somewhat shocked at hearing this pre-teen boy overtly resisting not only the authority of the National Park Service sign and his father, but the pervasive Euro-American myth of the actual and inevitable disappearance of Indians, be it through genocide, assimilation, integration, or the unstoppable dominance of Western Civilization. Perhaps not surprisingly, however, given both the complexity of the issue of the presence of Native Americans in the contemporary U.S. and the physical commotion of ten people getting out of two cars, the father managed a barely audible "well..." and that particular conversation came to an end.

We need to bolster the son's voice against those of his father, the Park Service, and Steward. Interpretive signs and brochures are one way to bolster that alternative narrative.

References Cited

Archaeology Southwest
2018 A Guest's Guide to the Painted Rock Petroglyph Site. Archaeology Southwest and Bureau of Land Management. Electronic document, https://www.archaeologysouthwest.org/wp-content/uploads/painted_rocks_brochure_web.pdf, accessed February 17, 2020.

Bettinger, Robert L., and Martin A. Baumhoff
1982 The Numic Spread: Great Basin Cultures in Competition. *American Antiquity* 47:485–503.

Bostwick, Todd W., and Peter Krocek
2002 *Landscape of the Spirits: Hohokam Rock Art at South Mountain Park.* University of Arizona Press, Tucson.

Francis, Julie
2005 Pictographs, Petroglyphs, and Paradigms: Rock Art in North American Archaeology. In *Discovering North American Rock Art,* edited by Lawrence L. Loendorf, Christopher Chippindale, and David S. Whitley, pp. 181–195. University of Arizona Press, Tucson.

Kumiega, Karen, and Gwen Walter
2001 Toquima Cave National Register of Historic Places Registration Form. 29 June. National Park Service, United States Department of Interior.

Kuwanwisiwma, Leigh J., and Stewart B. Koyiyumptewa
2018 Hopi Foootprints at the Crack-in-Rock Community. *Plateau—The Land and People of the Colorado Plateau* 10(1):29–32.

Lewis-Williams, J. David
2006 The Evolution of Theory, Method and Technique in Southern African Rock Art Research. *Journal of Archaeological Method and Theory* 13:343–377.

Nevada State Historic Preservation Office
2021 Toquima Cave. Nevada's State Historical Markers No. 136. Nevada State Historic Preservation Office (online). Electronic document, https://shpo.nv.gov/nevadas-historical-markers/historical-markers/toquima-cave, accessed May 19, 2021.

Rogers, Richard A.
2018 *Petroglyphs, Pictographs, and Projections: Native American Rock Art in the Contemporary Cultural Landscape.* University of Utah Press, Salt Lake City.

2020 "Your Guess is as Good as Any": Rock Art, Public Interpretation, and Ownership. In *American Indian Rock Art, Volume 46,* edited by Richard A. Rogers, Evelyn Billo, and Robert Mark, pp. 173–181. American Rock Art Research Association, Cupertino, California.

Sanger, Kay Kenady
1992 Making Our Work in Rock Art Count. In *American Indian Rock Art, Volume 18,* edited by Frank G. Bock, pp. 19–22. American Rock Art Research Association, San Miguel, California.

Smith, Benjamin
1998 The Tale of the Chameleon and the Platypus: Limited and Likely Choices in Making Pictures. In The *Archaeology of Rock-Art,* edited by Christopher Chippindale and Paul S. C. Taçon, pp. 212–228. Cambridge University Press, Cambridge.

Steward, Julian H.
1929 *Petroglyphs of California and Adjoining States.* University of California Publications in American Archaeology and Ethnology 24(2).

Taçon, Paul S. C., and Liam M. Brady
2016 The Place of Rock Art in the Contemporary World. In *Relating to Rock Art in the Contemporary World: Navigating Symbolism, Meaning, and Significance,* edited by Liam M. Brady and Paul S. C. Taçon, pp. 3–13. University Press of Colorado, Boulder.

Treuer, David
2021 Return the National Parks to the Tribes. *The Atlantic* (online). Electronic document, https://www.theatlantic.com/magazine/archive/2021/05/return-the-national-parks-to-the-tribes/618395/, accessed May 19, 2021.

Whitley, David S.
2011 *Introduction to Rock Art Research.* 2nd ed. Left Coast Press, Walnut Creek, California.

Whitley, David S., and Jean Clottes
2005 In Steward's Shadow: Histories of Research in the Far West and Western Europe. In *Discovering North American Rock Art,* edited by Lawrence L. Loendorf, Christopher Chippindale, and David S. Whitley, pp. 161–177. University of Arizona Press, Tucson.

Wright, Aaron M.
2017 *A Site Condition Assessment of the Painted Rock Petroglyph Site, Southwestern Arizona.* Archaeology Southwest Technical Report No. 2017-02. Archaeology Southwest, Tucson, Arizona. Electronic document, https://www.archaeologysouthwest.org/wp-content/uploads/tr2017-102_final_web.pdf, accessed May 25, 2021.

2019 Why You Should Experience the Painted Rock Petroglyph Site (videorecording). Archaeology Café (online). Archaeology Southwest, Tucson, Arizona. Electronic document, https://www.youtube.com/watch?v=C8Myf6y6p4o, accessed May 25, 2021.

Wright, Aaron M., and Maren P. Hopkins
2016 *The Great Bend of the Gila: Contemporary Native American Connections to an Ancestral Landscape.* Archaeology Southwest Technical Report No. 2016-101. Archaeology Southwest, Tucson, Arizona. Electronic document, https://www.archaeology-southwest.org/wp-content/uploads/2016/06/GreatBend.pdf, accessed May 27, 2021.

Aesthetic Response, Kant, and Rock Art

Livio Dobrez

How critical is our aesthetic response to rock art? This article examines the contemporary relevance of the philosopher Kant's contribution to the subject of aesthetics with special focus on rock art. It argues that anything at all may be the object of an aesthetic response. But what precisely is such a response? For a start, does it actually exist? I reply in the affirmative, with reference first to aestheticians, then anthropologists, in the process making a key distinction between a universal human capacity for aesthetic response and culture-specific "taste," eventually distinguishing between the aesthetic and like/dislike responses in general. I give an outline of central Kantian notions of aesthetic "feeling" and "pleasure," the highly original idea of a judgement that is "necessary" and, finally, "disinterested." In each case I critically examine Kant's argument, elucidating his terminology, bringing it up to date, in particular complicating his views about the relation of form and content, the nature of the supposed "pleasure" response, above all the fact that "disinterested" contemplation of art is inevitably coloured by ethical/political/sexual/religious considerations. In short, I am querying the idea of art as non-utilitarian. In the end, however, I am bound to note that Kant's thinking on aesthetics has so permeated Western culture that his views emerge in much of what we say about art, rock art included.

The Role of the Aesthetic in the Study of Rock Art

Since I am addressing myself to members of ARARA I may ask the question: why do we "do" rock art? No doubt there are many reasons and specific combinations of reasons. Some have professional reasons, linked directly or indirectly to an academic discipline, which might be a social science such as archaeology/anthropology (usually) or cognitive psychology (sometimes), or a hard science, say, neuroscience (sometimes), or a humanities discipline such as (occasionally) art history or (rarely) philosophy. Some go to rock art out of historical interest; some out of a passion for indigenous cultures. All this for, perhaps, largely intellectual reasons, the solving of puzzles (Who? When? Why?), aimed at the reconstruction of that elusive but deeply engaging past, or of speculation over remote origins. Equally, I surmise, most come to rock art out of aesthetic fascination, possibly, in some cases, something less intellectual or aesthetic than vaguely (or specifically?) "spiritual." This at a time and in a society surfeited with consumer materialism, liable as much to the Hippy Hopi syndrome as to sober reflection on an over-exploited planet. Add to the above the simple—or quite complex—pleasure of travel to every corner of the world where there are markings on rocks, the only exception being Antarctica. Given this, who would not want to be a member of ARARA or equivalent organizations in any number of countries? Certainly my own eclectic position encompasses almost all of the reasons listed here. However, I must add that without aesthetic absorption in the marks on the rock, I would find all those non-aesthetic reasons for "doing" rock art less than satisfying. I make the point in the knowledge that for some the aesthetic may not play such a central role, though my suspicion is that few researchers would want altogether to discount it.

Livio Dobrez
Australian National University,
Canberra, Australia,
Retired

American Indian Rock Art, Volume 48. Amy Gilreath, Ken Hedges, and Anne McConnell, Editors. American Rock Art Research Association, 2022, pp. 155–166.

A Focus on Reception: Aesthetic Response

As I noted on a previous occasion (Dobrez 2012), art (including rock art) may be studied from three equally valid starting points: (1) that of the making, (2) that of the made, and (3) that of its reception. In line with my own academic focus on phenomenology, what follows will deal not with what it is that generates the historical making of certain objects (on rock or any other support, in 2D or 3D form), nor on the objects themselves. The first starting point leads to discussion of culture-specific contexts (the who/when/why of the making). The second to a discussion of the problematical "art" object which I recently characterized as follows: "any sort of formal arrangement, meaningful insofar as structured, which some of us decide to call art, whether before or after the fact, and possibly not without dissent" (Dobrez 2021). This too is a culturally specific question, and a fraught one, as I indicate in the characterization, which is disturbingly open-ended, but accurately so. This leaves me the third option: that of the reception of the object, available to anyone at any time, including the maker of the object, regardless of historical context. I will not here rehearse the difficulties, and the ultimately philosophical and scientific justification for a universalist perspective. Elsewhere I have grounded it in Husserlian phenomenology, cognitive psychology, and neurophysiology (see especially Dobrez 2013). In this article my focus is on a presumed universal human capacity for aesthetic experience. Naturally the thesis will require to be given substance in what follows.

Questions crowd at this point, but they need to be tackled one at a time. For a start: aesthetic "response" to—what? The answer must be to *anything at all*, natural, man-made, "found," etc. Prior to the early twentieth century modernist revolution in Western art, it would have been "response either to a natural or to an art object," but once Duchamp (in New York: 1917) exhibited his urinal as art, the notion of the object necessarily extended to anything at all. It could be a thing (a 2D picture, a 3D object, a Brillo box, an Installation, a video), or, "Post-Object," an activity (a Happening, a Performance), or an idea ("Conceptual Art"). As with Duchamp's urinal, the object itself may amount to an idea (that art is what we decide to call art). In the terms of the present article, which does not bear directly on the notion of art, but focuses on response, we must make the parallel observation that an aesthetic response may be directed at whatever we choose to posit as aesthetic. It may be a fine, pressure-flaked lithic blade, a commercial west-coast T-shirt (Figure 1), a rock art panel (Figure 2). Or it may be any of the various options listed above, as well as many others. In the case of the Duchamp urinal, the object of aesthetic attention will be not the material object (unlikely to draw admiration), but the concept, that art is what we choose to regard as art (a concept now debased by constant reiteration in artworks of the last few decades). However, it must be stressed that, while anything at all may be made the object of aesthetic response, it need not follow that the choice is arbitrary: there has to be some quality in the aesthetic object (something as minimal as an idea) that will trigger aesthetic response. Or rather that it *may* do so, since, just as we choose to respond aesthetically, so

Figure 1. T-shirt, Vancouver, Canada.

Figure 2. Butler Wash, Utah.

we can choose to *refuse* the response—for example, on ideological grounds. We activate the aesthetic as an act of free choice.

A History of Aesthetics

Aesthetics, in its present Western form, is traceable to the late-eighteenth-century cult of "sensibility." We recall that Jane Austen wrote a novel entitled *Sense and Sensibility*, and that the equally dominant term "sentiment" had wide usage at the time, especially in English and German literature (Richardson, Sterne, Goethe). The Germans had their Storm and Stress *(Sturm und Drang)* movement, which led to the nineteenth-century cultural phenomenon of Romanticism. Changing social power configurations (the much discussed decline of the feudal aristocracy and concomitant rise of a new "middle" class), brought about a context in which the experience of overwhelming nature, e.g., towering mountains, previously avoided as wearisome and dangerous, became an aesthetic must-see. In the sphere of the man-made, aesthetic experience assumed its modern preeminence, along with the value-loaded notion of "art." The term "aesthetic" was coined by Baumgarten (Hammermeister 2002). But the definitive analysis of this unique manner of responding to given (subsequently clichéd) objects and situations was provided by the philosopher Immanuel Kant (Figure 3), notably in his *Critique of Judgment* (1914 [1790]). Since then, opinion has revised Kant, often opposed him, sought to dislodge his premises and conclusions, but with only partial success. After more than two hundred years, Kant remains central to the discourse of aesthetics, which, as an academic discipline, is established in both philosophy and art history. From the last few decades of the twentieth century, so-called postmodern theory has critiqued the aesthetic as a social construct peculiar to a phase of consumer capitalism, the fetishism of consumer gratification, a culture in which everything is simultaneously aestheticized and depoliticized (see Dobrez 2010). However, this makes continuing reference to Kant's work all the more pressing. In the context of rock art studies, it is surprising how frequently researchers, particularly from the social sciences, return to basic Kantian assumptions, usually unrecognized.

Aesthetic Response as a Specific Attentional Stance

So what precisely is this "aesthetic" response? To begin with: does it actually exist? Is there such a thing as an aesthetic experience? Stolnitz (1969), who thinks of it as a particular distinct attentional attitude, believes it does. (Appeal to "attention" is surely an area ready for mining, given contemporary developments in neurophysiology, and information unavailable to Stolnitz fifty years ago.) Dickie (1969), at least in this well-known essay, disputes the idea of a distinct form of attention we may term aesthetic, and he does so with painstaking, if deliberately and provocatively obtuse, insistence that aesthetic attention inevitably boils down to any old attention, and consequently that the aesthetic is an empty category. If you do not want to argue that the aesthetic is a non-category, you may opt for it being a heterogeneous category, not one but many (Charlton 1970). So much for aestheticians (the reader may make further reference to anthologies such as Margolis 1962 and Rader 1973).

What about anthropologists, significantly represented in rock art studies? Boas, who casts a long shadow, is worth quoting: "In one way or another esthetic pleasure is felt by all members of mankind" (1927:9). For more recent views I turn to three largely or entirely

Figure 3. Immanuel Kant. Portrait (detail) by Gottlieb Doebler (1791). Museum Stadt Königsberg, public domain.

anthropology-oriented anthologies: Jopling (1971), Otten (1971), and Borofsky (1994). In Jopling I find general support for an aesthetic stance presumed to be universal, notably from David Stout, Harold Schneider, George Mills, Roy Sieber, Herschel Chipp, Irwin Child and Leon Siroto, Daniel Crowley, and Robert Thompson. The Otten anthology, which focuses more on art than the aesthetic, is somewhat cautious, with reservations expressed in its introduction of a kind requiring to be addressed below. Interestingly, Borofsky's anthology, which spans the paradigm shifts from functionalist to so-called postmodern anthropologies, gives no particular space to aesthetics or to art. It therefore illustrates the gradual disciplinary turn to the still-current dominance of political theorizing of culture (focus on anthropological reflexivity, stress on power structures, etc.). To return to the issue of social science reservations regarding the aesthetic, the matter is clearly put, in all its complexity, by Jopling (1971:xv): "Some peoples have aesthetic ideas close or parallel to Western aesthetics; others cannot or do not express any opinions, or, at least, any that a field worker is able to interpret; and still others have a completely different but well articulated set of standards." This is helpful, but continues to blur an important distinction. The same is true for Child and Siroto (1971) in the Jopling anthology, who describe an experiment in which New Haven art experts and, subsequently, African BaKwele carvers passed aesthetic value judgement on BaKwele masks, with the two groups showing surprising agreement.

A Critical Distinction

The Heyd and Clegg (2005) collection of articles, deserving credit not least as pioneering the role of aesthetics in rock art research, seems to me to put in perspective a major stumbling block some anthropologists/archaeologists are likely to have in connection with the aesthetic. The book, which includes a piece by Howard Morphy (2005), an Australian anthropologist who has emphasised Indigenous examples of aesthetic appreciation, opens with an argument by the philosopher Peter Lamarque (2005). Lamarque references a 1994 debate at a Manchester anthropological conference on "aesthetics as a cross-cultural category." He notes that a conference motion supporting the premise was defeated two to one. Then he goes on lucidly to show that the views expressed by anthropologists to the effect that aesthetics is not at all cross-cultural chronically conflate two separate issues—which I would express as the vital distinction between (1) a universal human capacity for aesthetic judgement and (2) a non-universal, culture-specific application of a particular individual or group taste. The term "taste" is unfortunately often used in a way that blurs the distinction. Clearly the conclusion of the Child and Siroto experiment (that there may be agreement in judgements about African masks) concerns taste—in which case agreement *is* indeed surprising—not a fundamental human capacity for aesthetic experience—in which case agreement would be quite *un*surprising. Unfortunately Child and Siroto do not clarify this point. Likewise the otherwise unexceptionable comment by Jopling just quoted glosses over the distinction. Of course, though essential, the distinction is a theoretical one. In everyday practice, any aesthetic judgement will be coloured by a specific cultural or individual taste. A hypothetical person might well respond to a Mwai mask (Figure 4) from the middle Sepik in New Guinea, with some negativity. S/he may find it fearsome or aggressive, possibly ruggedly unsophisticated. I happen to register the mask as stylish, even effete, almost oversophisticated. The rightness or otherwise of these judgements is not the issue. The judgements agree insofar as both assume a capacity for aesthetic response, though the tastes they represent are in complete disagreement.

Figure 4. Mwai mask, middle Sepik, New Guinea.

One final point should be made at this stage, roughly in line with Jopling's comment: some cultures foreground the aesthetic, some do not. It is a (justified) platitude of anthropological thinking that the primary response to so-called art throughout human history has been religious. The Gothic cathedral has a spiritual/ritual rationale, though it is also able to be regarded aesthetically. The same is probably usually the case for all appreciable man-made objects, rock art included. Western culture increasingly foregrounded the aesthetic dimension as it moved in the direction of consumer materialism.

Towards a Definition of an Aesthetic Response: Kant

I now turn more specifically to the (for some) problematical and elusive aesthetic experience, which I have still to define, since I have so far merely argued that it exists. It may be that this existence is not exactly amenable to proof. It may be that—and I redirect/modify a comment by Charlton (1970:15)—"the only way of learning what an aesthetic response is like, is by having one." Be that as it may, any definition is bound to take me back to Kant. In what follows I ask rock art researchers to resist the usual observation that whatever we think about the aesthetic may bear no relation to what was thought by the makers of the art. My position is that the makers, whatever was in their minds, nonetheless had a capacity for aesthetic response to their own images, whether this experience was foregrounded or not.

Kant, in tune with the proto-Romanticism of the time, argued the aesthetic is a "feeling" *(Gefühl)*. Today's usage makes that word seem excessively vague, but Kant's point is that, as a feeling, it involves no idea or concept, i.e., is not a cognitive operation. Rather it is simple, immediate or spontaneous. You judge something as satisfying not because it conforms to an idea. For example, if you say a picture appeals because it features a dog and you love dogs, you are expressing a response due to some preexisting notion (your love of dogs). Since the aesthetic must be independent of any concept, your reply to the question "Why do you like the picture?" should be: "I just like it." Here the "why" question has no ready answer. Perhaps we could speak of an indeterminate concept (in philosophical language, "synthetic" rather than "analytic"). Likewise the aesthetic response is not exactly emotive. You can be excited in front of a panel of Dinwoody-style figures, or the face of Tsagiglalal at Horsethief Lake, but this excitement is of a special kind. Kant, appealing to terms we will need to revise, identifies the aesthetic as a feeling of "pleasure." But what pleasure does one feel in front of a picture depicting, for example, the horrors of war? Goya's *Tres de Mayo 1808 en Madrid* (AFPM 2021), which illustrates a Napoleonic firing squad cutting down terror-stricken civilians, is unlikely to evoke a pleasure response. At the same time, we do not react with *dis*pleasure, the obverse of the pleasure response: it is, in fact, a magnificent work.

Form and Content

One way out of the difficulty suggests itself: the distinction between form and content. Perhaps you respond positively to the formal qualities of the picture, its chaotically unbalanced, disturbing compositional masses, evocatively bleak tones, etc. So while touched by the negative content, you appreciate its masterly handling, i.e., its formal values. This formulation remains adequate in theory. In practice, it must be the case that you respond to form and subject matter simultaneously. That the two may be distinguished, after the fact, is easily shown by the knowledge that we are perfectly able to switch from one to the other, directing attention to each in turn. For example, we may focus on the design, then switch to the ugly depiction of humans being killed. Or we may switch from awareness of design to awareness of the image as a historical record (what happened in Madrid on May 3, 1808). In spite of these options, our initial, simple (non-conceptual) response must be not to form on its own, the immediate "look" of the thing, but to a fusion of form and content, say, a perception of something indeterminate we may loosely refer to as the vision or truth or idea or theme of the work, something that evokes and sustains a sense of empathy, an indignant response to depicted injustice—and is at the same time indissolubly linked to the simple "look" of the picture. At this point it is clear that terms like "pleasure" fail to do the job of accurate description.

The Beautiful and the Sublime

Not all descriptions are as challenging as the example given above. In the case of rock art various after-the-fact descriptive terms come to mind (elegance, power, strength, vitality, delicacy), some tending more to the side of formal qualities, some suggestive of the larger fusion of form and content just outlined. Leaping guanaco at Cueva de las Manos (Figure 5) suggest terms like vitality, delicacy; dancing Gwions in the

Australian Kimberley (Figure 6), or finely-delineated horses (the pride of their owners) in the northwest Plains of America (Figure 7), a term like elegance. Barrier Canyon Style figures in Utah (Figure 8) may be characterized as having strength, power, presence. (For discussion of aesthetic terminology in the context of style-analysis, see Dobrez and Dobrez 2019.)

Figure 5. Cueva de las Manos, Santa Cruz, Argentina.

Figure 6. Lower Mitchell, Kimberley, Australia.

Figure 7. Joliet, Montana.

Figure 8. Barrier Canyon, Utah.

Mention of Barrier Canyon figures raises a further question. Kant (1914 [1790]:147-148), following the British politician Edmund Burke (1757), distinguished between aesthetic response to the "beautiful" and to the "sublime." While the language is period-bound, it signals something of importance. I have avoided mention of the "beautiful," preferring more contemporary terminology. In the context of Barrier Canyon figures, Kant's "sublime" has some resonance, though again it is probably better to choose different terms. I would put it this way: in some instances, rock art *overwhelms* the observer. This is the case at Barrier Canyon; it is also the case at this shelter in Australian Arnhem Land (Figure 9); or in a close encounter at the innermost Quinkan shelter, Cape York, Queensland (Figure 10); or at Torrey Lake, Wyoming (Figure 11). In Kant's day the "sublime" was notably associated with alpine peaks, raging seas, and the like. It is relevant to recall that, in exposure to rock art, aesthetic admiration, perhaps

Figure 9. Mt. Borradaile, Arnhem Land, Australia.

Figure 10. Quinkan Shelter, Cape York, Australia.

Figure 11. Torrey Lake, Wyoming.

The Aesthetic as an "Ought" Judgement

I have put forward the Kantian notion of aesthetic pleasure, using more contemporary terms, with clarification through discussion of the form/content distinction. We are now at least in the initial stages of understanding that aesthetic response is a complex human phenomenon, one that is not reducible to a general like/dislike response, as, for example, evolutionary aesthetics, for lack of a better definition, assumes. (See especially Thornhill's article in Voland and Grammer 2010, as well as Dobrez 2011 commentary; see also an account of the neuroscientist Zeki's non-reductive attempt at locating neural substrates for the aesthetic experience [Dobrez 2016:163-164]). While the aesthetic, awe, is doubtless as much prompted by the natural setting as the marks on the rock. Huashan, China, would, by its magnitude and visibility, seem a likely candidate for this response. The same may be said of the spectacular Cueva de las Manos site. Rock art is sometimes hidden away, like the panels in the Spanish Levant. It is equally frequently positioned in inspiring fashion: at the head of a fjord at Alta, Norway, or, on a high ridge, twin feathered serpents overshadowing the observer at Tenabo, New Mexico (Figure 12a, b).

Figure 12. (a) The high ridge at Tenabo, New Mexico. (b) Twin feathered serpents on the high ridge.

viewed in evolutionary context, evidently relates to like/dislike judgements, it has equally evidently evolved into a very special type of like/dislike response. But how to continue to characterize this particular type?

Once more, I am bound to refer to Kantian accounts of the phenomenon. Kant points to a curious aspect of aesthetic judgement. If I judge delicate leaping guanaco from Patagonia or monumental Barrier figures to be "good," which I do, I am not merely asserting they are good *for me*. That is not the character of an aesthetic judgement. Rather I am asserting they are good for all. That is, any observer must ("necessarily") find them good. But this is indeed strange, because I know very well that some observers may not, perhaps will not, agree with me. Yet implicit in my "they are good" is the idea they are so in themselves, i.e., at least potentially "good" for any and all observers. If someone is so benighted or lacking in judgement as not to see how good they are, I am prepared to give them time to revise their faulty opinion, or to become better informed. No doubt about it: the aesthetic phenomenon has a peculiar structure. In philosophy, we would say it has an "ought" rather than an "is" structure, i.e., it assumes not that everyone *will* concur with the judgement, but that they *ought* to do so. That means that (as Kant believed) aesthetic judgement has some connection with ethical judgement, which also maps out for itself those "ought" areas of human experience. The ethical judgement assumes you ought to agree, it being (not so much "good" as) "right"—though it remains perfectly aware that everyone will not in fact agree about what is or is not right. In short, like ethics, aesthetics has a universalizing aspect to it. Kant thought it provided a bridge between cognitive ("is") judgements, that is to say factual ones, and ethical ("ought") ones, and accordingly that aesthetics had to be an important area of study.

The Key: Disinterestedness

It is now time to focus on the key aspect of the aesthetic as defined by Kant, and one that is especially polemical, though also to an extent inescapable. If when I observe Barrier Canyon art, or Andy Warhol Brillo boxes, I assign a particular kind of value to the object in question, one that is at least in part referrable to its formal properties and which is given universal validity in the form of an "ought" ("Even if you don't like it, you really ought to. Please reconsider!"), it follows I am assuming not a usual everyday attentional stance to it, but a unique form of attention. How to characterize this specific stance or attitude?

The Kantian answer is that the attitude is "disinterested," literally "without any interest" *(ohne alles Interesse)*. Of course this does not mean that when I view Barrier figures I am "uninterested" as in "lacking interest" (by contrast, fascination with Brillo boxes may soon flag!). It means that my interest is not personal, that I have nothing at stake in the matter, nothing to gain by it, that my attitude has something like the freedom implicit in an ethical position. In short, my attention to the "fine," "powerful," "imposing" images at Barrier Canyon is of a contemplative sort. Kant, though deeply committed to ethics and Christian ritual, has no feeling for the religious in the sense of "spiritual." Nonetheless the detached attitude he describes might be not unrelated to what the European mystical tradition (Meister Ekhart, the anonymous English fourteenth-century author of *The Cloud of Unknowing*, the sixteenth-century Spaniards Teresa of Avila and John of the Cross) would have referred to as the practice of contemplation. It may equally be thought of as not unrelated to aspects of the shamanic or vision-quest experience in the Americas; or to the stance of philosophical or scientific attention to an abstract line of thought—or a mathematical problem to be solved (hence the easy quip that philosophers and mathematicians live on another planet).

Be that as it may, the classical Kantian stance to the object of aesthetic attention focuses entirely on the object, distancing or detaching itself from the experiencing subject. Viewing Barrier art I forget myself in complete concentration on the images themselves. This is usually expressed as valuing the object "for its own sake," that is, not for any personal gratification: hence "disinterested." If someone insists on the personal delight I feel, my answer will be "Never mind *me*! I'm detached. I get nothing out of it! It's all about the Barrier images!" Of course this takes us back to the associated issue discussed above, namely that instead of asserting "I like it!" my formulation takes the impersonal form of "It's good!" This even as the experience may be taken as personally "pleasurable." But then it is not exactly pleasure, as we have stressed above (we recall the experience of contemplating the Goya depiction of a massacre). We likewise recall the original characterization of the aesthetic response as non-cognitive and non-emotive. Kantian "pleasure" is not an actual emotion any more than it is knowledge of something: that is the whole point of emphasis on disinterestedness. In connection with the example of Goya's picture: if I respond to the *El Tres de Mayo* picture by saying "I don't like violence," I am not responding aesthetically but cognitively and emotively (I have a *negative* emotional reaction to the concept of violence). If I respond (kinkily?) by saying "I like violence," I am not responding aesthetically but with a *positive* emotional reaction to the same concept of violence. The aesthetic judgement, in other words, is (qualitatively, not quantitatively) objective: it refers us not to personal beliefs, or emotions such as gratification, it stirs no desire on our part. Rather it has its eye solely on the valued object. So it is characterized by contemplative detachment: you don't want to eat the apple in the picture by Cézanne, just to admire it. Some very different examples: while you may be overawed by the hieratic figures at Butler Wash (Figure 2) or Barrier Canyon (Figure 8), or the huge snake on the ceiling of an Arnhem Land shelter (Figure 9), or the looming figures in the Quinkan cave (Figure 10), you are not actually *afraid* of them (assuming you are not a "believer"—a point to which I shall return). James Joyce, in his *Portrait of the Artist as a Young Man*, called the attitude one of stasis rather than kinesis, that is, as prompting no action (Joyce 1916:243). This means neither movement towards (attraction), nor movement away (flight, revulsion). In direct contrast to Thornhill in the *Evolutionary Aesthetics* collection, Dissanayake (1988:1992), equally committed to an evolutionary approach to the aesthetic, insists on aesthetic value as being for its own sake.

The Uses of the Aesthetic

This line of thinking leads, inexorably in the case of Kant, to a view of the aesthetic as non-utilitarian. In line with many in the nineteenth century who had absorbed Kant, no doubt at various removes, and who were out to shock a middle-class public anxious for morally uplifting art, Oscar Wilde flaunted the position in the preface to *The Picture of Dorian Gray*: "All art is quite useless" (Wilde 1891:vii). It goes without saying that put this way the idea of something admirable for its own sake would have also shocked the highly moral Kant. Nonetheless it follows from the premise of contemplative disinterestedness: strictly speaking, the Kantian aesthetic cannot have a purpose outside itself. The notion has so permeated Western thinking that it surfaces in unlikely contexts: for example, when anthropologists/archaeologists, taking the distinction between objects with and without use for granted, judge that a lithic is fragile and therefore probably for ritual use *only*, or that a tool (e.g., the famous Mas d'Azil spearthrower) is *over*-decorated, that is, more decorated than utility requires, the assumption being that use is one thing, embellishment or ornament another, and that the latter signals something done for the pleasure of it, in short, "for its own sake." It is also worth noting here that the IFRAO/AURA *Rock Art Glossary* defines rock art as "*non-utilitarian* anthropic markings on rock surfaces..." (Bednarik et al. 2010:14, emphasis added).

Naturally we may at this point argue that there are various kinds of uses, not all narrowly practical or material. In other words, we may query the Kantian argument as too black and white. After all, something may serve important functions and be at the same time an object of aesthetic admiration. Importantly, this does not mean wholesale abandonment of the notion of aesthetic detachment. The point may be valid, and useful, in any theory of aesthetic experience, as highlighting its specific, perhaps unique, character. At the same time it makes sense to allow that experience is never simple, that in practice the aesthetic may be combined with, or colored by, other forms of satisfaction, and that aesthetic judgement probably cannot ever be entirely divorced from judgements based on any number of other practical demands.

Take the case already foreshadowed above, that of the aesthetic and ethical/political. Goya's picture is judged aesthetically (not least insofar as we have chosen to put it in the Prado Museum), but it is clearly intended to stir moral/political indignation and indeed does just that. Picasso's *Guernica* (Figure 13) is a modern variant on the same theme, arousing distress and anger at the destruction of the Basque town in the Spanish civil war. At the same time the picture has hung in two museums, New York's MOMA and the Reina Sofia in Madrid, and so by common consent is to be regarded as suitable for aesthetic contemplation. The same was the case with Duchamp's urinal, which ceased to be an object of utility once placed in an exhibition. When I first saw it in London, I noted to my partner that one thing was certain: any attempt at use would be immedi-

Figure 13. Picasso's Guernica *(on a Spanish postage stamp).*

ately prevented by the gallery guard! Economic utility is obvious in the case of an attractive Canadian T-shirt (Figure 1): it serves the seller financially and the buyer as wearable. Political utility, a message invisible to uninformed outsiders, is clearly included in landscapes by central Australian Aboriginal artists who paint in watercolour: the apparently innocent landscapes function as titles to land, challenging European takeover of the country. Then there is the question of sexual desire, combined with aesthetic detachment, in so many European art objects, from Greco-Roman Apollos and Venuses to Renaissance nudes, and from these to nineteenth- and twentieth-century depictions of the human body. To what extent do these arouse "kinetic" desire, to what extent "static" contemplative detachment? Ads featuring desirable objects, for the purpose, say, of selling cars or shampoo, are found on billboards or on the screen; at least that was so, until fifties/sixties Pop Art relocated them to museums (think of pictures by Lichtenstein). That was in line with the Duchamp idea that anything may be matter for art or, as argued above, for aesthetics. Or the obverse: that *no* aesthetic object is without non-aesthetic, e.g., monetary, use (so much for *ohne alles Interesse!*).

The above returns us to earlier points concerning the relation of form and content, now redirected to discussion of Kant's idea of disinterestedness. We must reiterate that form and content can be distinguished (you may focus attention to each in turn, if you wish), but that in aesthetic contemplation they will be experienced together. Admiration, pleasure, satisfaction, etc., cannot be other than a response to content as well as form, implying utility (of some sort) as well as a "for its own sake" perspective. It is of course easier to see this logic working itself out in a familiar cultural context like the Western one from which I have just taken examples, less easy to do so in the case of rock art—unless content/context is known, which often it is not. Sometimes even the most straightforward question of rock art content remains unanswered (Figure 14: does this South African image depict rhino or wart hog?). However, since as observed above, rock art is generally (probably correctly) assumed to have a religious rationale, we are able to apply some observations to it in connection with the utility/non-utility critique of Kantian aesthetics. This striking image (Figure 15) is at the same time eminently useful: it probably aims at sorcery. So its spirituality is of a destructive kind. On the other hand, and like a crucifix or a Buddha statue, the Torrey Lake image (Figure 11) suggests a positive,

Figure 14. Injisuthi, KwaZulu-Natal, South Africa.

Figure 15. Cahill's Crossing, Kakadu, Australia.

eminently practical spirituality. It evokes awe, perhaps as a record of a special experience such as obtains in a vision quest. Finally, the contemporary observer is more likely right than wrong in reading spirituality, perhaps in shamanic form, into those Butler Wash or Barrier Canyon hieratics (Figures 2 and 8). For those in the know, e.g., Indigenous Australians or Native Americans, many depiction sites continue to be regarded more with actual fear and reverence than detached admiration. At Cave Hill, in the APY Lands of central Australia, as indeed at celebrated Kakadu sites, not to mention celebrated settings for rock art like Uluru (Ayers Rock), the visitor is made aware that s/he is on sacred ground. At the thunderbird cave at Writing-on-Stone, Alberta (Figure 16), as elsewhere, local people (here, Blackfoot) still leave offerings behind. For those observers, the site is not in the first instance aesthetic. However, this is not to say that those same indigenous folk experience no aesthetic "feeling" *(Gefühl);* in cultures not as yet dominated by materialism, they simply put it well behind religious experience.

The Centrality of Kant's Definition

Whatever else, Kant, an exceptionally intelligent, morally upright, politically bold yet totally respectable

Figure 16. Thunderbird Cave, Writing-on-Stone, Alberta, Canada.

citizen of eighteenth-century Königsberg who would have recoiled in horror from all the rock art I have illustrated, as well as from artful urinals and Brillo boxes, was correct in putting the spotlight on aesthetics as a critical aspect of human experience. Though I have wanted very much to modify his formulations, I have to stress that they continue to provide a basis for aesthetics. In this article, and focusing on observer-response rather than on the making of art or on the art object, I have argued that the aesthetic experience, clearly distinguished from the hopelessly open-ended notion of "art," may be prompted by any number of objects or situations, indeed by anything at all, material or immaterial. Making some distinction between "art" and "aesthetic response" is critical in this context. We may put the issue as follows: (1) anything may be called "art"; (2) likewise, aesthetic attention may be directed at any object, (3) but this does *not* mean that *any* like/dislike or pleasure/displeasure response may be called "aesthetic." The definition must fit the experience. Accordingly, I began at the beginning, arguing as a preliminary move, that the aesthetic response does indeed exist (though it may be, as with moral or spiritual or any other experience, e.g., falling in love, that the only satisfactory way of learning what it is like, is by having it). That, despite a turn to the political in art-history discourse, it remains important in that discipline, as in philosophy. That it is frequently unknowingly appealed to in social sciences discourse. That, contrary to the approach of some evolutionary aestheticians, it is not reducible, except at the cost of confusion, to a simple like/dislike response—though it no doubt has its adaptive roots in the development of the limbic system of the brain, i.e., our capacity for positive and negative emotions. That, as a universal human response, it must be distinguished from culture-specific "taste." That Western culture foregrounds it while historically most cultures have not done so.

Turning to Kant as a compelling, if by no means definitive, starting point, I have outlined his argument, which posits a specific structure for the aesthetic response: the aesthetic is defined as a "feeling," non-cognitive, non-emotive, but essentially a "pleasure" focused on the formal qualities of its object which, in eighteenth-century terms, may be either "beautiful" or "sublime." This response is value-laden and universalizing (like ethics, it presumes universal agreement, despite knowledge that this may not obtain). Above all it is "disinterested," free of personal interest, gratification—and utility. While I have disagreed with aspects of this and in addition have wanted to bring Kant into contemporary focus, I have acknowledged the relevance of his key ideas. In the process I have questioned terms like "beauty" and "sublimity" without dismissing their continuing significance; preferred to use terms other than "feeling" and "pleasure," noting that some aesthetically valid images provoke anything but pleasure; that there are limits to formal analysis, since form cannot be purely and simply divorced from content. Accepting Kant's perceptive analysis of the sense that aesthetic judgement is "necessary," even in situations of acknowledged disagreement, I have given an account of the central idea of "disinterestedness," to an extent criticizing it as another version of the problematical argument for form over content. This is not, however, to dismiss it, but merely to complicate it. Like all of Kant's basic postulates, the idea of detached, non-utilitarian contemplation, modified as required and adapted to twenty-first-century understanding, continues to speak to any definition of the aesthetic. At the same time, insisting that aesthetic response will be to content as well as to form, I have offered examples from Western art showing that ethical/political, sexual, and religious issues are bound to coexist with formal ones in the aesthetic experience. Throughout the article, I have sought to show the way in which the discourse of aesthetics in general and the Kantian perspective of it in particular may be judiciously applied to rock art.

Acknowledgments. Grateful thanks to Stuart Conner and James Keyser for the photograph of detail from the Joliet site, Montana. I owe a debt to Larry Loendorf for introducing me to Joliet, and once again to James Keyser for arranging a complex visit to the entire northwest in 2011, in the course of which Jack Brink introduced me to Writing-on-Stone.

References Cited

American Friends of the Prado Museum (AFPM)
2021 The 3rd of May 1808 in Madrid, or "The Executions," Goya. Masterpieces (online). American Friends of the Prado Museum, Minneapolis. Electronic document, https://www.afpradomuseum.org/the-3rd-of-may-1808-in-madrid-or-the-executions-goya, accessed August 24, 2021.

Bednarik, Robert G., Ahmed Achrati, Mario Consens, Fernando Coimbra, George Dimitriadis, Tang Huisheng, Alfredo Muzzolini, Dario Seglie, and Yakov A. Sher
2010 *Rock Art Glossary: A Multilingual Dictionary*. Occasional AURA Publication No.16. Australian Rock Art Research Association, Melbourne.

Boas, Franz
1927 *Primitive Art*. H. Aschehoug & Co., Oslo, and Harvard University Press, Cambridge. Unabridged facsimile reprint with new index 1955, Dover Publications, New York. Electronic document, https://archive.org/details/in.gov.ignca.17776/page/n5/mode/2up, accessed January 12, 2022.

Borofsky, Robert, ed.
1994 *Assessing Cultural Anthropology*. McGraw-Hill, New York.

Burke, Edmund
1757 *A Philosophical Enquiry into the Origin of our Ideas of the Sublime and Beautiful*. R. and J. Dodsley, London. Electronic document, https://archive.org/details/enqphilosophical00burkrich/page/n5/mode/2up. Accessed January 12, 2022.

Charlton, W.
1970 *Aesthetics: An Introduction*. Hutchinson University Library, London.

Child, Irvin L., and Leon Siroto
1971 BaKwele and American Aesthetic Evaluations Compared. In *Art and Aesthetics in Primitive Societies: A Critical Anthology*, edited by Carol Jopling, pp. 271–289. E. P. Dutton, New York.

Dickie, George
1969 The Myth of the Aesthetic Attitude. In *Introductory Readings in Aesthetics*, edited by John Hospers, pp. 28–45. The Free Press (MacMillan), New York.

Dissanayake, Ellen
1988 *What is Art For?* University of Washington Press, Seattle.

1992 *Homo Aestheticus: Where Art Comes From and Why*. University of Washington Press, Seattle.

Dobrez, Livio
2010 Framing and the Organization of Space in Representation. *Global Art FundhaMentos* IX:651–665. Fundação Museu do Homem Americano, São Raimundo Nonato, Brazil.

2011 Sex for its Own Sake. *Rock Art Research* 28(2):166–168.

2012 But what Exactly is the Aesthetic? *Rock Art Research* 29(2): 223–224.

2013 The Perception of Depicted Motion. *Arts* 2:383–446.

2016 Theoretical Approaches to Rock Art Studies. *Rock Art Research* 33 (2):143–166.

2021 The Possible Significance of Depicted Scenes for Cognitive Development. In *Making Scenes: Global Perspectives on Scenes in Rock Art*, edited by Iain Davidson and April Nowell, pp. 32–50. Berghahn, New York.

Dobrez, Livio, and Patricia Dobrez
2019 Vasari, Schapiro, Schaafsma: Three Points of Departure for a Discussion of Style in Rock Art. *Arts* 8(3). Electronic document, https://doi.org/10.3390/arts8030080, accessed June 25, 2021.

Hammermeister, Kai
2002 *The German Aesthetic Tradition*. Cambridge University Press, Cambridge, United Kingdom.

Heyd, Thomas, and John Clegg, eds.
2005 *Aesthetics and Rock Art*. Ashgate Publishing, Aldershot, United Kingdom

Jopling, Carol F., ed.
1971 *Art and Aesthetics in Primitive Societies: a Critical Anthology*. E. P. Dutton, New York.

Joyce, James
1916 *A Portrait of the Artist as a Young Man*. B. W. Huebsch, New York. Electronic document, http://www.archive.org/details/artistportraitof00joycrich, accessed January 5, 2022.

Kant, Immanuel
1914 [1790] *Critique of Judgment*. Translated by J. H. Bernard. Revised Second Edition. MacMillan, London. Originally published (in German) as *Kritik der Urteilskraft*, Lagarde und Friederich, Berlin, 1790. Electronic document, https://archive.org/details/cu31924028104085/page/n25/mode/2up, accessed January 5, 2022.

Lamarque, Peter
2005 Palaeolithic Cave Painting: A Test Case for Transcultural Aesthetics. In *Aesthetics and Rock Art*, edited by Thoman Heyd and John Clegg, pp. 21–35. Ashgate Publishing, Aldershot, United Kingdom.

Margolis, Joseph, ed.
1962 *Philosophy Looks at the Arts: Contemporary Readings in Aesthetics*. Charles Scribner's Sons, New York.

Morphy, Howard
2005 Aesthetics Across Time and Place: An Anthropological Perspective on Archaeology. In *Aesthetics and Rock Art*, edited by Thomas Heyd and John Clegg, pp. 51–60. Ashgate Publishing, Aldershot, United Kingdom.

Otten, Charlotte M., ed.
1971 *Anthropology and Art: Readings in Cross-Cultural Aesthetics*. American Museum Sourcebooks in Anthropology, American Museum of Natural History, The Natural History Press, Garden City, New York.

Rader, Melvin, ed.
1973 *A Modern Book of Aesthetics: an Anthology*. Holt, Rinehart and Winston, New York.

Stolnitz, Jerome
1969 The Aesthetic Attitude. In *Introductory Readings in Aesthetics*, edited by John Hospers, pp. 17–27. The Free Press (MacMillan), New York.

Thornhill, Randy
2010 Darwinian Aesthetics Informs Traditional Aesthetics. In *Evolutionary Aesthetics*, edited by Ekhart Voland and Karl Grammer, pp. 9–35. Springer-Verlag, Berlin.

Wilde, Oscar
1891 *The Picture of Dorian Gray*. Ward Lock and Co., London.

Rock Art Profile and Plan View Narratives, and Their Combination

Patricia Dobrez

This article discusses alternative ways of generating a perception of an unfolding event, with two perspectives, profile and plan view, identified as characterizing two basic narrative strategies. Examples are given of profile and plan being employed together, as in the often bi-angular compositions of Plains Indian Biographic art. It is argued that plan view narrative is tied to a hunter-gatherer dependence on the "readability" of real traces occurring in the landscape as a result of human or animal activity. In Australia this dependence has given rise to a tradition of sand drawing, the motif repertoire of which—sequenced tracks, motion lines, and so-called geometrics—bears close resemblance to that of an extensive "tracks-and-lines" petroglyph practice known in the discourse as Panaramitee (after a proposed type site). The implications for graphic representation of hunter-gatherer intimacy with animals and the landscape are considered, and an appeal made to researchers to reassess geometric forms deemed to be contentless "abstracts" in light of the well-documented iconic nature of Australian desert art in both its ancient and modern expressions.

I am proposing that two viewpoints, profile and plan, deliver two kinds of rock art event depiction, and, tellingly for their status as depictive options, that they may be employed together in the one composition. Profile view corresponds to our seeing, for example, the form of a warrior, hunter, or animal against the *horizon* (Figure 1), even though suggestions of depicted backdrops are almost non-existent (P. Dobrez 2021). In discussions of rock art animal depiction, profile view is often referred to as "canonical" or "typical" view in order to draw attention to the way in which it maximizes the presentation of salient features (Deregowski 1995; Dobrez and Dobrez 2013a, b; Hodgson 2013; B. Watson 2009). That this presentation has advantages—namely, ease and speed of recognition—is attested to by the proliferation of profile animal images in paleoart. As far as narrative compositions are concerned, profile cues directionality in a scene. Profile is not the only option in event depiction, however. The advantages of a "plan" view of the world (to date insufficiently discussed) come into focus when we acknowledge the key role *traces* of human and animal activity in the landscape play in the lives of hunter gatherers who possess the ability "to read the ground like a book" (Strehlow 1951:3, 1964; Wilkins 2016). Oversight of the landscape determines the viewpoint of a large body of both sand drawing and rock art in Australia where a hunter-gatherer lifeway prevailed for millennia prior to contact. Various descriptors are encountered in the discourse: "plan view" (P. Dobrez 2021; Sutton 1998a:363), "bird's eye" (rejected by Munn 1973b, 219, n. 24), "perpendicular viewpoint" (Sutton 1998a:363), "from above" (Strehlow 1951:3) or "aerial perspective" (Wilkins (2016:258; citing Strehlow 1951). In my own work on "tracks-and-lines" rock art and its relationship with sand drawing (Figure 2), I have used the expressions "map" and "trace" view (P. Dobrez 2018:56; 2021:56, 59), in addition to plan view.

Patricia Dobrez
Independent Scholar, Canberra, Australia

American Indian Rock Art, Volume 48. Amy Gilreath, Ken Hedges, and Anne McConnell, Editors. American Rock Art Research Association, 2022, pp. 167–185.

Figure 1. Hunting scene, Toca do Estevo III, Parque Nacional Serra da Capivara, Brazil. Photos by author unless otherwise credited.

Figure 2. Demonstration of plan-view sand-drawing narration in central Australia.

Should we be surprised that both viewpoints are at times brought into play in the one composition? In North America, Plains Indian Biographic art—where additional devices to suggest spatial relations are employed—provides a very clear example of the narrative usefulness of combining viewpoints. Kaiser and Keyser (2020:28) observe: "The most common example of using two-plane twisted perspective in Biographic rock art is illustrating a horse completely in side *profile* except for its hooked or C-shaped hooves (which are a representation of the animal's one-toed, C-shaped track) turned 90 degrees so as to be shown in *plan view* [emphasis added]." Since it has had more exposure in rock art studies, I shall discuss narrative profile view first, before turning to narrative plan view, and, finally, hybrid forms.

Profile Narratives

We take profile view for granted in what we generally recognise as narrative depictions, but the matter is worth bringing into the open. Profile is a necessary, though not sufficient, cue for visual narrative. Thus, for example, European Palaeolithic animals are shown in profile, but their depictions do not usually constitute narratives. (For discussion of these under the heading of Canonical Form see Dobrez and Dobrez 2013a, b). My concern here, however, is with compositions normally referred to as scenes, such as pictures of figures fighting, hunting, copulating, birthing, dancing, counting coup—all the activities that characterize a way of life. In rock art studies the tendency has been to define these as interactions between figures, that is, to think of all scenes as interactive. By contrast L. Dobrez (2013, 2021) has focused on the scene as a depiction of an event, which, among other things, allows for inclusion of single-figure narratives. In so doing, he has sought for a number of visual markers in addition to profile view, stressing the depiction of motion as necessary for reading a composition as an event.

From this perspective, various markers of movement come to the fore—asymmetries like bent limbs, often in rock art displaying "peak shift" (Ramachandran and Hirstein 1999), with profile representation maximizing the possibility of "the reading of motion in dynamic space *across* the viewer's visual field" (L. Dobrez 2013, 2021:35). Livio Dobrez also points to the necessity for coherence in the depiction of space between agents and targets (such as a spear-throwing hunter and his prey), and further suggests that figures seen in profile allow the viewer to observe a pictured event as if looking through a window, thus establishing contemplative distance from what is being viewed. The window effect often means that figure size in narrative compositions is small, and that there will be eye-level placement for optimal viewing. The focal point of this ongoing discussion is perceived motion in appropriately cued profile figures (L. Dobrez 2008, 2011, 2013, 2021).

We need to take on board the fact that our visual system responds in approximately the same way when confronted with representations as with real events. Whereas in real life we witness events unfolding in space and time, in art we respond to markers activating perception of something happening in terms of a narrative or story. Krekelberg et al. (2005) have shown that there is actually some neural sharing for real and pictured events (the same cell ensembles fire for both acts). In addition to neurophysiological evidence, there are psychology experiments demonstrating that a still image can trigger a perception of movement through the phenomenon of "Representational Momentum." In a number of publications examining how we read narratives in rock art, L. Dobrez has cited the work of Freyd (1983) and Freyd and Finke (1984) demonstrating the dynamic nature of mental representations. Both cognitive psychology experiments (Johansson 1973) and research into brain functioning (Ungerleider and Mishkin 1982) tell us that we see *movement* before the *content* of that movement. So, the depiction of movement is paramount in promoting the perception of an event unfolding. Aware that many visual narratives involve interaction, Livio Dobrez (2013, 2015) turns to the evidence Michotte (1963) provides to support the notion that these are directly perceived as cause-and-effect relationships.

One important fact that emerges from all the above is the Gibson (1950, 1979) idea of "direct perception." Seeing movement or cause and effect activities in a still image is not a matter of inference. In general, when viewing a rock art scene, we do not stop and ask, "are these figures in motion, etc.?" because, in the presence of appropriate markers, we grasp the facts immediately: that there is *something happening* is a matter of direct perception. It is in this context that I situate my discussion of profile-view representation.

An Alternative to Profile View Narrative

In his chapter titled "Decorative Art" in *Native Tribes of the Northern Territory of Australia* (1914)—valued as one of a handful of ethnographies written while cultural practices were still intact—Baldwin Spencer places "rock and bark drawings" in the one category, declaring them to be "superior" to artwork from central Australia (Spencer 1914:408). Spencer's chapter illustrations show exactly what it is that excites his enthusiasm for northern artistic practice, since the bark paintings he comments on all satisfy the criteria for visual narrative understood as the depiction of an event in profile view. Spencer takes pleasure in explicating his figures in terms of their narrative content. I am focusing on an Arnhem Land hunting scene as a representational category (Figure 3) because Spencer, who of all anthropologists writing about Australia has been most influential, is an interesting case of cultural blindness when it comes to recognizing that people from the desert heart of the continent are also taken up with visual storytelling. When we understand that everything in desert art

Figure 3. "Bark Drawing: a Kangaroo Hunt, (Kakadu Tribe)" (Spencer 1914:Figure 87).

depends on the way in which images are *connected*, it becomes apparent that Spencer and Gillen's illustrated miscellany (Figure 4) of discrete animal outlines and plant-form images, hand stencils and tracks, in addi-

Figure 4. Illustration of image types found in Australian desert art (Spencer 1896:Plate IV).

tion to "geometric" designs—the most "conspicuous" being the "concentric circle pattern" (Spencer and Gillen 1927:573, 576, Plate II)—presents an obstacle to our understanding the way in which stories may be pictured in plan view in order to make use of tracks trails in conjunction with general resemblance icons. Many decades after Spencer's uncomprehending dismissal, the potential of the desert repertoire to generate narrative has been found to equal (and arguably in several aspects to surpass) profile depiction. We now understand that desert artists employ very different strategies for communicating meaning, and this understanding has coincided with the emergence on the international art scene of modern desert acrylics, the motifs and narrative patterns of which are based on the very practices non-indigenous viewers in the early-contact situation were unable to comprehend. (For an overview of desert acrylic art see the catalogue of the *Dreamings* exhibition, Asia Society, New York [Sutton 1988a].)

With nothing from his own European tradition to prompt an understanding of visual storytelling without profile figures depicted in movement, it escaped

Spencer that there might be more than one way of narrating a story in visual terms. At the time of writing his monumental ethnographies (Spencer 1914; Spencer and Gillen 1899, 1927), he convinced himself that narrative representations are in fact absent in central Australia and that this is worthy of emphatic observation: "we nowhere amongst these tribes, so far as we know, meet with any of the more complicated drawings depicting scenes such as a kangaroo chase, or men spearing emus, or a corroboree dance" (Spencer and Gillen 1899:617, 1927:575). As it happens, central Australia is the heartland of an extant form of multimodal storytelling—communicated through speech, gesture, and sand drawing—whose antiquity is suggested by long-surviving rock art narratives which may well have their origins in its inscriptive practices (P. Dobrez 2017).

That Spencer (1914) has no difficulty in elucidating the action content of profile scenes is apparent from his commentary on his bark painting examples. Keyser et al. (2013) call just such pictures "explicit narratives." Spencer's matter-of-fact exposition of the event depicted in his Figure 87 ignores the inset upside-down figures to describe several activities focused on the image of a kangaroo (Figure 3):

> On the right-hand side there is a kangaroo, the main figure in the drawing. Behind it there are two male figures, upside down, who have nothing to do with the main scene. Behind them is a man with a spear-thrower in his hand, from which he has just thrown the spear that is entering the kangaroo. Behind him, again, follows a woman, whose sex is indicated by her breasts. She carries a digging stick in her hand and a dilly bag hanging from her head. Behind her is a man, evidently following the chase with a spear in his left hand and a spear-thrower in his right. In front of the kangaroo is the figure of a man who is supposed to be killing the wounded animal with a club [Spencer 1914:437–438].

It should be noted that a bark painting is a mobiliary object which can be viewed from any side, while rock art generally obeys the rule of up-and-down-ness, unless there is a special symbolic reason to do otherwise: to suggest death or sorcery, for example. If pressed, I think Spencer would have acknowledged that there are two scenes depicted in his Figure 87. One is the kangaroo spearing; the other appears to be a dance, perhaps the kind of ceremony that might be conducted to celebrate a successful hunt—this last suggested by the figures in the smaller scene wearing fans at their wrists and carrying spear-throwers and boomerangs.

Just how set we can become in our ways of seeing is shown in the judgment that the two scenes had to be entirely unrelated simply because they do not appear on the same ground line. When it came to desert art, the possibility of (more culturally remote) *plan-view narrative* as an alternative to *profile-view narrative* simply did not occur to Spencer and his colleague Gillen. This is perhaps owing to abbreviations that often occur in plan-view desert art, such as the omission of connecting paths in some compositions depicting journeys. Present-day visitors to New York's *Gagosian Gallery* or the *Kluge-Ruhe Aboriginal Art Gallery*, Charlottesville, Virginia, will have more insight than was previously possible into the way so-called geometrics and tracks or motion lines serve a storytelling function in the graphic practices of Australian desert communities. In what follows I shall concentrate on possible relations between sometimes ancient rock art, contemporary sand drawing, and acrylic paintings, arguing for the iconicity of images or marks employed, and for their essential connection with the landscape. But I begin by posing a question.

What If?

What if we took tracks, which Spencer and Gillen acknowledge occur in desert art, and *combined* them with circles, which Spencer and Gillen also illustrate in their display of representative, but isolated, images (1927, Plate II)? "Track and circle" (Edwards 1966), or alternatively "tracks and lines" (Clegg 1995), is in fact the definition of a major patterning of images: the "Panaramitee Tradition" (Flood 1997:179), named after a type site in South Australia significant in the developing discourse of this category of rock art. Because its manifestations are widespread, there would have been as many Aboriginal language words to describe tracks-and-lines communication as there were groups employing it. Since a *generic* descriptor is needed, Clegg's "tracks and lines" is as useful as any.

In this modern-day sand-drawing-derived acrylic by desert artist Michael Nelson Jagamara (Figure 5) we see displayed a very economical way of constructing a storyline through the utilization of dynamic (sequenced tracks) and stable (geometric range) motifs. The work is the artist's design for the remarkable mosaic granite pavement at the heart of the forecourt of Parliament House, Canberra, and reflects the traditional graphic practices of the Walbiri people. As the artist

Figure 5. Michael Jagamara (born 1945) Luritja/Warlpiri peoples, Possum and Wallaby Dreaming, 1985. Reproduced with permission of the Artist through the Aboriginal Artists Agency Ltd. Photography courtesy of the Parliament House Art Collection, Canberra, Australian Capital Territory. © The Artist licensed by Aboriginal Artists Agency Ltd.

described its message of reconciliation, it is the story of a coming together at a meeting place, with the tracks of wallaby, kangaroo, and goanna picturing a convergence (the tracks have clear iconic directionality) of peoples of different "Dreamings," and the circle at the core of the design standing for both a place significant in Jagamara's own landscape-embedded story and for the seat of Australia's federal government (Johnson 1997:85, 127).

The artist has adopted the sand drawing and related ceremonial ground-sculpture manner of representing topographical features in the form of circles joined by trails representing songline journeys. It is a feature of sand drawing that tracks trails representation or abbreviating motion lines will be impressed using parts of the hand or drawn with a finger or stick to communicate a route (Munn 1973a), whereas a ground painting or sculpture (illustrated by Spencer and Gillen 1927, Figures 245–247) marks the site of ceremonial activity in which actual paths are taken in the vicinity of the ground design by performers. Bardon (1979:43), who specifically relates their designs to those found in central Australian petroglyphs and pictograph panels, describes the making of a ground sculpture: "Sometimes various mounds are formed to create a miniature landscape appearance, and the designs of circles, spirals, and loops made from feathers, natural ochres and charcoal are arranged by a special team of men who have 'custody' relationship with that particular dreaming story." The predominance of circles in ceremonial art where no graphic link between the shapes is supplied except for the occasional line, no doubt explains why it is possible to overlook their (by no means adjunct) role in setting the scene for stories that are also embedded within real landscapes. While they are dazzled by multiplying circles, Spencer and Gillen (1927:576) see these as "geometric in nature," which has the unfortunate effect of putting an end to further investigation. Moreover, there is the further difficulty for the outsider that many designs, such as those appearing on sacred objects like *churingas*, are secrecy-guaranteed by virtue of their variations-on-a-geometric-theme graphics. On such objects an arrangement of circles will have spatial values relating to topography, but its reference points and their meaning will remain hidden. To the non-initiated, such a design, removed from its landscape context, will appear simply that: a *design*, an arrangement of circles. Only rightful custodians are allowed to disclose specific dreaming connotations.

What does not remain an enigma is the *general principle* behind the organization of the images. Sutton (1998:361) lists four "spatial cultural categories" in Aboriginal representation: 1) a mythologised "tract of country," 2) a "broad regional political geography," 3) "a cosmological category" (this might be earth or sky, for example), and 4) "a plan of a residential site" or "of a vessel," as well as the contents of each. Both on the small scale of sand-drawing storytelling, chiefly the domain of women, and on the large scale of ritual performance, chiefly that of men, the function of so-called geometrics is topographical contextualization, the equivalent of the landscape settings and backdrops found in many traditions of profile-narrative depiction, the difference being that for the first peoples of Australia the landscape is sacred, and in some social contexts its most important meanings will be withheld. For views on the gendering of the two manifestations of the same storytelling tradition, sand drawing and ground painting, see Johnson (2016), Mountford (1976), Munn (1973a), and C. Watson (2003). Since, historically, anthropology has itself been gendered, it is important that we do not overlook the possibility of a women's ceremonial ground-painting practice (P. Dobrez 2017). When Mountford was collecting crayon drawings from the Mann and Musgrave ranges (south of Uluru, on the border of the Northern Territory and South Australia), he was constrained to use a go-between when collecting women's drawings to allay any anxiety the men might have had that he was passing on men's stories to women (Mountford 1976:109). Mountford collected his drawings with the purpose of exploring a "living art" which might throw light on petroglyphs that had long fascinated him since he first learned of their existence from Basedow's descriptions of northern Flinders Ranges engraved pavements and vertical surfaces (Basedow 1914; P. Dobrez 2011; Mountford 1976:95). Since Mountford's documentation of desert storytelling, other sources of possible comparison between sand-drawing traditions and rock art have become readily available, notably through the advent of the desert acrylic art movement which issued from the cross-cultural mentoring interventions of Geoffrey Bardon at Papunya (1979, 1991; Bardon and Bardon 2004).

The present article is entirely concerned with the *graphic principles* of an art practice: those same principles that are frequently discussed in catalogues (see, for example, Anderson and Dussart 1988, and Sutton 1988b) and other texts such as Bardon's discussions of contemporary artworks using the traditional sand-drawing and ground-sculpture iconographic repertoire (Bardon 1979, 1991; Bardon and Bardon 2004). The art public has even had the opportunity of seeing desert practice in action. Witness, for example, *The New York Sandpainting Event* that inaugurated the 1988 *Dreamings* exhibition in Brooklyn where Michael Nelson Jagamara and fellow Western Desert artist Billy Stockman constructed ceremonial designs on the three tons of Brooklyn sand provided for them. An account of the event with illustrations is given in Johnson (1997:92–98). While Jagamara executed tracks-and-circles stories centered on ancestral travels, Stockman shaped a simple single concentric circle, edged by four large arcs within a large white circle. It was one of Stockman's ritual ground designs executed in the manner taught him by his elders. Myers (1994:679) has discussed this historic sand construction as "an ethnography for which anthropological knowledge is part of the event itself." Anderson and Dussart (1988:119) outline the levels of meaning in graphic designs. Artists will explain their works according to degrees of entitlement. A painting may be a "'proper dear one'—'dear,' in this sense, meaning religiously important, powerful, and potentially dangerous." Not everything is made known to everyone, or at any one time. However, secrecy surrounding particular mythic meanings does not extend to the graphic principle guiding the Stockman design. Sand drawing and ground sculpture practice makes it clear that his concentric circle exists for the artist and uninitiated viewers alike as an evocation of a sacred geography carrying information (in this case withheld) about an ancestral songline or trackway.

Although the storytelling function of tracks icons has been recognized since their widely-occurring trails first attracted anthropological notice (Basedow 1925; Mountford and Edwards 1963; Tindale 1932), to date there has been a reluctance among rock art researchers to go beyond the basic acknowledgement that circles, zigzags, arcs, "U" motifs, and related forms simply *co-present* with tracks at sites—without any *necessary connection* existing between them. At the same time, the fact that motifs have particular iconic meanings has been well understood by ethnographers concerned with media other than rock art. For example, in a chapter on Arunta "decorative art," and despite their tendency to see most motifs as non-iconic, Spencer and Gillen (1927:570), speculate about the "imitative" nature of "U" shapes used to "represent a group of individuals sitting down together." However, with rock art researchers inclined to concentrate on relative percentages of image type occurrence at different sites for the light these might throw on regional style variability (Franklin 2007, 2011; Mulvaney 2001), the relevance of iconicity and the possible *associations* of potentially iconic motifs with tracks has remained unexamined. Invariably non-tracks forms are referred to in the literature as "geometrics" or "abstracts." This terminology has the disadvantage of ignoring their resemblance to motifs made in sand drawing, as well as Aboriginal crayon drawings collected by Mountford, Tindale, and others. As Munn (1973a) has decisively shown, tracks and motion lines used in sand drawing and other media are associated with circles and other iconic forms to extend the meaning of a pedal sequence (P. Dobrez 2018).

If association is assumed and sand-drawing iconography is taken into account, this set of motifs from Panaramitee North, South Australia (Figure 6), is plausibly read as a man or woman traversing terrain where there are distinctive features pictured as circles.

Figure 6. A possible association of circles and tracks at a petroglyph site, South Australia.

A circular motif might denote any one of a range of topographical features, like a hill, waterhole, or campsite; although, without complementary information in the form of a spoken or sung story, we cannot know its exact meaning. Beyond the tentative speculations of Spencer and others about the possible iconicity of some desert graphics, Munn's study of sand-drawing iconography, augmented by the regionally relevant research undertaken by Green (2014) and C. Watson (2003), opens an ethnographic window on Panaramitee track and circle/lines petroglyph assemblages. Green (2014) has demonstrated that sand-drawn narratives centering on traces of motion actions made by the hand in the sand and used in conjunction with icons like circles to indicate a camp or waterhole are part of a method of communication in which speaking/singing and hand gestures accompany the ground narrations. This not only suggests that rock art inscriptions may also have been part of multimodal performances, but also that their so-called geometric forms have particular meanings. Even if at this distance it is impossible to retrieve some of these, we should be aware that a shape like a circle denotes a range of possible meanings relating to circularity. The critical comparative work involving linguists and rock art researchers remains to be done. I have previously (P. Dobrez 2017:160–162, Figures 11–14) sketched possible lines of inquiry, and provided some evidence to support a tracks-and-lines petroglyph lineage from 1) observed real tracks and other traces of activities in the landscape, to 2) imitative sand/ground designs, to 3) the "translation" of sand-drawing iconography into more enduring rock art images. The striking correspondence in motif repertoire between sand drawing and tracks-and-lines rock art suggests that a turn to iconicity in Panaramitee discourse is overdue.

Even in North America where there is no *prima facie* case for reconsidering the language of geometricity currently prevailing in descriptions of hunter-gatherer assemblages, the acknowledged presence of trace-simulated icons (footprints, tracks, hands) is a feature deserving renewed attention. Documenters (Keyser 2004:51; Malotki and Dissanayake 2018:154–155) record these elements (Malotki's term is "protoiconic"), with Schaafsma (1980:52) open to the idea of some abstracts as iconic on the basis of an Australian comparison.

Plan-View Narratives: Staging Action with Ground Surface Tracks and Lines

I turn now more specifically to the phenomenon of plan-view pictorial presentation and its eminent suitability for the construction of narrative—for the most part without the use of profile figures—especially for Australian desert peoples "where there is ample inscribable ground" (Green 2014:2). T. G. H. Strehlow's 1964 description of a performance of a cautionary tale concerning the punishment of a boy who has strayed from a camp illustrates how fingers, leaving trace marks in the sand, are employed to enact the part of the protagonist of the story. Unlike depicted movement in profile, real hand action across an area of sand cannot be taken in at a glance. As miniature theatre, it develops in real time and is imbued with the suspense of something actually happening. The dramatization begins with a circular impression to represent a campfire, and a "U" figure to represent a key actor sitting beside it. This gives us the *mise en scène*. On the entry of the truant into the story, the narrator commences walking her fingers across the sand to leave behind a series of dots. Soon the fingers take off at speed in pursuit of the boy: "The chase would begin—round and round the camp-fire; and the index finger would indicate the trail and pace of the pursuer by drawing a narrowing spiral more rapidly around the central circle that stood for the campfire. Suddenly the finger would stop: the boy had been clubbed and killed by the *njunja* woman" (Strehlow 1964:46). This crucial part of the story ends abruptly: "Suddenly the finger would stop," with no further marks to indicate the dénouement. Interaction between pursuer and pursued is not depicted, the cessation of movement having to do all the work of communicating the story's climax. This is typical of sand drawings made by people whose hunter-gatherer lifeway depends on a continuous scanning of the landscape for traces of events that have occurred in it. Narratives unfold as marks in the sand. I see a dingo's track that has intersected with that of a wallaby; the wallaby tracks have come to an end; only dog tracks leave the scene. I have a good idea as to the fate of the wallaby.

Kinesthetic Visuality

It requires only a short acquaintance with sand drawing for it to become apparent that it involves the *participation* of the narrator—and by proxy the viewer. More intensely than *static* images of dynamic action, sand-drawing *performances* elicit a motor response. Furthermore, we know from ethnographical sources that sand stories are cardinally oriented (Green 2014; Myers 1986): the sand-drawing narrator and viewer are situated in a storytelling space defined by actor-viewer embeddedness in actual landscapes (P. Dobrez 2021). In rock art, tracks sequences are also inscribed on surfaces to remain as trace-form imagery. If they were once elements in active performances, we have no way of retrieving knowledge of this. As static shapes they nevertheless activate neural responses conducive to understanding that an action is underway. What we "see" in the still images—for example, in a line-up of human feet or kangaroo tracks—is not constrained by their visually perceived iconic forms. Here I appeal to a recent turn to the *body* in aesthetics theory calling for an understanding of perception as multisensory. Gallese (2021:377), in his summary of important shifts in thinking about responses to art, stresses *motor input* as an overlooked aspect of the relationship between a work of art and its observer: "The aesthetics of images traditionally relies upon a unimodal notion of vision, conceived as the expression of the *visual* part of the brain... [emphasis added]." Changing the picture completely, however, "contemporary neuroscience proposes a radically different notion of vision, conceived as the expression of multimodal integration processes, whose key player is the motor system." As the theorizer of "simulative" responses to events and representations of events, Gallese comes to the subject from his discipline of cognitive neuroscience with a mission to change the way we understand perception:

> Contemporary neuroscience shows that what we see is not the simple "visual" recording in our brain of what stands in front of our eyes, but the result of a complex construction whose outcome is the result of the fundamental contribution of our body with its motor potentialities, our senses and emotions, our imagination and our memories. We must definitely abandon the outdated concept of solipsistic and "purely-visibilist" vision [Gallese 2017:48].

Any treatment of representations of movement cannot fail to take into account the relationship between what our bodies do and how we perceive motion. My previous work on tracks has been aligned to approaches that may be described as emphasizing kinesthetic visuality. There are many ways of coming to a body-centered position, and mine has been through an investigation of a role for *proprioception*, our awareness of the position and movement of our bodies, and our ever-readiness for action.

In contexts commenting on the iconographic matching of sand drawing and tracks-and-lines rock art images (P. Dobrez 2015, 2017, 2018), I have discussed what formal elements are required to facilitate the perception of an event unfolding. I have argued that while it is readable iconicity, supplied by footprints or tracks, that initially attracts our attention, we respond to something additional in the images capable of provoking a motor response. As Sognnes (2011:185) has observed of rock art footprints at Leirfall, North Trøndelag, Norway: they "seem to lure visitors to walk from panel to panel." The direction of tracks—transparent in the case of human footprints whose icons we understand from our "inside" proprioceptive knowledge of our own feet, as well as their ("outwardly") visually perceived form—establishes a trajectory for the eyes to follow (P. Dobrez 2018). Tracks sequencing delivers a perception of movement through forward displacement, a phenomenon observed by perceptual psychologists in experimental situations (Freyd and Finke 1984; Hubbard 2006; Hubbard and Bharucha 1988). In line with Gallese's post-visibilist challenge, my own argument for a *multisensory* delivery of meaning has been made via an appeal to the known plasticity of human body representation shown in the ready incorporation of prosthetic limbs, tools, and other aids requiring the mapping of an external object onto proprioceptive body awareness. In the tracking situation, it is the tracks themselves that are incorporated as the tracker reads part-for-whole. It should be stressed that—in contradistinction to the notion of "indexical *inference*" used by Summers (2003:27) to encapsulate the way we respond to footprints—my claims are for *perceived* movement and preconscious body schema transformation. So it is that the art whose modus operandi is precisely the replication of trace marks depends for its communication of movement on proprioceptive reorganization prompted by spontaneous visuomotor responses—a shapeshifting of one's body map.

In the North American context, and in the light of body schema plasticity, is there any wonder that bear paws and human prints appear merged in ambiguous images? Keyser and Klassen (2001:170) observe that some simulated handprints occurring in Foothills Abstract Tradition art can be seen as shapeshifters, in that they are "just as readily identified as bear tracks" (Keyser and Klassen 2001:172). I am suggesting that this kind of fusion takes place at the immediate *perceptual* level, prior to expressing a conscious act of symbolic identification. This makes anthropomorphization a fundamental dimension of human insight and awareness: our understanding of the world is wedded to our bodily experience. Because habitats ("country" in Australian indigenous thinking) are also mapped, identification will be more intense where environments are shared. Keyser and Poetschat (2015:36–37, 31, Figures 17 and 26) illustrate their discussion of Lucerne Valley therianthropes with examples of bear-men figures notable for their "bulbous heads" and "outsized bear paws with exaggeratedly long claws drawn for one or both feet." One bear-man (their Figure 26a) has a raised arm with "a bear paw hand." Citing Schaafsma (1992:105), Greer and Greer (1997:92) observe that in the Southwest "rock art depictions of a combination of bear-shaman usually have a human body with attached bear attributes such as feet, claws or teeth." Understanding such figures from the point of view of Gallese's multisensory delivery of meaning suggests a complex response to bear upright posture, imposing facial structure, plantigrade back paws, and a menacing capacity to dismember bodies with sharp teeth or claws (in the Lucerne Valley instance there are juxtaposed body parts). The turn to multisensory vision is only beginning to influence the way we understand the visual arts. In terms of my own argument, a remapped body schema generated by a visuomotor response to tracks has implications for our understanding of therianthropic imagery as the foundation of much story, myth, and ceremony.

Panaramitee Tracks-and-Lines and Sand Drawing: The Same System?

Without the contextualizing gestural and verbal commentary that accompanies sand drawing, it is not possible to know if some of the spirals depicted at rock art sites which are mostly consigned to the category of "geometric/abstract" imagery along with circles, meanders, zigzags, dots, etc., have a comparable narrative function to that of the spiral in Strehlow's sand story. For this reason, a chronicling-of-movement role for such lines is generally overlooked in rock art studies, along with their iconic possibilities. Munn (1973a:127) observes that in Walbiri sand stories the snake is "sometimes drawn as a spiral circle, suggesting the snake coiled in his hole, and then extended in a meander to depict the snake uncoiling and emerging." The petroglyph spirals illustrated here are tantalizing images (Figure 7). As dotted lines they resemble Strehlow's case of a sand-drawing trace form achieved by the diminutive performance of walking fingers. However, although we are entitled to conjecture that a dotted line

Figure 7. Pecked spirals (presenting with bird and other tracks) at a petroglyph site, South Australia.

in rock art might correspond to digital enactment of a story, it is necessary to proceed with caution. What we see now as a broken-line spiral might simply be explained as an unfinished motif. In any case, with spirals in general, broken line or otherwise, whether we are to take the image as iconic or as a narrative motion line will remain uncertain. As in Munn's ethnography-informed snake instance both iconicity and narrative may be intended. At the same time, given the perceived content correspondence of petroglyph and sand-drawn tracks motifs—and their sequencing which directly communicates a narrative trajectory—we can be confident that, notwithstanding the different media, tracks in rock art and sand story function identically as perceptual constants.

Returning to the line-as-movement possibility illustrated in the Strehlow performance, tracks may have stand-ins. Commenting on a variety of sand story-related media, Munn establishes the effectiveness of employing a *line* to convey the progress of a journey, and draws the obvious link between tracks and path lines:

> The print and the path line both signify marks made on the ground by the passage of individuals through the country. Moreover, Walbiri also think of campsites, or the features of the topography that emerged at these sites, as being ancestral marks. Both track prints and site-path figures depict what are in effect vestiges of the ancestor, marks in the country that he has left behind him. Walbiri can in this sense "follow" the ancestors through and recreating their *guruwari* designs [insignia-like composition condensing the important features of an ancestral narrative] just as they can follow animals by tracking them [Munn 1973a:137, glossed by present author].

We can be in no doubt that tracks and stand-in motion paths are central to sand drawing: there is no narrative without them. In view of this, we need to keep an open mind about the possible narrative function of *lines* (including spirals, meanders, and zigzags) in rock art. Unsurprisingly, however, because of their eminent iconic *readability,* it was track rather than motion-line narratives that first claimed the attention of researchers in Australia.

Panaramitee Rock Art's Conspicuous Pedal Narratives

While early much-publicized surveys of petroglyph sites in South Australia were motivated by quasi-paleontological interest in what were thought to be representations of extinct animals (for a discussion see P. Dobrez 2010–2011), excitement also surrounded the recording by Mountford and members of the newly formed *Anthropological Society* of human, macropod, bird, and lizard trails. In astonished tones, "N.C." (identity unknown) in the Adelaide *News* (January 10, 1939) revealed to the public the existence of indigenous plan-view trace-form imagery in the form of tracks: "The aborigines seem to see every thing in the shape of tracks—a man is represented by his footprints, rather than by a representation of the shape of his body" (N.C. 1939:6). Novel to the western eye, this is precisely the narrative possibility that had earlier escaped the notice of Spencer and Gillen in central Australia.

The *News* article on the petroglyphs at Panaramitee Station expresses amazement at the *specificity* of the images, providing the particular example of a representation of a "euro drinking" (the euro being a species of macropod): "Clearly shown are the two hind feet with the bar of the long tail between where it rested on the ground, and the fore-feet on which the animal lent as it drank" (N.C. 1939:6). Specification of detail is in fact a feature of petroglyph trails (Figure 8). Alternating right and left human footprints are shown (P. Dobrez 2017:Figures 5 and 11). With pecked trackways at Panaramitee sites, we can not only say with confidence "this is a macropod trail," but, as with the traces of animal activity in real life, appreciate exactly what the kan-

Figure 8. Alternating human feet and paired macropod tracks at a petroglyph site, South Australia.

garoo or wallaby is doing at any moment: sitting, grazing, or hopping (Mountford and Edwards 1963:Figure 9). "N.C." notes a sequence of human footprints which, through the size and frequency of the images, tells the tale of an adult leading a child by the hand: "With remarkable fidelity the artist of long ago has carved the little feet, taking two steps to every one of the big feet" (N.C. 1939:6). Further striking examples are given of what are described as "story pictures":

> There are two unusually well sustained "story pictures" in this area, one showing a man stalking a kangaroo right across a wide expanse of rock.

> This story, of course, is told in tracks only. On another large outcrop, extensively carved, can be traced the tracks of a big kangaroo hopping across the rock, and in places stopping to drink or feed, putting his forepaws to the ground [N.C. 1939:6].

The "pedal narrative" (P. Dobrez 2021) theme was later taken up by Clegg and his students at Sturt's Meadows petroglyph sites near Broken Hill, New South Wales, where many fascinating examples (discussed in P. Dobrez 2017:154–155) were recorded (Clegg 2009; McDonald 1982). Also mentioned in the *News* article (N.C. 1939:6) is the narrative of "an emu's nest full of eggs, with emu tracks leading away from it"—clearly an *association* of iconic shapes and a trail indicating motion. Arguably, this association of stable and dynamic forms provides the template not only for sand drawing and contemporary acrylic painting but for plan-view rock art narrative as well, which in turn raises the question of a possible genealogy.

A Genealogy

In a previous article (P. Dobrez 2017), I have provided some evidence to support the hypothesis of a derivation of plan-view narrative rock art from sand drawing in which forms are generated via affordances and constraints governing the use of the mark-making hand. I assert that the consequences of these affordances and constraints can be seen in the rock art whose motifs no longer appear as new inventions. In sand drawing everything depends on the dexterity of the hand, and the timing of the storytelling. Where the communication of speed is of importance, walking fingers in a miniaturized sand-story performance has clear communication advantages. At other times, the more deliberative action of making a series of tracks with parts of the hand will be brought to the task of narration. Munn (1973a:120) describes the making of a human footprint in sand drawing thus: "Fingers are clenched; hand held half closed. Footprint is made by impressing outer edge of hand in sand. Toe prints added with finger dabs" (see also Basedow 1925:72; C. Watson 2003:82). It is striking that petroglyph images can be found which precisely reproduce the shapes of footprint images made by this method (P. Dobrez 2017:Figures 5 and 11; 2018:Figure 2). This suggests that what we see in rock art is a version of an already existing sand-drawing lexicon later adapted to pecking, abrading, and incising technologies. It should be noted, however, that there is clearly more than one way to make the image of a footprint in petroglyph form, and that it is possible that marking the outline of a real foot before infilling may account for the appearance of some images (P. Dobrez 2017:Figure 8 and cover). Nonetheless, there are examples (see P. Dobrez 2017:160–161, Figures 11–14) of visual conformity of petroglyph tracks to sand-drawn images made by hand and finger maneuvers documented by Basedow (1925) and Munn (1973a) for emu, dingo, and macropod. The simple, easily inscribed tick mark (√) for the back foot of a macropod is found in sand drawing, rock art, and acrylic painting.

The question arises: what would motivate a desire to give sand-drawing motifs more endurable form as petroglyphs? Sand stories are ephemeral; they exist in the moment. As Munn (1973a:58) remarks: "To accompany one's speech with explanatory sand drawings is to 'talk' in the Walbiri manner." As each episode in a story is concluded, traces of it are erased with a sweep of the hand in the sand (Green 2014; Munn 1973a). Erasure ensures that "an indefinite number of scenes can be conveyed without expanding the pictorial space" (Munn 1973a:72). Rock art storytelling clearly does not have this advantage, but it does ensure durability. Although we can only guess at the motivation for the production of rock art images, making *lasting images* could be at the top of our list of conjectures. For a better understanding, researchers need to go beyond the recording of relative numbers of tracks and "geometrics" at Panaramitee sites in order to take in the larger picture. They might consider instances of distinctive *compositions* rather than counting individual motifs. In addition to trails of the kind noted above, and trails associated with linear forms, candidates for sand-drawing comparison would include possible "insignias" of the *guruwari* kind. Thus, a sitting emu with eggs at Sturt's Meadows might qualify: compare Munn (1973a:125, Figure 8C1), and Spencer and Gillen (1899:Figure 124). They might also include circles-only arrangements (for example, in South Australia at the sites of Orroroo, Moolooloo, and Sacred Canyon); likewise possible *site-path* type linkages of circles (there are linked circles on the bed of Yanyarrie Creek not far from Orroroo). Indeed, we might find the full complement of sand drawing, ground painting, and ceremonial object imageries in rock art: those associated with ancestral songline myths, *guruwari*-type insignia (Figure 9a, b, c), hunting stories, and pastime yarns. In our pursuit of a fuller understanding, we have to keep in mind the key realization that sand drawing and rock

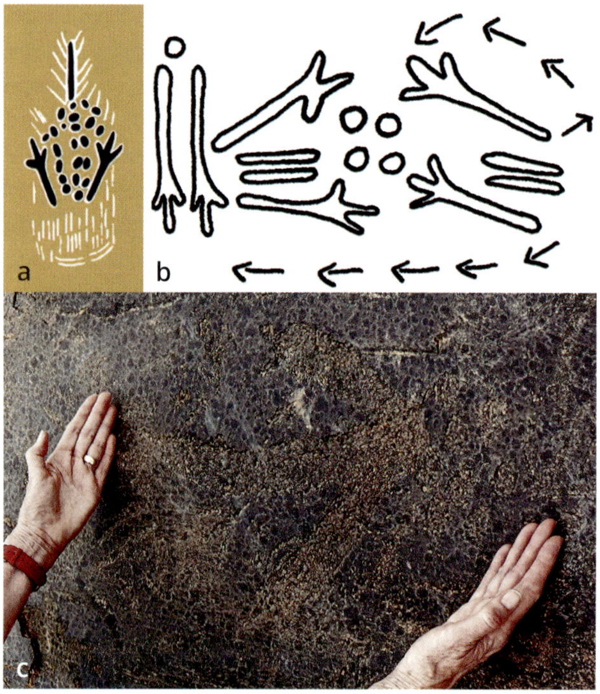

Figure 9. (a) Emu sitting on eggs seen from above, painting site (Spencer 1896:Plate IV, detail). (b) Men's ancestral design of emu. Eggs and tracks, painting site of Rugari, northwest Australia. After Nancy Munn (1973a:Figure 8Ca). (c) Petroglyph of emu track with eggs, New South Wales, Australia.

art tracks-and-lines have in common the replication of naturally occurring trace imagery so important to hunter-gatherers. The fact that contemporary canvases for sale and on display in galleries are also plan-view depictions of traces of activities in landscapes is evidence of an adaptable system able to be shaped to both new and old purposes. Indeed, in the contemporary situation such compositions often serve the political purpose of communicating connection to "country" (Myers 2002:47), and may be produced as evidence in land-rights claims and disputes related to mining. The research of Franklin (2007) suggests that in the past rock art may have played an important part in the negotiation of boundaries between groups.

Combined Profile and Plan Narrative Forms

For the way in which it makes use of an extensive stretch of rock surface to situate the story of the progress of a bear across a presumably icy landscape, this petroglyph composition at Alta, Norway, has to be one of the most spectacular known combinations of profile and plan-view narrative (Figure 10a, b). An assemblage of images dating from the hunter-gatherer period, it consists of a partially enclosed circle (interpreted as a den) from which trails emanate, and a single trackway culminating at an area where several bears of varying size are depicted in profile. Additionally, judging by its proximity to the bears, the frontal figure of a human wielding a pole (shaman's staff or hunter's weapon?) would also seem to be part of the scene. Thus, we have a composition conforming to the combination of viewpoints ("frontal, profile, and bird's eye view") identified by Keyser and Klassen (2001:250) as contributing to an overall suggestion of narrativity in American Northwestern Plains Biographic art petroglyphs. The striking example of the Biographic Tradition Rocky Coulee battle scene at Writing-on-Stone (Keyser and Klassen 2001:251–252, Figure 14.32), where trace-view motion lines "show a long journey from the raider's camp to the scene of the fight, and horse tracks show the path of the camp's mounted defenders," illustrates the hybrid combination of plan-view and profile scenic elements. Thus, in addition to trails (expressed as plan-view horses' hooves), we have across-the-visual-field motion lines (gunfire) between directionally oriented profile and semi-frontal figures (armed riders on horseback, a

Figure 10. (a) Combined tracks and profile figure. (b) Plan-view "den" and bear trackway linking with scene of bears and hunter pictured in (a). Bear hunt narrative, Alta petroglyph site, Norway.

swordsman, bowman, and two combatants with aimed guns)—all adding to the dynamism of the composition. In contrast to the Alta narrative, this extremely busy action picture is "drawn on a small, smooth rock face surrounded by large, deteriorated surface areas that serve to frame and contain the action, thereby helping to separate pictorial space from 'real' space" (Keyser and Klassen 2001:252). Such setting-off of the composition from the actual landscape conforms to the "window" effect L. Dobrez (2021) finds characteristic of profile narrative. The extent of the Alta trails across unusually wide terrain maintains a sense of real-landscape embeddedness. The only difference between the Alta composition and rock art or sand-drawing trace-view narratives is that a profile actor-figure (the travelling bear) is introduced.

Where a profile figure is introduced into a tracks narrative, the job of generating motion will fall to the profile figure or tracks or both. In terms of plan-view tracks dominance, a nearer composition to the Alta one in Biographic art would have to be the "Traveling bear meets a shaman" combination of profile bear, bear trails, and two frontal human figures at a Lucerne site illustrated by Keyser and Poetschat (2015:114, Figure 71). (It should be noted that frontality not only represents a significant canonical option for *human* representation, but also confers *status* on a figure by virtue of its confrontational posture.) Unlike the Alta narrative stretching for meters across the rock surface, the Lucerne bear and shaman scene is small: the total composition (described as "loosely but carefully structured") is just over a meter in width. Keyser and Poetschat explicate the narrative as a scene of shamanic identification with the bear:

> The small bear has travelled a long distance (represented by 19 paw prints) and encounters two humans, the larger of whom has his own bear paw feet. This human—who is obviously part bear himself—gestures toward the approaching bear, as does a smaller human just behind him. This smaller human then metaphorically "becomes" the bear by assuming its persona as evidenced by 11 tracks streaming from his head. Whether this "cerebral" trackway was intended only to metaphorically show the working of this man's mind, or instead to represent his allegorical transformation into a bear who then travels off on his own destiny cannot be determined [Keyser and Poetschat 2015:137–138].

On the remapped body schema thesis, emphasis will in the first instance be on the proprioceptive incorporation of the bear via its tracks—subsequently elaborated into a metaphor: becoming bear.

In many instances where there are bi- (or poly-) angular viewpoints, it will be sequenced tracks or their substitute motion lines that will deliver a sense of motion. In others the cueing of movement in profile (or semi-profile) figures will do the work. In some cases it will be both. The Alta bear narrative exemplifies dependence on trackways to convey passage across terrain since both human and bear figures lack markers of movement. This is true also of the Lucerne composition explicated by Keyser and Poetschat. The extremely interesting Boturini Codex example (Figure 11) from a manuscript illustrating the Aztec migration story is another case in point. Here the profile figures, while illustrating direction

Figure 11. Combined profile and plan-view narrative from Boturini Codex, Folio 3. Museo Nacional de Antropologia, Mexico. Public Domain via Wikimedia Commons. El Comandante, photographer.

of movement, lack actual movement markers, so the job is left to the tracks. Outside rock art, plan-view footprint routes are a major device in the dominantly profile art of Mexican codices (Brotherston 1995). In Australia, Crawford's example (1968:82, Figure 66) of a bi-angular profile and plan-view composition from the Kimberley region (where profile depictions proliferate) puts the emphasis on dynamic figure representation. This scene depicts a kangaroo hunt by means of a motion-cued profile hunter with spear and spear-thrower lunging towards his prey, also in profile. Surrounding both figures is a set of sequenced kangaroo tracks showing the animal's pathway. Both elements contribute to the dynamism of the scene, although the vigor of the hunter makes this figure dominant.

I shall give a revealing final example of a hybrid plan-and-profile view. Wilkins (2016:266), critiquing

Cox and Hill (1996), draws attention to the fact that Walbiri children have in recent times been "merging two drawing traditions due to contact with Anglo-Australian culture." The resulting artwork combines both Western-style side-on representation of trees and buses, while at the same time using "the traditional U-shaped icons...in such a way that they 'map' out the seating arrangements of the people." Unlike narrative examples discussed above, these are static pictures. Wilkins's Figure 10.6 (2016:267) shows larger and smaller **U** figures indicating adults, children, and babies. The babies are depicted as nested **U** figures within **U** figures to represent a cradling situation. These depictive choices tell us something about critical representational options available to central Australian children adapting to Western pictorial conventions: "the Western form of drawing seems to provide the background scene-setting of the pictures, but it is the traditional form of representation which is used to render their central theme (i.e., what and who the pictures are about") (Wilkins 2016:267). Wilkins (2016:269, Figure 10.7) reproduces a drawing by a child from an Arrernte (Spencer's Arunta) desert community in which a frontal stick figure is connected to a side-view bus by a motion path. Of these two examples, the first shows how "geometric" plan forms may be utilized as readily as trace view trails. However, the result is a picture of a state of affairs rather than a narrative scene.

In summary: profile and plan-view dynamic elements deliver two basic kinds of *event depiction* in rock art and, in some cultural contexts, they are employed together in the one composition—with the probability of one or the other being dominant. Depending on local conventions, profile figures may be more or less animated. Sequenced tracks and/or motion pathways—as illustrated by the Alta, American Plains, Aztec, Australian Kimberley, and Arrernte depictions—invariably provide the dynamic plan element in the case of combined forms. Because of the importance of *real* tracks in the human story—the survival value of a capacity to track is especially evident in Australia (Elkin 1974 [1938])—it should not surprise us to discover their images in world rock art. The role of tracks in animal recognition, for instance, is vividly on view in rock art depicting humans with track prints in place of feet. Keyser and Poetschat provide striking human (2015:30, Figures 16 and 17) and bear (2015:42, Figures 30 and 33) examples, and Keyser and Klassen bear (2001:151, Figure 11.1) and horse (2001:19, 1760–1850 group in Figure 2.2). Australian examples of human and horse tracks in the place of feet are given in "Their proper sphere: situating human feet in rock art" (P. Dobrez 2015:269, Figures 6 and 7, respectively). Rosenfeld (1982:205) makes the point that the feet of humans and animals are frequently depicted in tracks orientation, while Watson illustrates Australian and southern African examples, which, however, he discusses in terms of "typical contour" or canonical form rather than as tracks-view (B. Watson 2009:198, Figure 3.20). With tracks orientation in mind, we might legitimately ask the question: did plan-view narrative precede profile? I recently raised this question (P. Dobrez 2021:22–23) without coming to a conclusion: the story is a complex one.

A different kind of testimony to the importance of plan-view imagery (literally "from the ground up") as foundational, comes from the Arrernte child's pen-on-paper sketch of a girl, pictured as a stick figure, disembarking from a bus. Wilkins (2016:268–269, Figure 10.7) reports on the order in which the image was constructed. Unlike drawings by her non-indigenous counterparts, this five-year old began with a **U**-shape ("drawn in one stroke") for the legs (as we have seen, the trace-view icon normally used in desert art to represent legs in a seated position), proceeded to draw a body line, followed this with the arms, and added the head at the very end—the opposite to the drawing order of Western-educated children who begin with the head (Bassett 1977, cited by Wilkins 2016:268). Wilkins's argument relates to cross-cultural diversity. I wish to stress that, over and above this, the example of children's pictures shows diverse cultures working within a set of universal depictive options.

I shall give the final word on tracks to this eloquently bi-angular petroglyph image of a lion and its paw traces marks from Namibia (Figure 12). It tells us that tracks are as likely as body shapes to engage the attention of people who share habitats with animals.

Future Directions?

Let me conclude by 1) pointing out an important implication of the likeness I have posited between sand drawing and rock art tracks-and-lines imageries, 2) raising questions of possible relevance to American researchers, and 3) making a general "future-directions" appeal to the rock art research community. My first observation, based on acceptance of the similarity of the plan/trace view sand drawing and Australian Panaramitee rock art systems, is that researchers—not only

Figure 12. Profiled lion with identifying tracks features at Twyfelfontein, Namibia.

in Australia where associations between tracks-and-lines-based forms can be identified across many media—might review the tendency to automatically classify lines-based forms (circles, spirals, arcs, dots, zigzags, etc.) as non-figurative/geometrics/abstracts. Intentionally or otherwise, this terminology is not neutral. If we continue to classify along these minimalist lines, in Australia at least, we jettison the possibility of making discoveries from the most interesting area of ethnographic contextualization presently open to us. Much work needs to be done in this connection, but my own conclusion is that the Panaramitee, like sand drawing and modern-day sand-drawing-derived acrylics, is best regarded as an iconic system. Its geometric icons—e.g., circles—have perceivable general meaning and therefore do not need consigning to the too-hard basket.

This brings me to possible questions for American researchers. First, are there features of widely occurring, perhaps prematurely labeled "geometric/non-iconic," rock art assemblages that warrant re-examination? Is it possible that many images deemed unreadable ("enigmatic") are in fact iconics in plan view? An Oregon panel of "deeply carved dotted and concentric circles" reproduced as Figure 1.1 in Malotki and Dissanayake (2018:24) closely resembles the map-view circles compositions of desert acrylic art found in Australian homes, public buildings, and museums (Figure 13), and at rock art sites. Is it necessary to describe geometric patterns, so plentiful and widely distributed in the American west, in terms of their presumed randomness? While we need to make judicious allowance for the palimpsest nature of ancient art panels, does not the liberal use in Malotki and Dissanayake (2018) of such adjectives as "haphazard" (Figure 1.7), "unstructured" (Figure 5.20), "erratic" (Figure 5.35), and nouns like "medley" (Figure 1.8), "mélange," "jumble" (Figure 2.3), "scattering" (Figure 2.14), "scribbles" (Figure 2.15), "assortment" (Figure 3.2), "congeries" (Figure 3.23)—to cite just a few descriptors used in picture captions—overlook the all-important question of deliberate placement and possible combination, assuming that question to have been already answered? It is clear that for Malotki and Dissanayake (2018), we are meant to assume that such images are *necessarily* chaotic because they are the result of impulsive, spontaneously generated mark-making activities—explicable by reference to a version of phosphene theory, namely the idea of neural resonance. But this would seem to rule out consideration of an alternative systematic deployment of generalized icons and motions lines, in which context I would appeal to rock art researchers with expertise in linguistics to search for evidence of pre-contact speech, gestural, and inscriptive multimodality in storytelling.

Figure 13. Tim Payungka Tjapangati (1942–2000), Papunya, mythological sequence from the Tingari (lawmen), 1978. Acrylic paint on canvas. Western Desert, Australia. © Artist's estate licensed by Aboriginal Artists Agency, Ltd.

The question I would like to put to researchers globally is: what evidence do we have of iconics masquerading as content-less geometric/abstracts? I have made my own tentative contribution (P. Dobrez 2018:59) towards answering this question by arguing that circles-and-lines petroglyphs at the Lower Pecos region site of Lewis Canyon, Texas, previously described as "abstracts" and interpreted as being trance-induced "entoptics," might be read as iconic forms, since the motifs which present with them, such as tracks and atlatls, are indisputably iconic. It has been suggested that this site, which includes a *tinaja* or bedrock tank, was associated with water rituals (Turpin 2005). (For an overview of the Lewis Canyon petroglyphs and their landscape context see the impressive gigapan produced by Willis [2013].) In addition to the presence of iconic imagery, *location*, emphasized by Turpin, is another important consideration. The above-mentioned Australian Yanyarrie Creek site comes to mind for comparison with these Lower Pecos "abstracts": both feature linked circles and, because of their water contexts, suggest the possibility of a mapping of ponds. Often completely dry, the Australian creek would, after rain, be made up of a series of waterholes. Owing to the effects of water drainage, the Lewis Canyon rock surface is scored by obtrusive runnels and water-collection areas. We would require ethnographic information to support the notion of a rock art depiction of these natural pools and channels, and I offer the suggestion simply as a thought experiment, based on the unequivocal fact that it is possible to envisage a circle and line as *looking like something* (Figure 14). Allowing it would not preclude a shamanic element, though it would mean no longer assuming that any site featuring "abstracts" necessarily illustrates visual phenomena associated with trance.

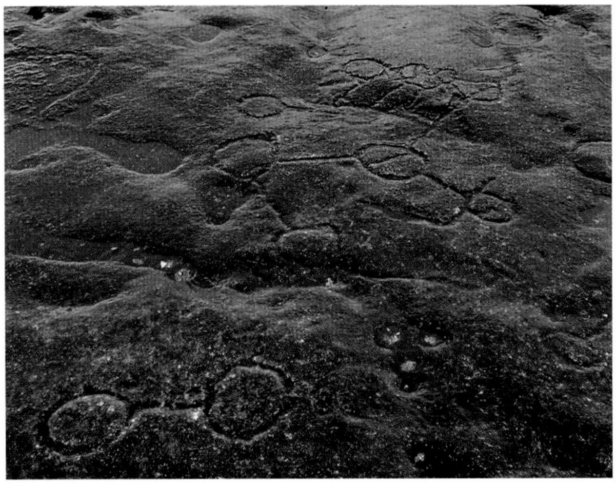

Figure 14. Linked circles. Lewis Canyon, Texas.

Taking a wider comparative overview, one in which motif types are compared on a global basis, we can at least say with confidence that the linked-circle design corresponds in appearance to the dominant site-path narrative strategy of a songlines tradition existing across a continent inhabited since the Pleistocene. Circular petroglyph motifs of various kinds in Australia have been identified as belonging to a Middle Palaeolithic tradition, although they have been deemed non-iconic by the strenuous arguer for their placement early in a construed sequence (Bednarik 2010). My argument has been that the *iconicity* of the multimodal sand-drawing tradition in Australia suggests that the function of these motifs was the representation of *general resemblance* (P. Dobrez 2017, 2018, 2021). Human cognition being both embodied and world-embedded, there is no impediment to thinking that it was the recognition of real-world forms (like handprints and footprints, tracks, and other ecologically meaningful shapes such as landscape features) that provided the catalyst for take-up of trace marks for purposes of human communication—hence my self-licensed Lewis Canyon water dreaming elicited by linked circles. Inscriptions of site-path routes or not, the Lower Pecos circles-and-lines petroglyphs—together with other "geometrics" such as those of the early Western Archaic Tradition—invite re-investigation.

References Cited

Anderson, Christopher, and Françoise Dussart
1988 Dreamings in Acrylic: Western Desert Art. In *Dreamings: The Art of Aboriginal Australia*, edited by Peter Sutton, pp. 89–142. Viking, New York.

Bardon, Geoffrey
1979 *Aboriginal Art of the Western Desert*. Rigby Limited, Sydney.
1991 *Papunya Tula: Art of the Western Desert*. Penguin Books, Ringwood, Victoria, Australia.

Bardon, Geoffrey, and James Bardon
2004 *Papunya: A Place Made After the Story*. The Miegunyah Press, Melbourne.

Basedow, Herbert
1914 Aboriginal Rock Carvings of Great Antiquity in South Australia. *The Journal of the Royal Anthropological Institute of Great Britain and Ireland* 44:195–211.
1925 *The Australian Aboriginal*. F. W. Preece and Sons, Adelaide.

Bassett, Elizabeth M.
1977 Production Strategies in the Child's Drawing of the Human Figure. In *The Child's Representation of the World*, edited by George Butterworth, pp. 49–59. Plenum Press, New York.

Bednarik, Robert G.
2010 Australian Rock Art of the Pleistocene. *Rock Art Research* 27(1):89–113.

Brotherston, Gordon
1995 *Painted Books from Mexico*. British Museum Press, London.

Clegg, John
1995 Tracks and Lines: A "New" Almost Anything to Study in Rock Art. *News 95 - International Rock Art Conference Proceedings* (CD: n. pag.). Centro Studi e Museo d'Arte Prehistorica, Pinerolo, Italy.
2009 *Sturt's Meadows Guide*. Self-published Fieldtrip Guide for 2009, AURA Inter-Congress Symposium in Broken Hill, Australia.

Cox, M., and R. Hill
1996 Different Strokes. *The Times Education Supplement*, August 9, p. 18.

Crawford, Ian M.
1968 *The Art of the Wandjina: Aboriginal Cave Paintings in Kimberley, Western Australia*. Oxford University Press, Melbourne.

Deregowski, Jan B.
1995 Perception—Depiction—Perception, and Communication: A Skeleton Key to Rock Art and its Significance. *Rock Art Research* 12(1):3–10.

Dobrez, Livio

2008 A Rock Art Typology: Narrative and Non-narrative Figural Representation. In *Aesthetics and Rock Art III Symposium*, edited by Thomas Heyd and John Clegg, pp. 29–33. Ashgate, Hampshire, United Kingdom.

2011 Looking at Our Looking: A New Approach to the Definition of a Rock Art Scene. In *American Indian Rock Art, Volume 37*, edited by Mavis Greer, John Greer, and Peggy Whitehead, pp. 251–264. American Rock Art Research Association, Glendale, Arizona.

2013 The Perception of Depicted Motion. In World Rock Art, Special Issue, edited by Robert G. Bednarik. *Arts* 2:383–446. Electronic document, https://www.mdpi.com/2076-0752/2/4/383/pdf, accessed April 15, 2022.

2015 Depicted Motion, Interaction and Causality in Rock Art. In *American Indian Rock Art, Volume 41*, edited by James D. Keyser and David Keyser, pp. 57–68. American Rock Art Research Association, San Jose, California.

2021 The Possible Significance of Depicted Scenes for Cognitive Development. In *Making Scenes: Global Perspectives on Scenes in Rock Art*, edited by Iain Davidson and April Nowell, pp. 32–50. Berghahn Books, New York.

Dobrez, Livio, and Patricia Dobrez

2013a Canonical Form and the Identification of Rock Art Figures. *American Indian Rock Art, Volume 39*, edited by William D. Hyder, pp. 115–129. American Rock Art Research Association, Glendale, Arizona.

2013b Rock Art Animals in Profile: Visual Recognition and the Principles of Canonical Form. *Rock Art Research* 30(1):75–90.

Dobrez, Patricia

2010–2011 Fossil Fever: Early Australian Rock Art Studies in Historical Context. *Purakala* 20–21:99–110.

2011 Deception Creek: An Architectural Petroglyph Site in South Australia. In *American Indian Rock Art, Volume 37*, edited by Mavis Greer, John Greer, and Peggy Whitehead, pp. 217–230. American Rock Art Research Association, Glendale, Arizona.

2015 Their Proper Sphere: Situating Human Feet in Rock Art. In *Proceedings of the XIX International Rock Art Conference IFRAO 2015* (Cáceres, Spain), edited by H. Collado Giraldo and J. J. García Arranz. *ARKEOS* 37 (CD):259–277.

2017 From Tracks to Gesture-derived Inscription: An Australian Genealogy for "Tracks and Lines" Petroglyphs. *Rock Art Research* 34(2):149–168.

2018 The Body as Intelligent Tool: The Making and Reading of Trace and Trace-derived Forms in Rock Art. *Time & Mind: The Journal of Archaeology, Consciousness and Culture* 11(1):41–66.

2021 Event Depiction in Rock Art: Landscape-Embedded Plan View Narratives, Decontextualized Profile "Scenes," and Their Hybrid Instances. In *Making Scenes: Global Perspectives on Scenes in Rock Art*, edited by Iain Davidson and April Nowell, pp. 51–66. Berghahn Books, New York.

Edwards, Robert

1966 Comparative Study of Rock Engravings in South and Central Australia. *Transactions of the Royal Society of South Australia* 90:33–38.

Elkin, Adolphus P.

1974 *The Australian Aborigines*. 5th Revised edition. Angus & Robertson, Sydney. Original publication (first edition) 1938.

Flood, Josephine

1997 *Rock Art of the Dreamtime: Images of Ancient Australia*. Angus & Robertson, Sydney.

Franklin, Natalie

2007 Discontinuous Dreaming Networks: Analysis of Variability in Australian Prehistoric Petroglyphs. *Rock Art Research* 24(10):79–103.

2011 Analyses of Panaramitee Tradition Engravings and Paintings. *Journal of the Anthropological Society of South Australia* 34:56–89.

Freyd, Jennifer

1983 The Mental Representation of Movement When Static Stimuli Are Viewed. *Perception and Psychophysics* 33:575–581.

Freyd, Jennifer J., and Ronald A. Finke

1984 Representational Momentum. *Journal of Experimental Psychology* 10:126–132.

Gallese, Vittorio

2017 Visions of the Body: Embodied Simulation and Aesthetic Experience. *Aisthesis* 1(1):41–50. Electronic document, https://oajournals.fupress.net/index.php/aisthesis/article/view/915/913, accessed August 25, 2021.

2021 Brain, Body, Habit and the Performative Quality of Aesthetics. In *Habits: Pragmatist Approaches from Cognitive Neuroscience to Social Science*, edited by Fausto Caurana and Italo Testa, pp. 376–394. Cambridge University Press.

Gibson, James J.

1950 *The Perception of the Visual World*. Houghton Mifflin Company, Boston.

1979 *The Ecological Approach to Visual Perception*. Houghton Mifflin Company, Boston.

Green, Jennifer

2014 *Drawn from the Ground: Sound, Sign and Inscription in Central Australian Sand Stories*. Cambridge University Press, Cambridge.

Greer, Mavis, and John Greer

1997 Bear Imagery in Central Montana Rock Art. In *American Indian Rock Art, Volume 23*, edited by Steven M. Freers, pp. 85–94. American Rock Art Research Association, San Miguel, California.

Hodgson, Derek

2013 The Visual Brain, Perception, and Depiction of Animals in Rock Art. *Journal of Archaeology*. Open Access. Electronic document, https://www.hindawi.com/journals/jarchae/2013/342801/, accessed August 25, 2021.

Hubbard, Timothy L.

2006 Bridging the Gap: Possible Roles and Contributions of Representational Momentum. *Psicológia* 27:1–34.

Hubbard, Timothy L., and Jamshed J. Bharucha

1988 Judged Displacement in Apparent Vertical and Horizontal Motion. *Perception & Psychophysics* 44:211–221.

Johansson, Gunnar

1973 Visual Perception of Biological Motion and a Model for its Analysis. *Perception and Psychophysics* 14:201–211.

Johnson, Vivien

1997 *Michael Jagamara Nelson*. Craftsman House, Sydney.

2016 *The Streets of Papunya: The Reinvention of Papunya Painting*. New South Publishing, Sydney.

Kaiser, David A., and James D. Keyser

2020 Hoofprints and Footprints: The Grammar of Biographic Rock Art. *American Indian Rock Art, Volume 46*, edited by Richard A. Rogers, Evelyn Billo, and Robert Mark, pp. 25–45. American Rock Art Research Association, San Jose, California.

Keyser, James D.
2004 *Art of the Warriors: Rock Art of the American Plains.* University of Utah Press, Salt Lake City.

Keyser, James. D., Livio A. C. Dobrez, Donald Hann, and David A. Kaiser
2013 How Is a Picture a Narrative? Interpreting Different Types of Rock Art. In *American Indian Rock Art, Volume 39,* edited by William D. Hyder, pp. 83–99. American Rock Art Research Association, Glendale, Arizona.

Keyser, James D., and Michael Klassen
2001 *Plains Indian Rock Art.* University of Washington Press, Seattle.

Keyser, James D., and George Poetschat
2015 *Seeking Bear: The Petroglyphs of Lucerne Valley, Wyoming.* Oregon Archaeological Society Press, Portland, Oregon.

Krekelberg Bart, Argiro Vatakis, and Zoe Kourtzi
2005 Implied Motion From Form in the Human Visual Cortex. *Journal of Neurophysiology* 94(6):4373–4386. Electronic document, https://www.physiology.org/doi/pdf/10.1152/jn.00690.2005, accessed August 25, 2021..

Malotki, Ekkehart, and Ellen Dissanayake
2018 *Early Rock Art of the American West: The Geometric Enigma.* University of Washington Press, Seattle.

McDonald, Josephine
1982 *On the Write Track.* B.A. (honors) thesis. University of Sydney, Australia.

Michotte, Albert
1963 *The Perception of Causality,* Translated by T. R. Miles and Elaine Miles. Methuen, London.

Mountford, Charles P.
1976 *Nomads of the Australian Desert.* Rigby, Sydney.

Mountford, Charles, and Robert Edwards
1963 Rock Engravings of Panaramitee Station, North-Eastern South Australia. *Transactions of the Royal Society of South Australia* 86:131–146.

Mulvaney, Ken
2001 Cultural Images: The Petroglyphs of a Sandstone Quarry, Helen Springs, Northern Territory, Australia. *Rock Art Research* 18(1):40–53.

Munn, Nancy D.
1973a *Walbiri Iconography: Graphic Representation and Cultural Symbolism in a Central Australian Society.* Cornell University Press, New York.

1973b The Spatial Presentation of Cosmic Order in Walbiri Iconography. In *Primitive Art and Society,* edited Anthony Forge, pp. 193–220. Oxford University Press, London.

Myers, Fred R.
1986 *Pintubi Country, Pintubi Self: Sentiment, Place, and Politics among Western Desert Aborigines.* Smithsonian Institution Press, Washington.

1994 Culture-making: Performing Aboriginality at the Asia Society Gallery. *American Ethnologist* 21(4):679–699.

2002 *Painting Culture: The Making of an Aboriginal High Art.* Duke University Press, London.

N. C. (identity unknown)
1939 Valley of Mysterious Ancient Art. *News* (Adelaide, South Australia), Tuesday10 January, p. 6.

Ramachandran, Vilayanur, and William Hirstein
1999 The Science of Art: A Neurological Theory of Aesthetic Experience. *Journal of Consciousness Studies* 6(6–7):15–51.

Rosenfeld, Andrée
1982 Style and Meaning in Laura Art: A Case Study in the Formal Analysis of Style in Prehistoric Art. *Mankind* 13(3):199–217.

Schaafsma, Polly
1980 *Indian Rock Art of the Southwest.* University of New Mexico Press, Albuquerque.

1992 *Rock Art in New Mexico.* Fully revised edition. Museum of New Mexico Press, Santa Fe.

Sognnes, Kalle J.
2011 These Rocks Were Made for Walking: Rock Art at Leirfall, Trøndelag, Norway. *Oxford Journal of Archaeology* 30(2):185–205.

Spencer, Baldwin (editor)
1896 *Report on the Work of the Horn Scientific Expedition to Central Australia, Part IV: Anthropology.* Dulau and Co., London, and Melville, Mullen and Slade, Melbourne.

1914 *Native Tribes of the Northern Territory of Australia.* Macmillan, London.

Spencer, Baldwin, and Frank J. Gillen
1899 *The Native Tribes of Central Australia.* MacMillan and Co. Limited, London. Electronic document, https://archive.org/details/nativetribescen02gillgoog/, accessed April 12, 2022. Facsimile reprint 1968, Dover Publications, New York.

1927 *The Arunta: A Study of a Stone Age People.* 2 volumes. Macmillan, London.

Strehlow, Theodor G. H.
1951 Foreword. In *Modern Australian Aboriginal Art,* edited by Reginald E. Battarbee, pp. 1–7. Angus and Robertson, Sydney.

1964 The Art of the Circle, Line and Square. In *Australian Aboriginal Art,* edited by Ronald M. Berndt, pp. 44–59. Ure Smith, Sydney.

Summers, David
2003 *Real Spaces: World Art and the Rise of Western Modernism.* Phaidon Press, London.

Sutton, Peter (editor)
1988a *Dreamings: The Art of Aboriginal Australia.* Viking, New York.

1988b The Morphology of Feeling. In *Dreamings: The Art of Aboriginal Australia,* edited by Peter Sutton, pp. 59–88. Viking, New York.

1998 Icons of Country: Topographic Representations in Classical Aboriginal Traditions. In *The History of Cartography, Volume 2.3: Cartography in the Traditional African, American, Arctic, Australian, and Pacific Societies,* edited by David Woodward and Malcolm Lewis, pp. 351–386. Chicago University Press.

Tindale, Norman B.
1932 Primitive Art of the Australian Aborigines. *Manuscripts* 3:38–42.

Turpin, Solveig
2005 Location, Location, Location: The Lewis Canyon Petroglyphs. *Plains Anthropologist* 50(195):307–328.

Ungerleider, Leslie G., and Mortimer Mishkin
1982 Two Cortical Visual Systems. In *Analysis of Visual Behavior,* edited by David J. Ingle, Melvyn A. Goodale, and Richard J. W. Mansfield, pp. 549–586. The Massachusetts Institute of Technology Press, Cambridge, Massachusetts.

Watson, Benjamin
2009 *Universal Visions: Neuroscience and Recurrent Characteristics of Palaeoart.* Ph.D. thesis, Centre for Classics and Archaeology, University of Melbourne.

Watson, Christine
2003 *Piercing the Ground: Balgo Women's Image Making and Relationship to Country*. Freemantle Arts Centre Press, Freemantle, Western Australia.

Wilkins, David P.
2016 Alternative Representations of Space: Arrernte Narratives in Sand. In *The Visual Narrative Reader*, edited by Neil Cohn, pp. 251–281. Bloomsbury, London.

Willis, Mark
2013 Lewis Canyon Petroglyph Site. GigaPan Systems, Portland, Oregon (online). Electronic document, http://api.gigapan.org/gigapans/136529, accessed April 26, 2021.